Building Science
Concepts and Application

Jens Pohl

Professor of Architecture
College of Architecture and Environmental Design
California Polytechnic State University (Cal Poly)
San Luis Obispo, California

⊛WILEY-BLACKWELL

A John Wiley & Sons, Ltd., Publication

This edition first published 2011
© 2011 John Wiley Ltd

Blackwell Publishing was acquired by John Wiley & Sons in February 2007. Blackwell's publishing programme has been merged with Wiley's global Scientific, Technical, and Medical business to form Wiley-Blackwell.

Registered office
John Wiley & Sons Ltd, The Atrium, Southern Gate, Chichester, West Sussex, PO19 8SQ, United Kingdom

Editorial office
9600 Garsington Road, Oxford, OX4 2DQ, United Kingdom
The Atrium, Southern Gate, Chichester, West Sussex, PO19 8SQ, UK
2121 State Avenue, Ames, Iowa 50014-8300, USA

For details of our global editorial offices, for customer services and for information about how to apply for permission to reuse the copyright material in this book please see our website at www.wiley.com/wiley-blackwell.

Library of Congress Cataloging-in-Publication Data

Pohl, Jens.
  Building Science : Concepts and Application / Jens Pohl, Professor of Architecture, College of Architecture and Environmental Design, California Polytechnic State University (Cal Poly), San Luis Obispo, California. – First.
      pages cm
  Includes bibliographical references and index.
  ISBN 978-0-470-65573-3 (pbk. : alk. paper)   1. Buildings–Environmental engineering.   I. Title.
  TH6021.P64 2011
  720'.47–dc22

                      2010042179

A catalogue record for this book is available from the British Library.

This book is published in the following electronic format Wiley Online Library [9781444392333]

Set in 10/12pt Palatino by Toppan Best-set Premedia Limited
Printed and bound in Malaysia by Vivar Printing Sdn Bhd

1   2011

Contents

The book's companion website at www.wiley.com/go/pohlbuildingscience contains freely download-able resources to support both students and lecturers:

Multiple choice questions and answers have been set for Chapters 2 to 11 and are designed to allow students to test their understanding of the concepts and principles of climate, heat, light, and sound, as well as their application in the design and construction of buildings.

PowerPoint slides have been prepared for lecturers to accompany Chapters 2 to 12 and are designed to highlight the underlying fundamental principles pertaining to the environmental aspects of build-ing science, with some practical examples from the natural and built environment.

Please feel free to use any of these resources with appropriate attribution.

Foreword

The design of buildings and the broader field of environmental design are often described as an art and a science. Design is an art because of both the complexity of the problem-solving and decision-making processes involved, and the innate desire of the designer to produce a solution that is unique and at the same time pleasing to our human senses. In the first instance, the complexity of the design process itself is not necessarily due to the complexity of any single issue or factor that must be considered – although some of these certainly demand in-depth subject-matter knowledge – but rather the many interrelationships among those factors.

For example, placing a window into the external wall of a building for the primary purpose of providing daylight may well have far-reaching implications on other areas of the overall design solution. The same window will also allow heat to either enter or escape from the building and in this way impact the thermal balance of the building interior. If located near an external noise source such as a freeway, the presence of the window may adversely affect speech communication within the space that is served by the window. In addition, the existence of the window may impact the building structure and it may also have privacy and security implications.

Clearly, the designer is faced with a very complex situation where a change in any one factor of the overall solution can impact a host of other factors and possibly unravel the current solution altogether. But why is dealing with such complexity considered an art rather than a science? The answer is perhaps surprising to the reader. While true and tried methods exist for solving most of these factors in isolation, there are really no such methods available for producing an optimum overall solution that satisfies all of the individual factors. Instead, the designer typically utilizes a rather time-consuming, iterative process that commences with the solution of the individual design factors more or less in isolation. These individual solutions are then tested in terms of their impact on each other, usually requiring major adjustments to be made based on progressively more clearly defined constraints. This is a cyclic process that has so far defied rigorous scientific explanation. However, we do have knowledge of at least some of the characteristics of this human design activity (Pohl, 2008).

- Even though the designer may assign weightings to the multiple issues and factors that appear to impact the design solution, the relative importance of these issues and their relationships to each other often changes dynamically during the design process. So also do the boundaries of the problem space and the goals and objectives of the desired outcome. In other words, under these circumstances decision making is an altogether dynamic process in which both the rules that govern the process and the required properties of the end result are subject to continuous review, refinement, and amendment.
- Observation of designers in action has drawn attention to the important role played by experience gained in past similar situations, knowledge acquired in the general course of design practice, and expertise contributed by persons who have detailed specialist knowledge in particular problem areas. The dominant emphasis on experience is confirmation of another fundamental aspect of the decision-making activity. Designers seldom start from first principles. In most cases, the designer builds on existing solutions from previous design situations that are in some way related to the problem under consideration. From this viewpoint, the decision-making activity involves the modification,

refinement, enhancement, and combination of existing solutions into a new hybrid solution that satisfies the requirements of the given design problem. In other words, building and environmental design can be described as a process in which relevant elements of past prototype solution models are progressively and collectively molded into a new solution model. Very seldom are new prototype solutions created that do not lean heavily on past prototypes.

- Finally, there is a distinctly irrational aspect to design. Donald Schön refers to a "… reflective conversation with the situation …" (Schön, 1983). He argues that designers frequently make value judgments for which they cannot rationally account. Yet, these intuitive judgments often result in conclusions that lead to superior solutions. It would appear that such intuitive capabilities are based on a conceptual understanding of the situation that allows the designer to make knowledge associations at a highly abstract level.

Based on these characteristics, the design activity can be categorized as an information-intensive process that depends for its success largely on the availability of information resources and, in particular, the experience, reasoning capabilities, and intuition capacity of the designer. The appropriate blending of these skills is as much an art as a science.

Much of the science of design falls under the rubric of building science, which includes climatic and thermal design determinants, daylighting and artificial lighting, and acoustics. The field of building science is built on solid rational foundations that are based on scientific concepts and principles. This does not mean, however, that an in-depth knowledge of science and mathematics is necessarily required for the application of consistent building science principles during the design process. In most cases an understanding of the higher-level technical notions involved is sufficient for the designer to make the necessary decisions during the early design stages, when the conceptual design solution is formulated. However, it is most important that those decisions are sound, so that they can be translated into detailed solutions during later design stages by consultants with specialized expertise.

Accordingly, the purpose of this book is to describe and explain the underlying concepts and principles of the thermal, lighting, and acoustic determinants of building design, without delving into the detailed methods that are applied by engineers and other technical consultants to design and implement actual system solutions. Nevertheless, there are some fundamental mathematical methods and scientific concepts that are a prerequisite for a full understanding of even those largely qualitative descriptions and explanations. For this reason Chapter 1 is dedicated to brief explanations of mathematical methods, such as the principal rules that govern the solution of equations, the notion of logarithms, and elementary statistical methods, as well as some basic scientific concepts such as the notion of stress and strain, the difference between objective and subjective measurements, temperature scales and other units of measurement that are used in building science, and the idealized notion of a *black body* in physics. Readers who have an engineering or science background may well wish to pass over this chapter.

Exploration of the thermal building environment is divided into four chapters. Chapter 2 deals with the principles of thermal comfort, and Chapter 3 translates these principles into conceptual building design solutions. Chapter 4 examines the heat-flow characteristics of the building envelope and explains *steady-state* design methods that form the basis of most building codes, with examples. Chapter 5 explores the sun as a natural heat source and describes the principles of active and passive solar building design solutions.

The treatment of light is divided into three chapters. Chapter 6 introduces the scientific principles of light, color, and vision. In particular, it provides an historical account of the difficulties that were encountered by physicists in formulating a scientifically plausible and consistent explanation of the nature of light. Chapter 7 stresses the importance of daylight in building design, presents the *Daylight Factor* design concept and methodology, and concludes with a discussion of glare conditions and their avoidance. Artificial lighting is the subject of Chapter 8. This chapter delves into the prominent role that electricity plays in the production of light by artificial means and compares the efficacy and characteristics of the various commercially available light sources in terms of the energy-to-light conversion ratio, lifespan, available intensity range, color rendition properties, and cost.

The various aspects of sound that impact the design of the built environment are also divided into three chapters. Chapter 9 discusses the nature of sound as a physical force that sets any medium through which it travels into vibration. This chapter lays the foundations for the treatment of sound as an important means of communication and source of pleasure in Chapter 10, and as a disruptive disturbance that must be controlled in Chapter 11.

Chapters 2 to 11 are largely historical, because they deal with the concepts and principles of building science that were mostly established during the emergence of this field of architecture in the post-World War II period of the 1950s and 1960s. Based on existing scientific premises in physics and other sciences, these foundations have gradually become an increasingly important component of the education and training of architects. However, it can be argued that except for some innovations in artificial light sources, relatively minor mechanical system improvements, and alternative energy explorations, little was added to this body of knowledge during the concluding years of the twentieth century.

There are strong indications that this will change quite dramatically during the twenty-first century, owing to an increased awareness of the human impact on the ecology of planet Earth. Clearly, the *sustainability* movement will have a major impact on the design and construction of the built environment during the coming decades. For this reason the final section of this book, Chapter 12, provides an introduction to ecological design concepts and describes both the objectives that are being established and the approaches that are emerging for meeting sustainability targets in building design and construction during the twenty-first century.

Multiple choice questions and answers for all chapters except Chapters 1 and 12 can be found on the website
www.wiley.com/go/pohlbuildingscience.

1 Technical Underpinnings in Mathematics and Physics

The field of building science is based on scientific concepts and principles. This does not mean, however, that an in-depth knowledge of science and mathematics is necessarily required for the application of sound building-science principles during the building design process. In most cases an understanding of the higher-level technical notions involved is sufficient for the designer to make the necessary decisions during the early design stages, when the conceptual design solution is formulated. However, it is most important that those decisions are sound, so that they can be translated into detailed solutions during later design stages by consultants with specialized expertise.

Accordingly, the purpose of this book is to describe and explain the underlying concepts and principles of the thermal, lighting, and acoustic determinants of building design, without delving into the detailed methods that are applied by engineers and other technical consultants to design and implement detailed system solutions. Nevertheless, there are some basic mathematical methods and scientific principles that the reader should be familiar with to easily follow the largely qualitative treatment of the subject matter of the subsequent chapters. The particular mathematical methods that are briefly reviewed include elementary linear equations and *normal distribution* statistics. In respect to Physics the fundamental concepts related to temperature scales and *black body* radiation have been selected for explanation in this introductory chapter, because they form the basis of discussions related to the thermal determinants of building design and artificial light sources, respectively.

1.1 Linear equations

Many problem systems in environmental design, planning, engineering, and management may be defined in terms of a set of equations or algorithms that can be solved mathematically. Naturally, the method of solution, the kind of solutions, and the question of solvability (i.e., whether or not the set of equations has a solution) will depend largely on the types of equations involved. We shall therefore briefly describe a simple, but also quite typical, type of equation known as the *linear equation*.

Building Science: Concepts and Application. Jens Pohl.
© 2011 John Wiley & Sons, Ltd.
Published 2011 by John Wiley & Sons, Ltd.

Also referred to as *first-degree* equations, linear equations obey the following two rules:

Rule 1: All variables or unknown quantities are to the exponent 1. Therefore, the equation $x^2 - 4y = 1$ is not a linear equation (because the variable x is raised to power 2).

Rule 2: Variable or unknown quantities appear only once in each term. For example, in the equation $ax + by + cz = k$, each of the terms on the left side of the equation contains a constant (i.e., a, b, and c) and a variable (i.e., x, y, and z), but there is never more than one variable in any of the terms. Therefore this is a linear equation with three variables. However, in the equation $8xy = -14$ the variables x and y appear in the same term and therefore this is not a linear equation. If we were to plot this equation on graph paper with y on the vertical axis and x on the horizontal axis, for multiple values of x and y, then the resulting graph would be a curve. On the other hand a linear equation, by virtue of its name, will always result in a straight line when plotted on graph paper.

The general form of a linear equation is $A_1X_1 + A_2X_2 + A_3X_3 + \ldots A_iX_i = C$, where A_1 to A_i and C are constants and X_1 to X_i are variables. The following are examples of linear equations and all of these will result in straight lines when plotted on graph paper:

$7x = -16$; or $2x - 6y = 8$; or $x - 3y + 17z = -3$.

There is another very useful rule in Algebra that applies to not just linear equations, but to all equations.

Rule 3: Whatever operation is applied to one side of an equation must also be applied to the other side. Restating this rule in a more positive form: any mathematical operation such as multiplication, division, addition, or subtraction can be applied to an equation as long as it is applied to both sides of the equation. We will use this rule repeatedly in Section 1.1.2 to solve equations involving two unknowns.

1.1.1 What are unknown quantities?

It is generally considered convenient in Algebra to categorize equations according to the number of unknown quantities (or more commonly the number of *unknowns*). This refers simply to the number of different variables contained in the equation. For example:

$12x - 16 = 0$	has *1* unknown
$2x + 17y = -66$	has *2* unknowns
$-114x + 212y = 22z + 9$	has *3* unknowns
$A_1X_1 + A_2X_2 +$ $A_3X_3 + \ldots A_iX_i = C$	has *i* unknowns

A set or *system* of equations that are to be considered together for the solution of the same problem are known as *simultaneous equations*. It is a fundamental and very important rule in mathematics that to be able to solve a system of simultaneous equations *there must be at least as many equations as there are unknowns.*

1.1.2 Simultaneous equations with two unknowns

A problem that has only two linear variables can be solved quite easily in Algebra as a set of two simultaneous equations. The approach is to eliminate one of the two unknowns by utilizing one of the following three alternative methods:

Method A: Elimination by addition or subtraction. Multiply one or both of the equations by a constant and then add or subtract the equations to eliminate one of the unknowns. For example, solve the following two equations for the unknowns x and y: $5x + 2y = 32$ and $2x - y = 2$.

$5x + 2y = 32$	[1]
$\underline{4x - 2y = 4}$	[2] multiply equation [2] by 2
$9x = 36$	add equation [2] to equation [1]
$x = 4$	divide both sides of the equation by 9
$20 + 2y = 32$	substitute for $x = 4$ in equation [1]
$2y = 12$	subtract *20* from both sides of the equation
$y = 6$	divide both sides of the equation by 2

Method B: Elimination by substitution. Using one of the equations, find the value of one unknown in terms of the other, then substitute. For example, solve the following two equations: $2x + 4y = 50$ and $3x + 5y = 66$:

$2x + 4y = 50$	[1]
$3x + 5y = 66$	[2]
$2x = 50 - 4y$	subtract $4y$ from both sides of equation [1]
$x = 25 - 2y$	divide both sides by 2 to find x in terms of y

$3(25 - 2y) + 5y = 66$ substitute for x in equation [2]

$75 - 6y + 5y = 66$ expand the brackets on the left side

$-y = -9$ subtract 75 from both sides of the equation

$y = 9$ multiply both sides of the equation by -1

$2x + (4 \times 9) = 50$ substitute for $y = 9$ in equation [1]

$2x + 36 = 50$ expand the brackets on the left side

$2x = 14$ subtract 36 from both sides of the equation

$x = 7$ divide both sides of the equation by 2

Method C: Elimination by comparison. From each equation find the value of one of the unknowns in terms of the other, and then form an equation of these equal values. For example, solve: $3x + 2y = 27$ and $2x - 3y = 5$:

$3x + 2y = 27$ [1]

$2x - 3y = 5$ [2]

$3x = 27 - 2y$ subtract $2y$ from both sides of equation [1]

$x = (27 - 2y)/3$ divide both sides of the equation by 3

$2x = 5 + 3y$ add $3y$ to both sides of equation [2]

$x = (5 + 3y)/2$ divide both sides of the equation by 2

$(27 - 2y)/3 = (5 + 3y)/2$ equate the two values of x

$27 - 2y = 3(5 + 3y)/2$ multiply both sides of the equation by 3

$54 - 4y = 15 + 9y$ multiply both sides of the equation by 2

$-4y = -39 + 9y$ subtract 54 from both sides of the equation

$-13y = -39$ subtract $9y$ from both sides of the equation

$13y = 39$ multiply both sides of the equation by -1

$y = 3$ divide both sides of the equation by 13

$3x + 6 = 27$ substitute for $y = 3$ in equation [1]

$3x = 21$ subtract 6 from both sides of the equation

$x = 7$ divide both sides of the equation by 3

In all of these examples we have dealt with simultaneous equations that have only two unknowns, and already the solution methods described become rather tedious. In architectural design, building science, and construction management many of the problems encountered, such as the structural analysis of a building frame, or the analysis of an electrical circuit, or the solution of a work-flow management problem, will often involve a set of linear equations with three or more unknowns. Such systems of equations are normally solved using methods that require the equations to be formulated as a matrix of variables and constants, as shown below.

$$A_{11}X_1 + A_{12}X_2 + \ldots\ldots A_{1n}X_n = C_1$$
$$A_{21}X_1 + A_{22}X_2 + \ldots\ldots A_{2n}X_n = C_2$$
$$A_{31}X_1 + A_{32}X_2 + \ldots\ldots A_{3n}X_n = C_3$$
$$. \quad . \quad . \quad . \quad + \qquad . \quad . \quad . \quad .$$
$$. \quad . \quad . \quad . \quad + \qquad . \quad . \quad . \quad .$$
$$A_{n1}X_1 + A_{n2}X_2 + \ldots\ldots A_{nn}X_n = C_n$$

where:

A_{11} to A_{nn} are the known coefficients of the unknowns (or variables);
C_1 to C_n are the known constants;
X_1 to X_n are the unknowns for which the equations are to be solved.

The subscripted format is also referred to as an *array*, and is a very convenient mathematical notation for representing problems that involve many linear relationships.

1.2   Some statistical methods

The word *statistics* was first applied to matters of government dealing with the quantitative analysis of births, deaths, marriages, income, and so on, necessary for effective government planning. Today, statistics is applied in a number of ways to any kind of objective or subjective data, whether this be a small sample or the total available information. There are basically two kinds of statistics:

Descriptive statistics deal with the classification of data, the construction of histograms and other types of graphs, the calculation of means, and the analysis of the degree of scatter within a given sample.

Inferential statistics may be described as the science of making decisions when there is some degree of uncertainty present (in other words, making the best decision on the basis of incomplete information).

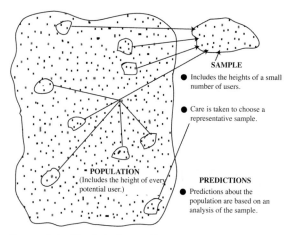

SAMPLE
● Includes the heights of a small number of users.

● Care is taken to choose a representative sample.

POPULATION
(Includes the height of every potential user.)

PREDICTIONS
● Predictions about the population are based on an analysis of the sample.

Figure 1.1   Statistical sampling.

For example, a large contracting firm may wish to embark on the manufacture of standard, mass-produced, precast concrete balustrades for staircases, balconies, and similar structures. On the assumption that the required height of a comfortable balustrade is directly related to the heights of human beings, the contracting firm considers it necessary to conduct a survey of the heights of potential users in various countries of the world. Obviously, to measure the height of every potential user (even if this were possible) would be very costly and time-consuming. Instead, a small number of potential users constituting a sample of the total population are selected for measurement. The selection is usually by a random process, although a number of other kinds of sampling procedure exist. However, what is most useful and important is that on the basis of this relatively small set of measurements we are able to make predictions about the range and distribution of heights of persons in the sampled countries. The accuracy of our predictions will depend more on the representativeness than the size of the sample (Figure 1.1).

1.2.1   Ordering data

It is very difficult to learn anything by examining unordered and unclassified data. Let us assume that in the example under considera-

Table 1.1 Sample of the heights of persons (in inches).

72	67	65	70	82	76	60	62	68	59
50	78	67	68	68	68	64	80	54	49
67	64	71	75	60	70	69	69	65	79
67	69	65	69	68	78	59	64	72	72
81	76	52	53	56	82	71	68	63	59

Table 1.2 Frequency distribution table.

Class no.	Class limits	Class frequency
1	45.5 to 50.5	2
2	50.5 to 55.5	3
3	55.5 to 60.5	6
4	60.5 to 65.5	8
5	65.5 to 70.5	16
6	70.5 to 75.5	6
7	75.5 to 80.5	6
8	80.5 to 85.5	3

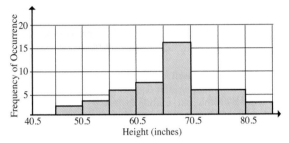

Figure 1.2   Histogram (or bar chart).

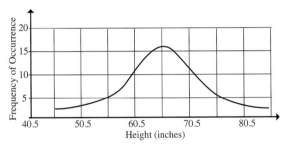

Figure 1.3   Distribution curve.

tion, the following sample (Table 1.1) of the heights of persons has been collected (i.e., measured to the nearest inch):

These measurements may be represented graphically in the form of a histogram (i.e., a bar chart) or a distribution curve, as shown in Figures 1.2 and 1.3, respectively.

To facilitate the preparation of either of these two graphs it is convenient to prepare a frequency distribution table, in which the measurements are grouped into clearly defined classes. Class limits are carefully chosen so that no measurement can be allocated to more than one class (see Table 1.2).

In addition to the construction of graphical representations of data, there are a number of arithmetically calculated measures of central tendency that are frequently used to convey a quantitative sense of a set of data with a single numerical value. Four of these are discussed below in order of increasing importance:

Mid-Range is the value halfway between the smallest and largest observation. For the sample of human heights in Table 1.1 the mid-range is calculated to be:

$$\text{Mid-Range} = (49 + 82)/2 = \textbf{65.5 IN}$$

Mode is defined as the observation in the sample that occurs most frequently. This means, of course, that some sets of data may not have a mode because no single value occurs more than once. In the sample shown in Table 1.1 there are several heights that occur more than once.

$$\text{Mode} = \textbf{68 IN} \text{ (occurs six times)}$$

Median is defined as the middle observation if the sample observations are arranged in order from smallest to largest. Again, with reference to the sample shown in Table 1.1: 49, 50, 52, 53, 54, 56, 59, 59, 59, 60, 60, 62, 63, 64, 64, 64, 65, 65, 65, 67, 67, 67, 67, 68, **68**, **68**, 68, 68, 68, 69, 69, 69, 69, 70, 70, 71, 71, 72, 72, 72, 75, 76, 76, 78, 78, 79, 80, 81, 82, 82

But the total number of observations in Table 1.1 is 50, which is an even number; therefore there are two middle observations. Typically, under these conditions the median is calculated to be halfway between the two middle observations. In this case the two middle observations are the same.

$$\text{Median} = (68 + 68)/2 = \textbf{68 IN}$$

Mean (or Arithmetic Mean) is the average value of the sample. It is calculated simply by adding the values of all observations and dividing by the number of observations. In reference to Table 1.1:

$$\text{Mean } (\bar{x}) = 3360 / 50 = \textbf{67.2 IN}$$

The manual calculation of a mean using this method tends to become tedious if the sample is quite large, as it is in this case. Therefore, for samples that contain more than 30 observations, it is common practice to draw up a frequency distribution table with an expanded set of columns, as shown in Table 1.3 below.

where:

t = [group mid-value – assumed Mean $(\bar{x}_o)$] / class interval (c);
$\bar{x}_o$ = any assumed Mean (63 in this case);
c = the class interval (5 in this case).

Based on the frequency distribution table, the true mean $(\bar{x})$ of the sample is given as a function of an assumed mean $(\bar{x}_o)$ plus a positive or negative correction factor.

$$\textbf{Mean } (\bar{x}) = \bar{x}_o + c\,[\Sigma(ft)]/[\Sigma f] \qquad \textbf{[1.1]}$$

Applying equation [1.1] to the sample of heights shown in Tables 1.1 and 1.3, we calculate the true mean $(\bar{x})$ of the sample to be:

$$\bar{x} = 63 + 5\,(40/50)$$
$$\bar{x} = 63 + 4.0$$
$$\bar{x} = \underline{\textbf{67.0 IN}}$$

It should be noted that the smaller the class interval, the more accurate the result will be. In this case, with a class interval (c) of 5, the error is 0.2 (or 0.3 percent).

1.2.2 The normal distribution curve

We have seen that frequency distributions are of great value for the statistical analysis of data. Moreover, there would appear to be considerable merit in the standardization of frequency distributions leading, for example, to the tabulation of coordinates and so on. In fact, such systems have been devised, and one of them relies on a rather distinctive natural phenomenon. There are a large number of distributions that appear to have a symmetrical, bell-shaped distribution (e.g., the heights, intelligence, and ages of persons) of the type shown in Figure 1.4.

This unique distribution, which is known as the Normal Distribution Curve, or the Error

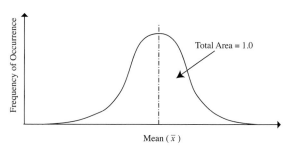

Figure 1.4   The normal distribution curve.

Group boundaries	Group mid-value	f	t	(ft)
45.5 to 50.5	48	2	−3	−6
50.5 to 55.5	53	3	−2	−6
55.5 to 60.5	58	6	−1	−6
60.5 to 65.5	63	8	0	0
65.5 to 70.5	68	16	+1	+16
70.5 to 75.5	73	6	+2	+12
75.5 to 80.5	78	6	+3	+18
80.5 to 85.5	83	3	+4	+12
		$\Sigma f = 50$		$\Sigma(ft) = 40$

Table 1.3   Expanded frequency distribution table.

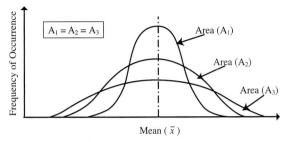

Figure 1.5   Various distributions.

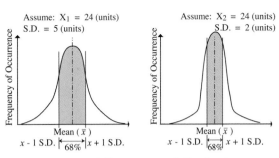

Figure 1.7   Two different normal distributions.

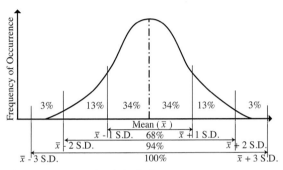

Figure 1.6   Standard deviations.

Law, or the Gaussian curve, occupies a prominent position in statistical theory. It has the following characteristics:

- The total area under the normal distribution curve is assumed to be unity (i.e., 1.0), as shown in Figure 1.4.
- The exact shape of the curve may vary from distribution to distribution, although the area will always remain the same (Figure 1.5).
- The Normal Distribution Curve has been arbitrarily divided into three major sections (with subsections), so that judgments may be made regarding the exact variation (i.e., the shape of the curve) for each distribution. These sections are defined as standard deviations from the mean (Figure 1.6).

Accordingly, the Standard Deviation (SD) of a sample provides a method for calculating the amount of scatter or variation in a sample. For example, we are readily able to distinguish

between the two Normal Distributions shown in Figure 1.7, by reference to their standard deviations.

For the first distribution 68 percent of the sample observations lie between 19 units (i.e., $24 - 5$) and 29 units (i.e., $24 + 5$). In the case of the second distribution 68 percent of the sample observations lie between 22 units (i.e., $24 - 2$) and 26 units (i.e., $24 + 2$). Obviously, the first distribution has greater variation among the observations of the sample than the second distribution. The calculation of the standard deviation of a sample is basic to virtually all statistical procedures dealing with the Normal Distribution Curve. It allows us to proceed with further predictions relating to the degree of scatter or variation likely to be encountered in the population from which the sample was drawn, and the probable accuracy of these predictions.

1.2.3   The standard deviation of a sample

There are basically three methods available for the calculation of the Standard Deviation of a sample. The first method is used whenever a Frequency Distribution table has been drawn up (i.e., when the number of observations in the sample is large). In reference to the sample of the heights of persons discussed previously in Section 1.2.1 (Table 1.1), the Frequency Distribution table may be extended to calculate the Standard Deviation of the sample of 50 measured heights according to the following formula:

$$S = c\,[((\textstyle\sum(ft^2)\,/\,\sum(f)) - ((\textstyle\sum(ft)\,/\,\sum(f))^2]^{1/2} \quad [1.2]$$

Group boundaries	Group mid-value	f	t	(ft)	(ft^2)
45.5 to 50.5	48	2	-3	-6	18
50.5 to 55.5	53	3	-2	-6	12
55.5 to 60.5	58	6	-1	-6	6
60.5 to 65.5	63	8	0	0	0
65.5 to 70.5	68	16	+1	+16	16
70.5 to 75.5	73	6	+2	+12	24
75.5 to 80.5	78	6	+3	+18	54
80.5 to 85.5	83	3	+4	+12	48
	H	$\Sigma f = 50$		$\Sigma(ft) = 40$	$\Sigma(ft^2) = 178$

$$S = 5\,[(178/50) - (40/50)^2]^{1/2}$$
$$S = 5\,[3.56 - (0.8)^2]^{1/2}$$
$$S = 5\,[3.56 - 0.64]^{1/2}$$
$$S = 5\,[2.92]^{1/2}$$
$$S = 5\,[1.71]$$
$$\mathbf{S = 8.55\ IN}$$

Accordingly, with a Mean of 67.2 IN and a Standard Deviation of 8.55 IN, we have now defined the sample within the following boundaries:

68% of the measured heights will lie in the range:

$(67.2 - 8.55)$ to $(67.2 + 8.55)$; i.e., **58.7 to 75.8 IN**

94% of the measured heights will lie in the range:

$(67.2 - 17.1)$ to $(67.2 + 17.1)$; i.e., **50.1 to 84.3 IN**

100% of the measured heights will lie in the range:

$(67.2 - 25.7)$ to $(67.2 + 25.7)$; i.e., **41.5 to 92.9 IN**

The second method for calculating the Standard Deviation of a sample is often used when the size of the sample is greater than 10 but less than 30 (i.e., a Frequency Distribution table has not been drawn up).

$$S = [(\Sigma(x^2)/\Sigma(f)) - (\bar{x})^2]^{1/2} \qquad [1.3]$$

where:

x = each observation in sample;
Σf = total number of observations;
$\bar{x}$ = Mean of sample.

Let us consider the following sample, containing measurements of the ultimate compressive strengths of 10 concrete test cylinders:

i.e., 2000, 2500, 4000, 1800, 2100, 3000, 2600, 2000, 2900, and 1900 psi.

x	x^2
2000	4 000 000
2500	6 250 000
4000	16 000 000
1800	3 240 000
2100	4 410 000
3000	9 000 000
2600	6 760 000
2000	4 000 000
2900	8 410 000
1900	3 610 000
$\Sigma(x) = 24\ 800$	$\Sigma(x^2) = 65\ 680\ 000$

Step (1) – find the Mean ($\bar{x}$):

$$\bar{x} = \Sigma(x)/\Sigma(f)$$
$$\bar{x} = 24\ 800/10$$
$$\mathbf{\bar{x} = 2480\ psi}$$

Step (2) – find the Standard Deviation (S):

$$S = [(65\ 680\ 000/10) - (2480)^2]^{1/2}$$
$$S = [(6.568 \times 10^6) - 6.150 \times 10^6]^{1/2}$$
$$S = [0.418 \times 10^6]^{1/2}$$
$$S = [41.8 \times 10^4]^{1/2}$$
$$\mathbf{S = 646.5\ psi}$$

The third method is often used when the sample is very small (i.e., less than 10). For example, consider the following measurements taken of the permanent expansion of six brick panels (in thousandths of an inch):

i.e., 22, 24, 26, 28, 25, and 22×10^{-3} IN.

$$S = [(\sum(x - \bar{x})^2) / \sum(f)]^{1/2} \qquad [1.4]$$

where:

x = each observation in sample
$\sum f$ = total number of observations
$\bar{x}$ = Mean of sample (i.e.,
$\bar{x} = (147/6) \times 10^{-3} = 24.5 \times 10^{-3}$ IN).

$S = [((22 - 24.5)^2 + (24 - 24.5)^2 + (26 - 24.5)^2$
$\quad + (28 - 24.5)^2 + (25 - 24.5)^2$
$\quad + (22 - 24.5)^2) / 6]^{1/2} \times 10^{-3}$

$S = [((-2.5)^2 + (-0.5)^2 + (1.5)^2 + (3.5)^2 + (0.5)^2$
$\quad + (-2.5)^2) / 6]^{1/2} \times 10^{-3}$

$S = [(6.25 + 0.25 + 2.25 + 12.25 + 0.25 + 6.25) / 6]^{1/2}$
$\quad \times 10^{-3}$

$S = [27.5/6]^{1/2} \times 10^{-3}$

$S = [4.58]^{1/2} \times 10^{-3}$

$\mathbf{S = 2.14 \times 10^{-3}}$ **IN**

The square of the Standard Deviation is referred to as the *Variance* and is therefore another measure of the degree of scatter within a sample.

1.2.4   The standard deviation of the population

Having calculated the Standard Deviation of a sample with any one of the three methods available (i.e., equations [1.2], [1.3] or [1.4] in Section 1.2.3) we are able to predict the Standard Deviation of the entire population (i.e., all possible observations) from which the sample has been drawn. If the Standard Deviation of the sample is *S*, then the best estimate of the Standard Deviation of the population (σ) is given by:

$$\sigma = S[\sum(f) / (\sum(f) - 1)]^{1/2} \qquad [1.5]$$

Obviously, the value of the correction factor $[\sum(f)/(\sum f - 1)]^{1/2}$ is very much influenced by the size of the sample (i.e., $\sum(f)$). For example:

If the sample size is 6, then $[\sum(f)/(\sum(f) - 1)]^{1/2}$
$\quad = 1.096$

If the sample size is 30, then $[\sum(f)/(\sum(f) - 1)]^{1/2}$
$\quad = 1.017$

If the sample size is 100, then $[\sum(f)/(\sum(f) - 1)]^{1/2}$
$\quad = 1.005$

If the sample size is 900, then $[\sum(f)/(\sum(f) - 1)]^{1/2}$
$\quad = 1.001$

Accordingly, samples containing 30 or more observations are normally considered to be large samples, while samples with fewer than 30 observations are always described as small samples. To summarize: while the Standard Deviation of a small sample (S) is used as the basis for estimating the Standard Deviation of the population (σ) utilizing equation [1.5], the Standard Deviation of a large sample is expressed directly as σ and the correction factor $[\sum(f)/(\sum(f) - 1)]^{1/2}$ is not used.

1.2.5   The coefficient of variation

The Coefficient of Variation (*v* or *V*) is a further measure of the degree of variation or scatter within a sample. It is expressed as a percentage and provides a simple method of obtaining a measure of the correlation among a set of experimental results, such as concrete specimens that are tested to destruction to verify the strength of the structural concrete members in a building.

For a small sample: $v = [(S/\bar{x}) \times 100]\%$ **[1.6]**

For a large sample: $V = [(\sigma/\bar{x}) \times 100]\%$ **[1.7]**

where:

S = Standard Deviation of sample
σ = Standard Deviation of population
$\bar{x}$ = Mean of sample for [1.6] and population for [1.7].

Naturally, the smaller the value of *v* or *V*, the better the correlation will be. At the same time, the appropriate interpretation of the Coefficient of Variation value is largely governed by the type of material being tested and the experimental procedure that was employed. In the case of concrete, it is very difficult to achieve a v value below 10%, even under the most stringent experimental procedures.

1.2.6   What is a standard error?

It is accepted as a general rule in statistics that *the scatter of means is always much less than the scatter of individual observations*. The reader may wish to verify this rule by comparing the individual and mean results of tossing a coin. If the Standard Deviation of individual observations in a population (σ) is known, then the best estimate of the standard error (or deviation) of the means of samples (σ_m) taken from the same population is given by:

$$\sigma_m = [\sigma / \Sigma(f)]^{1/2} \qquad \textbf{[1.8]}$$

where:

σ_m = Standard Error of Means
σ = Standard Deviation of single observations
$\Sigma(f)$ = total number of observations in sample.

1.2.7   What are confidence limits?

So far we have used the parameters of small samples, such as the Mean ($\bar{x}$) and Standard Deviation (S), to predict the parameters of the populations from which these samples were obtained. Let us assume for a moment that the Standard Deviation (S) of a small sample of size 10 is 2.4. Then using equation [1.5], the Standard Deviation of the population is predicted to be:

$$\sigma = 2.4 \, [10/(10-1)]^{1/2} = \textbf{2.53}$$

Of course, we have no reason to believe that the Standard Deviation of the population (σ) is exactly 2.53; we have simply estimated it to be very close to that value. It is frequently desirable to know the probability that a certain estimate based on a small sample is in fact correct. Similarly, we may wish to ascertain the actual probability that a certain observation (or mean)

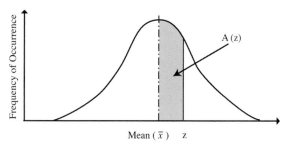

Figure 1.8   Standard normal distribution.

could be contained in a particular population. For example, if the lengths of a small sample of 10 tiles were measured to be:

7.30, 7.20, 7.25, 7.28, 7.32, 7.46, 7.50, 7.22, 7.54,
   and 7.28 IN,

what is the probability that the Mean of the population (i.e., the entire stack of tiles from which the sample of 10 was selected at random) is 7.27 IN or less?

We are able to calculate such probabilities by reference to the Normal Distribution curve (Figure 1.8), based on the following four criteria:

Criterion A: Any distribution (X_1) is said to have been standardized when it has been adjusted so that its Mean ($\bar{x}$) is zero and its Standard Deviation (σ) is 1.

Criterion B: A Normal Distribution with the Mean equal to zero and the Standard Deviation equal to unity is known as the Standard Normal Distribution.

Criterion C: The Standard Normal Variable (z) refers to the area under the Normal Distribution curve and is given by:

$$\pm z = (x_1 - \bar{x})/\sigma \qquad \textbf{[1.9]}$$

where:

x_1 = a single observation
$\bar{x}$ = the Mean
σ = the Standard Deviation of the population.

Criterion D: When considering the probable accuracy of the prediction of the Mean of the population, equation [1.9] is rewritten in the following form in terms of the calculated Mean ($\bar{x}$), the Mean (x') for which a probability is to be determined, and the Standard Deviation of Means (σ_m):

$$\pm z = (\bar{x} - x') / \sigma_m \qquad \text{[1.10]}$$

where:

$\bar{x}$ = the Mean
x' = a Mean
σ_m = the Standard Deviation of Means.

Areas under the Normal Distribution Curve are frequently needed and are therefore widely tabulated (Table 1.4).

Let us denote by $A(z)$ the area under the Normal Distribution curve from 0 to z, where z is any number (i.e., z may have a positive, negative, or zero value). As shown in Figure 1.9, some Normal Distribution tables give the value of $A(z)$ for positive values of z in steps of 0.01 from z = 0 to z = 0.5, and others give the value of $A(z)$ from z = 0.5 to z = 1.0, depending on

Table 1.4   The normal probability integral A(z).

z	0	1	2	3	4	5	6	7	8	9
0.0	.5000	.5040	.5080	.5120	.5160	.5199	.5239	.5279	.5319	.5359
0.1	.5398	.5438	.5478	.5517	.5557	.5596	.5636	.5675	.5714	.5753
0.2	.5793	.5832	.5871	.5910	.5948	.5987	.6026	.6064	.6103	.6141
0.3	.6179	.6217	.6255	.6293	.6331	.6368	.6406	.6443	.6480	.6517
0.4	.6554	.6591	.6628	.6664	.6700	.6736	.6772	.6808	.6844	.6879
0.5	.6915	.6950	.6985	.7019	.7054	.7088	.7123	.7157	.7190	.7224
0.6	.7257	.7291	.7324	.7357	.7389	.7422	.7454	.7486	.7517	.7549
0.7	.7580	.7611	.7642	.7673	.7704	.7734	.7764	.7794	.7823	.7852
0.8	.7881	.7910	.7939	.7967	.7995	.8023	.8051	.8078	.8106	.8133
0.9	.8159	.8186	.8212	.8238	.8264	.8289	.8315	.8340	.8365	.8389
1.0	.8413	.8438	.8461	.8485	.8508	.8531	.8554	.8577	.8599	.8621
1.1	.8643	.8665	.8686	.8708	.8729	.8749	.8770	.8790	.8810	.8830
1.2	.8849	.8869	.8888	.8907	.8925	.8944	.8962	.8980	.8997	.9015
1.3	.9032	.9049	.9066	.9082	.9099	.9115	.9131	.9147	.9162	.9177
1.4	.9192	.9207	.9222	.9236	.9251	.9265	.9279	.9292	.9306	.9319
1.5	.9332	.9345	.9357	.9370	.9382	.9394	.9406	.9418	.9429	.9441
1.6	.9452	.9463	.9474	.9484	.9495	.9505	.9515	.9525	.9535	.9545
1.7	.9554	.9564	.9573	.9582	.9591	.9599	.9608	.9616	.9625	.9633
1.8	.9641	.9649	.9656	.9664	.9671	.9678	.9686	.9693	.9699	.9706
1.9	.9713	.9719	.9726	.9732	.9738	.9744	.9750	.9756	.9761	.9767
2.0	.9772	.9778	.9783	.9788	.9793	.9798	.9803	.9808	.9812	.9817
2.1	.9821	.9826	.9830	.9834	.9838	.9842	.9846	.9850	.9854	.9857
2.2	.9861	.9864	.9868	.9871	.9875	.9878	.9881	.9884	.9887	.9890
2.3	.9893	.9896	.9898	.9901	.9904	.9906	.9909	.9911	.9913	.9916
2.4	.9918	.9920	.9922	.9925	.9927	.9929	.9931	.9932	.9934	.9936
2.5	.9938	.9940	.9941	.9943	.9945	.9946	.9948	.9949	.9951	.9952
2.6	.9953	.9955	.9956	.9957	.9959	.9960	.9961	.9962	.9963	.9964
2.7	.9965	.9966	.9967	.9968	.9969	.9970	.9971	.9972	.9973	.9974
2.8	.9974	.9975	.9976	.9977	.9977	.9978	.9979	.9979	.9980	.9981
2.9	.9981	.9982	.9982	.9983	.9984	.9984	.9985	.9985	.9986	.9986
3.0	.9987	.9987	.9987	.9988	.9988	.9989	.9989	.9989	.9990	.9990
3.1	.9990	.9991	.9991	.9991	.9992	.9992	.9992	.9992	.9993	.9993
3.2	.9993	.9993	.9994	.9994	.9994	.9994	.9994	.9995	.9995	.9995
3.3	.9995	.9995	.9996	.9996	.9996	.9996	.9996	.9996	.9996	.9997
3.4	.9997	.9997	.9997	.9997	.9997	.9997	.9997	.9997	.9998	.9998
3.5	.9998	.9998	.9998	.9998	.9998	.9998	.9998	.9998	.9998	.9998
3.6	.9998	.9998	.9999	.9999	.9999	.9999	.9999	.9999	.9999	.9999

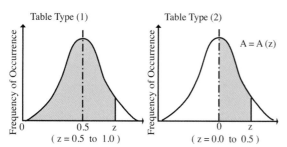

Figure 1.9   Normal distribution table formats.

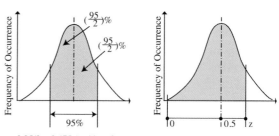

Figure 1.10   Confidence limits of the mean compressive strength of concrete.

whether the area under the curve is measured from the Mean or from the left side. It is readily seen that Table 1.4 is of table type (1) in Figure 1.9 and therefore starts with an $A(z)$ value of 0.5 (as opposed to 0.0) in the top left-hand corner of the table.

Summarizing, we conclude that equation [1.9] is always used to find the probability that a single random observation may occur in a population. Equation [1.10] is used to find the bounds of the Mean of a population.

1.2.8   Predicting the strength of concrete

On a large concrete dam construction project, 121 concrete test cylinders were taken and subjected to compressive strength tests, with the results shown below. What is the probability that a random test cylinder will have a compressive strength of more than 1800 psi?

$$\text{Mean compressive strength } (\bar{x}) = 2160 \text{ psi}$$
$$\text{Standard Deviation } (\sigma) = 252 \text{ psi}$$
$$\text{Random observation } (x_1) = 1800 \text{ psi}$$

Apply equation [1.9]: $\pm z = (x_1 - \bar{x}) / \sigma$
$$\pm z = (1800 - 2160) / 252$$
$$\pm z = (-360) / 252$$
$$z = 1.43$$

From Table 1.4 we obtain a probability of 0.9236 for a z-value of 1.43. Thus the probability of obtaining a strength greater than 1800 psi is 92.36% (i.e., approximately 92 percent).

For the same 121 concrete test cylinders of the above example, find the 95 percent confidence limits of the Mean compressive strength of all of the poured concrete deduced from this large sample of 121 test cylinders.

$$\text{Sample Mean } (x') = 2160 \text{ psi}$$
$$\text{Standard Deviation } (\sigma) = 252 \text{ psi}$$

Step (1): Apply equation [1.8] to determine the Standard Deviation of the Mean (σ_m).

$$\sigma_m = [\sigma / \Sigma(f)]^{1/2}$$
$$\sigma_m = [252 / 121]^{1/2}$$
$$\boldsymbol{\sigma_m = 23 \text{ psi}}$$

Step (2): Apply equation [1.10] to determine the 95 percent confidence limits of the Mean compressive strength of the whole population ($\bar{x}$).

$$\pm z = (\bar{x} - x') / \sigma_m$$

Transposing equation [1.10] to make (x) the subject of the equation, we obtain:

$$\bar{x} = x' \pm z (\sigma_m)$$

The value of z is obtained for the required 95 percent probability, as shown in Figure 1.10, to be 0.975.

The corresponding z-value for a probability of 0.975 is given in Table 1.4 as 1.96; therefore, substituting in the transposed equation:

$$\bar{x} = x' \pm z (\sigma_m)$$
$$\bar{x} = 2160 \pm (1.96 \times 23)$$
$$\bar{x} = 2160 \pm 45$$

Accordingly, the 95 percent confidence limits of the Mean compressive strength of all of the poured concrete in the dam are between **2115 psi** and **2205 psi**.

1.3   Foundational concepts in physics

The chapters that follow assume some knowledge of the scientific concepts and principles that underlie current understanding of the nature of the physical phenomena that we refer to as heat, light, and sound, and how these environmental stimuli are perceived by us as human beings. Most of these stimuli have been studied for centuries as the various specialized fields of science emerged. In the following sections a few selected members of this foundational group of scientific principles are briefly explained in layperson terms. We will start with units of measurement because they are fundamental to all scientific and technical endeavors (Cardarelli, 1997).

1.3.1   Units of measurement

Measurement of length and volume became an important early concern as civilization evolved with an increasing focus on agriculture, trade, specialization, and collective aspirations that led to more and more community endeavors. The earliest length measurement of major consequence was most likely the Egyptian *cubit*, which was based on the length of the human arm from the elbow to the finger tips. While this provided a basis for measuring relatively short lengths such as those associated with plants, animals, and manmade artifacts, two additional needs soon surfaced. First, as communities grew in size and influence the need for standardization became paramount. By 2500 BC the Egyptians had already seen the need for the establishment of a Master Cubit made of marble. Second, as the roots of science emerged so also did the need for the accurate measurement of a host of additional quantities beyond length, area, volume, and time (Klein, 1975).

The national standardization of units of measurement progressed somewhat more slowly than might have been expected. In England, units of measurement were not effectively standardized until the early thirteenth century; however, deviations and exceptions continued long thereafter. For example, total agreement on the volume measure, the *gallon*, was not reached until the early nineteenth century. Until then there existed the different ale, wine, and corn *gallons* (Connor, 1987).

The US adopted the English system of weights and measures, with some specific exceptions. For example, the wine-gallon of 231 cubic inches was adopted in preference to the English *gallon* of 277 cubic inches. France officially adopted the metric system in 1799, with the *metre*[1] as the unit of length. The *metre* was defined as one ten-millionth part of the quarter of the circumference of the Earth. Later this basis for defining a standard *metre* was replaced by a more exact and observable physical phenomenon,[2] as the metric system became the *Système International (SI)* (i.e., le Système International d'Unités) in 1960. Today almost all nations, with the notable exception of the US, have adopted the SI system of units (United Nations, 1955). However, even in the US the scientific community has to all intents and purposes unofficially migrated to the SI standard.

SI units of measurement: The SI standard is based on seven categories of unit, from which many other units are derived.

Category	Name	Abbreviation
Length	metre	m
Mass	kilogram	kg
Time	second	s
Electric current	ampere	A
Temperature	Kelvin	K
Amount of substance	mole	mol
Luminous intensity	candela	cd

Each of these base units is clearly defined as a fraction of some measurable physical phenomenon. For example, the *kilogram* is based on the weight of a platinum–iridium cylinder maintained under constant environmental conditions in Sèvres, France, and the *second* is defined as the length of time taken by 9 192 631 770 periods of vibration of the caesium-133 atom. SI units that are derived from these base unit categories include: the *farad (F)* for electrical capacitance; the *hertz (Hz)* for the frequency of a periodic vibration such as sound; the *joule (J)* for work and energy; the *newton (N)* for force; the *ohm (Ω)* for electrical resistance; the *pascal (Pa)* for pressure; the *volt (V)* for electric potential; and the *watt (W)* for the rate of doing work or power.

In addition, the SI standard utilizes specific prefixes to serve as convenient multiplication factors for increasing or reducing the relative size of these units in multiples of 1000. Commonly used prefixes are *K* for thousand, *M* for million, *G* for billion, *m* for thousandth, *μ* for millionth, and *n* for billionth. Therefore, *kW* stands for kilowatt or 1000 watt, and *mm* stands for millimeter or 1000th of a metre.

US system of units: Following the official adoption of the SI metric system of measurement by Britain in 1995, the US stands virtually alone with its continued use of what was originally known as the United Kingdom (UK) System of Measurements. With only a few specific differences, the US system of measurements is the same as the pre-1995 UK system. However, whereas in the UK system the base measures of *yard*, *pound*, and *gallon* were originally defined by physical standards, in the US system these are all now defined by reference to the SI *metre*, *kilogram*, and *litre*. The US system recognizes nine distinct categories of units, as follows:[3]

Length: *inch (IN)*, *foot (FT)*, *yard*, *furlong*, and *mile*.

Area: *square inch (SI)*, *square foot (SF)*, *acre*, *square mile* or *section*, and *township* (i.e., 36 square miles or 36 sections).

Volume: *cubic inch (CI)*, *cubic foot (CF)*, and *cubic yard*.

Capacity (dry): *pint*, *quart*, *peck*, and *bushel*.

Capacity (liquid): *fluid ounce*, *gill*, *pint*, *quart*, and *gallon*.

Mass: *grain*, *ounce*, *pound (LB)*, *stone*, *hundredweight*, and *ton*.

Troy weights: *grain*, *ounce*, *pennyweight*, and *pound (LB)*.

Apothecaries' measures: *minim*, *dram*, *fluid ounce*, and *pint*.

Apothecaries' weights: *grain*, *scruple*, *dram*, *ounce*, and *pound (LB)*.

It should be noted that among the mass units there are various versions of the *ton* unit, all of which are different from the original UK *ton*. A standard US *ton* is equal to 2000 LB instead of the original 2240 LB, so a US *ton* or *short ton* is equal to 2000 LB, while a US *metric ton* is equal to 1000 LB, and a US *long ton* is equal to 2240 LB. To make matters even more confusing, a US *measurement ton* has nothing to do with mass, but refers to a volume of 70 CF.

Conversion factors that must be applied to convert one unit of measurement to another are readily available in the form of published tables. Horvath (1986) has included conversion factors covering both historical and current units. Cardarelli (1997) provides more than 10 000 conversion factors in his more recent publication, which claims to be the most complete set of tables dealing with unit conversion.

1.3.2 Temperature scales and thermometers

Temperature provides a measure of the degree of hotness or coolness as perceived by our human senses. The desire to measure the precise degree of this sensation has led to a rich history of temperature scales and measurement instruments, the latter commonly referred to as thermometers.

As might be expected, the various physical states of water have served as a convenient set of reference points up to the present day for defining alternative temperature scales. One of the earliest records of a temperature scale dates back to 170 AD when Galen, in his medical writings, proposed four degrees of heat and four degrees of cold on either side of boiling water and ice. In 1610 Galileo constructed a simple apparatus consisting of a glass tube with a bulb at one end and open at the other end. Holding the tube upright, he placed the open end into a container of wine, and extracted a small amount of the trapped air so that the wine would rise some distance above the level of the wine container inside the glass tube. The contraction and expansion of the air above the column of wine with changes in temperature would force the level of the wine in the glass tube to likewise rise and fall, correspondingly. The first attempt to use a liquid, rather than a gas, for recording temperature is credited to Ferdinand II, Grand Duke of Tuscany, in 1641. He proposed a device that held a quantity of alcohol in a sealed glass container with gradations marked on its stem. However, his device failed to reference the scale to a fixed point such as the freezing point of water.

In 1724, the Dutch instrument maker Gabriel Fahrenheit used mercury as a temperature-measuring medium. Mercury has several advantages as a thermometric medium. First, it has a relatively large coefficient of thermal expansion that remains fairly constant (i.e., linear) over a wide range of temperatures. Second, it retains its liquid form at temperatures well below the freezing point of water and well above the boiling point of water. Third, it does not easily separate into bubbles that might adhere to the glass surface as the column of mercury rises and falls with increasing and decreasing temperatures. On his scale, Fahrenheit fixed the boiling and freezing points of water to be 212° and 32°, respectively, providing an even 180 divisions in between. The Fahrenheit temperature scale was adopted as the basis of measuring temperature in the British system of units, which has now become the US system of units. Measurements recorded with this scale are referred to as *degrees Fahrenheit (°F)*.

In 1745 Carolus Linnaeus of Sweden proposed a temperature scale in which the freezing point of water is fixed as 0° and the boiling point of water is fixed at 100°, with 100 divisions in between these two reference points. This reversed the temperature scale that had been proposed a few years earlier by Anders Celsius, who had set 0° as the boiling point and

100° as the freezing point of water. Maintaining Linnaeus' reversal the name *Centigrade* was replaced by *Celsius* in 1948.[4] The conversion of Fahrenheit to Celsius degrees and vice versa proceeds as follows:

$$°C = 5/9 \ (°F - 32) \qquad [1.11]$$

$$°F = 9/5 \ (°C) + 32 \qquad [1.12]$$

There is one other scale that has relevance to temperature. It is related to the concept of a *thermodynamic temperature*. In 1780 the French physician Jacques Charles (1746–1823) demonstrated that for the same increase in temperature all gases exhibit the same increase in volume. In other words, the coefficient of thermal expansion of all gases is very nearly the same. Using this fact it is possible to devise a temperature scale that is based on only a single fixed point, rather than the two fixed points that are necessary for the Fahrenheit and Celsius scales. This temperature is referred to as the *thermodynamic temperature* and is now universally accepted as the fundamental measure of temperature. The single fixed point in this temperature scale is an *ideal gas* pressure of zero, which is also defined as *zero temperature*. The unit of measurement on this scale is called the *Kelvin*, named after Lord Kelvin (i.e., William Thompson, 1824–1907). The symbol used is K without the degree (°) symbol. To convert degrees Celsius to Kelvin units we simply add 273.

$$K = °C + 273 \qquad [1.13]$$

$$K = 5/9 \ (°F - 32) + 273 \qquad [1.14]$$

$$°C = K - 273 \qquad [1.15]$$

$$°F = 9/5 \ (K) - 241 \qquad [1.16]$$

1.3.3 Objective and subjective measurements

With very few exceptions, buildings are designed and constructed to be occupied by human beings. Therefore, in the study of building science we are concerned as much with how the human occupants of buildings perceive their environment as we are with the physical nature of the environment itself. While the perception of heat, light, and sound is of course directly related to the stimuli that are received and processed in the human cognitive system, the measurement of what was received and what is perceived may differ widely. For example, while the amount of sound produced by a person speaking on a cell phone in a public place such as a restaurant can be measured objectively with a sound-level meter, the degree of annoyance that this telephone conversation may cause to nearby customers depends very much on the sensitivity, current activity and emotional state of each person who is forced to overhear the telephone conversation. These individual perceptions are subjective reactions.

Objective information can normally either be measured with an instrument, or counted. It is typically information that is observable and factual. Examples include the measurement of light with a light meter, sound with a sound-level meter, and temperature with a thermometer. If the instrument is true and properly calibrated, then the measurement of exactly the same sound should not vary from one sound-level meter to another. However, the subjective perception of that sound may very widely from one person to another, and even for the same person under different circumstances.

Both objective and subjective data can be collected in experiments or in assessing some particular aspect of a building environment. For example, based on complaints received about the stuffiness of a particular building space from the occupants of a new building, it may become necessary to conduct a survey of opinions to determine the degree of dissatisfaction. The data collected will likely be based on responses to a questionnaire and therefore subjective in nature. However, the survey may be followed by a systematic assessment of actual environmental conditions, including measurement of the density of occupation, temperature, relative humidity, and degree of air movement in the space. All of these are objective measurements.

Methods that are normally used to collect objective data include: measurements taken with an instrument; recorded data (e.g., sound, light, heat, humidity, and air movement); and direct, objective measurements of a physical product, or natural event, phenomenon, or object. Such measurements are reproducible and factual. However, the methods used for collecting subjective data are quite different in nature. They include ranking and rating methods, questionnaires, and interviews. The interpretation of subjective data must be undertaken with a great deal of caution because they are subject to human bias (Cushman and Rosenberg, 1991). For this reason alone it is considered good practice to collect both objective and subjective data during experiments, surveys, and assessments of environmental conditions involving human subjects.

1.3.4 Stress and strain

The relationship between stress and strain is one of the fundamental concepts in the fields of material science and structural engineering. When a material is subjected to some kind of external force, then it will in some manner respond by changing its state. For example, if we walk on a suspended platform, such as the concrete floor of a multistory building, then the force applied by our weight will produce a physical strain within the concrete material. The resulting strain may result in a visible deflection of the floor. Similarly, if we blow air into a rubber balloon, then the air pressure will result in a stretching of the balloon material, with the result that the balloon increases in size. If we continue to blow air into the balloon, then eventually the strain in the rubber material will exceed the strength limit of the material and the balloon will burst.

In 1678 the English scientist Robert Hooke showed by means of a series of experiments that within the elastic range of a material the degree of strain produced is directly proportional to the amount of stress imposed. This relationship has come to be referred to as Hooke's Law and is easily verified with a very simple apparatus.

If we freely suspend a thin metal wire from a nail at some height above the ground and then progressively load the lower end of the wire with more and more weights, we will observe that the wire will slightly increase in length after each weight has been added. When the increases in weight and length are plotted on graph paper a straight line will be the result, indicating a linear relationship between the load (i.e., stress) imposed and the resulting deflection (i.e., strain).

The relationship between stress (i.e., stimulus) and strain (i.e., reaction) applies generally to all kinds of situations, although the relationship is not necessarily linear when we move out of the field of material science into the biological domain. For example, in the field of building lighting increases in illumination level tend to increase the ability to see details. For this reason the recommended task illumination level for fine machine work (e.g., sewing) is much higher than for casual reading. However, if we continue to increase the illumination level, then a point will eventually be reached when the light level is so intense that we can no longer see any details. This condition is referred to as *disability glare*.

Similarly, the thermal environment can produce stresses that will produce physiological strain in the occupants of buildings. Examples of such strain include an increased heart rate, the dilation or constriction of blood vessels, and perspiration or shivering. It is important to note that the stress imposed by a building environment is cumulative. For example, slightly inadequate lighting conditions in a building space may not by themselves produce any observable human discomfort. However, when this condition is coupled with a slightly elevated room temperature and perhaps also a moderately excessive level of background noise, the resultant cumulative strain may exceed the comfort level of the building occupant by a disproportionately high degree.

1.3.5   Black-body radiation

A *black body* is a concept in physics that the non-technical reader is unlikely to be familiar with.

Since it is of significance in some aspects of the thermal environment – in particular in respect to the utilization of solar energy, and also in respect to artificial light sources – it warrants some explanation. When the temperature of any material is raised above the temperature of its surroundings it will radiate heat to its surroundings.[5] On the other hand, when an object is at a lower temperature than its surroundings, then the surroundings will radiate heat to the object, which will absorb some of the heat and reflect and transmit the remaining heat. A *black body* is a theoretical object that absorbs all of the radiant energy that falls on it. It is an idealized concept, because no such material exists in the real world. The material that comes closest is the graphite form of carbon, which absorbs close to 97 percent of the radiation that is incident on its surface.

Therefore, an ideal solar collector surface would be a black body. Water at any depth is, for practical purposes, considered to act as a black body and this phenomenon underlies the principle of solar ponds. A solar pond is essentially a shallow pool of water that may or may not have a single glass sheet placed at a small distance above the water surface for added efficiency. Because of the near black-body characteristics of the water, even without the single glazing, the pond acts as a very efficient absorber of solar heat radiation.

In the case of a standard flat-plate solar collector, the upper surface of the metal plate is typically provided with a matte black finish. However, sometimes a more expensive *selective surface* coating with special heat-absorbing characteristics is applied. A *selective surface* is a surface finish that has a large solar heat absorptance and a small solar emittance.[6]

A black body is also a radiator of heat if its temperature is higher than the temperature of its surroundings. The radiation produced consists of a continuous spectrum of wavelengths. In fact, a black body at any temperature will emit energy at all wavelengths, but to varying amounts. As shown in Figure 1.11, the theoretical energy emission curve is asymptotic[7] to the X-axis.

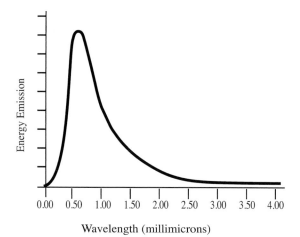

Wavelength (millimicrons)

Figure 1.11   Black body curve for 5000 K.

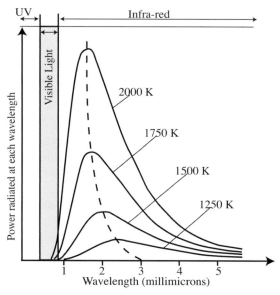

Figure 1.12   The black-body radiation spectrum at increasing temperatures with the maximum emission wavelength moving toward the visible range.

In other words, at very long wavelengths the curve never quite reaches zero emission. However, the actual amount of radiation varies both with the wavelength and the temperature of the *black body*. The precise radiation spectrum produced by a black body can be calculated mathematically and is referred to as the *black-body radiation* for that temperature (Figure 1.12).

Standard *black-body radiation* curves have been drawn for each temperature, based on the Kelvin temperature scale. In this way, for example, the spectral distribution of an artificial light source can be rated according to its equivalent black-body radiation curve. This is referred to as the *color temperature* of the light source, because it characterizes the color rendition properties[8] of the light source. As the temperature of the black body increases, the maximum of the radiation spectrum moves toward the shorter wavelengths (Figure 1.12).

Therefore, at some temperature the radiation spectrum of a black body will maximize the amount of light produced, because light is a narrow bandwidth within the full electromagnetic spectrum of radiation. This ideal color temperature is around 6000 K.[9]

Endnotes

1. The US has adopted the alternative spelling of *meter*.
2. In the SI standard the *metre* is defined as the distance light travels in 1/299 792 458th of a second.
3. Where abbreviations are shown they refer to the abbreviations used throughout this book (in the absence of a standard US notational convention).
4. Apart from the name change, there are also some very small differences in the precise temperature values of the freezing and boiling points of water. Under standard atmospheric conditions the boiling point of water is defined on the Celsius scale as 99.975°C, as opposed to 100° on the Centigrade scale.
5. This of course applies only to those surfaces of the material that are not in direct contact with the surfaces of other objects. In the case of surfaces that touch each other heat is transferred by conduction from the object that is at a higher temperature to the object that is at a lower temperature.
6. The efficiency of the flat-plate solar collector increases if either the absorptance increases or the emittance decreases. A maximum efficiency is reached when the emittance is zero. In the case of a *selective surface* the absorptance is greater than the emittance, while for a *non-selective surface* the absorptance is equal to the emittance (Kreider and Kreith, 1975, pp. 42 and 96).

7. An *asymptotic curve* never crosses the axis, but comes infinitesimally close to that axis.

8. The term *color rendition* refers to the appearance of colored surfaces under a light source with a particular spectral distribution. For example, a red surface under a blue light will appear almost black, because most of the blue light is absorbed by the red surface. However, a red light will accentuate the redness of a red surface because much of the red light will be reflected.

9. As explained in a later chapter on artificial lighting, *color temperature* must not be confused with the operating temperature of an artificial light source.

2 Principles of Thermal Comfort

Almost all buildings are designed and constructed for the purpose of sheltering and facilitating the activities of human beings. In most cases these activities are performed within the building itself and therefore require the designer to carefully consider the thermal comfort needs of the occupants. One can further argue that if the building occupant is the focus of our attention, then the starting point for the thermal design of a building should be the human body and its thermal interactions with the immediate environment.

2.1 Heat transfer between body and environment

The human being is a form of heat engine that derives its energy from the combustion of food, a process referred to as *metabolism*. To achieve comfort under varying climatic conditions it is necessary to regulate the amount of heat lost from, or gained by, the human body (Figure 2.1).

From a general viewpoint our body is able to lose heat in three ways:

- through outward radiation to colder surroundings, such as colder surfaces and a colder sky;
- through outward convection or conduction to air below skin temperature and by direct contact with colder objects (e.g., bare feet on a concrete floor);
- through evaporation from the respiratory tract and from skin perspiration.

When exposed to the external environment the human body is involved in heat transfer driven by infra-red radiation of short wavelength (i.e., solar radiation) and long wavelength (i.e., thermal radiation). The intensity of direct solar radiation can be in excess of 300 BTU/SF per hour on a horizontal surface. The amount of surface of the human body exposed to the sun varies with the altitude of the sun and the posture assumed. Generally speaking, for a standing person the maximum exposure to radiation in a warm climate will occur between 9 to 10 am in the morning and between 2 to 3 pm in the early afternoon.

The ground and surrounding objects will exchange radiant heat with the human body if their temperatures are at variance with that of the body surface. For example, in hot, dry climates the ground and surrounding surfaces may become appreciably warmer than the human body, so that the amount of heat gained by radiation can become critical. Unfortunately, this radiation tends to be of the long-wavelength type and is therefore readily absorbed by the skin. Transfer of heat between the skin and surrounding air will occur by convection and conduction, with the rate of transfer depending very much on the degree of air movement. The latter tends to replace the air next to the skin with fresh air, thereby increasing the amount of heat lost from the human body if the temperature of the air is less than that of the skin. Air movement also increases the amount of heat lost by evaporation, since it replaces

Building Science: Concepts and Application. Jens Pohl.
© 2011 John Wiley & Sons, Ltd.
Published 2011 by John Wiley & Sons, Ltd.

> The human body is a form of heat engine that derives its energy from the combustion of food (i.e., metabolism).

- Thermal comfort depends on heat transfer between human body and environment.

- Heat loss may occur through outward radiation (to sky and colder surroundings), evaporation (from breathing and perspiration), and outward convection (air below skin temperature) or conduction (feet on cold floor).

- Direct solar radiation may exceed 300 BTU/SF/HR on a horizontal surface.

- Deep body temperature (i.e., temperature of blood) is approximately 98.6°F (skin temperature is about 92°F).

Figure 2.1   The human heat engine.

> Environmental temperature is one of the most critical factors governing human comfort and survival.

- Our ability to survive in environmental temperatures ranging from –60°F to 130°F is due to our technical skills (shelter and clothing).

- Our deep body temperature must not vary by more than 1% for thermal comfort and –2°F to +6°F for health and survival.

- Clothing is an effective mechanism for insulating the body in cold climates and for providing some individual control under most conditions.

Figure 2.2   Environmental adjustment.

the saturated air in contact with the skin with fresh air.

Therefore, to achieve a comfortable thermal environment it becomes necessary to regulate the heat lost from the human body by cooling or heating the air directly surrounding the skin or the surface of the skin. The fact that we have been able to adjust to a surprisingly wide range of climates (i.e., from the cold, ice-bound Arctic regions to the hot and humid tropical rainforests) is largely due to a number of technical skills that we have been able to apply in the construction of shelters and the manufacture of clothing (see Figure 2.2).

While the shelter must be considered the more important means of environmental control, at least from a qualitative point of view clothing provides a highly desirable degree of individual control within the sheltered environment.

2.2   Some physiological considerations

The range of temperatures to which the human body can adjust without discomfort is actually quite small. This is because the zone of thermal comfort for the human body is restricted to the temperature range in which the deep body temperature can be regulated by the control of blood flow in the skin and underlying tissue. In medical terms this is referred to as the *vaso-motor control* mechanism. Should the temperature gradient between the skin and surrounding air be negative (i.e., if the air temperature is lower than the body temperature), the vaso-motor control mechanism will constrict blood vessels so that the amount of heat lost from the blood is reduced. Conversely, in the case of a positive temperature gradient blood vessels will automatically dilate, and so proportionally increase heat loss from the blood (Figure 2.3).

The normal deep body temperature of the human body is approximately 98.6°F, which is kept constant by the vaso-motor control mechanism to within 1 percent in the case of a healthy person. While virtually any fall in deep body temperature can have disastrous consequences, a little more latitude exists on the high side. The human body can operate with reasonable efficiency up to a deep body temperature of about 103°F.

Deep body temperature is regulated by the control of blood flow in the skin and underlying tissue (i.e., vaso-motor control).

- Colder Environment

  Vaso-Motor Control will constrict blood vessels to reduce the flow of blood and in this way reduce heat loss.

- Warmer Environment

  Vaso-Motor Control will dilate blood vessels to increase the flow of blood and heat loss.

- Control of the rate of blood flow also controls the metabolic rate of the human body (or vice versa).

Figure 2.3   Vaso-motor control mechanism.

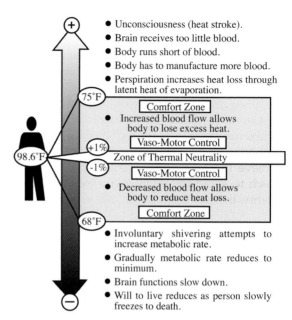

Figure 2.4   Human comfort and discomfort.

Immediately outside the vaso-motor control range the body resorts to involuntary muscular activity in the form of shivering to increase heat production, and evaporation from the skin and respiratory system (as well as insensible or osmotic perspiration) for increased heat loss (Figure 2.4). Both shivering and sweating are, however, associated with discomfort and must therefore be regarded as emergency measures (Figure 2.5). Furthermore, they must be described as inexact, slow in response and wasteful to the body in either food or water and salt intake.

From a general point of view, the operation of the human body as a heat engine that exchanges heat with the environment by convection, radiation and evaporation is described by the following equation:

$$M = E \pm C \pm R \pm S \qquad [2.1]$$

where:

M = heat produced by metabolism
E = heat exchanged by evaporation
C = heat exchanged by convection
R = heat exchanged by radiation
S = storage.

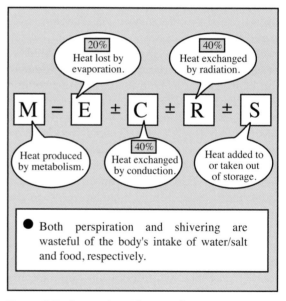

Figure 2.5   Proportional heat exchange.

It is an essential requirement of comfort that any variations in the amount of storage are made solely to meet involuntary physiological responses, such as the diurnal temperature rhythm, and that the heat exchange due to evaporation should be as small as possible. Subject to these restrictions, however, some flexibility and therefore convenient degree of control may be obtained by the adjustment of the remaining variables in equation [2.1].

Although the rate of metabolism is normally almost entirely governed by the work performed or the activity of the person, there is no doubt that adjustments can be and often are made to achieve thermal comfort. The architect can do much to avoid the unnecessary expenditure of energy, thereby limiting the rate of metabolism. For example, in residential buildings consideration of floor levels (e.g., avoidance of split floor levels), space layout (e.g., minimization of walking distances and comfortable-height shelving), ceiling height, and natural air movement provide the designer with some control over the metabolic rate of the occupants.

Heat exchange by evaporation will involve sweating and must therefore be avoided wherever possible. However, thought must also be given to the facilitation of perspiration under conditions that require a considerable amount of heat loss from the body. High levels of humidity tend to occur in laundries, kitchens, and bathrooms, as well as in a large number of industrial manufacturing environments. Where these conditions exist, the body must rely on its ability to lose large amounts of heat by evaporation (Figure 2.5). Since the rate of evaporation depends on air movement and vapor pressure, the importance of orientation, ventilation, and dehumidification cannot be overstated (Figure 2.6).

The rate of convection is very much influenced by air movement, and although it is normally desirable to facilitate heat loss by convection in hot, humid climates, care must be taken to avoid exposure to winds of high velocity in hot, dry climates. The latter would cause the skin to dry out and could ultimately lead to dermatitis or similar skin complaints (Figure 2.6).

The degree of solar radiation control that may be exercised by orientation, shading, reflective surfaces, and so on is well known and will be elaborated on in later sections. It suffices here

---

> Building orientation, insulation, sun shading devices, window openings, material selection, and space layout, are primary architectural design tools.

- Rate of metabolism is normally determined by physical work performed.

- Perspiration is uncomfortable and should be avoided where possible.

- However, perspiration can be facilitated through air movement to decrease discomfort under hot/humid conditions.

- Air movement under hot/dry conditions dries out the skin (e.g., dermatitis) and should be minimized.

Figure 2.6   Thermal comfort control factors.

---

to mention that careful consideration of the use of trees, screens, sunshading devices, and especially treated glass to produce a comfortable thermal environment is mandatory during the early planning stage of any building project.

Fortunately, in a given work space most of the occupants will be expending approximately equal amounts of energy. Furthermore, fashion has a tendency to restrict individual clothing variations, although the absence of one or more garments, such as a coat or cardigan, will allow some degree of individual control. This small degree of personal control seems to be essential, since it is most unlikely that any centrally controlled environment will satisfy more than two-thirds of the occupants.

For normally clad, sedentary adults the preferred temperature that will satisfy approximately 80 percent of building occupants is 72°F. Of the remainder, half will consider this temperature to be too warm and half too cold (Figure 2.7). Accordingly, compliance with a federally (US Government) mandated internal temperature standard of 68°F (i.e., in winter) for all public buildings will require most building occupants to wear more clothing.

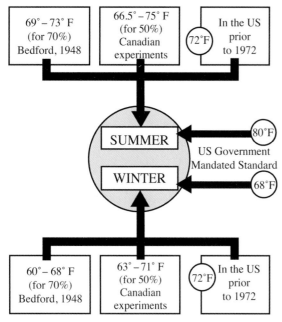

Figure 2.7   Objective comfort temperatures.

We may then define the zone of thermal neutrality for a person as the condition or range of conditions in which the body is not required to take any particular action to maintain its heat balance. Should the rate of heat loss increase through a fall in air temperature or increased air movement, the flow of blood through the skin will decrease. Consequently, the temperature of the skin will fall so that the deep body temperature can remain constant. With further increases in heat loss, the rate of metabolism will be increased by involuntary shivering or voluntary muscular activity (Figure 2.4). Conversely, if the rate of heat dissipation is reduced, the flow of blood through the skin will increase and balance will be achieved by a proportionate rise in skin temperature. Beyond this point, evaporative cooling is brought into play by operation of the sweat glands.

The zones of thermal neutrality for adult persons at rest under varying clothing conditions may be broadly defined as follows:

normally clothed	70°F to 75°F
lightly clothed	80°F to 85°F
without clothing	81°F to 86°F

During sleep the metabolic rate is at its lowest value, and therefore a warmer environment is required. The temperature of an occupied bed is approximately 85°F, although bedroom temperatures around this value are found to interfere with sleep owing to excessive environmental warmth. In cold conditions the body temperature during sleep can be maintained only by increased insulation. Such insulation is normally provided in the form of blankets. If hot-water bottles or similar unit heaters are used in bed, they are preferably applied to the feet. If these methods fail, then the body will resort to shivering for the production of heat energy. In hot conditions we have to ask the question: "What is the highest temperature compatible with sleep?" Observations have shown that for sound sleep, entirely devoid of covering, the temperature in still air must exceed 80°F. The presence of any substantial degree of air movement will increase this temperature considerably.

2.3   More about individual differences

Generally speaking, women require slightly warmer conditions than men both in winter and in summer. However, experiments have shown that such differences can be explained in terms of clothing (Figure 2.8).

It was found that interchange of the clothing appropriate to each sex produced negligible differences in the thermal sensations experienced by men and women.

Little is known about the preferences of children. The main difficulty here is that the metabolic rate of children varies appreciably from moment to moment, owing to rapid changes in activity. Infants are particularly susceptible to changes in environmental temperature. Both heat and cold can be equally disastrous, especially since infants are unable to call attention to their needs.

The elderly form another group who are particularly sensitive to extremes of temperature. It is generally recognized that with increasing age the temperature span to which elderly persons can adapt narrows down appreciably.

> The desire of women for slightly warmer conditions in both winter and summer is due to differences in clothing.

Age: The elderly are particularly sensitive to extremes in temperature.

Diet: Very high and very low calorie diets appear to slightly reduce heat tolerance.

Health: Any infection will reduce the ability to resist thermal stress.

Work Efficiency: The amount of muscular activity is directly related to individual heat tolerance. This is the most important factor contributing to individual differences.

Acclimatization: Appears to be due to behavioral adjustments (e.g., greater work efficiency) and not due to physiological changes.

Figure 2.8 Impacts on thermal comfort.

Further, it is well known that even individuals of the same sex and age vary in their susceptibility to heat. These differences may be attributed to a number of contributing factors (see Figure 2.8), as follows.

Diet: There is reason to believe that a high-calorie diet somewhat reduces heat tolerance generally. The same applies to a very low-calorie diet.

Efficiency: The mechanical efficiency with which a person performs a task appears to be one of the most important factors contributing to individual differences of heat tolerance. In other words, the amount of muscular activity bears a direct relationship to individual heat tolerance.

Health: Any disease or infection within the body system will reduce the ability of the body to resist stress.

Acclimatization: The belief that in tropical countries persons will be satisfied with higher temperatures in a controlled building environment than persons living in temperate climates, appears to be quite erroneous. The role played by acclimatization in heat tolerance can be explained in terms of short-range and long-range conditioning factors.

> According to Hooke's law, strain (e.g., physiological reactions) is proportional to stress (e.g., temperature).

- Stresses are usually cumulative (e.g., temperature, noise, glare, distractions) so that even low levels of a number of environmental stresses may cause discomfort, even though any one of these factors by itself may be quite tolerable.

- Strain is the physiological reaction of the human body to any imposed stress (e.g., shivering, perspiration, pulse rate, blood pressure, headache).

Figure 2.9 Hooke's law applied to the thermal environment.

Improvement in the means of losing heat from the body occurs in the short term, while reduction in heat production due to greater efficiency in the performance of work occurs over a longer term. However, it has been found that when acclimatized subjects are given a free choice of temperature, their preferences vary little from those persons who are not acclimatized.

When the human body fails to lose heat at the same rate as it is gaining heat, the results can be disastrous and we are said to be suffering from heat stress. In this sense stress is an attribute of the environment, and by analogy with Hooke's law it is the pressure applied (Figure 2.9).

Strain, though, is an attribute of the occupants of the environment and is related to the physiological deformation resulting from the application of the stress. Stresses such as high or low temperature, glare and noise are usually cumulative, so that even low levels of a number of these factors, although innocuous in themselves, may give rise to a high level of discomfort when summated.

Even though vaso-motor control provides us with an excellent heat-regulating mechanism that seldom allows the body temperature to rise to a dangerous level, this mechanism makes severe demands upon our body. In hot climates, it is these demands of temperature regulation whenever we experience difficulty in dissipating heat that will eventually lead to heat stress in the following stages (see Figure 2.4):

- By virtue of the vaso-motor control mechanism, the blood vessels of the skin and underlying tissues dilate to increase the rate of heat loss from the body.
- More blood passes through the skin to cool it; thus more blood must be manufactured.
- The ability to make blood is, however, limited, with the result that there will tend to be a blood shortage.
- The brain being at the highest point of the body may be deprived of a sufficient supply of blood. Heat exhaustion will eventually result, accompanied by the characteristic symptoms of headache, nausea, and finally unconsciousness.

While the human body has a remarkable sweating capacity and is able to lose as much as four gallons of water per day, this must be replaced by drinking. Under such circumstances the already precarious blood supply is still further depleted and the affinity to heat exhaustion is precariously increased.

2.4 Measurement of the thermal environment

The assessment of the thermal environment is one of the oldest judgments made by humans, although it is only since the German physicist Gabriel Fahrenheit (1686–1736) devised a satisfactory temperature scale in 1714 that we have been able to assign numerical values to prevailing environmental conditions. The Industrial Age focused attention on the assessment of environmental stress by determination of the intensity of thermal stress present in a given situation. This change in outlook was accompanied by the emergence of standards of accept-

---

Stress

- Typically only low levels of thermal stress occur in buildings.

- Currently comfort zones are established mainly on the basis of only four of the six thermal parameters (i.e., air temperature, humidity, air movement, and rate of work performed).

Strain

- Physiological strain factors include heart rate, blood pressure, rate of respiration, oxygen consumption, fatigue level, body temperature, and survival time.

- These measures of physiological strain are really only useful when the level of thermal stress is very high.

Figure 2.10 Thermal stress and strain relationships.

---

able working conditions accepted by employers, driven by the demands of workers and their unions.

Stress may be measured either in physical terms using the parameters of temperature, humidity, pressure, and so on, or by determining the physiological strain produced. In the latter case, heart rate, blood pressure, rate of respiration, oxygen consumption, fatigue, body temperature, and survival time are all available parameters for the measurement of strain (Figure 2.10).

However, these measures of physiological strain are satisfactory measures of stress only when the level of stress is very high. Accordingly, if and when it can be satisfactorily measured, comfort remains the most useful measure of the lower levels of stress that normally occur in buildings.

While the influential role of temperature, humidity, air movement, and mean radiant temperature in determining thermal comfort was already well established, the interest in production rates added two further thermal parameters: namely, the rate of work performance and

To date no single measurement scale that combines the six thermal comfort parameters into one index of thermal stress has been devised.

Air Temperature: The temperature of the air measured with a thermometer in the shade.

Humidity: The moisture content of the air typically expressed as a percentage in terms of relative humidity.

Air Movement: The speed at which air moves across the human body greatly influences thermal comfort.

Mean Radiant Temperature: The radiation that is received from surrounding surfaces (note: radiation is not influenced by air movement).

Rate of Work Performed: Muscular activity directly impacts the metabolic rate (and therefore the heat production).

Clothing Worn: The insulating characteristics of clothing inhibit heat loss from the human body.

Figure 2.11   **The thermal comfort parameters.**

None of the available indices combines all six parameters. The most commonly used index represents only one parameter.

Dry-Bulb Temperature: (Measures 1 parameter)

Measures only air temperature in the shade, but remains the most important single measure of thermal stress because it is readily available to everyone.

Wet-Bulb Temperature: (Measures 2 parameters)

Takes into account air temperature and humidity. Provides a reasonable index for hot humid climates.

Effective Temperature: (Measures 3 parameters)

Based on experimental data collected from groups in two test chambers, the Effective Temperature scale provides equal comfort curves (on a psychrometric chart) that take into account air temperature, humidity, and air movement.

Figure 2.12   **Very common thermal indices.**

the clothing worn. To date, it has not been possible to combine all six of these parameters into a single *index of thermal stress*, although there are a number of indices that incorporate at least two or three of the parameters (Figure 2.11).

Accordingly, comfort zones are established mainly on the basis of four of the six parameters of thermal stress: namely, air temperature, humidity, air movement, and rate of work performed. The question then remains: "Which of the available indices should be applied to assess the severity of any particular environment?" Before we can delve into this question more deeply it is appropriate to briefly survey the principal indices available today.

Dry-Bulb Temperature: Despite its obvious shortcomings, since it takes into account only one parameter (i.e., temperature), dry-bulb temperature remains the most important single measure of thermal stress (Figure 2.12). Weather forecasts that we hear daily on our radios and see on our television screens utilize temperature (i.e., dry-bulb temperature) as one of the principal indicators of tomorrow's weather conditions.

Wet-Bulb Temperature: This thermal indicator takes into account two factors: namely, temperature and humidity, while the important effects of air movement and radiation are disregarded. It provides a reasonable measure of the physiological effects of hot, humid environments.

Effective Temperature: The Effective Temperature scale was initially established as a series of equal comfort curves, based on experimental data by Houghton and Yaglou (1923). The temperature and humidity in one test chamber were adjusted until the degree of comfort or discomfort experienced by a trained group of observers was judged to be identical to that experienced in an adjacent test chamber maintained at a different temperature and humidity (Figure 2.12). Combinations of dry-bulb and wet-bulb temperatures were then plotted on a psychrometric chart to obtain curves of equal comfort. The intersection of any one of these curves with the dew point defined an *effective temperature*. These early experiments on Effective Temperature were followed by further work that also took into account such factors as clothing and muscular activity. Today, effective temperature may be described as an index that provides in a single numerical value a convenient measure of the interrelated effects of temperature, humidity and air movement. Further, by the provision of a normal and basic scale, it makes some allowance for the effect of clothing. In the mid-1950s it was demonstrated that by the addition of a simple monogram, Effective Temperature can also take into account the rate at which a person is performing work.

Equivalent Temperature: Proposed in the early 1930s, Equivalent Temperature is defined as the temperature of a uniform enclosure in which, in still air, a sizeable black body at 75°F would lose heat at the same rate as in the environment in question (Figure 2.13).

Accordingly, equivalent temperature is a measure of the combined effect of the temperature and movement of the air and the temperature of the surroundings. An instrument called a *eupathoscope* was invented to measure Equivalent Temperature. It consists of a blackened copper cylinder 22 inches high and 7.5 inches in diameter, the surface

---

Equivalent Temperature:
(Measures 3 parameters)

The temperature of an enclosure in which a Black Body at 75°F will lose heat at the same rate as the environment under consideration. Takes into account air temperature, air movement, and mean radiant temperature. (Black Body is a theoretical concept in Physics; absorbs all wavelengths of radiation equally.)

Predicted 4-Hour Sweat Rate (P4SR)
(Measures 5 parameters)

Combines air temperature, humidity, air movement, rate of work, and clothing worn (i.e., five of the six thermal parameters) into a single index. P4SR expresses the stress imposed by a hot thermal environment by measuring the amount of sweat secreted by fit, young persons when exposed to the environment under consideration for four hours.

Figure 2.13   Less common thermal indices.

---

of which is maintained by internal electric heaters at a constant temperature of 75°F. A few years later Bedford (1936, 1951) devised a monogram to more conveniently determine the Equivalent Temperature of an environment if the individual thermal parameters are known.

Globe-Thermometer Temperature: This thermal index was introduced in the late 1920s as a means of measuring the combined effect of air temperature, air movement and mean radiant temperature. Unfortunately, the Globe-Thermometer Temperature index can give misleading measurements under certain thermal conditions. First, in cold climates an increase in air movement will produce a rise in the temperature reading. Second, when the air and surrounding walls are at the same temperature the globe-thermometer will continue to show that temperature, regardless of changes in air movement. For these reasons its use as a measure of thermal stress has been largely abandoned, although it remains to the present day one of the most successful methods of determining the mean radiant temperature of the surroundings of a building space.

Predicted 4-Hour Sweat Rate (P4SR): This index was developed at the National Hospital, London in the late 1940s. Basically, P4SR is in the form of a monogram that is derived from experimental data and expresses the stress imposed by a hot environment in terms of the amount of sweat secreted by fit, acclimatized, young men when exposed to the environment under consideration for a period of four hours (Figure 2.13).

As such, P4SR represents a considerable advance over other previous indices, since it takes into consideration not only the environmental parameters of temperature, air movement and humidity, but also the rate of energy expended and the clothing worn. However, P4SR is not suitable as a comfort index because it applies only when perspiration occurs.

Wet-Bulb Globe-Thermometer Index: This index was devised in the 1950s for the US Army as

```
┌─────────────────────────────────────────────────┐
│    ████ Indices based on physical factors. ████   │
│                                                   │
│            Dry-Bulb Temperature                   │
│  e.g.,     Wet-Bulb Temperature                   │
│            Equivalent Temperature                 │
│  ┌─────────────────────────────────────────────┐ │
│  │ Provide no direct measure of the physiological effect of │ │
│  │ the environment.                            │ │
│  └─────────────────────────────────────────────┘ │
└─────────────────────────────────────────────────┘

┌─────────────────────────────────────────────────┐
│   ████ Indices based on physiological strain. ████ │
│                                                   │
│            Effective Temperature                  │
│  e.g.,     Predicted 4-Hour Sweat Rate            │
│  ┌─────────────────────────────────────────────┐ │
│  │ Based on Hooke's Law, which states that conditions of │ │
│  │ equal environmental stress produce equal physiological │ │
│  │ strain.                                     │ │
│  └─────────────────────────────────────────────┘ │
└─────────────────────────────────────────────────┘

┌─────────────────────────────────────────────────┐
│ ████ Indices based on heat exchange calculations. ████ │
│                                                   │
│        Indices that attempt to calculate the heat │
│  e.g., exchange between the human body and its    │
│        surroundings.                              │
│  ┌─────────────────────────────────────────────┐ │
│  │ Potentially the most promising approach to the │ │
│  │ development of a single thermal comfort index, but │ │
│  │ depends on the ability to accurately model the human │ │
│  │ body.                                       │ │
│  └─────────────────────────────────────────────┘ │
└─────────────────────────────────────────────────┘
```

Figure 2.14   Groups of thermal indices.

a means of preventing heat casualties at military training centers. As a single thermal index, it incorporates the effects of air temperature, humidity, air movement, and solar radiation as defined by the following equation:

$$\mathbf{WBGT = 0.7\,WB + 0.2\,GT + 0.1\,DB} \qquad [2.2]$$

where:

WB = wet-bulb temperature
GT = globe-thermometer reading
DB = dry-bulb temperature.

This index has considerable merit owing to its simplicity and the fact that it can be applied out of doors.

These are only some of the many available indices for the assessment of the thermal environment. MacPherson (1962) describes 19 indices. Since many of these indices are based on similar principles, it is convenient to establish three fundamental groups (Figure 2.14), as follows:

Indices based on the measurement of physiological factors such as Dry-Bulb Temperature,

Wet-Bulb Temperature, Equivalent Temperature, and Globe-Thermometer Temperature. Although all of these indices take into account air temperature and some combine this with air movement or humidity, they provide no direct measure of the physiological effect produced by the environment.

Indices based on physiological strain, including Effective Temperature and later modifications, Predicted Four-Hour Sweat Rate (P4SR), and the Wet-Bulb Globe-Thermometer index are based on the assumption, by analogy with Hooke's law, that conditions of equal environmental stress will produce equal physiological strain. It is common practice to express the relationship between stress and strain in the form of monograms.

Indices based on the calculation of heat exchange such as Operative Temperature and Standard Operative Temperature, Index for Evaluating Heat Stress, and the Thermal Acceptance Ratio, which attempt to calculate the heat exchange between the human body and its surroundings. Although the precise calculation of the quantity of heat transferred is fairly uncertain, and the relationship between this and the severity of the environment is a matter of debate, there seems little doubt that these indices potentially provide the most satisfactory approach to the development of a single comfort index.

We are therefore confronted with a wide range of indices of thermal stress, from which we must make a choice for the measurement of any particular environment. Furthermore, the assessment of the environment must be based on the measurement of all of the parameters, whether they are directly due to the environment, such as air temperature and air movement, or are attributes of the exposed persons, as in the case of clothing and work performance.

2.5   Selecting the appropriate index

The guidelines set out in Figure 2.15, while perhaps oversimplifying the problem, are generally

Rule 1: The index must cover the correct range of temperatures (e.g., Equivalent Temperature does not extend above 75°F, P4SR applies only to those conditions where sweating occurs).

Rule 2: If two environments are to be compared then the index does not need to include thermal parameters that are the same in each environment. (e.g., there may be no air movement in an office environment).

Rule 3: If there is a choice of indices then always select the simpler index (e.g., in air-conditioned offices the Dry-Bulb Temperature index may suffice).

Figure 2.15 Index selection rules.

accepted for the selection of indices of thermal stress for specific conditions.

- The index must cover the correct range of temperatures. The Equivalent Temperature scale (Figure 2.13), for example, does not extend beyond 75°F, while the Predicted 4-Hour Sweat Rate (Figure 2.13) and the Wet-Bulb Temperature (Figure 2.12) apply only to conditions where sweating occurs.
- If an index is required for the comparison of two or more situations in which a number of factors are identical (e.g., rate of work and air movement), then there is no advantage in selecting an index that incorporates these factors.
- If there remains a choice of two indices, the simpler one should be chosen. For example, in some cases the Dry-Bulb Temperature will suffice as an index. Often when defining comfort conditions of office workers for the purpose of air conditioning, air temperature alone will provide a satisfactory measure of the environment. The occupants are usually clad alike and engaged in similar physical tasks, while air movement would normally not vary greatly in a sealed environment. Further, there will not be any significant dif-

ference between the temperature of the air and enclosing walls unless the latter embody a heating system. Humidity may be safely disregarded on the basis that since we are dealing with comfort conditions, sweating must not occur and therefore any evaporative heat loss that could be affected by the ambient humidity is mainly confined to water loss from the lungs. Such heat loss constitutes less than 25 percent of the total heat transfer in comfort conditions. This is confirmed by the experimental work of Bedford, Yaglou, and Koch, who have demonstrated that changes of up to 50 percent in relative humidity will produce a change of less than 2°F in the Dry-Bulb Temperature. Obviously these circumstances are considerably altered in the hot, wet environments encountered in mills, laundries, and mines. There, the heat exchange is chiefly due to evaporation and it is likely that Wet-Bulb Temperature, which takes into account air temperature and humidity, will provide an adequate means of assessing the environment.

- If considerable variations in air movement are likely to occur in the environment under consideration, or if the air is hot and dry, then both the Predicted 4-Hour Sweat Rate and the Effective Temperature may be applied. However, if such an environment contains a significant radiation component, the Effective Temperature scale must be corrected for radiation.

2.6 Thermal comfort factors

While the similarity between the comfort zone and the zone of thermal neutrality (at which, by definition, the human body takes no particular action to maintain its heat balance) is evident, both are very much subject to individual preferences, clothing, activity, and age. In fact, the problem of individual differences encountered in the assessment of the comfort zone has become increasingly more complex. Although clothing can be effectively used to provide individual variation, it is well to remember that our garments serve many other purposes besides thermal comfort (i.e., social convention, fashion, availability of materials, and so on). Recent investigations in the Arctic region have demonstrated that in the absence of social convention the human being is able to adjust by means of clothing to any reasonable indoor temperature. Under these circumstances it was found to be quite useless to define a comfort or preferred temperature zone. Obviously a certain amount of latitude exists in the case of protection against cold conditions. In hot climates, people usually wear the minimum clothing that convention will permit and thus there exists far less latitude in the adjustment of individual differences by means of clothing.

In general terms, we can define the requirements of a comfortable thermal environment, as follows:

General Thermal Effects of the environment attributable to the parameters of air temperature, relative humidity, and air movement. According to Bedford, a habitable space should be as cool as is possible within the comfort zone; should be subject to adequate air movement, although both monotony and local drafts must be avoided; and should have an ambient relative humidity within the wide range of 30 to 70 percent. Further we can distinguish between two overall thermal problems. If a space is *too cold*, then this is most likely due to a low air temperature, with or without excessive air movement. On the other hand, if a space is *too hot*, then this may be attributable to either of the combinations of high air temperature and high humidity, or insufficient air movement and excessive radiation.

Local Thermal Effects such as excessive local warmth are to be avoided. Undue temperature gradients that may occur due to differences in temperature at different heights of a space will cause discomfort, although it is generally accepted that the floor should be at the highest temperature, with the temperature gradient gently decreasing toward the ceiling. Excessive loss of heat from body extremities such as the feet, and the local overheating of the heads of occupants by radiant heat, are two common sources of discomfort.

Density of Occupation will not only have an effect on air temperature and humidity by virtue of the heat and moisture contributed to the environment by the occupants, but also will strongly influence the subjective concepts of *freshness* and *stuffiness*. As our standards of thermal comfort become more sophisticated, a thermally comfortable environment will not be acceptable unless it is accompanied by a quality of freshness. Although it is generally recognized that freshness is related to coolness, absence of unpleasant odors, slight air movement, and a psychologically desirable feeling of change, and that stuffiness is partly defined by a degree of hotness, the presence of unpleasant odors, and the absence of air movement, little scientific information has been collected on either of these comfort factors.

Activity of the Occupants may involve muscular activity, which will increase the metabolic rate and therefore the body will produce more heat. This additional heat must be dissipated by the body at an increased rate, so that thermal neutrality is immediately restored. Accordingly, the comfort zone for persons engaged in heavy physical work is different from that required for office workers (Figure 2.16).

The approximate rates of heat production for various degrees of activity have been established on the basis of experiments, as shown below:

sleeping person = 300 BTU/hr.

sitting person = 400 BTU/hr.

typing or writing = 600 BTU/hr.

walking slowly = 800 BTU/hr.

walking briskly = 1200 BTU/hr.

hand sawing = 1800 BTU/hr.

medium jogging = 2300 BTU/hr.

severe exertion = 4800 BTU/hr.

Figure 2.16 Typical metabolic rates.

Most of the attendant heat loss from the body takes place by radiation (40 percent) and convection or conduction to air (40 percent). However, since the surface of the body is always slightly moist, a further loss will take place by evaporation (20 percent). The latter component will substantially increase whenever large-scale perspiration sets in.

3 Thermal Control by Building Design

Although acute physiological breakdowns such as heat stroke and heat cramps will normally occur only at very high temperatures, it has been found that even moderately high temperatures can appreciably affect the capacity of persons to perform work. Studies conducted after World War II, involving both laboratory experiments and industrial surveys, have confirmed this beyond any reasonable doubt. Seasonal production statistics collected in heavy and light industries, such as steel and textile manufacturing plants, have consistently shown that excessive temperature and humidity will result in reduced output. Although increased temperature seems to have the greatest effect on the performance of physical work, both high and low temperatures will affect manual dexterity, concentration, and the occurrence of accidents. For example, the statistics represented graphically in Figure 3.1 emphasize the effect of high temperatures on the rate of accidents in coalmines in England during the 1940s.

It is interesting to note that in this work environment temperature also appears to influence the distribution of accidents in the various age groups. In the coolest mines the accident rate declined with increasing age, since under reasonably comfortable conditions the greater experience of older persons will tend to diminish their accident risk. On the other hand, in the hottest mines the rate of accidents increased sharply for the 35 to 55 age group. This age group is likely to be more easily fatigued, accompanied by greater loss of concentration and resulting in a higher accident rate.

3.1 How important is the thermal environment?

There is ample statistical evidence indicating that every improvement made in an uncomfortable thermal environment not only will result in an increase in production, but will also improve the quality of the product, reduce the accident risk, and provide better labor relations. It is therefore essential that every effort be made at the design stage of a building to provide a comfortable thermal environment.

Before the advent of the energy crisis in the early 1970s, it was already recognized that even if a building is to be fully air-conditioned by mechanical means careful consideration must be given to building orientation, solar heat protection, adequate thermal insulation, and the appropriate choice of construction materials. While the improvement of living and working conditions has become a well-established social criterion, the necessity for energy conservation has rather abruptly forced the owners and designers of buildings to abandon mechanical environmental conditioning aids in favor of natural means whenever possible. Although the degree of thermal control that can be achieved by building design alone is constrained by climatic conditions, very significant savings in energy (often exceeding 50 percent) are nearly always possible. In hot climates such design measures can ensure that the internal building environment will be at least no worse than conditions in the shade out of doors. In many cases,

Building Science: Concepts and Application. Jens Pohl.
© 2011 John Wiley & Sons, Ltd.
Published 2011 by John Wiley & Sons, Ltd.

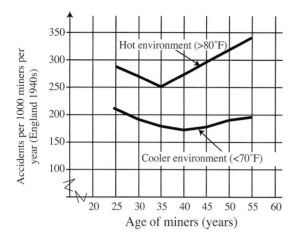

(Source: Bedford, T. (1946); 'Environmental Warmth and Its Measurement'; Medical Research Council, War Memorandum #17, HMSO.)

Figure 3.1   Accident rates in British coal mines during the 1940s.

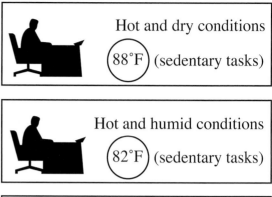
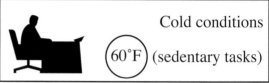

Figure 3.2   Limits of barely acceptable thermal conditions.

conditions that are considerably better may be achieved at little extra cost by the use of certain methods of construction. Nevertheless, as a rule, it is unlikely that completely unconditioned buildings will provide a comfortable thermal environment if the external climatic conditions are well outside the comfort zone. It is therefore necessary not only to establish optimum conditions, but also the upper and lower limits beyond which conditions are likely to produce an unacceptable degree of thermal discomfort.

According to studies undertaken in Australia (Drysdale, 1967), the upper limit of acceptable thermal conditions under hot-dry conditions for persons engaged in sedentary tasks is approximately 88°F (Figure 3.2).

In hot-humid conditions this upper limit is likely to lie closer to 82°F, owing to the negative influence of humidity. The lower threshold is less clearly defined, owing to the latitude provided by clothing, but it is probable that air temperatures below 60°F will produce definite discomfort. It has been argued that repeated exposure to conditions outside these limits is likely to have detrimental effects on the physi-

cal health of persons, but to date that does not seem to have been proven medically.

3.2 Thermal building design strategies

Both the heat capacity and thermal resistance of external walls will have a significant effect on the ability to regulate the internal environment by building design alone. Depending on the construction of the wall, some of the heat gained during the day will be absorbed by the wall material before the wall can pass on heat to the inside of the building. At night, the heat stored in the wall will naturally dissipate to the outside before the cooling of the building interior can commence. Accordingly, an external wall capable of absorbing a considerable amount of heat during a hot day will allow the building environment to remain relatively cool. Conversely, during the night the same wall will need to lose much of the stored heat before it can have an appreciable cooling effect on the interior. Heavyweight wall construction tends to produce the required effects, since the heat-storing capacity for most types of walls is proportional to the weight per unit surface area of the wall. This is clearly demonstrated in experiments performed by Roux and others (1951) in South Africa, in which variations in outdoor and indoor air temperatures and heat flows at the outside and inside surfaces of the east wall of a test building were plotted for a mild summer day in Pretoria, South Africa (Figure 3.3).

In this example, approximately five times more heat appears to have entered the outside surface of a 9 in. thick, unshaded brick wall than was passed into the interior of the building from the inside surface. It should be noted that since Pretoria is located in the southern hemisphere the sun is inclined to the north, and not the south as is the case in the northern hemisphere.

It can be seen from Figure 3.3 that there is a time delay between the maximum heat entry into the wall and the maximum dissipation of this heat into the building environment. This time lapse is related, of course, to the resistance to heat flow posed by the construction (i.e., the U-value of the wall). Generally speaking, heavyweight construction will reduce the ability of a building environment to follow any but the most considerable changes in outdoor conditions, and then only after an appreciable time lapse. This property of heavy wall construction is an advantage in those regions where there exist sharp differences between day and night temperatures (commonly referred to as the diurnal temperature range). Having been cooled at night, the wall will be able to absorb considerable heat before the temperature of the interior is raised. If the cool night air can be used to accelerate the cooling of the structure and interior by the provision of floor and ceiling openings to achieve ventilation at night, perhaps with the addition of a fan, then a very economical system of natural thermal control can be achieved.

As shown in Figure 3.4, heavyweight construction is particularly useful in hot-dry climates, which are characterized by high

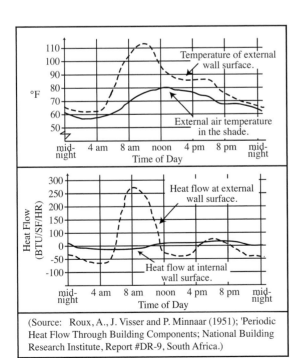

(Source: Roux, A., J. Visser and P. Minnaar (1951); 'Periodic Heat Flow Through Building Components; National Building Research Institute, Report #DR-9, South Africa.)

Figure 3.3 **Heat flow through a heavyweight building envelope (idealized) in a *hot-dry* climate.**

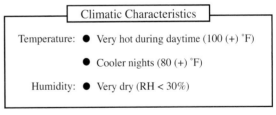

Climatic Characteristics

Temperature: ● Very hot during daytime (100 (+) °F)

● Cooler nights (80 (+) °F)

Humidity: ● Very dry (RH < 30%)

Design Strategies

Utilize the building envelope as a buffer and heat sink. Seal the building during the day and open it up at night to cool the envelope from the inside and the outside. Then repeat the cycle at sunrise.

● Heavy construction with high heat capacity for walls and roof.
● Small windows deeply recessed into the walls.
● Reflective external envelope (surfaces).
● Thermal insulation in walls (inside surface) and roof (also reflective foil).

Figure 3.4 **Design strategies for a *hot-dry* climate.**

temperatures during the day, significantly lower temperatures at night, and a relative humidity that rarely exceeds 30 percent. In such desert-like environments the building envelope per-forms the functions of a thermal buffer between the external and internal environments. Small windows, and a thermal insulation layer placed on the inside surface of the walls, allow the building to be virtually sealed off from the heat of the daytime hours. In addition, the windows are recessed deep into the walls so that the window reveal can act as a sunshading device. A light-reflective external wall finish ensures that at least some of the solar radiation is reflected back from the envelope.

For hot-humid climates, an elongated east–west building shape with large openings in the elongated north and south elevations is in order (Figure 3.5).

The large openings are required to facilitate air movement across the bodies of the build-ing's occupants. As discussed in the previous chapter, if the ambient temperature rises beyond the ability of the human vaso-motor control mechanism to maintain a normal deep body

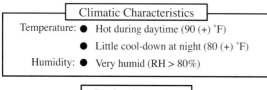

Climatic Characteristics
Temperature: ● Hot during daytime (90 (+) °F)
● Little cool-down at night (80 (+) °F)
Humidity: ● Very humid (RH > 80%)

Design Strategies
Single-banked building plan with large openings to maximize air-movement at the occupant level. Typically an elongated plan on an east–west axis.
● Since external air is used for cooling purposes the internal building temperature cannot be lower than the external air temperature in the shade.
● Lightweight construction with more than 50% of wall openings.
● Thermal insulation is required only in surfaces exposed to direct solar radiation (east, west and roof).
● Sunshading devices are recommended for south walls. (north walls in Southern Hemisphere).

Figure 3.5   Design strategies for an (idealized) *hot-humid* climate.

temperature (by losing heat at approximately the same rate as the body is gaining heat), then perspiration will set in. However, the ability of the body to lose more heat through the conver-sion of the liquid perspiration to gaseous water vapor (i.e., the energy used up in the latent heat of evaporation process) is severely limited, because the humid air is already nearly satu-rated with water vapor. Therefore, the small amount of moisture that each particle of air can soak up from the skin will be multiplied by the movement of many particles across the skin. The result is a slightly accelerated loss of heat from the body.

There are several building design implica-tions of this strategy. First, to facilitate the movement of air between the north and south walls, care must be taken to avoid any physical obstructions such as intermediate partitions. This virtually mandates a building layout with single-banked rooms. The typical natural wind speeds that are found in hot-humid climates rarely exceed 6 to 8 mph and even a fly wire screen can reduce this by as much as 40 percent. Second, since external air is being used to cool the building interior, clearly the temperature inside the building will not be lower than the temperature in the shade of the external air. Accordingly, thermal insulation in hot-humid climates is necessary only for those sections of the building envelope that are exposed to direct solar radiation – namely, the roof and the east and west walls. The south wall (in the northern hemisphere) is easily and effectively shaded from the sun, and the north wall will not be subjected to solar radiation. Third, as long as air movement serves as a primary cooling mecha-nism, little purpose would be served by provid-ing a heavyweight construction system. In fact, massive walls with their attendant heat capacity would tend to add an undesirable heat source during prolonged hot spells. Therefore, the pre-dominant construction solution in hot-humid climates is lightweight, with homes often raised at some height above ground level to maximize air movement (i.e., wind speed is normally slightly reduced at ground level owing to veg-etation). Finally, since up to 90 percent of the heat transfer through roofs subjected to intense sunshine is by radiation, it is important to utilize a highly reflective layer (e.g., aluminum foil) facing an air space as the first barrier to heat transmission in the roof. As this reflective layer heats up, it becomes a heat radiator on its own account. Therefore, several inches of thermal insulation are normally provided directly on the underside of the reflective foil to prevent the transmission of this heat into the building.

Cold climates are characterized by low day and night temperatures, snowfall during winter in some regions, and a wind-chill factor due to air movement that can easily lower the perceived temperature by another 5°F to 10°F (Figure 3.6).

Under these adverse thermal conditions, the available design strategies are all aimed at minimizing the loss of heat from the building interior to the external environment. First, the building envelope must be well insulated. In the case of the roof the insulation layer is often provided with reflective foil facing both upward and downward, so that in winter heat radiated from interior sources is reflected back into the building, and in summer excessive solar radiation is reflected back out of the building. Several such double-sided thermal insulation panel systems are commercially available. They typically consist of two to seven inches thick insulation bats lined on both sides with very thin aluminum foil. It is of course necessary for these double-sided panels to be installed so that they face an air space on each side. Second, care must be taken to minimize the infiltration of cold air into the building by sealing doors and windows with weather stripping. Third, attention now focuses on the windows as the least insulated component of the building shell. As will be seen in the next chapter, double-glazed windows will reduce the outward heat loss to less than half the heat loss through single-glazed windows. Fourth, a compact building plan will minimize the ratio of external wall and roof area to internal floor area. This leaves relatively less external surface area from which the building can lose heat.

Finally, in cold climates the sun must be looked upon as an important natural asset. Advantage can be taken of the difference in altitude of the sun during winter and summer. In winter the altitude of the sun during the midday hours may be as much as 40 degrees lower than in the summer months. This allows horizontal shading devices on south elevations (north elevations in the southern hemisphere) to be designed to prevent solar radiation from penetrating windows in the summer, and to serve as a welcome natural source of heating in the winter (Figure 3.6). However, despite all of these design measures some form of supplementary, non-natural heating will be required in virtually all cold climates.

3.3 Importance of sunshading devices

Heat transmission through glass is virtually instantaneous and is very much aided by the penetration of direct solar radiation. At first sight it would appear that the most effective way of reducing this type of direct heat gain is to keep the sun off windows entirely by using

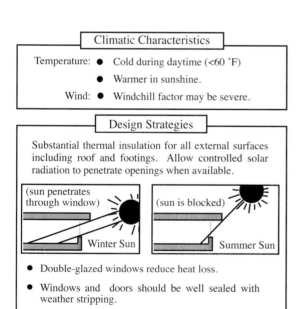

Figure 3.6   Design strategies for an (idealized) *cold* climate.

various types of sunshading devices. This solution may be appropriate to reduce summer heat gains and, at the same time, quite inappropriate for winter conditions. In winter, and perhaps throughout the year in colder climates, the sun is most useful as a heating device. As mentioned in the previous section, since the elevation or altitude of the sun is considerably lower in winter than in summer it is possible to design horizontal sunshading devices on south-facing windows to allow some direct solar radiation to penetrate through windows during the winter, and totally exclude the sun during the summer (Figure 3.6).

The heat gain that can be achieved by capturing solar radiation through closed windows in winter is magnified by the greenhouse effect (Figure 3.7).

The cause of this increased build-up of heat in spaces with large glazed areas is often misunderstood. It is a common misconception that the wavelength of the solar radiation changes as it passes through the glazing, and that the resultant radiation becomes trapped in the enclosed space because it cannot easily pass back through the glass. The correct explanation is quite different. In fact, when the solar radiation passes into the space it is readily absorbed by the objects in the space. Naturally, as these objects heat up they become heat radiators themselves. However, this radiation is of a longer wavelength and therefore cannot pass easily back through the window glass to the exterior. Most of it becomes trapped in the space, causing the space to progressively heat up beyond the contribution of the direct solar radiation.

There is no doubt that external shading is the most efficient form of solar protection from the point of view of heat control, since the heat radiation can be completely blocked if necessary. Unfortunately, it carries with it the disadvantages of interference with interior daylighting and natural ventilation. Furthermore, precautions must be taken to ensure that the shading device itself does not become unnecessarily hot, thereby assisting the transmission of heat by direct conduction to the wall or convection to the air surrounding the window opening (Figure 3.8).

Accordingly, the device should have a reflective finish and allow free air flow over its surface for cooling purposes.

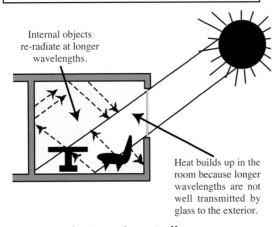

After solar radiation passes through a window (glass) it is absorbed by the objects inside the building space. These objects heat up and re-radiate heat at a longer wavelength that is partially blocked by the window glass.

Internal objects re-radiate at longer wavelengths.

Heat builds up in the room because longer wavelengths are not well transmitted by glass to the exterior.

Figure 3.7   The "greenhouse" effect.

- The altitude of the sun is much lower during the winter (about 30° at noon) than in summer (about 70° at noon).

- Heat transmission through glass (single-glazing) is virtually instantaneous.

- External sunshading devices are the most efficient form of solar heat protection.

- However, external sunshading devices interfere with interior daylighting (and possibly air movement).

- External sunshading devices should have a reflective finish and allow free air flow over their surface, because they can become a heat source.

Figure 3.8   Sunshading design considerations.

Fixed horizontal sunshading devices can be used to advantage in SOUTH orientations because the altitude of the sun is high.

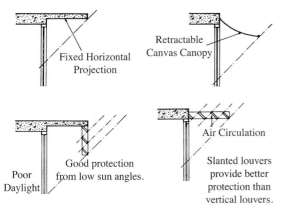

Figure 3.9   Horizontal sunshading devices.

Movable vertical sunshading devices can effectively block solar penetration on EAST and WEST orientations where the altitude of the sun is low.

Fins at right angles to wall.

Fins oblique to wall.

Separation of fins from wall avoids heat transmission.

Movable vertical fins can shade the whole wall or open up in different directions according to the position of the sun.

Figure 3.10   Vertical sunshading devices.

While horizontal sunshades may be used to advantage (i.e., summer shading and winter heating) for south-facing windows (Figure 3.9), they are definitely not appropriate for east and west orientations, where the altitude of the rising and setting sun is low. For these orientations vertical sunshading devices (Figure 3.10),

Internal shading devices are only as effective as the relative amount of direct solar radiation that they are capable of reflecting back through the window glass.

Approximate reduction in heat transfer due to selected internal and external shading devices:

Internal curtains		10% to 20%
Internal roller shades	(dark color)	20%
	(light color)	60%
Internal Venetian blinds	(dark color)	25%
	(light color)	.45%
External canvas awnings	(with sides).	.65%
	(without sides)	.75%
External louvers	(light color)	85%

Figure 3.11   Internal shading devices.

particularly if they are movable, are able to exclude the sun and yet allow the penetration of daylight.

Internal shading devices are only as effective as the relative amount of direct solar radiation that they are capable of reflecting back through the opening. The approximate percentage reductions in total heat transfer resulting from typical internal shading devices in comparison with similar externally applied devices are shown in Figure 3.11 (ASHRAE, 1989).

In recent years much research has been undertaken by glass manufacturers and allied industries, aimed at the development of glass and window units capable of substantially reducing heat transmission without proportional reductions in light transmission and transparency (Figure 3.12).

One of the first of these glass products was the green-tinted, heat-absorbing or non-actinic glass. Heat-absorbing glass, in conformity with its name, absorbs a large proportion of the solar energy falling upon it, with the result that its temperature is substantially raised and it can act as a radiator. Despite this drawback, it has many applications in industrial and commercial

Heat absorbing glass can be a severe radiator unless it is installed as a double-glazed unit with ordinary glass on the inside and a ventilated cavity.

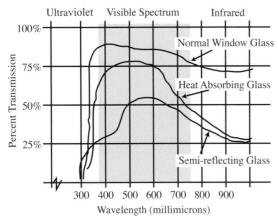

Figure 3.12 Transmission spectrum of various types of window glass.

buildings where occupants are unlikely to be in close proximity to the glazing (e.g., it is used as external sunshades in the UNESCO building in Paris). Although there are problems in its use for offices where staff are required to sit close to a window wall, many of these can be overcome if a sheet of ordinary glass is fitted parallel to but on the inside of the heat-absorbing glass and provision is made for ventilation of the air cavity between the two sheets, so that the hot air can be removed.

The next development in the reduction of solar heat transmission was to seal a series of small, metal louvers between two sheets of glass. Such glasses incorporating built-in shading devices were initially used to advantage in a number of buildings in the US, but never gained widespread acceptance owing to their relatively high cost. Probably the most notable achievement in this field has been the development of thin coatings that will transmit light but reflect heat. It has long been known that very thin films of some metals, such as gold and copper, have these properties, and by combining this effect with techniques developed for attaching electrically conducting coatings to

glass (e.g., for use as de-icing devices in aircraft wind screens), a completely new product known as semi-reflecting glass became commercially available in the 1970s. Figure 3.12 shows the properties of this type of glass when used in the form of a double glazed unit.

More recently, during the early 2000s, several window systems with low-emissivity (Low-E) glass have become commercially available. They typically utilize a special glass with low solar heat gain and high transparency properties. For example, the Solarban 60 glass manufactured by PPG Industries (Pittsburgh, Pennsylvania) relies on a 17-layer coating to reduce heat gain by 60 percent and heat loss by 75 percent in a double-glazed window assembly. There are two types of Low-E glass. In hard-coat Low-E glass tin is applied directly to the molten glass, providing a hard coating that is difficult to scratch off. Soft-coat Low-E glass is manufactured by applying a thin layer of silver while the glass is in a vacuum. Since this coating is delicate, the soft Low-E glass is sandwiched with another layer of glass.

3.4   Radiation through roofs

Transmission of heat through roofs is a legitimate concern even in moderately warm climates. It is now well known that most of this heat transfer occurs by radiation and that therefore the ventilation of roof spaces will contribute little to ameliorating the conditions. It is advisable to provide reflection by using a light-colored finish on the outside of the roof, and to provide some form of reflecting foil suspended on the underside of the roofing surface in conjunction with six or more inches of insulating material. It is essential that this reflecting foil faces an air space between itself and the underside of the roof.

Perhaps another effective method is provided by spraying water onto the outside roof surface. Although, this method makes use of the evaporative cooling effect of a fluid, it has as yet found little practical application owing to reasons of maintenance and capital cost.

On the other hand, a similar system has been applied with success to multi-story buildings, where the entire roof surface is flooded with a permanent pool of water up to 12 inches deep. In this way a reinforced concrete roof slab covered with layers of bituminous felt, which under severe solar exposure would act as a radiator, can be economically insulated. In addition, the water layer protects the otherwise inevitable deterioration of the asphalt binder in bituminous roofing material under cyclic exposure to solar radiation. Normally, flat roofs are typically covered with mineral chippings to mitigate the deterioration of the roofing material. Unfortunately, over time the mineral chippings are either blown off the roof during windy conditions or sink into the asphalt when it softens during hot summer days.

Studies conducted by Richards (1957) in the 1950s in South Africa have shown that high ceilings have no significant effect on ventilation, indoor temperature, or the subjective sensation of radiation from the internal ceiling surface. It was concluded that from a thermal viewpoint a minimum ceiling height of around eight feet should be acceptable in any part of the world.

3.5   Sun position and orientation

Although we may reduce the heat exchange between the external environment and the building interior through the judicial use of thermal insulation, it is nevertheless very important that careful consideration be given to building orientation during the earliest design stages. By using readily available computer programs or solar charts, it becomes a relatively simple matter to calculate the degree of exposure to solar radiation of walls, windows, and the roof. The results of these calculations provide the basis for optimizing the shape and orientation of the building, and the design of external sunshading devices.

Based on the supposition that solar radiation is of importance both positively in cold periods and negatively in hot periods, Olgyay (1952)

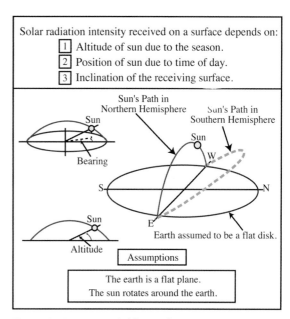

Figure 3.13   Sun variables and assumptions.

has divided the year into *underheated* and *overheated* periods. This allows the optimum orientation of a building to be determined by the point where the average radiations for the underheated and overheated periods are a maximum and minimum, respectively.

From a general point of view, and as shown in Figure 3.13, the amount of solar radiation received on a surface is dependent on three factors: (1) the altitude of the sun due to the season; (2) the position of the sun due to the time of day; and, (3) the inclination of the receiving surface. It has been found expedient to make two fundamental assumptions for purposes of simplifying the calculation of the sun's position in relationship to a building: namely, that the sun rotates around the Earth; and, that the Earth is flat.

The Earth's axis is tilted at 23.5°, which accounts for the seasons (Figure 3.14) and forms the basis for the equinox and solstice designations. As illustrated in Figure 3.15, the spring equinox and fall equinox occur on March 21 and September 21, respectively. On those dates the sun is directly overhead (90°) at the equator, the sun's altitude at noon anywhere on the

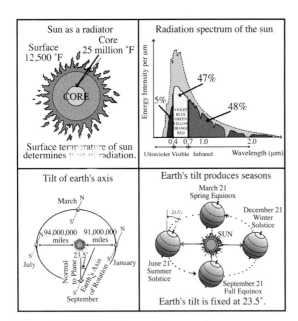

Figure 3.14   Radiation spectrum and seasons.

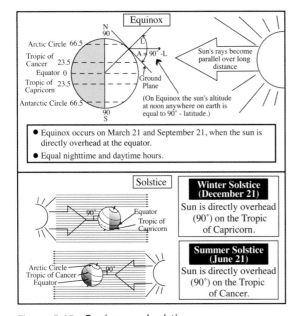

Figure 3.15   Equinox and solstice.

Earth is exactly 90° minus the latitude of that location, and daytime hours are equal to nighttime hours. Similarly, the summer solstice and winter solstice occur on June 21 and December 21, respectively. During the summer solstice the sun is directly overhead (90°) at the Tropic

of Cancer and during the winter solstice the sun is directly overhead (90°) at the Tropic of Capricorn. The equinox and solstice designations are more historical and mystical then technical in nature. Their significance stems mainly from pagan rites that were performed on these days to persuade gods to provide a plentiful harvest or a mild winter. The ancient goddess, Eostre, a Saxon deity who marked not only the passage of time but also symbolized new life and fertility, was a key symbol of the equinox celebration.

Based on the expedient assumptions that the Earth is flat and that the sun rotates around the Earth, it is necessary to ascertain only the altitude (A) and the bearing or azimuth (B) of the sun to plot shadows or predict the degree of penetration of the sun into a building space. These two parameters of the sun's position at any time of day on any date can be either mathematically calculated (ASHRAE, 1978; Duffie and Beckman, 1974) or determined graphically (Libby-Owens-Ford, 1951; Hand, 1948) on the basis of readily available solar charts.

As shown in Figure 3.16 the algebraic solution of the sun path is given by two principal equations, based on the latitude (LAT) of the observation point, the declination of the sun (D) and the difference in latitude between the observation point and the sun (H):

$$\sin (A) = \cos (90° \pm LAT) \cos (90° \pm D)$$
$$- (\sin (90° \pm LAT) \sin (90° \pm D) \cos (H) \qquad [3.1]$$

$$\cos (B) = \cos (90° \pm D) - \sin (A) \cos (90° \pm LAT) /$$
$$(\cos (A) \sin (90° \pm LAT)) \qquad [3.2]$$

$$D = 23.45 (\sin (360° (284 + day \ of \ the \ year) / 365) \qquad [3.3]$$

$$H = (\text{difference in latitude between} $$
$$\text{sun and observation point}) \qquad [3.4]$$

In equations [3.1] and [3.2], to the north is given by "90°+" and to the south is given by "90°– ". While the bearing (or azimuth) is usually measured from the south, the altitude is always measured as the angle from the point of observation between the horizon and the sun.

Only the altitude and bearing of the sun at any point in time are required to plot shadows and determine the penetration of the sun through a window.

$$\sin(\text{altitude}) =$$

$$\cos[90\pm\text{latitude}]\,\cos[90\pm\text{declination}]$$
$$+\,\sin[90\pm\text{latitude}]\,\sin[90\pm\text{declination}]\,\cos H$$

$$\cos(\text{bearing}) =$$

$$\frac{\cos[90\pm\text{declination}] - \sin[\text{altitude}]\,\cos[90\pm\text{latitude}]}{\cos[\text{altitude}]\,\sin[90\pm\text{latitude}]}$$

declination $= 23.45\,\sin[360\,(284 + \text{day of year})\,/\,365]$

H $=$ difference in latitude between the sun and the observation position.

(To the north is given by "90+" and to the south by "90-".)

Figure 3.16   Algebraic sun path solution.

A number of solar design charts have been developed over the years (e.g., Burnett, Baker and Funaro, Pleijel).

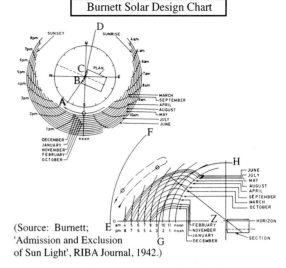

Burnett Solar Design Chart

(Source: Burnett; 'Admission and Exclusion of Sun Light', RIBA Journal, 1942.)

Figure 3.17   The Burnett sun path chart.

Clearly, the algebraic solution is rather laborious and is unlikely to be performed by architects. However, it is readily translated into computer software code and therefore forms the basis of several computer-aided design (CAD) programs that perform sun-path calculations as part of their shadow- or daylight-rendering capabilities. If the required computer program is not available, then graphical sun charts provide a practical alternative. A number of solar design charts have been prepared by various authors in past years, such as the Burnett chart and the Baker–Funaro chart.

The Burnett system consists of two diagrams that are available in printed form, and may be used to solve most sun-penetration problems as soon as small-scale plans and sections are available.

The first diagram (upper left in Figure 3.17) shows the position of the sun in plan, at different times of the day and season. The second diagram (lower right in Figure 3.17) shows the altitude of the sun and is intended to be used in conjunction with the section of a building or room. The plan diagram consists of parts of concentric circles each representing the center day (i.e., the 15th) of a month, the hours of the day,

sunrise and sunset, and the points of the compass. The plan of the building or room under consideration (drawn to a suitable scale) is positioned on the chart as shown in Figure 3.17, so that the hours of the day during which the sun can penetrate that particular building space can be read off for any month of the year between the boundaries AB and CD. Since the plan diagram cannot provide any information about the depth of the room, the second (section) diagram shows the altitude of the sun for the center day of each month in relationship to a reference point (Z). The times indicated by the boundaries AB and CD in the first (plan) diagram are drawn on a section diagram (i.e., GH and EF), so that the sunlight available for admission to the room is represented by the month and time curves enclosed between the boundaries EF and GH.

A third possibility available to the building designer for determining sun angles is to build a small-scale model of a room or entire building. Such a model can be simply constructed out of cardboard, with the only requirement that it be geometrically fairly accurate. Model analyses of the sun path are particularly valuable for visualizing the impact of the sun path

The Heliodon, developed by the U.K. Building Research Station, has been one of the most used scale model tools since the 1940s.

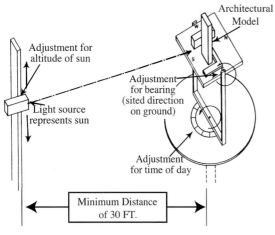

Figure 3.18   The UK Heliodon.

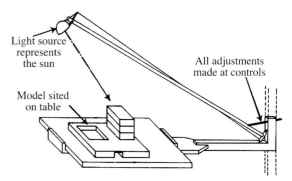

Figure 3.19   The Australian Solarscope.

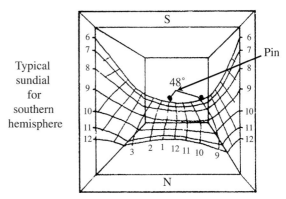

Figure 3.20   Pleijel's sundial.

on a particular building design; however, they do depend on access to a testing facility. One of the most popular sun-path model testing facilities is the Heliodon developed by the UK Building Research Station during the 1930s (Figure 3.18).

The model is placed on a movable platform, which is easily tilted or rotated to simulate the particular latitude and time of day under consideration. A pin-hole light source, placed at a specified distance from the model (normally 30 feet) may be moved vertically to allow for the seasons of the year.

An Australian modification of this basic test arrangement is the Solarscope (Figure 3.19), which allows all variables to be controlled at the light source. The Solarscope is a very convenient, simplified, and less expensive version of the Heliodon. However, it is also less accurate, owing to the relatively small distance between the light source and the model (i.e., the light rays are not parallel).

The sundial shown in Figure 3.20 was designed by the Swedish architect Gunnar Pleijel, who had developed a sun-path diagram as early as the 1940s (Pleijel, 1954). It consists of a small box that

is open at the top and has inclined internal sides, with a pin at the center of the bottom surface. The box is placed on the model, which is tilted until the tip of the pin's shadow touches the desired time of day on the sundial. However, a different sundial is required for each latitude.

3.6   Solar design steps

Whether or not mechanical or natural means of air conditioning are employed in a building, the need for energy conservation requires careful consideration of sun control for all window areas. While the glass element in walls is by far the most vulnerable source of heat transmission and glare, it is also the largest single factor that lends itself to simple preventive measures. In warm and hot climates it is usually cheaper to keep heat out of the building environment initially, than to remove it from the interior by mechanical cooling equipment. Accordingly, in summer, the protection of windows from solar radiation is of primary importance, even when the actual window area is small.

In winter, and particularly in colder climates, the sun can become a useful source of heat, and its inclusion or exclusion must therefore be given careful consideration. The design steps that should be followed to optimize this aspect of environmental control are summarized below:

Step 1: A fundamental decision must be made regarding the type and degree of solar control required (i.e., reflection, diffusion, part or complete exclusion).

Step 2: The building layout and the orientation of all elevations must be considered next, before an attempt is made to settle the secondary question of shading. Should all solar radiation be excluded in summer? How much solar penetration is desirable in winter?

Step 3: The size and location of window areas will largely determine the amount of heat transmission through the external walls, and the amount of cooling and ventilation that can be provided by non-mechanical air movement. Consideration should also be given at this stage to glare and levels of illumination. Every attempt must be made to provide at least sufficient daylight for background lighting in the majority of building spaces.

Step 4: Finally, the selection of suitable shading devices will be largely a matter of economics. Available means of solar control in the form of fixed or movable devices, with or without remote control, must be analyzed in respect to capital cost, savings in energy, reliability, and durability.

Datta and Chaudri (1964) published a very elaborate system of charts and graphs that furnish the required data for the design of numerous types of shading device for tropical regions. Although the charts are rather complicated, they were useful for establishing the following rules of thumb for practical guidance:

- For east and west orientations, where the altitude of the sun is likely to be low, inclined vertical louvers are most effective. If the inclination is perpendicular to the critical altitude of the sun, then the shadow coverage provided by the louvers will be a maximum.
- Horizontal shades are effective for the south orientations (or north orientations in the southern hemisphere), where the altitude of the sun is normally high. However, if these shades are inclined at less than 45° to the face of the wall, they are likely to interfere excessively with desirable solar penetration during the winter months.
- Orientations to the east and west of south (or north-east and north-west in the southern hemisphere), where the altitude of the sun is considered to be intermediate, will require a combination of horizontal shades and vertical shades. The latter may be inclined to be perpendicular to the critical altitude, while the horizontal shades take care of the higher altitudes of the sun, for which the vertical shades are ineffective.

3.7   Achieving air movement naturally

In the absence of temperature and humidity control, the only remaining natural means of cooling a building environment is by means of air movement. It is understood, however, that the exposure of building occupants to air movement is most desirable in a hot-humid climate where the perspiration mechanism of the human body is assisted by the accelerated passage of air over the skin. In hot-dry climates air movement would normally be restricted to the late afternoon and evening, for the purpose of cooling the building shell from the inside.

Research into aspects of natural ventilation has been mainly confined to a study of the size, shape, and position of air inlets and outlets in building walls, and the geometry of the building plan in relationship to the air flow produced by naturally occurring winds. The artificial production of air movement by means of thermal currents has been largely abandoned as an

- Air is sucked rather than pushed through a building.
- Air movement at low speeds (< 8 mph) is easily obstructed.

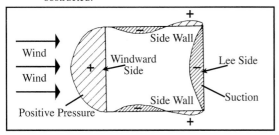

- For efficient summer cooling the air must pass over the occupants.
- For maximum air flow the inlets and outlets should be of equal size.
- Each opening and bend will produce a disproportionate reduction in air flow.

Figure 3.21   Impact of wind on buildings.

effective measure for producing cooling in low structures.

When wind impinges on a building shell a region of high pressure (positive) is normally produced on the windward surface of the building. As the air is deflected around the building it accelerates, thereby causing regions of low pressure (suction) to be set up just behind the windward surface on the side walls and along the entire leeward side (Figure 3.21).

Fundamentally, it would therefore appear to be necessary only to provide air inlets in the walls that experience high pressure, and air outlets in the walls subjected to low pressure or suction. Unfortunately, complications due to the inertia of the air, turbulence, and the extremely variable nature of architectural planning arise, and have necessitated much experimental work on scale models. Sufficient test data has now been collected to make some general predictions about the nature of the parameters that control the desired air-flow patterns for effective summer cooling.

Effects of landscaping: In regions of varying topography, microclimatic considerations may dictate the appropriate orientation and internal planning of a building. For example, depending on the slope of a site it is likely that at night cool air will move downhill independently of the orientation, thereby producing air currents that may be utilized for ventilation purposes. Such air currents normally do not exceed speeds of three mph, but even at these low speeds they are capable of removing substantial quantities of heat from an exposed building shell.

Similar microclimatic influences occur in coastal regions, where periodic land and sea breezes are produced by the unequal rates of heating and cooling of the adjacent land and sea masses. During the day, under solar radiation, the land becomes warmer than the sea, thereby generating onshore winds, while during the cooler night the reverse procedure occurs.

Most of the research dealing with the effects of wind breaks and their influence on the microclimate has been related to agriculture. However, in the mid-1950s the Texas Engineering Experiment Station published the results of an empirical study focused on the screening effects of hedges of various sizes and trees in the proximity of buildings, as shown in Figure 3.22.

Effects of building design: There are five factors that determine the air-flow pattern within building spaces: namely, the location, dimensions, and type of inlets, and the location and size of the outlets. Of these, the location and type of inlet are by far the most important aspects. For example, Caudill and Reed (1952) have demonstrated (Figure 3.23) with wind-tunnel tests that the position of the inlet has a significant impact on the air pattern.

When the opening is located symmetrically, similar pressures will exist on either side of the opening, resulting in a fairly straight air flow. However, if the inlet is located asymmetrically the pressures on either side of the opening will be unequal, forcing the air stream to enter diagonally. Similarly, in the case of a two-story building such pressure differences can decisively affect the air-flow pattern. As

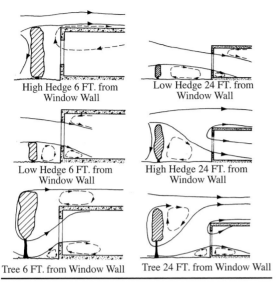

High Hedge 6 FT. from Window Wall

Low Hedge 24 FT. from Window Wall

Low Hedge 6 FT. from Window Wall

High Hedge 24 FT. from Window Wall

Tree 6 FT. from Window Wall

Tree 24 FT. from Window Wall

Source: White R.; 'Effects of Landscaping on Natural Ventilation of Buildings and Their Adjacent Areas'; Texas Engineering Experiment Station, Report #45, 1954.

Figure 3.22   **Effect of external vegetation.**

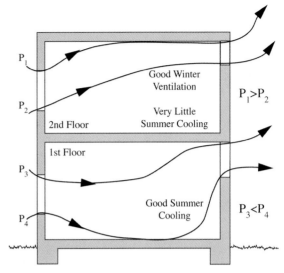

Figure 3.24   **Impact of vertical room location on air-flow patterns.**

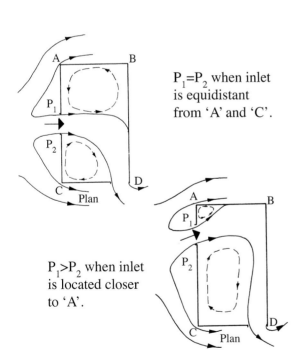

$P_1 = P_2$ when inlet is equidistant from 'A' and 'C'.

$P_1 > P_2$ when inlet is located closer to 'A'.

Figure 3.23   **Impact of door location on air-flow patterns.**

shown schematically in Figure 3.24, within the same building, rooms featuring identical location, size, and type of inlets will be subjected to quite different air-flow patterns, depending on whether they are situated on the first or second floor of the building.

These and similar studies have produced some useful building design and floor plan layout guidelines.

1 To achieve maximum air flow, inlets and outlets should be of approximately equal size. However, the concept of air change or ventilation rate has little bearing on summer cooling. The latter is influenced by the air-flow pattern. To achieve a satisfactory degree of summer cooling the air flow must pass over the occupants of the building and should therefore be directed downward to a level that is about two to five feet above the floor. For good winter ventilation, on the other hand, the air flow should be directed upward to the ceiling, so that the building occupants are not exposed to an undesirable cold draft. However, if air flow of a certain speed produces the required cooling effect, then the air-change

requirements are likely to be more than satisfied. The design dilemma posed by a building space that must cater for both summer cooling and winter ventilation can be resolved by the judicious use of window panes that can be pivoted and movable louvers.

2 The popular practice of locating extremely large openings on the windward wall of a building, as a means of increasing air flow within the building, is completely erroneous. In fact, slightly higher air speeds may be obtained whenever the outlet is larger than the inlet. This is because air is sucked, rather than pushed, through a building.

3 Openings that are partly obstructed will reduce air flow by a disproportionate amount, especially at low wind speeds. For example, a 16-mesh mosquito screen will reduce the air flow by about 60 percent when the wind speed is 1.5 mph, and by only about 30 percent when the wind speed is 4 mph.

4 Each opening and bend to be negotiated by an air stream will produce a reduction in flow. Accordingly, the optimum flow is obtained by uninhibited cross-ventilation. Further to this, air flow within building spaces is very much reduced if the direction of the wind is inclined more than about 30° to the normal axis of the inlet.

5 City and regional planning, landscaping, and architectural variables, such as building clusters, vegetation, and overhangs, will normally have a significant effect on the air-flow pattern around buildings.

3.8   Removal of heat by ventilation

Apart from the permanent ventilation requirements stipulated by building codes (i.e., number of air changes per hour), which are aimed at preserving the health and efficiency of the occupants, ventilation provides a means of removing heat from a building environment.

In quantitative terms, the ventilation rate (V_R cubic feet per hour) required to remove heat (Q British Thermal Units per hour) is given by the following equation (Figure 3.25):

The ventilation rate (V CF/HR) required to remove a heat load (Q BTU/HR) is given by:

$$V = \frac{Q}{PS\,(T_1 - T_2)}\,(CF/HR)$$

where:

P = average air density (approx. 0.075 LB/CF at an indoor temperature of 70°F)

S = specific heat of air (0.24 BTU/LB/°F)

T_1 = indoor temperature (°F)

T_2 = temperature of ventilation air (°F)

Figure 3.25   Ventilation rate formula.

Problem

Determine the required ventilation rate for:
Volume of room (V) = 1,345 CF
Indoor temperature (T_1) = 70° F
Outdoor temperature (T_2) = 65° F
Heat load to be removed (Q) = 12,000 BTU/HR

Ventilation Rate

Required ventilation rate is calculated as:

$$V = \frac{Q}{PS\,(T_1 - T_2)}\,(CF/HR)$$

$$V = \frac{12,000}{0.075 \times 0.24\,(70 - 65)}\,(CF/HR)$$

$$V = 133,333\ (CF/HR)$$

Air Changes

Number of air changes per hour are given by:

$$A = \frac{\text{ventilation rate}}{\text{room volume}} \qquad A = \frac{133,333}{1,345}$$

$$A = 99\ \text{(air changes per hour)}$$

Figure 3.26   Ventilation rate calculation.

$$V_R = Q / [(P\,S)\,(T_1 - T_2)] \qquad [3.5]$$

where:

V_R = Required ventilation rate (CF/HR)
Q = Total heat load to be removed by ventilation (BTU/HR)

P = Average air density (0.075 LB/CF at 70° F indoor temperature)

S = Specific heat of air (0.24 BTU/LB/°F)

$(T_1 - T_2)$ = The total rise in temperature of the incoming air (°F).

(Since the ventilation rate is inversely proportional to $(T_1 - T_2)$, it will not be possible to remove all of the heat liberated within the building environment.)

An example application of equation [3.5] is shown in Figure 3.26, where the number of air changes per hour, required to maintain an indoor temperature of 70°F by removing a heat load of 12 000 BTU/HR in a room 12 FT by 14 FT and 8 FT in height, while the outside air temperature is 65°F, is calculated to be just under 100 (air changes per hour).

4 Heat Flow and Thermal Insulation

This chapter will examine the exchange of heat between a building and the external environment. In industrialized countries the energy used to heat buildings in winter, and to a lesser extent cool buildings in summer since fewer homes have air conditioning facilities, constitutes a significant portion of the total energy consumption. For example, in the US more than 25% of the total energy consumption is attributable to buildings. About two-thirds of this energy is used for heating and cooling purposes. Even today, in the year 2010, more than 80% of this energy is still produced by fossil fuels, such as oil and coal.

4.1 The need for energy conservation

Prior to the energy crisis that was precipitated by the Middle East oil embargo of the early 1970s, energy was considered to be an inexpensive commodity in the US. As a consequence architects had little opportunity to apply their creativity and skills to building designs that utilized natural means for the heating, cooling, and lighting of buildings. The impact of an abrupt shortage of oil and dramatic escalation of the cost of energy was twofold. First, there was an immediate call for the conservation of energy, and second, the Government sponsored many concurrent research programs aimed at devising methods for maximizing the use of natural sources of energy such as the sun, wind, and daylight in buildings.

It was noted with alarm by the California State Utilities Commission that at the current rate of consumption all of the remaining natural gas would need to be diverted from commercial and industrial uses to residential heating by

1979. At the same time, the availability of fuel oil was becoming increasingly limited owing to political and economical factors, while the conversion of coal to a more directly useful form of energy, such as electricity, carried with it the problem of unacceptable levels of pollution. Faced with this potentially serious situation the US Government mobilized all of its responsible agencies and embarked on a massive program of research and incentives to drastically reduce the reliance on foreign imports of energy. To a large extent this program has continued to the present day and is unlikely to subside to any appreciable extent over the foreseeable future.

Three strategies were immediately implemented in the architecture, engineering and construction industry as a means of conserving the world's dwindling supplies of fossil fuel.

Strategy A: **Utilize all energy as efficiently as possible.** This strategy placed the emphasis on thermal insulation. Prior to 1970, the thermal insulation of buildings had not been mandatory in states such as California. It was realized that if by the stroke of a magic wand all existing building envelopes in the US could be provided with the equivalent of three inches of polyurethane insulation over-

Building Science: Concepts and Application. Jens Pohl.
© 2011 John Wiley & Sons, Ltd.
Published 2011 by John Wiley & Sons, Ltd.

night, then from the next day onward this would decrease the total national energy consumption by more than 10 percent A second focus was placed on improving the efficiency of heating systems such as electric resistance heaters and fireplaces, and household appliances such as refrigerators.

Strategy B: **Utilize less energy.** The requirement for energy could be reduced by careful planning, design and construction, as well as the reevaluation of comfort standards. It was realized that an emphasis on daylighting could substantially reduce the need for artificial lighting with a consequential reduction in cooling loads. Research showed that it was not unusual for high-rise office buildings in colder climates to require cooling in winter, due to the heat produced by artificial lights. It was estimated that through the provision of more daylight it would be possible to reduce the average artificial light design loads in office buildings by 50 percent (i.e., from the prevalent 4 watt per square foot to less than 2 watt per square foot).

Strategy C: **Utilize alternative energy sources.** Natural sources such as solar energy, wind, nuclear power, geothermal energy, and natural gas were targeted as promising alternatives to fossil fuel. Of these, solar energy immediately assumed a prominent position as an attractive source of hot water and space heating for single-family houses.

The need for adequate thermal insulation cannot be overstated. Buildings are normally exposed to direct solar radiation and therefore walls and roof will be subjected to temperatures of 120°F or more. This temperature in the sun is also referred to as the sol-air temperature. By providing adequate insulation in the building shell, the rate at which heat is transferred can be limited, with subsequent reduction in the capital and operating cost of heating and refrigeration plants. The major purpose of insulation then becomes the conservation of heat or cold within a building environment by maintaining temperature differences between this environment and ambient external conditions.

4.2 How is heat transferred?

Heat is a form of energy and is therefore a physical quantity that may be measured objectively. In the American system of units (i.e., formerly the British system, before the United Kingdom adopted the metric system of units) heat is expressed in terms of British Thermal Units (BTU). One BTU is defined as the amount of heat required to raise the temperature of one pound of water by one degree Fahrenheit. Similarly, in the metric system the Calorie heat unit is defined as the amount of heat required to raise the temperature of one kilogram of water by one degree Centigrade. The heat required for this one-degree rise in temperature is to a slight extent dependent on the actual temperature of the water, and therefore for precise measurements the temperature of the water should be around 60°F (or 15°C).

Heat may appear in either of two forms, namely:

- *Sensible heat*, which is associated with a change of temperature of the substance involved. By virtue of its name, changes in sensible heat are perceived by the senses.
- *Latent heat*, which is the thermal energy used during a change of state of a substance while the temperature remains unaltered. Latent heat cannot be perceived by the senses.

For example, when ice is heated, the heat is absorbed as sensible heat until the melting point is reached. At this stage any further addition of heat will not cause a rise in temperature until all of the ice has melted. Latent heat is therefore absorbed to produce a change of state from ice to water. The addition of more heat to the water will be accompanied by proportionate increases in temperature until boiling point is reached. Thereafter, latent heat will be absorbed by the water to facilitate a further change of state, until all of the water has been converted to steam.

The concepts of heat and temperature are closely interrelated. In fact, it is very difficult to provide a satisfactory definition for either heat or temperature without implying the other. To overcome this difficulty, it has been suggested

 Thermal conduction is the direct transmission of heat through a material or between two materials that are in contact with each other.

The rate of heat transfer by conduction (Q_C) depends on the thermal conductivity of the material(s):

$$Q_C = \frac{\left[\begin{array}{c}\text{thermal}\\\text{conductivity}\end{array}\right] \times \left[\begin{array}{c}\text{surface}\\\text{area}\end{array}\right] \times \left[\begin{array}{c}\text{temperature}\\\text{difference}\end{array}\right]}{[\text{ material thickness }]} \quad (\text{BTU/HR})$$

● Assumes that all of the heat is transferred through the material, while in fact some of the heat is absorbed and the temperature of the material is raised.

● The amount of heat stored depends mainly on the specific heat and mass of the material.

Figure 4.1 Heat transfer by conduction.

that the concept of thermal equilibrium might form a convenient starting point. Accordingly, for purposes of definition, two bodies are said to be at the same temperature if they remain in thermal equilibrium when brought into contact with each other, and scales of temperature are related to certain measurable physical properties such as the volumetric expansion of mercury (e.g., in a thermometer).

Heat is said to pass from one system or substance to another if the two systems are at different temperatures and in contact with each other. This heat transfer, which always occurs from a region of high temperature to a region of low temperature, may proceed by conduction, convection, radiation, or any combination of these.

4.2.1 Conduction

Thermal conduction is the direct transmission of heat through a material or between two materials in direct contact with each other (Figure 4.1).

All substances, whether solid, liquid, or gas will conduct heat, the rate of transfer depending on the thermal conductivity of the substance.

$$Q_C = k\,A\,(T_1 - T_2)/t \qquad [4.1]$$

where:

Q_C = total heat transfer by conduction
k = thermal conductivity of material
A = contact surface area
t = thickness of material
$(T_1 - T_2)$ = temperature difference.

Equation [4.1] applies to a homogenous material under steady-state temperature conditions, when a temperature differential (i.e., $(T_1 - T_2)$) exists between the two opposite faces of the material. The assumption of steady-state temperature conditions is a significant and convenient one. It implies that all of the heat is transferred through the material; while in fact some of the heat is absorbed, thereby raising the temperature of the material. The amount of heat stored in any material is referred to as its heat capacity and depends mainly on the specific heat and density of the material (i.e., heat capacity is equal to specific heat multiplied by density).

4.2.2 Convection

Heat is transmitted by convection in fluids and gases as a result of circulation. For example, when air is heated it expands and rises, thus allowing colder air to take its place. In the case of buildings, heat transfer by convection takes place at roof and wall surfaces, around heating and cooling units, or wherever a material is exposed to air at a different temperature. Consequently, heat loss by convection is a function of the surface coefficient of heat transfer and depends largely on the degree of air movement, the shape and dimensions of the surface, and the temperature differential that exists between the air and the surface (Figure 4.2):

$$Q_E = S_C(T_1 - T_2)^{5/4} \qquad [4.2]$$

where:

Q_E = total heat transfer by convection
S_C = coefficient of convective heat transfer
S_c = 0.4 for horizontal surface (face up)
S_c = 0.3 for vertical surface
S_c = 0.2 for horizontal surface (face down).

Heat is transferred by convection in liquids and gases as a result of circulation.

The rate of heat transfer by convection (Q_E) depends on the surface coefficient of heat transfer, the degree of air movement, the configuration of the surface(s) and the temperature difference.

$$Q_E = \left[\begin{array}{c}\text{surface}\\\text{coefficient of}\\\text{heat transfer}\end{array}\right] \times \left[\begin{array}{c}\text{temperature}\\\text{difference}\end{array}\right]^{5/4} \text{(BTU/HR)}$$

● Typical surface coefficients of heat transfer:

horizontal surface (face up) = 0.4
horizontal surface (face down) = 0.2
vertical surface = 0.3

● Most hot air and hot water heating systems operate on the basis of convection currents.

Figure 4.2   **Heat transfer by convection.**

In radiant heat transfer heat energy is converted into electro-magnetic radiation and reconverted to heat through absorption by another substance in its path.

The rate of heat transfer by radiation (Q_R) depends on the emissivities of the surfaces involved and the temperature difference between the surfaces.

$$Q_R = \left[\begin{array}{c}\text{emissivity}\\\text{factor (E)}\end{array}\right] \times \left[\begin{array}{c}\text{surface}\\\text{area}\end{array}\right] \times \left[T_1{}^4 - T_2{}^4\right] \text{(BTU/HR)}$$

● For two parallel surfaces whose emissivities are 'e_1' and 'e_2', respectively, the emissivity factor is given by:

$$E = \frac{e_1 \times e_2}{e_1 + e_2 - 1}$$

● Radiant heat transfer is not impacted by air movement.

Figure 4.3   **Heat transfer by radiation.**

Apart from the operation of hot-air and hot-water heating systems in buildings, convection has far-reaching effects on climatic conditions. Near the equator intense solar radiation will produce considerable thermal air currents, while ocean currents such as the Gulf Stream are also largely produced by convection.

4.2.3   Radiation

Radiant heat transfer is the process of the conversion of heat energy in a substance into electro-magnetic radiation, and the subsequent reconversion of this radiant energy into heat of absorption by another substance in its path. The intensity of radiation emitted by a substance is very much dependent on the type of material and the temperature (Figure 4.3).

The net heat radiation between two surfaces at different temperatures is given by:

$$Q_R = E_e \, A \, (T_1^4 - T_2^4) \qquad [4.3]$$

where:

Q_R = total heat transfer by radiation
A = surface area

E_e = factor that takes into account the emissivities of the surfaces involved (dimensionless). If "e_1" and "e_2" are the respective emissivities of two parallel surfaces, then:

$$E_e = (e_1 e_2)/(e_1 + e_2 - 1),$$

Particular values of E_e for specific situations, such as two square surfaces at right angles to each other, and so on, may be obtained from the ASHRAE Handbook of Fundamentals, 1989.

($T_1 - T_2$) = temperature difference.

Generally speaking, light surfaces are better reflectors than dark surfaces, although bright metallic surfaces are much more efficient in reflecting short-wavelength solar radiation than long-wavelength, low-temperature radiation (Figure 4.4). On the other hand the opposite is true for white paint.

The reader may feel that there exists an apparent anomaly in relation to the dark skin color prevalent among indigenous people in the tropics. One would expect a light-colored skin

● Light surfaces are better reflectors of radiation than dark surfaces.

● Bright metallic surfaces are very efficient in reflecting solar radiation (i.e., more efficient than white paint).

● Reflectivity = (1 − emissivity).

Type of Surface Material	Reflectivity in Respect to Solar Radiation
aluminum	0.80
galvanized steel	0.45
white paint	0.70
black paint	0.10
cream bricks	0.40
red tiles	0.30

Figure 4.4   Reflectivity and emissivity.

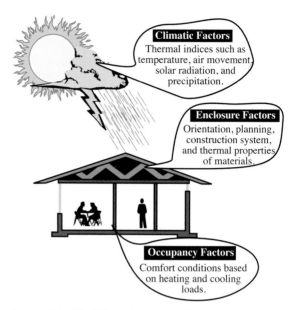

Figure 4.5   Heat-transfer parameters.

to have better reflecting properties and therefore provide more protection to the human body. In fact, in dark-skinned races, the pigment is deposited in the superficial layers of the skin and serves as a screen to filter out the potentially harmful rays in solar radiation. Ultraviolet light is emitted by the sun, and is even more abundantly reflected from a blue sky. If applied to the skin suddenly and in large doses, inflammation, whealing, and blistering (i.e., sunburn) will result. Consequently, pigmentation of the skin is believed to lessen the possibility of injury from solar radiation.

4.3 Steady-state heat-transfer assumptions

Since the desired thermal building environment is at most times different from ambient atmospheric conditions, there will exist a temperature differential between indoor and outdoor regions. Accordingly, the amount of heat transferred through the building envelope must be closely related to the heat-exchange parameters at the surfaces of the envelope layers (if composite) and the thermal properties of the materi-

als. These parameters may be conveniently grouped into three broadly defined categories, as shown in Figure 4.5:

Enclosure factors such as the thermal properties of materials of construction, orientation, planning, and design specifications.
Climatic factors involving thermal indices such as temperature, radiation, and air movement.
Occupancy factors such as the functional use of a building space that will establish the required comfort conditions and resultant internal heat loads.

While all of these parameters may be assigned numerical values at any particular time, some of them, in particular the climatic factors, are subject to considerable short-term change. Strictly speaking, therefore, heat transfer through building walls and roofs is of an unsteady character. However, to avoid the relatively complex calculations that are necessary to determine the time-dependent properties of systems of construction, it is common practice to assume very much simplified thermal boundary conditions: namely, that the indoor temperature is constant and that either steady heat flow or periodic heat flow conditions apply.

Simplifying Assumptions

A The temperature difference between the outdoor and indoor environments is large, and short-term outdoor temperature changes are small.

B The thermal capacity of the building shell is small in comparison to the total heat transfer.

Figure 4.6   Steady-state assumptions.

The rate of heat transfer through a construction component is determined by the thermal resistance of the material and the thermal resistance of the two surfaces of the material.

These are combined into a single thermal transmittance or U-Value.

The rate of heat transfer (Q) under Steady State Conditions is given by:

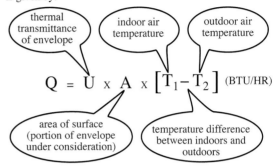

Figure 4.7   Steady-state heat transfer through the building envelope.

Although steady-state heat transfer does not exist in practice, since the outdoor climate fluctuates continuously, nevertheless it does provide a reasonable estimate of the heat flow through a building envelope if the following two conditions are satisfied (Figure 4.6):

Condition 1: When the temperature difference between the outdoor and indoor environments is large and short-term changes in outdoor temperature are small.

Condition 2: When the thermal capacity of the building shell is small in comparison with the total heat transferred.

In practice, heat is transferred through a building envelope by more than one mode of heat transfer. For example, in the case of prefabricated concrete wall panels heat is first transmitted from the air on one side of the panel to the nearest surface, mainly by convection; then the heat is conducted through the wall panel; and finally the heat is transferred from the opposite surface by convection to the surrounding air. Accordingly, the rate of heat transfer through a building component is determined not only by

the thermal resistance of the material, but also by that of the two surfaces. It is normal practice to combine these various resistivities into a single factor, known as the thermal transmittance or U-value (Figure 4.7).

$$Q = U A (T_1 - T_2) \qquad [4.4]$$

where:

Q = total heat transfer (BTU/HR)
U = overall thermal transmittance value (BTU/SF-HR-°F)
A = surface area (SF)
$(T_1 - T_2)$ = temperature difference (°F).

As shown in Figure 4.8, the thermal transmittance for a composite building wall is the reciprocal of the sum of the thermal resistances of the external surface, each layer of material, cavity (if any), and the internal surface. Since the thermal resistance of any material of specified thickness is given by the ratio of the thickness (d) to the thermal conductivity (k), the total resistance of "i" layers of a composite element is given by:

The U-Value of a composite building element is the inverse of the sum of the thermal resistances (R) of each material layer, cavity (if any), and the external and internal surfaces.

$$U = \frac{1}{R_T} \quad \text{(BTU/SF-°F)}$$

Where:

$$R_T = R_E + R_{M1} + R_C + R_{M2} + R_I$$

And:

R_E = external surface R_{M2} = second material

R_{M1} = first material R_I = internal surface

R_C = air cavity

$$R = \frac{[\text{thickness of material (d)}]}{[\text{thermal conductivity of material (k)}]} \quad \text{(SF-°F-HR/BTU)}$$

Figure 4.8   Calculation of the thermal transmittance or U-value of a Construction assembly.

The thermal conductivity of a material is influenced by its structure (density and porosity), moisture content and temperature.

Structure: Good thermal insulation materials have closed cells with the internal and external surface resistance of each cell (i.e., cavity) contributing to the overall thermal resistance of the material.

Density: Heavy materials are better heat conductors than light materials (light materials tend to contain more air).

Moisture Content: The conductivity of water is about 25 times greater than air. Therefore, insulating materials must be kept dry at all times.

Temperature: Although the conductivity of materials tends to increase at higher temperatures, this is negligible over the range of temperatures normally encountered in buildings.

Figure 4.9   Influences on the thermal conductivity of materials.

$$R_{total} = (\text{resistance of external surface})$$
$$+ d_1 / k_1 + d_2 / k_2 + \ldots d_i / k_i$$
$$+ (\text{resistance of internal surface})$$

4.4   The nature of thermal conductivity

The thermal conductivity of a material is influenced by a considerable number of factors including density, porosity, moisture content, and temperature (Figure 4.9).

Structure: Normally, the thermal conductivity of a cellular material is higher than that of a granular material. The explanation is that in cellular materials the cells tend to form a continuous path, while in granular materials the path is broken at the surface of each granule. In Figure 4.10 we see that the thermal resistance of an air cavity is approximately 0.91 and that 0.78 (i.e., 86 percent) of this value is made up by the thermal resistance of the surfaces of the enclosure.

Building Envelope Material/Component	Thermal Resistance (SF-°F-HR/BTU)
single brick (4-1/2" thick)	0.79
vert. boards (3/4" thick)	0.50
cement sheets (3/16" thick)	0.04
metal roofing (1/32" thick)	0.00
window glass (1/8" thick)	0.02
window glass (1/4" thick)	0.05
external surface	0.17
internal surface	0.61
air cavity	0.91
concrete (dense)	0.09 per inch
concrete (vermiculite)	1.25 per inch
timber	1.37 per inch
hardboard	0.71 per inch
fiberboard	2.50 per inch
polystyrene	3.57 per inch
polyurethane	6.25 per inch
mineral wool	3.86 per inch

Figure 4.10   Thermal resistance of common building materials.

Accordingly, the ideal thermal insulation material is one that has many closed air cells. By virtue of its enclosing surfaces, each of these cells will contribute to the overall thermal resistance of the material. The contribution will of course not be as much as 0.91, but sufficient to provide a closed-cell plastic foam material such as polyurethane with a thermal resistance of 6.25 per inch thickness.

Density: Light materials have in general a low conductivity and heavier materials are the better thermal conductors. Materials of low density are apt to contain more air between the pores or particles, thereby lowering the thermal conductivity as long as the pores are closed and not open.

Moisture content: The conductivity of water is some 25 times greater than that of air. Since the low thermal conductivity of porous materials is largely due to the air enclosed by the pores, the replacement of some of this air by water must result in an increase in conductivity. Particularly, insulating materials such as mineral wool are capable of absorbing large volumes of water, thereby nullifying most of their insulating effect.

Temperature: Thermal conductivity tends to increase as the temperature of the material increases, and this is more pronounced for lightweight, porous materials. However, generally speaking, the effect of temperature on the conductivity of materials of construction is negligible over the range of temperatures normally encountered in buildings.

Although we have used the analogy to many air cavities, for describing the superior heat-resistance characteristics of closed-cell plastic foam materials, these cells are not exactly the same as air cavities in building construction assemblies such as walls. The thermal insulation value of a one-inch-thick polyurethane foam slab is less than the sum of the resistances of all of the small closed air cells that lie between its opposite surfaces, each taken as contributing the full thermal resistance value of an air cavity (i.e., 0.91). This is due to the small size of the cells and the conductivity of the enclosing material.

The air cavity in a timber frame or brick cavity wall construction is typically continuous, vertically from floor to ceiling and horizontally at least from stud to stud. Some two-thirds of the heat transfer across this large cavity will occur by radiation, to which air will offer little resistance. Accordingly, the insertion of reflective foil can lower the conductivity of the air space in a cavity wall by some 50 percent. With respect to the optimum thickness of an air cavity, it has been established experimentally that there is little difference in the thermal conductivity of air spaces varying between 0.75 inches and six inches. For thicknesses less than 0.75 inches, the conductivity increased rapidly.

4.5 Building heat-flow calculations

As shown in Figure 4.11, the heat exchange between a building interior and its exterior environment is dependent not only on the thermal resistance of the envelope, but also on the heat gain or loss due to air infiltration and

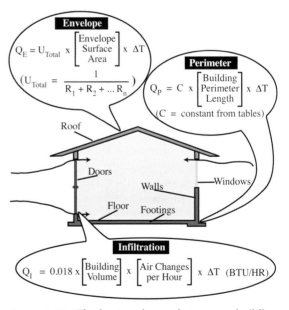

Figure 4.11 The heat exchange between a building and its external environment.

the perimeter of the footings. The degree to which each of these components contributes to the total heat exchange is estimated in different ways.

Envelope component: The thermal transmission or U-value of a composite building element is an approximate measure of the thermal insulation provided by that element, and can therefore be used to compare the insulation characteristics of different systems of construction, according to equations [4.4] and [4.5].

$$Q = U A (T_1 - T_2) \qquad [4.4]$$

where:

Q = total heat transfer (BTU/HR)
U = overall thermal transmittance value (BTU/SF-HR-°F)
A = surface area (SF)
(T_1 - T_2) = temperature difference (°F).

$$U = 1/(R_{ext} + R_{mat(1)} + R_{cavity} + R_{mat(2)} + R_{int}) \quad [4.5]$$

where:

R_{ext} = resistance of external surface
$R_{mat(1)}$ = resistance of material layer(s)
R_{cavity} = resistance of air cavity
$R_{mat(2)}$ = resistance material layer(s)
R_{int} = resistance of internal surface.

A building envelope normally consists of several elements that may contain different materials and may be assembled in quite different ways. For example, roof assemblies are nearly always very different from wall assemblies, doors typically consist of a single material layer, and windows are certainly made of different materials from the walls in which they are located. Each of these elements has its own U-value. It therefore makes a great deal of sense to calculate the heat transfer of the building envelope in five sequential steps (Figure 4.12).

First, we calculate the area of each different element; then we calculate the thermal resistance, U-value, and proportional thermal impact of that element; and finally we multiply the sum of all of those thermal impacts by the temperature difference between the inside and the outside of the building.

The building Envelope is composed of elements such as roof, solid walls, doors, windows, and floor. Each has its own U-Value and area.

① Calculate area (A) of each envelope element:

area of roof = A_{Roof} (SF)
area of solid wall partition = A_{Wall} (SF)
area of windows = A_{Window} (SF)
area of doors = A_{Door} (SF)
area of above-grade floor = A_{Floor} (SF)

② Calculate thermal resistance (R) for each element.

③ Calculate U-Value for each element.

④ Calculate $U \times A$ for each element.

⑤ Calculate heat flow (Q_B) for entire building:

$$Q_B = [\Sigma UA] \times \Delta T \ (BTU/HR)$$

Figure 4.12   Steps for estimating the heat gain or loss through the building envelope.

As an example of the influence of an air cavity in a wall assembly, we will compare the heat transfer through a solid brick wall (e.g., 9 inches thick) and a cavity brick wall (e.g., 11 inches thick) when the external and internal air temperatures are 140°F (e.g., sol-air temperature of the external surface of a wall exposed to direct solar radiation on a hot summer day) and 80°F, respectively.

For solid brick wall: external surface resistance = R_{ext} = 0.17

resistance of 9-inch brick wall = R_{mat} = 1.58

internal surface resistance = R_{int} = 0.61

total thermal resistance of solid brick wall = R_{total} = 2.36

U-value = $1/R_{total}$ = 0.43

Total heat gain through solid brick wall = Q_{total} = **25.6** BTU/SF-HR

For brick cavity wall: external surface resistance = R_{ext} = 0.17

resistance of external = $R_{mat(1)}$ = 0.79
brick leaf wall

resistance of air cavity = R_{cavity} = 0.91

resistance of internal = $R_{mat(2)}$ = 0.79
brick leaf wall

internal surface = R_{int} = 0.61
resistance

total thermal resistance = R_{total} = 3.27
of brick cavity wall

U-value = $1/R_{total}$ = 0.31

Total heat gain through = Q_{total} = **18.4** BTU/
solid brick wall   SF-HR

The impact of the air cavity is considerable, leading to a 40 percent reduction in the calculated heat gain. However, as discussed earlier, it must be remembered that the heat loads calculated in this manner will not necessarily provide an accurate account of conditions in practice. They are at best only a reasonable estimate of the actual expected heat flows. First, some of the quantities involved – such as the thermal conductivities of the materials – are not constant under normal climatic conditions. Second, the fundamental assumptions of steady-state conditions are very much an oversimplification of the actual nature of these heat-transfer parameters.

Air infiltration component: Depending on the tightness of the building, the air infiltration component can be considerable. Certainly in a hot-humid climate, where the achievement of thermal comfort by natural means relies mostly on the movement of external air over the building occupants, air infiltration will be the dominant heat-transfer component. In colder climates special precautions, such as weather stripping around doors, are taken to minimize the infiltration of cold air into the building. As shown in Figure 4.13, the air infiltration component is a direct product of the building volume, the number of air changes per hour, and a constant that represents the heat capacity of air (i.e., density times specific heat).

Recommended air change rates are available from reference tables, such as the ASHRAE Handbook of Fundamentals (1989), and are

based on the estimated tightness of the building envelope and the external design temperature.

Perimeter component: The heat-transfer calculation procedure for the portion of the building that connects to the ground depends on the type of construction employed (Figure 4.14).

In the case of a concrete slab on grade, the perimeter component is a direct product of the linear building perimeter, the temperature difference between the internal and external environments, and a modifier that may be obtained from reference tables such as those provided by the ASHRAE Handbook of Fundamentals (1989). This modifier is based on three parameters, two of which are rather vague estimates based largely on the expected quality (i.e., materials and workmanship) of construction: namely, type of wall construction and degree of insulation. The third parameter represents an approximate assessment of the severity of the climate in terms of the number of Degree Days (to base 65°F).

In the case where the lowest floor of the building is elevated above the ground (i.e., for floors above grade) the calculation of the estimated heat loss (perimeter heat gain is normally not considered) proceeds in exactly the same manner as for the building-envelope component.

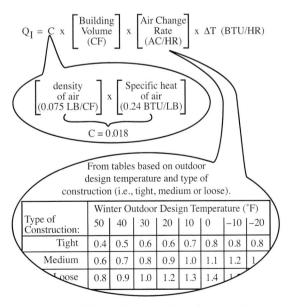

Figure 4.13 Calculation procedure for the air infiltration component.

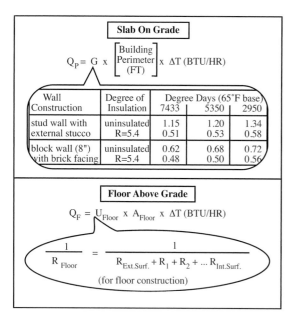

Slab On Grade

$$Q_P = G \times \begin{bmatrix} \text{Building} \\ \text{Perimeter} \\ \text{(FT)} \end{bmatrix} \times \Delta T \text{ (BTU/HR)}$$

Wall Construction	Degree of Insulation	Degree Days (65°F base)		
		7433	5350	2950
stud wall with external stucco	uninsulated R=5.4	1.15 0.51	1.20 0.53	1.34 0.58
block wall (8") with brick facing	uninsulated R=5.4	0.62 0.48	0.68 0.50	0.72 0.56

Floor Above Grade

$$Q_F = U_{Floor} \times A_{Floor} \times \Delta T \text{ (BTU/HR)}$$

$$\frac{1}{R_{Floor}} = \frac{1}{R_{Ext.Surf.} + R_1 + R_2 + \ldots R_{Int.Surf.}}$$

(for floor construction)

Figure 4.14   Calculation procedure for the perimeter (footings) component.

4.6   Energy conservation standards

Over the past several decades the increasing cost and dwindling supplies of fossil fuels have forced most countries to adopt stringent energy standards for buildings. These standards are compiled into building codes that are enforced at local, state, and national government levels. In the US such building codes exist both at the state and national levels. For example, in California the Building Energy Efficiency Standards (Title 24) divide buildings into two main categories: residential buildings and, non-residential buildings. These two building types are covered by different compliance manuals.

What is particularly progressive about the Californian energy standards is that they incorporate the concept of allowing the building designer to select either of two alternative approaches for complying with the standards. The first approach is *prescriptive* in nature. This is the simpler of the two approaches, but offers little flexibility. Each individual component of the building must meet a prescribed minimum energy efficiency. A small degree of flexibility exists in as much as the compliance of major building-envelope components, such as walls, may be area-weighted. In other words, even though a portion of the external walls of a building may exceed the specified energy consumption, the wall as a whole could still comply.

The *performance* approach is more complicated but offers considerably more design flexibility. It requires the use of an approved computer program to establish an allowed energy budget for the building under consideration. The same program is used during the design process to calculate the expected energy usage of the building and verify the compliance of the evolving design. In the *performance* approach the designer is able to consider window orientation, thermal mass, zonal control, and building plan configuration as variables that can be manipulated into an overall solution that does not exceed the allowed energy budget.

However, with either the *prescriptive* or *performance* approach there are some specific mandatory requirements that must be complied with. These deal typically with infiltration control, lighting, minimum insulation levels, and equipment efficiency. Whenever the mandatory requirements exceed either the *prescriptive* requirements or the *performance* proposals, the mandatory requirements will prevail.

The *prescriptive* requirements are divided into packages that stipulate a set of pre-defined performance levels for various building components. Each building component must meet or exceed the minimum energy efficiency level specified by the package. During periodic updating cycles, Packages A and B were eliminated in the 2001 revisions of the standards. Package C applies to locations where natural gas is not available and an all-electric solution is necessary. Package D applies to locations where both natural gas and electricity are available. Also, Package D serves as the basis of the standard design in the *performance* approach to determine the energy budget of the building.

To provide a basis for presenting the *prescriptive* requirements and standardize the energy calculations, California is divided into 16 climate zones. The climate zone definitions and data are the same for both the residential and non-residential building types. Where cities extend into more than one climate zone, the local government authority will normally determine the applicable climate zone and data set.

4.7   Insulation and insulating materials

The main purpose of thermal insulation is to retard heat flow, thereby ultimately influencing the degree of discomfort experienced by the building occupants, or the size of heating or cooling plant and the consumption of fuel that will be required to mitigate this discomfort. Accordingly, thermal insulation and heat reflection measures have the following important applications in building design:

- to maintain temperature differences between the building environment and the external climate;
- to minimize heat transfer by conduction and radiation (reflective foil) through roofs and walls when these are exposed to direct solar radiation;
- to maintain temperature differences between fluids flowing in pipes (e.g., hot water) or ducts (e.g., warm air) and the surrounding environment;
- to control condensation.

A note of caution: materials such as polyurethane, which are good thermal insulators, are typically very poor sound insulators. As will be explained in more detail in later chapters, sound is a form of vibration. In air these vibrations take the form of pressure differences. Therefore, the transfer of sound through a barrier such as a solid wall occurs through the physical movement of the wall. In other words, as the sound impinges on one side of the wall it sets the whole wall into vibration. This movement of the wall, as slight as it may appear, is sufficient to produce pressure differences (i.e., sound waves) on the opposite side of the wall. Accordingly, a good sound insulator is a heavy barrier, because the heavier the barrier, the

| The first 3" of thermal insulation provide the greatest return on investment. |

Calculations based on the heat transfer through 1SF of the building envelope per hour, where the outdoor temperature is 40°F and the indoor temperature is 70°F (i.e., 30°F temperature difference).

Construction Component	Thermal Resistance (R)	Heat Flow Calculation	Heat Loss (Q) (BTU/SF-HR)
single glass (1/8")	0.80	Q = 1(1/0.80) (70–40)	37.50
double glass (1/8" + 1/8")	1.73	Q = 1(1/1.73) (70–40)	17.40
concrete wall (6")	1.32	Q = 1(1/1.32) (70–40)	22.73
(+) 1" polyurethane	(+) 6.25	Q = 1(1/7.57) (70–40)	3.90
(+) 3" polyurethane	(+) 18.75	Q = 1(1/20.07) (70–40)	1.50
(+) 10" polyurethane	(+) 62.50	Q = 1(1/63.82) (70–40)	0.66
For external stucco (3/4") and internal drywall on 2" x 4" stud frame:			
with no insulation	2.00	Q = 1(1/2.00) (70–40)	15.00
with 1" polyurethane	(+) 6.25	Q = 1(1/8.25) (70–40)	3.50

Figure 4.15   Thickness as a measure of the efficiency of thermal insulation.

more of the incident sound energy will be converted into mechanical energy, leaving less sound energy to be passed on to the other side. This requirement for mass is directly opposed to the requirement for closed air cells in an effective thermal insulator.

Figure 4.15 compares the heat transfer through some typical building construction assemblies. As might be expected, the heat transfer through a double-glazed window unit is disproportionately less than through a single-glazed unit, even if only standard window glass is used. The double-glazed window is in excess of 50 percent more efficient. A six-inch-thick solid concrete wall is not a good thermal insulator, even though intuitively to the layperson the opposite may appear to be true. The reason is that owing to the relatively high heat capacity of the concrete material, it takes an appreciable amount of time for the temperature within a concrete wall to be uniformly distributed throughout the wall. However, the heat energy will eventually reach the opposite wall surface and produce either a heat gain (in a warm climate) or a heat loss (in a cold climate). As discussed previously, this heat-absorption

Assume a 1,600 SF home with an external surface area (envelope) of around 3,000 SF (including an allowance for the perimeter footings).

IF:

cost of polyurethane (in place)   = $0.50/SF
cost of electricity ($1.80/therm)   = $0.000018/BTU
30°F temp. diff. for 15 HR on 200 days = 3,000 HR

home (uninsulated) =
      15.00 x 3,000 x 3,000 x 0.000018 = $2,430/year

home (with 1" polyurethane) =
      3.50 x 3,000 x 3,000 x 0.000018 = $566/year

cost of 1" polyurethane = 0.50 x 3,000 = $1,500

**Even 1" of polyurethane insulation pays
for itself in less than one year.**

Figure 4.16   Return on investment of thermal insulation in a typical home.

characteristic of most heavy building materials is commonly used to advantage in hot-dry climates with a significant diurnal temperature range, where the building envelope can serve as a buffer between the outside and the internal building environment during day–night temperature fluctuations.

As shown in Figure 4.16, thermal insulation is a very effective measure for reducing the heat flow through the building envelope. Even a very thin layer of insulation material can reduce the annual heating costs of a home by more than 70 percent (e.g., 77 percent in Figure 4.16 for just one-inch-thick polyurethane).

Basically, building envelopes may be insulated by providing one or more layers of insulating material and air spaces between the external and internal surfaces of the envelope. Air spaces are most effective when faced with reflective foil, so that heat transfer by radiation is kept to a minimum. Obviously, multiple air spaces are more effective than a single air space, provided that each air space is at least 0.75 IN wide. There are a large variety of insulating materials commercially available today:

- Spray-on insulation, such as polyurethane foam, for interior or exterior applications. May be sealed with a silicon spray for exterior applications. Spray-on insulation also includes sprayed lightweight aggregate, which has the dual function of thermal insulation and fireproofing.
- Organic fiber-board manufactured from wood pulp, cane, or other organic fibers. Normally treated with water-proofing additives and sometimes coated with bitumen. Available in standard sheet sizes.
- Inorganic fiber-boards such as fiberglass products, which incorporate small air cells. Fine glass fibers are sprayed with resin, passed under compression rollers and then cured under heat.
- Cork board was for many years the principal insulation material used for refrigeration plants and cool-rooms. More recently, mainly due to cost, the use of cork board has been diminishing.
- Vermiculite is a magnesium silicate, processed with Portland cement to produce pellets suitable for placing into wall spaces.
- Lightweight concretes incorporating vermiculite, perlite, or similar aggregates, are normally used as structural materials for floors, ceilings, and walls.
- Sponge rubber provides a flexible covering for pipes and may be secured with air-drying adhesive.
- Fabricated panels such as metal-faced, box-like panels and metal or concrete faced sandwich panels with insulating cores.

The choice of any insulating material or laminated component for a particular situation will depend on a number of conditions, such as the nature of the surface to be insulated, the temperature of that surface or the surrounding air, and the purpose and cost of the insulation. For example, the underside of stagnant solar collectors can easily reach a temperature in excess of 160°F. Since polyurethane has a fairly low melting point, it may be necessary to apply a layer of fiberglass foam between the collector surface and the polyurethane insulation.

4.8 The cause and nature of condensation

Moisture problems in buildings are normally due to the movement of a mixture of water vapor and air around and through the building shell. The quantity of water vapor in the external atmosphere depends on ambient climatic conditions, while the quantity in the air inside a building also depends on the rate of ventilation and the occupancy. The amount of water vapor that can be held by a given volume of air before saturation occurs (i.e., before the dew point is reached) increases with higher temperatures (Figure 4.17).

It is no longer a matter of debate that dampness in buildings can have a negative effect on the health of the occupants. In particular, dampness supports the growth of molds that produce allergic reactions. However, just as importantly, damp conditions will seriously affect the performance of building materials. It is therefore necessary to control moisture movement, whether in the form of vapor or liquid, so as to keep the components of a building as dry as possible. Dampness arising from the upward passage of moisture through walls, and the penetration of rain water through openings in the building envelope, can be effectively controlled by means of damp-proof courses. There remains however, the problem of surface condensation and the flow of water vapor through insulation, which may be caused by:

- the addition of moisture to the air due to the occupancy of the building;
- the intentional humidification of air by mechanical means for reasons of safety, comfort, or industrial expediency;
- humid air coming into contact with cold surfaces.

As shown in Figure 4.18, there are fundamentally two kinds of condensation in buildings. Surface condensation will occur whenever the temperature of any exposed surface within a building is below the dew point of the surrounding air. According to the nature of the surface and material, the condensation will be visible in the form of water droplets or absorbed by the material. Commonly affected surfaces are window panes, metal window frames, and poorly insulated external walls and ceilings.

The ability of air to hold moisture increases with higher temperatures. Condensation occurs whenever the air temperature falls below the Dew Point.

Surface condensation and interstitial condensation may occur due to:

- The addition of moisture to the air due to the occupancy of the building (e.g., cooking, rigorous exercising, industrial processes, etc.)

- The intentional humidification of air for reasons of comfort or safety.

- Humid air coming in contact with much colder surfaces.

Figure 4.17   Causes of condensation.

Cold surfaces and steep temperature gradients are likely to produce condensation.

Surface Condensation: Occurs whenever the temperature of any exposed surface (e.g., window pane) within a building falls below the Dew Point of the indoor air.

Remedies: (1) Adequate thermal insulation
(2) Absorbent surface finishes

Interstitial Condensation: May occur within the layers of the building envelope whenever the temperature difference between the indoor and outdoor air is very large, and the reduction in vapor pressure across the envelope is abrupt.

Remedies: (1) A vapor barrier (foil or plastic membrane on the warmer side of the envelope).
(2) Avoidance of materials that are impervious to moisture (causing an abrupt vapor pressure drop).

Figure 4.18   Types of condensation.

Surface condensation is particularly prominent in cold climates where humidification of the indoor air is often desirable. To ensure that condensation will not occur on the internal surface of a building envelope, it is necessary to provide adequate insulation within the envelope, so that the temperature of the surface remains below the dew point of the indoor air. If it is likely that at odd times the humidity of the indoor air will be very high, it becomes advantageous to provide an absorbent surface finish, capable of retaining a limited amount of moisture for short periods without deterioration.

Interstitial condensation may occur within the thickness of the building envelope whenever the temperature gradient between the indoor air and the outside atmosphere is very large and the reduction in vapor pressure across the envelope is abrupt. When the system of construction includes materials that are impervious to moisture, thus preventing the diffusion of water vapor within the thickness of the material, the reduction in vapor pressure will not be gradual and condensation is likely to occur within the thickness of the construction. Metal, asphalt, and bituminous-felt roofs, and metal and glass curtain walls, will bring about this situation. Since the primary function of these elements is the exclusion of rain water, they are normally located at the external face of a building. For a heated building the temperature of this external face may often be below the dew point of the indoor air. It is therefore likely that condensation will occur at times, although as soon as the external temperature rises the absorbed moisture will evaporate. Commonly a vapor barrier (i.e., foil or plastic film) is included on the warmer side of the envelope, or at times within a wall, to prevent the passage of water vapor.

4.9 Heat-flow calculation example

In the following example of a building heat-flow calculation sequence, we are going to determine the heat-flow parameters that apply to the envelope (i.e., external walls and roof) of a single classroom in a multi-classroom build-

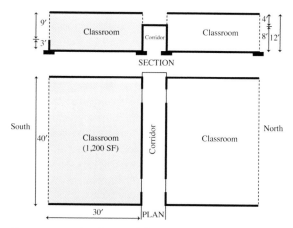

Figure 4.19 Section and floor plan of a portion of a classroom building.

ing, and will then explore the thermal behavior of the same classroom under three different climatic conditions. First, we will consider a cold climate and establish the need for substantial thermal insulation. Second, we will consider a hot-humid climate and determine whether reasonably comfortable conditions can be maintained inside the classroom through natural air movement alone. Third, we will consider a hot-dry climate and explore the potential for using the building envelope as a heat sink and buffer between external and internal conditions during daytime hours (i.e., from sunrise to sunset).

In the typical classroom building shown in Figure 4.19, which will form the basis of our heat-flow calculations, the large window wall of the classroom on the left side of the plan and section views faces due south.

Also, we will assume the following R-Values for the materials used for the construction of the walls and roof:

Classroom walls:

external surface resistance	$= R_{ext} = 0.17$
internal surface resistance	$= R_{int} = 0.61$
¾-IN stucco	$= R_{mat} = 0.15$ (or 0.20/IN)
2-IN by 4-IN timber studs	$= R_{mat} = 3.15$
3-IN polystyrene	$= R_{mat} = 11.55$ (or 3.85/IN)
½-IN drywall	$= R_{mat} = 0.45$ (or 0.90/IN)

Classroom windows:

external surface resistance $= R_{ext} = 0.17$

internal surface resistance $= R_{int} = 0.61$

$\frac{1}{8}$-IN normal glass pane $= R_{mat} = 0.02$ (or 0.16/IN)

Classroom roof:

external surface resistance $= R_{ext} = 0.17$

internal surface resistance $= R_{int} = 0.61$

$\frac{3}{8}$-IN built-up roofing $= R_{mat} = 0.33$ (or 0.88/IN)

5-IN polystyrene $= R_{mat} = 19.25$ (or 3.85/IN)

$\frac{1}{2}$-IN plasterboard ceiling $= R_{mat} = 0.45$ (or 0.90/IN)

Step 1: Adjust the thermal insulation provided by 3 IN of polystyrene in the solid portions of the external walls to allow for timber studs at 16-IN centers.

$$\frac{14.5 + 1.5}{14.5/11.55 + 1.5/3.15} = \frac{16}{1.26 + 0.48} = \frac{16}{1.74} = 9.2$$

It is interesting to note that the presence of the studs reduces the effective thermal insulation value of the wall by about 20 percent (i.e., 9.2 / 11.55 × 100 = 79.7%)

Step 2: Calculate the U-Value of the solid wall sections.

$$R_{total} = 0.17 + 0.15 + 9.2 + 0.45 + 0.61 = 10.58$$
$$U_{wall} = 1/10.58 \qquad = 0.09$$

Step 3: Calculate the U-Value of the window portions of the walls.

$$R_{total} = 0.17 + 0.02 + 0.61 = 0.80$$
$$U_{window} = 1/0.80 \qquad = 1.25$$

Step 4: Calculate the U-Value of the roof.

$$R_{total} = 0.17 + 0.33 + 15.4 + 0.45 + 0.61 = 16.96$$
$$U_{roof} = 1/16.96 \qquad = 0.06$$

Step 5: Determine the total thermal transmittance of the external portion of the classroom's building envelope (i.e., the west wall, the south wall, the upper portion of the north

wall, and the roof). For the purpose of this limited example we will neglect the heat transfer due to air infiltration and the perimeter of the floor slab.

Building Element	U-Value	Surface Area (A)	UA
solid wall	0.09	360 + 120 = 480	43
Windows	1.25	360 + 160 = 520	650
Roof	0.06	1200	72
			Total: 765

Step 6: Calculate the total heat loss in the case of a *cold* climate, assuming an external temperature of 50°F and an internal temperature of 68°F.

$$Q_{cold} = 765 \times (50 - 68) = -13\,770 \text{ BTU/HR}$$

Step 7: Calculate the total heat gain in the case of a *hot-humid* climate, assuming an external temperature in the shade of 78°F (for walls), a sol-air temperature on the roof of 110°F, and a desired internal temperature of 80°F. Then calculate the ventilation rate and wind speed required to maintain an internal temperature of 80°F.

$$Q_{wall} = 693 \times (78 - 80) \qquad = -1386 \text{ BTU/HR}$$
$$\underline{Q_{roof} = 72 \times (110 - 80) \qquad = +2160 \text{ BTU/HR}}$$
$$\text{Net heat gain } (Q_{hot-humid}) \qquad = +774 \text{ BTU/HR}$$
$$V_{rate} = Q_{hot-humid}/[0.018 \times (78 - 80)]$$
$$= 774/0.036 \qquad = 21\,500 \text{ CF/HR}$$

Assuming 160SF of open windows (i.e., 4FT × 40FT = 160SF):

$$W_{speed} = V_{rate} / [88 \times 0.6 \times 160]$$
$$= 21\,500 / 8448 = 2.5 \text{ MPH}$$

Step 8: Calculate the total heat gain in the case of a *hot-dry* climate, assuming an external temperature in the shade of 95°F (for walls), a sol-air temperature on the roof of 130°F, and a desired internal temperature of 80°F. Then determine whether the building envelope could function as a heat sink to buffer the inside of the building from the hot external environment during daytime hours. To increase the heat capacity of the building envelope, and at the same time reduce the direct heat flow through the window areas, four constructional modifications will be assumed. First, the external timber stud walls will be replaced by 3-IN thick concrete with ½-IN drywall on the inside. Second, the timber roof structure will be replaced with a 4-IN concrete slab and a ½-IN plasterboard ceiling. Third, the solid part of the wall on the south side will be raised to an 8-FT height, leaving only a 4-FT high strip of windows similar to the north wall. Fourth, all of the single-glazed windows will be replaced by double-glazed windows.

Modified walls:

external surface resistance $= R_{ext} = 0.17$

internal surface resistance $= R_{int} = 0.61$

3-IN concrete $= R_{mat} = 0.27$ (or 1.09/IN)

½-IN drywall $= R_{mat} = 0.45$ (or 0.90/IN)

Modified windows:

external surface resistance $= R_{ext} = 0.17$

internal surface resistance $= R_{int} = 0.61$

⅛-IN normal glass pane $= R_{mat} = 0.02$ (or 0.16/IN)

air cavity between two sheets of glass $= R_{cavity} = 0.91$

Modified roof:

external surface resistance $= R_{ext} = 0.17$

internal surface resistance $= R_{int} = 0.61$

⅜-IN built-up roofing $= R_{mat} = 0.33$ (or 0.88/IN)

4-IN concrete $= R_{mat} = 0.36$ (or 1.09/IN)

½-IN plasterboard ceiling $= R_{mat} = 0.45$ (or 0.90/IN)

Calculate the U-Value of the modified solid wall sections:

$$R_{total} = 0.17 + 0.27 + 0.45 + 0.61 = 1.50$$
$$U_{wall} = 1/1.50 \qquad\qquad = 0.67$$

Calculate the U-Value of the modified window portions of the walls:

$$R_{total} = 0.17 + 0.02 + 0.91 + 0.02 + 0.61 = 1.73$$
$$U_{window} = 1/1.73 \qquad\qquad = 0.58$$

Calculate the U-Value of the modified roof:

$$R_{total} = 0.17 + 0.33 + 0.36 + 0.45 + 0.61 = 1.92$$
$$U_{roof} = 1/1.92 \qquad\qquad = 0.52$$

Determine the total thermal transmittance of the external portion of the classroom's modified building envelope (i.e., the west wall, the south wall, the upper portion of the north wall, and the roof). Again, for the purpose of this limited example we will neglect the heat transfer due to air infiltration and the perimeter of the floor slab.

Building Element	U-Value	Surface Area (A)	UA
solid wall	0.67	360 + 320 = 680	456
Windows	0.58	160 + 160 = 320	186
Roof	0.52	1200	624
			Total: 1266

Total heat gain for an external temperature in the shade of 95°F (for walls), a sol-air temperature on the roof of 130°F, and a desired internal temperature of 80°F is given by:

$$Q_{wall} = 642 \times (95 - 80) \qquad = +9630 \ BTU/HR$$
$$Q_{roof} = 624 \times (130 - 80) \qquad = +31\,200 \ BTU/HR$$
$$\text{Net heat gain } (Q_{hot\text{-}dry}) = +40\,830 \ BTU/HR$$

For a 10-hour day the external building envelope will need to be able to absorb at least 408 300 BTU (i.e., 40 830 × 10). With a weight of 140 LB/CF for concrete, the heat capacity ($Q_{capacity}$) of the external building shell is approximately equal to:

$$Q_{capacity} = (\text{total concrete mass}) \times (\text{specific heat})$$
$$\times (\text{temperature difference})$$
$$Q_{cap\text{-}wall} = (680 \times 3/12 \times 140) \times 0.22$$
$$\times (95-80) \qquad = 78\,540 \text{ BTU}$$
$$Q_{cap\text{-}roof} = (1200 \times 4/12 \times 140) \times 0.22$$
$$\times (130-80) \qquad = 616\,000 \text{ BTU}$$

Total heat capacity $(Q_{capacity}) = 694\,540$ BTU

Therefore, the total heat capacity of the concrete portions of the external building shell is some 70 percent greater than the estimated daily heat load and, therefore, the building shell will be able to function as an effective buffer between the external and internal environments during the daytime.

5 Solar Energy: The Beckoning Opportunity

This chapter will investigate the potential of solar energy as a natural source of energy for buildings. From the beginning of the energy crisis in the early 1970s solar energy has been heralded as a readily available source of heat for virtually any application. Closer examination shows that while solar energy may be a very useful and convenient source of energy for some applications, it is not at all appropriate for other applications.

5.1 Opportunities and limitations

Although solar energy is the world's most abundant source of energy, and although it is free, and although it is completely unpolluted (Figure 5.1), it is unlikely that solar energy will account for more than 20 per cent of the entire energy consumption in the US by the year 2020 (Figure 5.2).

The fact is that the collection and utilization of solar energy carries with it a number of problems:

- Solar energy constitutes a low-quality source of heat. Most of the energy released by the sun is either intercepted or deflected away from the Earth's surface, leaving only some 2000 BTU/SF to impinge on a horizontal surface during a clear summer day, in California. Without any form of concentration, the temperature generated by this insolation is, at most times, less than 160°F (i.e., sol-air temperature). While such diluted energy may be perfectly adequate for residential hot-water services and most space-

heating systems, it is totally inadequate for the majority of industrial applications.

- Solar energy is only available for a portion of each 24-hour day. In most regions useful solar energy is limited to no more than 8 to 12 hours on a clear day, depending on the season. Also, clouds diffuse and therefore further dilute solar radiation to an extent that can render it almost useless for collection purposes. Therefore, in view of the discontinuity and unreliability of solar energy, all solar systems require heat storage facilities and many require conventional back-up provisions.
- The collection of solar energy is relatively expensive. A typical active solar system, including collector, heat storage unit and facilities for the transmission of the collected heat, costs more than a comparable fossil-fuel heating system.

We might well then ask ourselves, "Why bother with solar energy if it is such a problematic source of heat?" There are a number of reasons why we should not disregard solar energy altogether. First, although solar energy is not suitable for satisfying all energy needs, it may still be the most appropriate solution for some applications. In fact, the low-quality nature of

Building Science: Concepts and Application. Jens Pohl.
© 2011 John Wiley & Sons, Ltd.
Published 2011 by John Wiley & Sons, Ltd.

The effective utilization of solar energy can make at least the 'sunshine states' of the USA virtually independent of fossil fuel for homes.

Solar energy is ...

- Abundantly available in most regions of the world.

- A natural source of energy that is available most of the time.

- A direct source of heat that can be readily captured through absorption.

- A free and completely unpolluted source of heat.

- Controllable through shading devices and/or reflection (i.e., special glass).

- Not impacted by air movement since it is transmitted by radiation.

Figure 5.1   **Solar energy promises.**

Solar energy is unlikely to provide more than 20% of the entire US energy consumption by 2020.

Solar energy is ...

- A low-intensity (i.e., low-temperature) heat source that is not adequate for most industrial heat requirements.

- Available for only a portion of the 24-hour day (i.e., 8 to 12 hours/day).

- Relatively expensive to collect, control, and store.

- Sometimes not available for days due to inclement weather.

- Often (mostly) not an acceptable solution without a back-up system.

Figure 5.2   **Solar energy reality.**

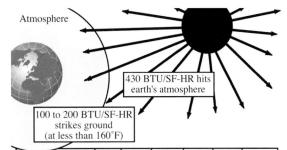

Location		JAN	MAR	MAY	JUL	SEP	NOV
Santa Maria	CA	970	1779	2343	2509	1934	1155
Los Angeles	CA	897	1609	2048	2402	1845	1037
Fresno	CA	679	1576	2387	2517	1882	923
Davis	CA	642	1439	2306	2517	1819	819
Las Vegas	NV	1022	1915	2590	2491	2033	1173
Boston	MA	476	1070	1642	1793	1232	502
Cleveland	OH	461	1118	1852	2074	1026	520
Pittsburgh	PA	347	797	1583	1834	1251	435
Seattle	WA	277	978	1856	2089	1196	384

Figure 5.3   **Availability of solar energy.**

if it were to be confined to that application alone. Second, even if solar energy systems are more expensive than conventional systems, we still have to consider the sun to be an attractive, non-polluting source of heat.

In other words, the arguments for and against solar energy cannot be based purely on economic criteria. The fact is that the world is rapidly depleting all available fossil-fuel sources and, therefore, we need to explore the potential applications of solar energy and other non-fossil-fuel sources, such as wind energy and geothermal energy, regardless of whether or not such alternative sources are immediately cost-competitive.

As shown in Figure 5.3, solar energy is incident on the Earth's surface at the rate of about 100 to 300 BTU/SF-HR. Owing to its diluted nature, relatively large collection areas are required. The actual amount of solar radiation incident on a surface is dependent on the time of day, the season of the year, the condition of the sky (i.e., in respect to clouds and pollution), and the inclination of the surface. Therefore, the initial capital cost of a solar system is normally greater than that of a conventional system utilizing fossil fuel.

solar energy is not a deterrent for water- and space-heating applications, where temperatures seldom exceed 150°F. Therefore, it was postulated in the 1970s that solar energy could easily account for more than 5 percent of the total annual energy consumption in the US by 1990,

5.2   Two types of solar collection system

The simplest way of using solar energy for space-heating purposes is to allow the sun to penetrate directly into the building. In this manner, the building acts as a solar collector, by absorbing solar radiation when it needs heat and rejecting it when no heat is required. Such solar systems are known as passive or direct systems, not because they do not incorporate any mechanical components (in fact they often do), but because they rely totally on the passive absorption or rejection of solar radiation (Figure 5.4).

To date, passive solar systems have been particularly successful in mild climates, not subject to prolonged cold winters. It is likely that most applications of solar space-heating systems in the single-family residential sector will in time come to rely more and more on passive principles.

Active solar systems typically utilize one or more manufactured collector units, normally located on the south-facing side of an inclined roof (for the northern hemisphere, and north side for the southern hemisphere), to collect heat and transport it either in circulating water or air into the building. This type of solar system is known as an active or indirect system, since it consists of components that do not form an integral part of the building envelope. In view of the low temperatures required for hot-water services and space heating, most active solar systems incorporate non-concentrating or flat-plate solar collectors. However, virtually all active solar systems require a fairly large heat-storage facility, a water pump or air fan, pipes or ducts, controls, and valves or dampers.

5.3   Flat-plate solar collectors

The most important component of an active solar system is the collector. Of the many types of solar collector that have been developed in recent years, the flat-plate liquid or air collector has found the widest application.

As shown in Figure 5.5, a typical flat-plate collector consists of a flat metal, plastic, or rubber absorbing plate that is painted black or subjected to a special surface treatment for maximum absorption of the sun's heat. Underneath, or in tubes forming an integral

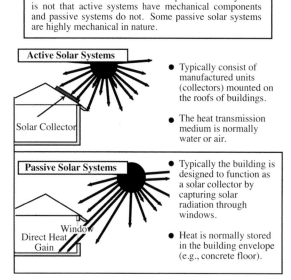

Figure 5.4   Active or passive systems?

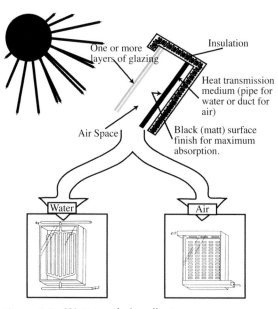

Figure 5.5   Water and air collectors.

part of the absorber plate, a fluid such as water or air is circulated to transfer the collected heat into the building or storage facility. To minimize the heat lost from the collector and circulating fluid, the underside and sides of the collector are well insulated with a several-inches-thick layer of insulating material such as polyurethane or polystyrene foam. Finally, one or more layers of glass with interstitial air spaces are placed above the collector plate to reduce the outward reflection of heat and take advantage of the *greenhouse effect*.

The efficiency of a flat-plate collector (i.e., the percentage of incident radiation that the unit is capable of collecting) is closely related to the number of glazing layers provided, as well as, the temperature difference between the fluid entering and leaving the collector unit (Figure 5.6).

Accordingly, collector efficiencies that are stated independently of the specific temperature differential under consideration may be very misleading.

- Liquid flat-plate collectors are available in many variations. Most utilize water with or without an anti-freeze solution as the heat-

transfer medium. The liquid typically circulates (i.e., is pumped) in pipes that form an integral part of the absorber plate. Problems associated with liquid flat-plate collectors are related to leakages, corrosion, freezing, and the relatively high cost of the necessary plumbing work.

- Air flat-plate collectors are also available in many forms. All utilize air as the heat-transfer medium, which is blown by fans through one or more ducts located underneath the absorber plate. Advantages of air collectors include freedom from freezing and corrosion, as well as lower maintenance costs. However, these advantages are offset by the relatively large duct size and electricity requirements of the fan, necessary for the transfer of the air from the collector unit to the building interior or heat-storage facility.

The choice between an air or water flat-plate collector will require consideration of the nature of the intended application, as well as the ambient climatic conditions with respect to the likelihood that freezing conditions may occur in winter. Water collectors are usually favored for domestic hot-water services because of the relatively inefficient transfer of heat from air to water.

On the other hand, hot water from a solar collector entering a water-storage tank is diffused throughout the water by convection currents. Accordingly, the temperature of the water in the tank may not be high enough to be useful as a hot-water service. For example, on a summer day the temperature of the water leaving the solar collector may be as high as 140°F. However, as this water flows into the storage tank it is quickly diffused throughout the tank, with the result that the temperature of the water may not exceed 100°F throughout the day. Water at 100°F is hardly satisfactory for a shower. One way of overcoming this problem, caused by the lack of heat stratification in water, is to use two storage tanks. The hot water from the solar collector is pumped directly into a small tank and from there into the larger tank. With this arrangement a small supply of water

Collector Type (based on construction)	Typical Temp. (°F)	Efficiency (%)
No insulation and no glazing — black garden hose	90°F	20%
No glazing (but insulated)	130°F	30%
Single glazing (and insulated)	160°F	50%
Double glazing (and insulated)	180°F	60%
Triple glazing (and insulated)	212°F (boiling)	70%

Figure 5.6 Typical collector efficiencies.

at a high temperature (i.e., in the small tank) is available at most times. The disadvantage of this arrangement is the additional cost associated with the requirement for two water tanks and the associated piping.

From an architectural planning viewpoint the principal feature that distinguishes between solar water and air collectors is the size of the associated pipes or ductwork. While small-diameter water pipes can be easily hidden from sight inside walls and vertical plumbing shafts, air ducts are likely to measure at least 6 IN in the smallest dimension, making them too wide to fit into a normal wall. This leaves the designer with few options other than either to provide vertical and horizontal casements for the air ducts, or to expose the ducts as a special feature that contributes to the aesthetic ambience of the building. In the latter case, the ducts could of course be exposed on either the interior or the exterior of the building envelope. A comparative summary of water and air flat-plate solar collectors is presented in Figure 5.7.

5.4 Solar heat-storage systems

Since solar radiation is not available for all hours of the day, it is necessary to store heat for later use. In passive solar-heating systems the heat capacity of the entire building shell can be used as a convenient storage facility. Unfortunately, in the case of active solar systems the heat-storage facility is normally looked upon as a self-contained unit that must be accommodated somewhere within, or in the proximity of, the building. To allow for a storage period of one to two days, the required storage unit can be quite large, even for a single-family residential building. Storage-unit sizes of 100 to 200 CF (i.e., 750 to 1500 gallons) for water and 300 to 600 CF (i.e., 20 to 40 TON) for rock are not uncommon. Architectural planning problems and the not insignificant cost associated with heat storage are an incentive for the development of less bulky storage systems.

As shown in Figure 5.8, the heat capacity of a material, such as water or rock, is given by the

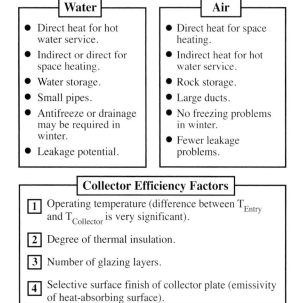

Water	Air
• Direct heat for hot water service.	• Direct heat for space heating.
• Indirect or direct for space heating.	• Indirect heat for hot water service.
• Water storage.	• Rock storage.
• Small pipes.	• Large ducts.
• Antifreeze or drainage may be required in winter.	• No freezing problems in winter.
• Leakage potential.	• Fewer leakage problems.

Collector Efficiency Factors

1 Operating temperature (difference between T_{Entry} and $T_{Collector}$ is very significant).

2 Degree of thermal insulation.

3 Number of glazing layers.

4 Selective surface finish of collector plate (emissivity of heat-absorbing surface).

Figure 5.7 Comparison of water and air collectors and efficiency factors.

The ability of a material to store heat is a function of its heat capacity, which is a product of the specific heat and the density.

Storage Material	Specific Heat (BTU/LB-°F)	Density in Container (LB/CF)	Heat Capacity (BTU/CF-°F)
Water	1.00	62	62 (0% void)
Air	0.24	0.075	0.018
Rock*	0.21	130	27 (25% void)
Concrete	0.23	140	32 (0% void)
Brick	0.20	140	27 (5% void)
Scrap Iron	0.12	490	41 (30% void)
Sand	0.19	120	16 (30% void)

* Rock is really gravel (i.e., pebbles).

Figure 5.8 Heat storage potential of common building materials.

product of the specific heat and the density (in the container). Although the term *rock storage* is in common use, it actually refers to stone pebbles that typically vary in size from about 0.75 IN to 3 IN, depending on the particular design conditions. Therefore, in the case of rock storage the effective density is very much reduced owing to the many air pockets between the adjoining rock particles. In other words, 20 to 30 percent of a rock storage unit may consist of voids, which have negligible heat capacity (i.e., the specific heat and density of air are 0.24 BTU/LB/°F. and 0.075 LB/CF, respectively).

Another approach to reducing the required heat-storage volume is to take advantage of the latent heat that is absorbed by materials during a change of phase. For example, Glaubers salt absorbs 100 BTU/LB and paraffin absorbs 65 BTU/LB when they melt at temperatures just above normal room temperature. Although these materials are more expensive and there are problems associated with their typically imperfect re-solidification, desiccant beds can be used effectively in hot-humid climates to extract moisture from the air stream. The resultant reduction in relative humidity can result in a significant improvement of the thermal comfort conditions inside the building.

A further problem associated with such systems is that, following passage through the desiccant, the temperature of the outlet air stream has usually increased by 40°F to 60°F (i.e., exhaust temperatures of 100°F are common), and consequently it must be cooled. Without such cooling the effectiveness of the desiccant system is greatly reduced. Possible remedies include the incorporation of a passive heat sink in the desiccant system, or the use of a sensible cooling system such as heat exchangers connected to a roof pond. A cooling system that utilizes ambient air may be feasible during the nighttime if the temperature consistently drops to around 80°F.

One- or two-bed systems are typically used. One-bed systems are suitable for conditions where the daytime load is low and beds can be regenerated by solar radiation. Otherwise, the one-bed system has to be regenerated during the high solar radiation period of the day, during a 24 hour cycle. Such systems are more suitable for inland regions where daytime dew points are relatively lower. In two-bed systems each bed operates in opposing and alternating cycles of 12 hours of adsorption and three hours of regeneration.

Currently, water and rock (i.e., pebbles) constitute the most popular solar heat-storage materials for active solar systems.

Using water: Water is readily available in the quantities required for heat storage; it is cheap and it has a high heat capacity of 62 BTU/CF/°F (see Figure 5.8). As a rule of thumb, approximately 1 to 10 gallons of water are normally required per square foot of solar collector. Water has the advantage of not requiring a heat exchanger when used in conjunction with liquid flat-plate solar collectors for a typical residential hot-water service. Furthermore, the circulation of water uses less energy than the circulation of air with comparable heat content, and piping is conveniently routed to remote places and around sharp bends. On the other hand, water-storage tanks are subject to leakage, freezing, and corrosion, as well as a relatively higher initial installation cost.

A typical water-storage facility is shown in conjunction with a liquid flat-plate collector system in Figure 5.9.

The coolest water from the bottom of the tank is pumped through the collector, where it is heated and then returned to the top of the tank. The warmest water at the top of the tank is circulated directly through baseboard radiators or heating panels inside each room. Owing to convection currents, the temperature difference between any two points in the water tank is seldom more than 25°F. This is a disadvantage, since no appreciable heat stratification can be maintained in the tank.

Using rock: Rock storage is most commonly used in conjunction with active-air solar systems. Pebble beds or rock piles normally require two and one half times the volume of an equivalent water-storage tank. The sizes

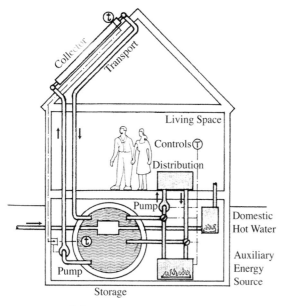

Figure 5.9   Solar water system components.

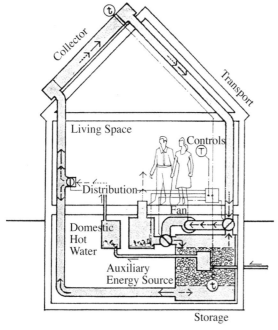

Figure 5.10   Solar air system components.

of typical pebbles range from 0.75 IN to 3 IN in diameter, and the preferred rock type is of the igneous variety.

The smaller the pebble size, the greater is the resistance to air flow, requiring larger fans and more electric power. A typical rock-

storage facility is shown in conjunction with an air flat-plate collector system in Figure 5.10.

During the day, while the sun is shining, hot air is blown from the collector through ducts into the top of the rock-storage unit. There, the heat is quickly absorbed by the pebbles, leading to a high degree of heat stratification. At night the cycle is reversed, so that air is blown from the hottest section of the storage unit into the rooms to be heated.

Every heat-storage system, whether using air or water, requires a large amount of thermal insulation. Thermal resistance values in the range of R20 to R30 (i.e., 3 IN to 5 IN of polyurethane foam) are recommended, depending on the location of the storage tank or rock container. Naturally, all pipes and ducts must be equally well insulated, to minimize the heat losses from the solar system as a whole.

5.5   Sizing a solar hot-water service

As a rule of thumb and under favorable weather conditions, we would expect approximately one square foot of a single-glazed solar collector to heat one gallon of water per day from a mains temperature of 60°F to about 120°F. More accurately, the required collector area (A) for a domestic hot-water service is given by:

$$A = 834 \, W \, (T_H - T_M)/(I \, E) \qquad [5.1]$$

where:

A = required collector area (SF)
W = total hot water required per day (GAL)
T_H = temperature of hot water (°F)
T_M = temperature of cold water (°F)
 I = daily insolation at collector tilt (BTU/SF)
 E = collector efficiency (%).

Currently, in the US, the average daily consumption of hot water is about 12 gallons per person. An example of the application of equation [5.1] is shown in Figure 5.11. Another example is shown below.

Allowing for a storage capacity of two days, a typical family of three would require 144 gallons of water to be heated by solar radiation.

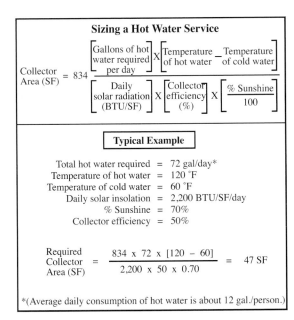

Sizing a Hot Water Service

$$\text{Collector Area (SF)} = 834 \frac{\left[\begin{array}{c}\text{Gallons of hot}\\\text{water required}\\\text{per day}\end{array}\right] X \left[\begin{array}{c}\text{Temperature}\\\text{of hot water}\end{array} - \begin{array}{c}\text{Temperature}\\\text{of cold water}\end{array}\right]}{\left[\begin{array}{c}\text{Daily}\\\text{solar radiation}\\\text{(BTU/SF)}\end{array}\right] X \left[\begin{array}{c}\text{Collector}\\\text{efficiency}\\\text{(\%)}\end{array}\right] X \left[\dfrac{\text{\% Sunshine}}{100}\right]}$$

Typical Example

Total hot water required	=	72 gal/day*
Temperature of hot water	=	120 °F
Temperature of cold water	=	60 °F
Daily solar insolation	=	2,200 BTU/SF/day
% Sunshine	=	70%
Collector efficiency	=	50%

$$\text{Required Collector Area (SF)} = \frac{834 \text{ x } 72 \text{ x } [120 - 60]}{2,200 \text{ x } 50 \text{ x } 0.70} = 47 \text{ SF}$$

*(Average daily consumption of hot water is about 12 gal./person.)

Figure 5.11   Sizing a solar hot-water system.

Assuming an average daily insolation of 2200 BTU/SF, 70 percent of possible sunshine (i.e., allowing for clouds) and a collector efficiency of 40 percent, we obtain on the basis of equation [5.1]:

$$A = 834 \times 144 \times (120 - 60) / (2200 \times 0.70 \times 40)$$
$$= 117 = 120 \text{ SF (approx.)}$$

5.6   The degree–day concept

The Degree–Day (DD) concept serves as a convenient and useful measure of the severity of a climate. While it is most commonly applied to determine heating requirements, it can be equally well applied to cooling requirements in warmer climates. It is based on the concept that there exists an equilibrium external temperature at which no supplementary heating (or cooling) will be required inside a building. For the same climate this base temperature is likely to be slightly different for assessing the heating and cooling requirements.

The normal DD base temperature for heating is 65°F. If another base temperature is chosen, then this is always indicated in the calculations. It is assumed that no heating will be required if

The Degree-Day (DD) concept provides a simplified procedure for calculating the size of a solar collector system. It assumes that there is no heating requirement if the external temperature is higher than a certain temperature (e.g., 65°F).

● Each degree below the 'DD base temperature' (e.g., 65°F) is considered to be one DD.

● If the mean monthly temperature for May in a particular locality is 60°F, then each day of May has 5 DD (i.e., 5 DD/day or 155 DD/month).

● If the heat loss for a building (in the same locality) is 1,000 BTU/HR/°F, then:

heat loss = 24 x 1,000 x [65 – 60] = 120,000 BTU/DD

heat loss = 120,000 x 155 = 18.6 x 10^6 BTU/month

Figure 5.12   The degree–day concept.

the external temperature is above the DD base temperature. Each degree below the base temperature is considered to be one DD. Therefore if the mean temperature during the month of November in a particular region is 56°F, then this region will have 270 DD for that month (i.e., (65°F – 56°F) × 30 days = 270 DD). The calculation of an actual heating requirement in BTU/DD is shown in Figure 5.12.

It simply requires the estimated heat loss in BTU/HR-°F to be multiplied in turn by the DD/day (i.e., 9 DD/day in the above example) and by the number of hours during which this heat loss is expected to persist on a particular day. This calculation tends to lead to conservative results, since it assumes that the estimated heat loss (BTU/HR-°F) applies throughout the entire 24-hour period of a day. Nevertheless, it is commonly accepted as a sufficiently accurate measure of the size of a solar collector facility.

5.7   Sizing a solar space-heating system

To determine the size of the collector area and storage volume required for an active solar heating system it is necessary to:

1 Determine the heat loss that will be experienced by the building each month.
2 Establish the amount of solar radiation that can be collected each month. This will depend on the latitude of the site location, and the percentage of sunshine, as well as the inclination and efficiency of the collector.
3 Calculate the percentage of the total heating requirements that can be catered for by solar energy each month. The deficit must be supplied by an auxiliary heating facility, or alternatively the collector area can be increased.
4 Select the heat-storage medium and determine the volume of the storage facility.

The approximate solar collector area (A SF) required to provide P percent of the total heating requirements for a particular month (Q_M BTU/ month), is then given by the following formula:

$$A = 100\, Q_M\, P\, /(I\, E\, S_M)\qquad [5.2]$$

where:

A = required collector area (SF)
Q_M = heating requirement (BTU/month)
P = percentage heat requirement supplied by sun (%)
I = monthly insolation at collector tilt (BTU/ SF)
E = collector efficiency (%)
S_M = monthly percentage of sunshine (%).

Also, the required heat-storage volume (V CF), for a storage period of D days, is given by:

$$V = Q_D\, D\, /(H_C\, (T_S - T_U))\qquad [5.3]$$

where:

V = required heat-storage volume (CF)
Q_D = daily heating requirement (BTU/day)
D = storage period in days
H_C = heat capacity of storage material (BTU/ CF-°F)
T_S = maximum temperature of heat storage material (°F); normally 130°F to 160°F
T_U = minimum temperature of usable heat (°F); normally 90°F to 110°F.

Owing to the relatively large volume of storage required, architectural planning problems encountered in accommodating this storage

volume, and the cost involved, storage periods of one to two days are normally considered adequate. Example applications of equations [5.2] and [5.3] are shown in Figures 5.13 and 5.14, respectively.

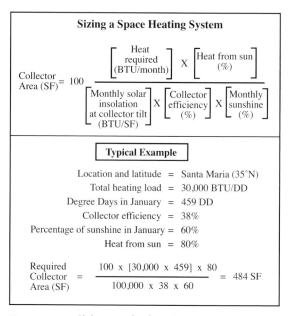

Figure 5.13   Sizing a solar heating system.

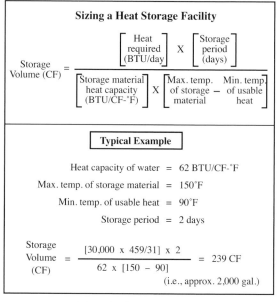

Figure 5.14   Sizing the heat-storage facility.

Ideally, the angle between the incident rays of the sun and a flat-plate solar collector should always be 90°. However, since in our view (i.e., as it appears to us from the Earth) the position of the sun continuously changes in both altitude and bearing from sunrise to sunset, to maintain this optimum 90° angle would require the collector to track the sun. To date such tracking devices have been considered to be too expensive for flat-plate solar collectors. In other words, the efficiency (i.e., lack of efficiency) of a flat-plate collector simply does not warrant the sophistication and expense of a tracking mechanism. On the other hand, such mechanisms are considered appropriate and have been used successfully with concentrating solar collectors. In these collectors the collection surface is typically concavely curved and highly reflective (i.e., like a mirror) to focus the sun's rays onto a target at the focal point.[1] These concentrating collectors are much more expensive than flat-plate collectors owing to the cost associated with the production of a relatively large, curved, mirror-like surface. To fully exploit these higher production costs it becomes important to maintain an optimum profile angle between the curved collector mirror and the sun. This justifies the addition of a tracking mechanism.

In the case of a flat-plate collector (i.e., fixed in position) we select an orientation and slope that optimizes the exposure to the sun. The optimum orientation is due south, and the optimum slope is dependent on the latitude of the location, and also whether the solar heat is being collected for use year-round or just in winter. For example, a solar hot-water service would need to collect solar energy throughout the year, while a solar space-heating facility might be needed only during the winter months. As shown in Figure 5.15, the optimum collector angles recommended for these different applications differ by as much as 15°.

Several rules of thumb for approximate sizing of flat-plate solar collector systems and heat-storage facilities are listed in Figure 5.16. It should be noted, however, that these rules are useful only as order-of-magnitude estimates

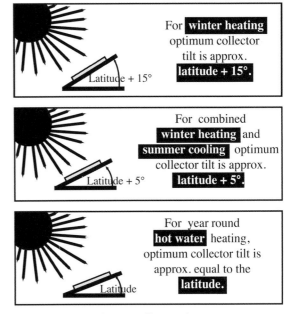

Figure 5.15   Optimum collector slopes.

√ Approximately 1 to 10 gallons of water are normally required per SF of collector area for heat storage.

√ Rock heat storage is approximately 2.5 times larger in volume than water storage.

√ Pebble sizes in rock storage normally range between 0.75 and 3 inches.

√ Heat storage facilities require substantial thermal insulation (R20 to R30, i.e., 3 to 5 inches of polyurethane foam).

√ Under good weather conditions 1 SF of single-glazed solar collector should be able to heat 1 gallon of water from 60° to 120°F.

Figure 5.16   Rules of thumb.

and cannot substitute for the application of equations [5.1], [5.2] and [5.3] in the design of a specific solar installation.

5.8 Integrating building structure and heat storage

An interesting concept for combining the structural support system of a residential building with the storage requirements of a typical active solar heating system was investigated during the mid-1970s in a full-size test building constructed by students in the School of Architecture and Environmental Design at the California Polytechnic State University (Cal Poly), San Luis Obispo, California.

The building incorporates an innovative, fluid-supported structure, consisting of a central 5-FT diameter column fabricated from 18-gauge galvanized steel sheeting and filled with a mixture of sand and water. It is the dual function of the sand–water mixture to support the building loads and to act as a convenient heat store for solar energy collected at roof level (Figure 5.17).

Structurally, the column is classified as a thin-walled cylindrical shell, which is subject to local buckling (i.e., crinkling or folding of the thin column wall) under excessive vertical loads. The resistance to buckling of such a column can

be very much increased by pressurizing the column interior with a fluid, such as air, water, or even sand. The initial structural concept called for water to be used as the pressurizing medium. Unfortunately, two attempts to render the column waterproof by inserting a plastic bag inside the column failed. Each time the plastic bag developed a leak, either before or during the filling operation. Therefore, it was decided to substitute sand for water as the pressurizing medium. Although sand is not commonly described as a fluid, it does display a number of fluid properties. When a bucket of dry sand is poured onto the ground, it forms a heap with sides sloping at an angle of approximately 45°, governed by the friction between individual sand grains. This indicates that sand has limited shear strength and therefore transmits a proportion of superimposed vertical loads sideways. Accordingly, the sand in the building column produces pressure on the inside surface of the column wall, thereby resisting the formation of local buckles (i.e., wrinkles or folds) in the column wall. In addition, the sand has the ability to directly support the vertical load of the building as long as it is contained by the column wall.

The column wall is welded at all joints and sealed top and bottom with circular mild-steel plates (i.e., 0.25 IN thick). At roof level, eight open-web steel joists or trusses are welded to the top column plate. The trusses are fabricated from mild-steel angles (i.e., 2 IN by 3 IN by 0.25 IN thick) that cantilever approximately 10 FT out from the central column.

The suspended floors are approximately 22 FT in diameter and of octagonal shape. Each floor consists of eight wedge-shaped prefabricated panels constructed with 1-3/4 IN thick rigid polystyrene foam sheets sandwiched (i.e., glued) between two layers of 3/8-IN plywood sheets. Each floor panel is provided with a frame of standard 2-IN by 4-IN timber beams laid flat around the perimeter. Individual panels were joined by gluing together overlapping plywood skins. The final panel thickness is 2.25 IN. The floors are suspended from roof level by means of 16 mild-steel suspension rods, attached to the radial roof trusses and prestressed to the

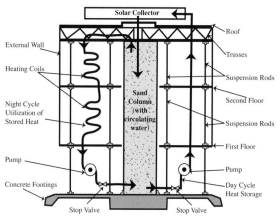

Figure 5.17 System diagram of the sand-column concept.

footings by means of turnbuckles. The rods are of 5/8 IN diameter.

The solar collector consists simply of a 1300 FT long, ¾-IN diameter, black polyethylene hose laid onto the roof surface in the form of a spiral and glazed over with a single layer of translucent tedlar-coated panels. With an estimated efficiency of 35 percent, the 330 SF solar collector is capable of providing 100 percent of the space-heating requirements in January, while the central sand column has a heat-storage capacity of five days.

The principal advantages of this type of fluid-supported building are related to the ability to integrate the structural and environmental functions into one efficient component, thereby obviating the need to accommodate a separate, large heat-storage unit. Moreover, the structural efficiency of the fluid-supported column itself can lead to additional cost savings, particularly on sloping sites.

5.9 Passive solar systems

Active solar systems, whether flat-plate or concentrating collectors, are typically manufactured units that are attached to the external envelope of a building. A much more elegant approach is to design the building itself as a solar heat collector. This is the objective of a passive solar system. Ideally, the design of a passive solar system should allow the building not only to collect solar energy, but also to store it and to distribute it when needed. Unfortunately, in practice this ideal objective is difficult to achieve. The kinds of problem encountered by the designer include difficulties associated with controlling the penetration of the sun into the building, and the even distribution of the collected heat within the interior spaces.

Four principal passive solar approaches will be discussed: namely, Direct Gain systems; Trombe Wall systems; Sunspace systems; and, Roof Pond systems (Figure 5.18).

Of these only one, the Roof Pond system, is capable of winter heating and summer cooling. The other three approaches, apart from providing little (if any) relief in summer, suffer from

the compounding problem of potentially allowing excessive heat to enter the building spaces during the summer months.

Direct Gain passive solar systems rely largely on the greenhouse effect for trapping heat in the building. There are many parts of a building, such as south-facing windows (Figure 5.19),

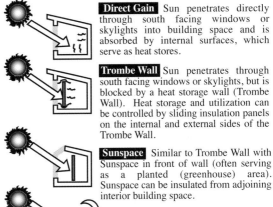

In passive solar systems the building itself is designed to be a solar collector.

Direct Gain Sun penetrates directly through south facing windows or skylights into building space and is absorbed by internal surfaces, which serve as heat stores.

Trombe Wall Sun penetrates through south facing windows or skylights, but is blocked by a heat storage wall (Trombe Wall). Heat storage and utilization can be controlled by sliding insulation panels on the internal and external sides of the Trombe Wall.

Sunspace Similar to Trombe Wall with Sunspace in front of wall (often serving as a planted (greenhouse) area). Sunspace can be insulated from adjoining interior building space.

Roof Pond Water pool on roof is exposed to sun during day and covered with insulation panels at night during Winter. Strategy is reversed for Summer cooling.

Figure 5.18   Typical passive solar systems.

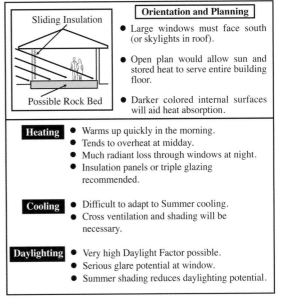

Sliding Insulation

Possible Rock Bed

Orientation and Planning
- Large windows must face south (or skylights in roof).
- Open plan would allow sun and stored heat to serve entire building floor.
- Darker colored internal surfaces will aid heat absorption.

Heating
- Warms up quickly in the morning.
- Tends to overheat at midday.
- Much radiant loss through windows at night.
- Insulation panels or triple glazing recommended.

Cooling
- Difficult to adapt to Summer cooling.
- Cross ventilation and shading will be necessary.

Daylighting
- Very high Daylight Factor possible.
- Serious glare potential at window.
- Summer shading reduces daylighting potential.

Figure 5.19   The direct gain system.

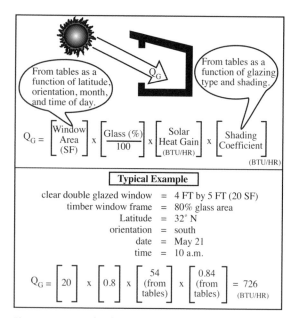

From tables as a function of latitude, orientation, month, and time of day.

From tables as a function of glazing type and shading.

$$Q_G = \begin{bmatrix} \text{Window} \\ \text{Area} \\ \text{(SF)} \end{bmatrix} \times \begin{bmatrix} \dfrac{\text{Glass (\%)}}{100} \end{bmatrix} \times \begin{bmatrix} \text{Solar} \\ \text{Heat Gain} \\ \text{(BTU/HR)} \end{bmatrix} \times \begin{bmatrix} \text{Shading} \\ \text{Coefficient} \end{bmatrix}$$
(BTU/HR)

Typical Example

clear double glazed window	=	4 FT by 5 FT (20 SF)
timber window frame	=	80% glass area
Latitude	=	32° N
orientation	=	south
date	=	May 21
time	=	10 a.m.

$$Q_G = \begin{bmatrix} 20 \end{bmatrix} \times \begin{bmatrix} 0.8 \end{bmatrix} \times \begin{bmatrix} 54 \\ \text{(from} \\ \text{tables)} \end{bmatrix} \times \begin{bmatrix} 0.84 \\ \text{(from} \\ \text{tables)} \end{bmatrix} = 726 \; \text{(BTU/HR)}$$

Figure 5.20   Solar heat gain through glass.

roof lights, and even attached greenhouses (Figure 5.20), that may be used as built-in solar heat traps.

To avoid overheating of the building space, care must be taken to facilitate the absorption of heat by materials with good heat capacities, such as concrete, brick, tile, or stone floor and walls. If well designed, these masonry elements will have just the right amount of heat capacity to maintain a thermally comfortable building environment during the night.

Also, there is a need for a fairly open-plan floor layout so that the solar heat will be well distributed throughout the building. Internal subdivision of the building space into several smaller rooms will tend to concentrate the collected heat in those spaces that directly adjoin the south-facing windows.[2]

Direct Gain systems respond quickly to external solar radiation conditions. On the positive side, this facilitates the warming of the building interior in the morning after a cool night. However, on the negative side, it also tends to lead to overheating by midday and may require the provision of some shading mechanism (e.g., external solar shades and/or internal blinds) to control the amount of solar heat penetration. In

other words, Direct Gain systems are difficult to adapt to summer conditions in climatic regions where cooling will be required. Under such conditions the principal control mechanisms available to the designer are restricted to:

- Reduction of the size of the south-facing openings. This requires careful calculation of the actual solar heat gain through a window opening. As shown in Figure 5.20, the solar heat gain through glass (Q_G BTU/HR) can be estimated by applying the following formula:

$$Q_G = A \times (G_P / 100) \times Q_R \times S \qquad [5.4]$$

where:

Q_G = estimated heat penetration into building (BTU/HR)
A = window area including frame (SF)
G_P = percentage of window that is glass (%)
Q_R = solar heat gain (BTU/HR) (from tables as a function of latitude, orientation, month, and time of day)
S = shading coefficient (from tables, as a function of glazing type and degree of shading).

- Provision of movable, reflective insulation panels or blinds that can be applied manually or automatically to the internal surface of the window as a heat shield during the overheated periods of the day.
- Facilitation of cross-ventilation in much the same manner that this measure is used for cooling in hot-humid climates. The degree to which this approach may be successful will depend largely on the prevalence and dependability of natural breezes during the part of the day when overheating is likely to occur.

Trombe wall systems utilize the thermosyphoning concept to circulate the heat stored in a wall or roof structure by means of naturally occurring thermal currents.

As shown in Figure 5.21, a heat-absorbing wall (e.g., masonry) is placed within a few inches of the inside surface of a window. The surface of the wall facing the window is painted black for maximum heat absorption, and the

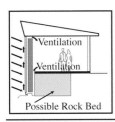

Orientation and Planning	

- Trombe wall can be masonry or water.
- Large windows must face south.
- Outdoor view is blocked.

Heating
- Unvented systems are slow to warm by day and slow to cool at night.
- Comfort is best near the Trombe wall surface.

Cooling
- Cross-ventilation is difficult because of wall obstruction.
- High risk of evening overheating.
- Good mass capacity where such is desirable.

Daylighting
- Most of the daylight is blocked by wall.
- High glare potential around wall perimeter.
- Diffuse light transmission possible through water wall.

Figure 5.21   The Trombe wall system.

Orientation and Planning
- Large glass wall must face south.
- Planted sunspace area adds pleasant character.
- Sunspace can be insulated from adjoining spaces.
- Outdoor view blocked from adjoining space(s).

Heating
- Sunspace thermal characteristics similar to Direct Gain systems, but more extreme temperature swings.
- Accentuated radiant heat loss at night.

Cooling
- Cross-ventilation potential reduced by wall to adjoining space(s).
- Stack ventilation may be effective.

Daylighting
- Very high Daylight Factor in sunspace.
- Very low Daylight Factor in adjoining space(s).
- Summer shading reduces daylight potential.

Figure 5.22   The Sunspace system.

interstitial air space is vented over the top of the wall into the building space. Note the cold air return located at the bottom of the wall to facilitate the thermosyphoning effect.

The principal disadvantages associated with this passive solar system are related to the blocking of daylight by the Trombe wall itself, the slow response to warming in the morning, the equally slow response to cooling at night, and the difficulties associated with combating potential overheating with cross-ventilation. However, on the positive side the Trombe wall system provides a high thermal-mass capacity in colder climates where the intensity of solar radiation may be limited and the daytime temperatures are relatively low.

The characteristics of Sunspace systems (Figure 5.22) are very similar to Direct Gain systems.

Differences are related to the nature of the sunspace itself, which serves as the primary heating element of the building. On the one hand, this space can be treated as a greenhouse with attractive plantings that can greatly enhance the character of the building interior. On the other hand, the separation of the sunspace from the other building spaces restricts

the penetration of daylight into those interior spaces and also reduces the cross-ventilation potential. Experience has shown that the Sunspace system is prone to more extreme temperature swings then the Direct Gain system, and to considerable radiant heat losses during the night.

The Roof Pond system, invented by Harold Hay under the name of SkyTherm™, is an ingenious concept (Figure 5.23).

It overcomes virtually all of the overheating and temperature swings that characterize the other three passive solar design approaches. Its relatively low acceptance to date is not due to any lack of solar performance, but is related to an entirely different set of problems. The maintenance requirements related to the need for movable insulation panels, and the ultraviolet radiation degradation of the clear plastic bags that are required to contain the water on the roof, have proven to be strong deterrents within the context of current building practices.

A solar pond is a fairly shallow pool of water, often contained in one or more plastic bags, which can serve both as a solar collector and a heat-storage facility. Water at any depth acts as Black Body (i.e., absorbs all incident radiation).

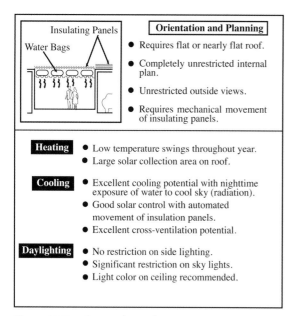

Insulating Panels
Water Bags

Orientation and Planning
- Requires flat or nearly flat roof.
- Completely unrestricted internal plan.
- Unrestricted outside views.
- Requires mechanical movement of insulating panels.

Heating
- Low temperature swings throughout year.
- Large solar collection area on roof.

Cooling
- Excellent cooling potential with nighttime exposure of water to cool sky (radiation).
- Good solar control with automated movement of insulation panels.
- Excellent cross-ventilation potential.

Daylighting
- No restriction on side lighting.
- Significant restriction on sky lights.
- Light color on ceiling recommended.

Figure 5.23   The roof pond system.

The SkyTherm concept utilizes the solar pond principle to collect solar heat during winter days and radiate heat to the colder night sky in summer.

Movable insulation panels are activated by differential thermostats to cover the solar ponds during times when neither heating nor cooling of the water is required. At other times the roof ponds remain exposed to the sun, so that they can collect heat. During a typical winter day–night cycle the insulation panels will automatically slide over the roof ponds in the late afternoon (or during cloudy daytime periods) to minimize the loss of heat from the water during the cold night. Then, when the sun rises in the morning and there is sufficient radiation to collect heat, the panes slide to one side of the

roof (normally over the garage area) to allow the water to collect solar energy. During the summer the day–night cycle is simply reversed. The insulation panels automatically slide over the roof ponds during the day to avoid over-heating under intense solar radiation, and slide away from the roof ponds after sunset to facilitate the cooling of the water through nighttime radiation to the relatively cool sky. At sunrise the same cycle is repeated, with the insulation panels again automatically sliding over the water bags.

The Roof Pond system has several additional advantages, apart from its ability to provide both winter heating and summer cooling. First, it does not impose any restrictions on the building plan in respect to orientation, internal layout, or the size and location of windows. Second, the system does not in any way impact the availability of daylight, nor does it restrict the provision of cross-ventilation. Third, testing of several full-size structures over extended periods has shown that the Roof Pond system experiences the least temperature swings of any of the passive solar systems. And, this applies to both summer and winter conditions (Hay and Yellott, 1970; Hay, 1973).

Endnotes

1. The alternative approach to a curved collector mirror is a concentrating lens that focuses the sun's rays onto a target. In this case the high cost of the concentrating collector is derived from the cost of the lens.
2. South-facing windows in the northern hemisphere and north-facing windows in the southern hemisphere.

6 Light, Color, and Vision

Vision is one of the five physical senses (i.e., touching, tasting, hearing, smelling, and seeing) that connect us human beings to our environment. It allows us to detect approaching danger, enjoy the beauty of our surroundings, and communicate in a very personal manner with fellow human beings. While light is only one component of a building design, it is a very important consideration. In particular, the maximum utilization of daylight, leading to energy conservation efficiencies, can be a dominant factor in the layout of spaces and the planning of the building as a whole. The constraints that may be imposed on a floor plan, if the optimization of daylight is a primary design criterion, can be quite severe. For example, most architects would agree that for classrooms to be adequately served by daylight alone they should receive this light from two opposite sides. This will require each classroom to have at least two partial external walls (i.e., partial, because both daylight sources could be highlights above party walls).

6.1 Some historical background

We understand today that vision is made possible by the interaction of a physical entity called light and a biological organ called the eye, which is sensitive to light and in combination with the brain, allows us to see. This understanding was achieved only gradually.

The ancient Greeks thought that vision was produced by something traveling between an object and the beholder. Pythagoras explained vision as images traveling from objects to the eye. Euclid, some 200 years later, reversed the travel direction by suggesting that visual rays travel from the eye to the object. A few years later Aristotle advocated a more sophisticated theory. He suggested that apparently transparent substances such as air and water become transparent only in the presence of some light source. That was a very clever concept, which provided a plausible explanation of our inability to see in the dark. According to the theory, air is made transparent by the light from the sun (or some other source, such as a fire or a candle) and this allows us to see, because the colors of the objects in the environment are able to travel to our eyes.

It took another 1,300 years for the understanding to emerge that the eye is a detector of light. This decisive distinction between a physical entity and a biological detector, first proposed by the Arab scholar Alhazen, set the stage in the Middle Ages for the investigation of the characteristics of light within a new field of science, called to this day geometrical optics. Knowledge of the rules of geometrical optics was acquired relatively rapidly and allowed the design and fabrication of optical devices such as lenses, microscopes, and telescopes. However, the question of what light itself is lingered into the twentieth century.

Building Science: Concepts and Application. Jens Pohl.
© 2011 John Wiley & Sons, Ltd.
Published 2011 by John Wiley & Sons, Ltd.

6.2 Light speed and color

If light is a mobile physical entity, then it should be possible to measure its speed. Early in the seventeenth century the Italian philosopher and astronomer, Galileo,[1] devised an experiment to measure the speed of light. He positioned himself and an assistant separately on two hilltops at night. The hilltops were several kilometers apart, with a clear line of sight between them. By flashing light signals back and forth between himself and his assistant, Galileo sought to measure the round-trip travel time of the light signals. Taking into account the human reaction time, he found that there was no time interval left to attribute to the movement of the light. He realized that the speed of light must be very high and could therefore not be measured with this kind of earthly line-of-sight experiment.

The solution to the problem came indirectly through astronomical observations in the later part of the seventeenth century. While observing the movement of the moons of Jupiter through a telescope, the Danish astronomer Roemer[2] discovered that the prediction of the eclipses of the moons by Jupiter (i.e., whenever Jupiter is located directly between one of its moons and the Earth) was consistently incorrect. The prediction was based on the measurement of the orbital periods of the moons, which could be calculated with reliable precision. Roemer reasoned that the error might be due to the changing distance between the moons and the Earth, as they travel in their orbits around Jupiter. Since these astronomical distances are very large, they could affect the time it takes for light to transmit the image of the moon's location at any particular time to the eyes of the observer on Earth. As further explanation, it should be noted that we can see an event occurring only when light from that event reaches our eyes. Roemer was absolutely correct in his supposition. Today, using very precise instruments, we know the speed of light to be close to 300,000 km/sec or 186,000 miles/sec. No wonder that Galileo failed with his experiment! Even if the two hilltops had been 20 miles apart,

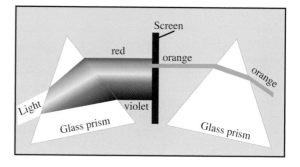

White light is made up of a spectrum of colors ranging through red, orange, yellow, green, blue, indigo, and violet.

When any one of those separate color beams is passed through a second prism, it remains unchanged.

Figure 6.1   A second prism has no effect on the color of any one of the spectrum components.

the time taken for a return-trip light signal would have been less than a thousandth of a second.

At around the same time in the seventeenth century the renowned English scientist Isaac Newton shed light on the nature of color. The origin of color had been another perplexing issue. While it was already known that when light is passed through a glass prism it clearly separates into the colors of a rainbow, Newton took this experiment a step further (Figure 6.1).

He showed that when he passed one of these separate color beams through a second prism, it had no effect on the color of that beam. He inferred from this experiment that color was not due to any change in the nature of the light as it passes through the prism, but that the prism simply separates the light beam into a spectrum of colors. In other words, all of the colors are contained in light. He further proved this point by reuniting the separated colors into the original white light by passing them through a second inverted prism (Figure 6.2).

Newton proceeded to place objects of various colors in the path of a colored light beam. He

If the spectrum of colors is passed through a second inverted prism, the colors recombine into white light.

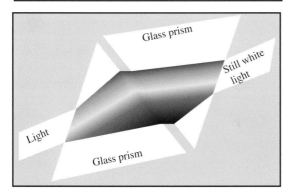

A rainbow is produced by refraction and internal reflection when sunlight passes through millions of raindrops.

Figure 6.2   A second inverted prism will recombine the spectrum into white light.

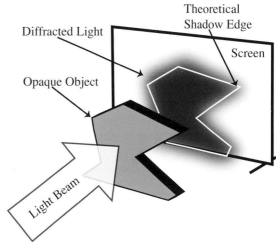

Figure 6.3   Diffraction of light around an object.

found that a colored object would effectively reflect light of the same color, but absorb light of another color. For example, a blue object would appear blue under blue light, but nearly black under a red light. Newton correctly concluded that objects have color because of the way in which they reflect certain colors of the spectrum while absorbing the light of other colors.[3]

6.3   What is light?

The question of what exactly light is turned out to be a more difficult issue, which was not fully resolved until the twentieth century. During the seventeenth century there had been two prevailing theories about the nature of light. The first theory, advocated by Newton, held light to be a flow of particles, while the second theory postulated light to be a form of wave motion. There was the obvious need for advocates of either theory to be able to explain the optical phenomena that were known at that time. These included:

- *Reflection*, which occurs when light strikes a polished surface and is reflected away from the surface in such a way that the angle of incidence is equal to the angle of reflection.
- *Refraction*, which occurs when light passes from one transparent or translucent medium to another. In other words, the light appears to bend slightly as it enters the second medium.
- *Diffraction*, according to which light bends slightly around corners. For example, if we place an opaque object between a light source and a screen, then the light will bend slightly around the object, resulting in the projection of a shadow that is smaller than might be expected (Figure 6.3).
- *Polarization*, which occurs when light passes through some transparent medium and only a portion of light appears to be transmitted. For example, looking through polarized sunglasses eliminates the glare normally seen when light is reflected from a shiny surface, such as the water surface of the ocean (Figure 6.4).

Both theories provided quite plausible explanations of the reflection, refraction, and diffraction phenomena. However, the polarization of light constituted a challenging problem. Newton, as

Figure 6.4   Polarization of light.

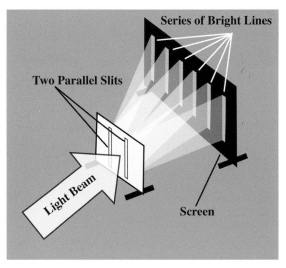

Figure 6.5   Young's double-slit experiment.

the principal proponent of the particle theory, argued that light consists of slightly elongated particles that are oriented in random directions in normal light, but in the same direction in polarized light. The advocates of the wave theory simply could not explain the polarization phenomenon, because they incorrectly regarded light to be a *longitudinal*[4] wave form. Therefore, for almost 100 years the particle theory was accepted as providing the best explanation of the nature of light.

It was not until the nineteenth century that a decisive experiment by the English scientist Thomas Young (1773–1829) gave new life to the wave theory. He showed that when light is passed through two narrow slots, not two as might be expected, but a series of alternating lines of light and dark are projected onto a screen (Figure 6.5).

He argued correctly that this phenomenon was caused by the interference of two sets of light waves passing through the two narrow slits (Figure 6.6). Based on Young's experiments, the French physicist Augustin Fresnel (1788–1827) developed a detailed mathematical explanation of transverse light waves that very quickly replaced the particle theory.

Even though the wave theory of light had now triumphed, there was still a great deal of speculation about the nature of the medium that could support the propagation of transverse light waves. The separate contributions of two British physicists, Michael Faraday[5]

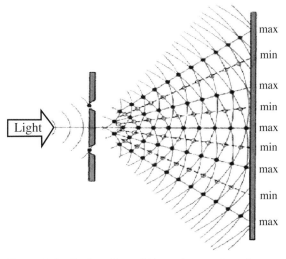

Figure 6.6   Explanation of Young's experiment.

and James Maxwell, and the German physicist Heinrich Hertz (1857–1894) finally led to the understanding that light waves are electromagnetic waves. Essentially, light waves are produced by electric charges that can travel through any transparent or translucent medium. Unlike sound waves, which are transmitted by the progressive oscillation of the particles in the medium, the transmission of light waves does not require the physical particles of the medium to be set into vibration. Therefore, while sound cannot exist without a medium made up of particles (i.e., atoms and molecules), light can travel through a vacuum.

As shown in Figure 6.4, a light wave can be characterized as a beam that consists of a bundle of waves at all angles like the spokes of a bicycle wheel, so that the plane of each wave is perpendicular to the direction of the light beam. When this bundle of light waves passes through a Polaroid filter, then all of the light waves in one plane (i.e., either the vertical or the horizontal plane) are blocked and only the waves in the other plane are transmitted.[6]

The realization that light is a form of electromagnetic radiation constituted a major break with the nineteenth-century view in physics that any phenomenon could and should be explained in mechanical terms. Contrary to this prevailing view, Maxwell had shown that physical objects could influence each other through lines of force (i.e., electrical or magnetic field lines) without being in direct contact with each other. However, even the understanding of light as electromagnetic radiation was insufficient. Not all of the characteristics of light could be described in terms of wave motion. Particularly troubling was the large discrepancy between the theoretically predicted and measured emission of light from an object raised to a high temperature. This puzzle was solved at the turn of the twentieth century by Albert Einstein (1879–1955), building on the earlier work of the German physicist Max Planck (1858–1947). Planck had proposed that electromagnetic radiation is produced in discrete units called photons, rather than as a continuous flow. Einstein used this concept to explain the photoelectric effect,[7] postulating that light behaves like a wave and also like a flow of particles, thereby adding credence to the quantum theory[8] of physics that began to emerge at that time.

The photons that light consists of can be looked upon as discrete bundles of energy. Therefore, light is a form of energy just as heat, electricity, and sound are other forms of energy. One of the properties that the various forms of

energy share is the ability to change from one form to another. For example, when we take a photograph with a non-digital camera light energy is converted into chemical energy in the film of the camera.

6.4 Light viewed as mechanical waves

Although it is now accepted that light consists of discrete units of energy, it does obey to a limited extent the laws of wave motion. Photons can interfere with each other like the waves shown in Figure 6.6, in the explanation of Young's experiment. They can also diffract around corners, as seen in Figure 6.3, or be polarized (Figure 6.4) like transverse waves. In fact, so many of the properties of light can be quite accurately described in terms of wave motion that it has become common practice to refer to light as electromagnetic waves. While this oversimplification of the nature of light is quite acceptable for the lighting design of buildings, there are properties of light in the realm of physics that can be explained only by treating light as a stream of individual energy bundles (i.e., photons).

The ability of electromagnetic waves to travel through a vacuum is due to the fact that they are produced by a vibrating electric charge. However, electric charges also generate magnetism – hence the term "electromagnetic". In other words, electromagnetic waves have both an electric and a magnetic component. Like mechanical waves, they can be characterized in terms of just three attributes (Figure 6.7).

Amplitude is a measure of the intensity of the wave, *wavelength* is equal to the distance between two successive crests (i.e., maxima) or troughs (i.e., minima), and the number of complete wavelengths passing a particular point in one second is referred to as the *frequency*.

While the electromagnetic spectrum ranges over an enormously large number of wavelengths, the part of that spectrum that stimulates the retina of our eyes and is therefore visible to us is a very narrow band of microscopically

> Wavelength is the distance from the crest of one wave to the crest of the next wave.

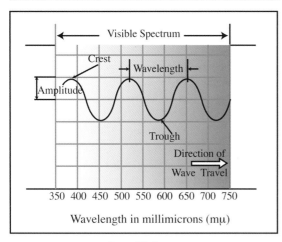

Figure 6.7   Properties of light waves.

> Light waves are very small waves.

Unit	Symbol	US Equivalent	Approximate Size	
Meter (measures radio waves)	m	1 m = 39.37 in.	A small child	
Centimeter	cm	0.01 m (or 10^{-2} m) = 0.3937 in.	A sunflower seed	
Millimeter	mm	0.001 m (or 10^{-3} m) = 0.039 in.	A grain of sand	
Micron	μ	0.000001 m (or 10^{-6} m) = 0.000039. in.	A small bacterium	
Millimicron	mμ	0.000000001 m (or 10^{-9} m) = 0.000000039 in.	A benzene molecule	

Figure 6.8   Comparative measures of wavelength size.

small wavelengths. The wavelengths that constitute light are measured in millimicrons (also referred to as nanometers), ranging from approximately 350 mμ to 750 mμ, where one millimicron (mμ) or nanometer (nm) is equal to one-billionth of a meter (see Figure 6.8).

As shown in Figure 6.9, each individual wavelength within the spectrum of light is representative of a particular color, ranging from red to violet in descending wavelengths. The reason why Isaac Newton was able to demonstrate that light contains the colors of the rainbow (Figures 6.1 and 6.2) when it passes through a translucent prism is because each wavelength will bend to a slightly different degree as it passes through the prism. When all of the wavelengths of the visible spectrum are perceived by our eyes at the same time, then we refer to this as white light. However, strictly speaking white is not a color at all but simply the presence of the complete spectrum of light. Similarly, neither is black a color, but is rather the absence of all of the wavelengths of the visible spectrum.

There are many forms of electromagnetic energy, the effect of each depending on its

> White light may be dispersed into its spectral components by passing it through a prism.

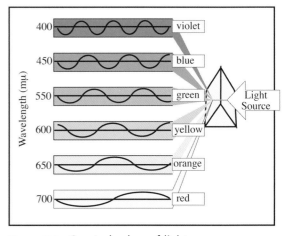

Figure 6.9   Spectral colors of light.

According to the Quantum Theory in Physics, light is a form of electromagnetic radiation (i.e., energy), obeying the laws of wave motion.

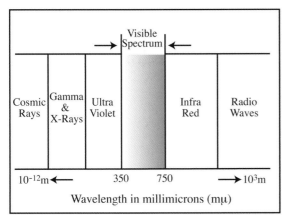

Figure 6.10 The full spectrum of electromagnetic radiation.

The human eyes measure brightness differences and not objective light levels like a photometer (i.e., light meter).

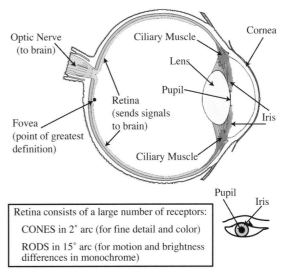

Retina consists of a large number of receptors:

CONES in 2° arc (for fine detail and color)

RODS in 15° arc (for motion and brightness differences in monochrome)

Figure 6.11 Section through the human eye.

energy content, so that high-frequency radiation will have high energy content and low-frequency radiation will have correspondingly lower energy content.

As shown in Figure 6.10, the visible spectrum or light as we perceive it occupies a very narrow band (i.e., 350 to 750 mµ), although it is possible by means of fluorescence to create perceptible light from ultraviolet radiation. We will discuss the latter in some detail in a later chapter dealing with the creation of light by artificial means. However, in the study of natural lighting we are concerned only with the visible spectrum of electromagnetic radiation as perceived by the human eye.

The eye is not a photometer and does not measure absolute physical brightness levels. Objects are perceived through the eyes by virtue of their brightness and color or, more precisely, by the differences in brightness and color. In other words, our eyes measure brightness differences. When we drive a car at night on a two-way road the headlights of an oncoming car tend to temporarily blind us. This will be particularly the case if the driver of the oncoming car forgot to dip his or her headlights and

they remain on full beam. If we were to encounter the same car on the same road during the day in bright sunshine, we would be hard pressed to even recognize whether the car has its headlights on full beam or not. Obviously the amount of light emitted by the headlights is exactly the same during nighttime and daytime. What is different is the background illumination level. During a dark night the headlights of a car, particularly if on full beam, will be several orders of magnitude brighter than the ambient illumination level. However, during a bright day under a clear sky, even the full-beam headlights of a car are unlikely to be much brighter than the sunlight reflected from the asphalt paving of the road. Consequently, the headlights of an oncoming car will appear to be much dimmer during the day than at night.

The central area of the retina (Figure 6.11), called the fovea, is covered by cones in an approximately 2° arc. Cones are required for fine detail and color vision.[9] Therefore, the very small fovea region is also the area of greatest definition. Outside this area we enter into the para-fovea region, in which the number of rods increases. Rods are used in the perception of brightness differences and motion, but in monochrome. Accordingly, color vision is limited to some 15° of arc around the fovea. Both cones and rods are light receptors that pass the light stimulus through the optic nerve to the brain for interpretation.

Although the eye is sensitive to a very wide range of luminosity (i.e., brightness) it takes time to see. However, the time it takes for the eyes to adjust is reduced by higher luminance. We experience this in our daily activities. For example, if we decide to see a movie during the daytime and have to enter the theater after the start of the show, we find that it takes a minute or two until our eyes adjust to the semi-darkness and we are able to vaguely make out the shapes of people, empty seats, and steps. Conversely, when we leave the cinema at the end of the show we are able to adjust to the bright sunshine of the exterior much more quickly. While vision speed increases with higher levels of illumination, visibility increases with greater object brightness.

Increased illumination also increases visual acuity (i.e., the ability to see fine details). However, this does not mean that we can simply increase the illumination of the task area at will, to improve our ability to resolve small visual details. At some point the difference between the brightness of the task area and the immediate surround will become a source of glare. This is due to the fact that our eyes measure brightness differences, and if these brightness differences are excessive then the rods in the para-fovea area of the eye will be overstimulated.

As shown in Figure 6.12, the sensitivity of the human eye varies considerably within the visible range. Our eyes are most sensitive to yellow-green light with a wavelength of around 550 mμ. Below wavelengths of 480 mμ and above 620 mμ our sensitivity is reduced by more than 50 percent. For this reason, in most countries, highway signs are given a green background color. However, it must be noted that the Standard Luminosity Curve shown in Figure 6.12 represents a statistical average. Individual persons vary slightly in their response to

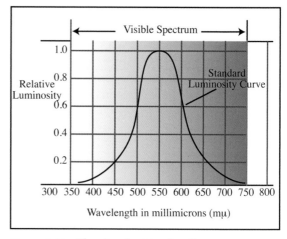

Figure 6.12 The standard luminosity curve.

luminosity and this may contribute to individual differences in taste, particularly as far as color preferences are concerned.

The fact that the human eye perceives subjective brightness differences forms the basis of the Apparent Brightness Theory of lighting design, which will be discussed in some detail later in this chapter. It suffices here to define apparent brightness as the subjective perception (i.e., through the human eye) of physical brightness. Accordingly, the apparent brightness of any area in the visual field is determined by the luminance (i.e., physical brightness) of the field and the average luminance of all objects in the field. The average luminance of all objects in the visual field is further known as the adaptation level.

In summary, the following characteristics of the human eye are of particular interest:

- Individuals vary in their response to luminosity, a fact that may largely contribute to differences in taste among persons.
- Although the eye is sensitive to a very wide range of luminosity, it takes time to see and this time is reduced by higher luminance.

- Visual acuity is the ability to resolve small visual details. An increase in luminance increases visual acuity.
- Vision speed increases with higher levels of illumination, and visibility improves with increased object brightness.
- Pictures or images received by the eye are inverted.
- The retina consists of a very large number of receptors known as rods and cones. Cones are concentrated in the actual fovea area and are responsible for our ability to see fine details and color. Rods increase in number in the para-fovea area and are responsible for the detection of brightness differences and movement.
- The retina sends signals to the brain, where the images received by the receptors in the retina are interpreted.
- The fovea is the point of greatest definition.

The subjective aspects of vision are related to the more general concept of sensation and stimulus. By sensation we understand a sensing or feeling by a human being, purely on a subjective basis. For example, when the level of illumination in a room is measured with a light meter, the reading will not be a measure of the sensation produced by the light, but the physical stimulus. Accordingly, the physical stimulus measured in units of physical energy gives rise to subjective sensations, which are related in magnitude to the amount of stimulation.

6.5   Measurement units of light

Since the perception of light is related to the sensitivity of the eye, it is only appropriate that the units of light should be quite separate from the normal units of power and energy found in the thermal, electrical, and mechanical fields. There are essentially only four characteristics of light that are directly relevant to the lighting design of building spaces: namely, light flux; luminous intensity; illumination level (also referred to as illuminance); and luminance.

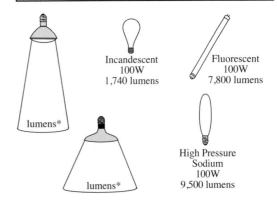

Flux is the quantity of light emitted by a light source, irrespective of direction or distribution. It is measured in **lumens**.

Incandescent
100W
1,740 lumens

Fluorescent
100W
7,800 lumens

lumens*

High Pressure
Sodium
100W
9,500 lumens

lumens*

*(Although both lamps may emit the same amount (flux) of light, the intensity and width of the light beams may be very different.)

Figure 6.13   **Light flux.**

Flux is the quantity of light emitted by a light source, irrespective of direction or distribution (Figure 6.13). Strictly speaking the units of flux should be lumen per second, but it is common practice to neglect the time element. The performance of a lamp is stated in terms of the number of lumen it emits, and its efficiency in terms of the number of lumen emitted per watt of input energy.

Luminous intensity is the property of a source to emit light in a given direction, and is measured in candela, where one candela is approximately equal to the light emitted by a single candle[10] (Figure 6.14). Light flux (F lumen) from a point source is related to the luminous intensity (I candela) of the source by the expression:

Light flux (F) = luminous intensity (I)
× solid angle (W)   lm   [6.1]

A solid angle is a spherical angle that is subtended by a surface to the center of a sphere.[11] In the case of the luminous intensity of light, the "surface" is the area illuminated by the light source and the "center of the sphere" is the light source itself.

Luminous intensity is particularly useful for describing the characteristics of artificial light

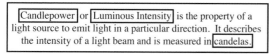

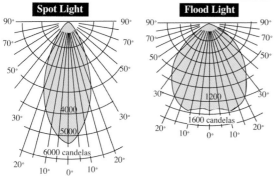

Plotted on a polar diagram the distance from the center determines the intensity of light (candelas) in that direction.

Light Flux = Luminous Intensity x Solid Angle (lm)

Figure 6.14   Luminous intensity.

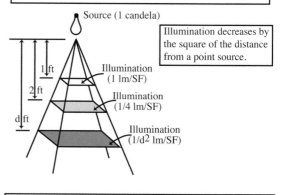

Figure 6.15   Illumination or illuminance.

sources. As shown in Figure 6.14, the distribution of light provided by a luminaire can be plotted on a polar diagram as concentric rings of luminous intensity, measured in candela. However, it should be noted that the area depicted on the polar diagram is not a measure of the amount of light emitted by the lamp, but simply represents the distribution of light. In other words, a larger area does not indicate that a given luminaire provides more light than a luminaire with a smaller area. What it does indicate is that the available light is spread over a larger or smaller area, respectively.

Illumination level or illuminance is the amount of light flux falling on a surface area (A SF) and is measured in lumen/SF (lm/SF) or footcandle (fc).[12] Accordingly, illumination (E) is given by the formula:

$$\text{illumination (E)} = \text{flux (F)} / \text{area (A)}$$
$$\text{lm}/\text{SF or fc} \qquad [6.2]$$

As shown in Figure 6.15, illumination decreases by the square of the distance for a point source.[13] Therefore, the illumination (E) at a distance (D) from a point source of luminous intensity (I) acting through a solid angle (W), is expressed by:

$$\text{illumination (E)} = \text{flux (F)} / \text{area (A)} = \text{I} \times \text{W} / \text{A}$$
$$= \text{I}/\text{D}^2 \text{ lm}/\text{SF or fc} \qquad [6.3]$$

If the surface is inclined at some angle θ to the direction of the emitted light, then:

$$\text{illumination (E)} = \text{I} \cos\theta / \text{D}^2 \text{ lm}/\text{SF or fc} \quad [6.4]$$

The concept of unit sphere defines the relationship between luminous intensity and illumination level. Imagine a candle flame at the center of a sphere that has a radius of one foot. The amount of light flux falling on any one square foot of the surface of that sphere is one lumen/SF or one footcandle. Since the total surface area of the sphere is equal to 4π, then the amount of light flux generated by the candle is 4π lm or 12.57 lm.

Luminance is the intensity per unit area of a surface seen from a particular direction and is measured in candela/SF or foot Lambert (fL). The performance of a large light source may be determined by dividing it up into a number of elements, each of which could have a different intensity distribution. Accordingly, the concentration of flux emitted in a given direction from the projected area of each of these elements is

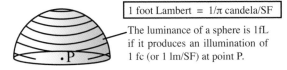

Luminance is the intensity per unit area of a surface seen
from a particular direction and is measured in candelas/SF
(cd/SF) or foot Lambert (fL).
(1cd/SF = 3.14 fL and 1fL = 0.32 cd/SF)

1 foot Lambert = 1/π candela/SF

The luminance of a sphere is 1fL
if it produces an illumination of
1 fc (or 1 lm/SF) at point P.

- Luminance is the amount of light that is reflected off
  a surface and reaches the eye.

- Luminance is an objectively measured quantity and
  brightness is its subjective counterpart.

- Luminance is dependent on: (1) illumination level;
  (2) location of viewer in respect to light source;
  (3) specularity of light source (i.e., mirror-like
  reflection); and, (4) color of surface.

Figure 6.16   Luminance.

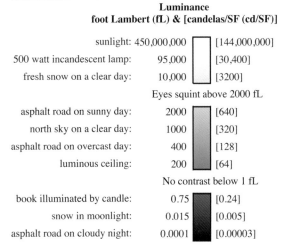

The human eye can detect luminance over a range of more
than a trillion (10^{12}) to one. However, the perceived
brightness of any luminance is relative and subjective.

Luminance
foot Lambert (fL) & [candelas/SF (cd/SF)]

	fL	cd/SF
sunlight:	450,000,000	[144,000,000]
500 watt incandescent lamp:	95,000	[30,400]
fresh snow on a clear day:	10,000	[3200]

Eyes squint above 2000 fL

asphalt road on sunny day:	2000	[640]
north sky on a clear day:	1000	[320]
asphalt road on overcast day:	400	[128]
luminous ceiling:	200	[64]

No contrast below 1 fL

book illuminated by candle:	0.75	[0.24]
snow in moonlight:	0.015	[0.005]
asphalt road on cloudy night:	0.0001	[0.00003]

Figure 6.17   Perception of luminance as brightness
by the human eye.

referred to as the luminance of that element
(Figure 6.16).

It can be shown that if the surface of a sphere
has a uniform luminance, then a numerically
equal illumination is produced by that luminance at the center of the sphere. This means
that a uniform sky with a luminance of 1000 fL
will produce an outdoor illumination on a horizontal surface of 1000 lm/SF (or 1000 fc).

Luminance, illumination, and reflectance are
closely related in the following manner. The
illumination on a surface may be defined as the
incident luminous flux per unit area expressed
in lumen per square foot (or footcandle).
However, some of the light flux falling on this
surface is reflected so that the amount of light
reaching the eyes of the observer is proportional
to the amount of flux falling on the surface, and
the ability of the surface to reflect light.
Accordingly, the luminance of this surface is a
function of the incident flux per unit area and
the reflectance of the surface.

As shown in Figure 6.17, the human eye can
detect luminance over an enormously wide
range that extends from the more than 450
million fL generated by the sun to under 1 fL
under moonlight. Of course looking directly

into a light source with a very high luminance,
such as direct sunlight, must be avoided because
it can cause permanent damage to the retina of
the eye. In fact, our eyes already start to squint
involuntarily when subjected to a luminance of
around 2000 fL. While luminance is an entirely
objective quantity that can be measured with a
luminance meter, the perception of luminance
by our eyes is relative and subjective. This subjective equivalent of luminance is referred to as
brightness, and is relative to the adaptation
level of the surroundings.

A comparison of metric and American[14] lighting units of measurement is shown in Figure
6.18, with the respective conversion factors. For
both light flux (lumen or lm) and luminous
intensity (candela or cd) the units of measurement are the same in both the metric and
American systems. However, in the case of illumination and luminance conversion factors are
necessary as follows:

For illumination or illuminance: 1 lm/SF or 1 fc
  is approximately equal to 10 lux.
For luminance: 100 fL is approximately equal to
  3 cd/m^2.

As a rule of thumb: 1fc ≈ 10 lux

Lighting Property	American Units (AS)	Metric Units (SI)	Conversion Factor
light flux	lumens (lm)	lumens (lm)	(not required)
illumination (or illuminance)	footcandles (fc)	lux (lx)	1fc = 10.764 lux
luminous intensity	candelas (cd)	candelas (cd)	(not required)
luminance	cd/SF foot Lamberts	cd/m²	1cd/SF = 0.09 cd/m² 1 foot Lambert = 0.03 cdm²

Figure 6.18   Comparison of metric and American units of measurement.

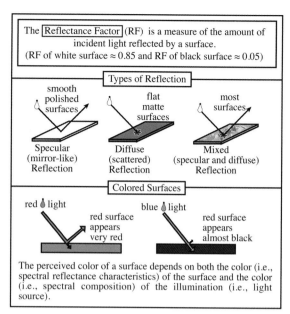

Figure 6.19   Reflectance factor (RF).

6.6   Light reflection, absorption, and transmission

When light is incident on any opaque material, then some of the light will be reflected and the remaining light will be absorbed. If the material is translucent, then some of the light will also be transmitted. The proportions of light that are reflected, transmitted, and absorbed depend on the characteristics of the material and the nature (i.e., the spectral distribution) of the incident light. To determine exactly how much light is reflected we must know not only the reflectance curve of the material,[15] but also the intensity of the incident light at each wavelength of its spectrum. Therefore, if light with an intensity of 20 candela in the red wavelength (i.e., around 700 mμ) is incident on a predominantly blue material that has only 10 percent reflectance at the red wavelength, then only 2 (i.e., 0.1 × 20 = 2) candela will be reflected at that wavelength.

The reflectance of a surface is defined as the percentage of light incident on the surface that is reflected from the surface, and the Reflectance Factor (RF) is simply the decimal equivalent of the reflectance percentage.

As shown in Figure 6.19, there are two basic types of reflection, which depend on the size of the surface irregularities in relationship to the wavelength of the incident light. A smooth or polished surface produces specular reflection, in which light is reflected in a single direction and the angle of incidence is equal to the angle of reflection. If the surface is rough in relationship to the wavelength of the incident light, then the light will be scattered and this is referred to as diffuse reflection. A perfectly diffuse reflector is known as a lambertian surface,[16] with the property that its reflected brightness is the same when viewed from any direction. Of course most surfaces, including those listed in Figure 6.20, exhibit both specular and diffuse reflection characteristics.

When light is transmitted through a translucent material some of the light may be absorbed and some of it may collide with particles inside the material and be deflected (i.e., scattered) into another direction (Figure 6.21).

Successive scattering inside the material may actually return some of the light back to the incident surface as reflected light. It is interesting to note that the absorption of light, while it is being transmitted through a translucent material, is also due to a form of collision. In

Reflectance: The percentage of light falling on a surface that is reflected (the remainder is absorbed and/or transmitted).

$$\text{Luminance (fL)} = \left[\begin{array}{c}\text{illumination}\\\text{level (fc)}\end{array}\right] \times \left[\frac{\text{reflectance (\%)}}{100}\right]$$

Material or Surface Finish	Reflectance* (%)	Material or Surface Finish	Reflectance* (%)
Metals:		Glass:	
Aluminum, brushed	60%	Clear or tinted	5%
Aluminum, etched	80%	Reflective	25%
Aluminum, polished	70%	Ground cover:	
Stainless steel	55%	Asphalt	5%
Tin	70%	Concrete	40%
Masonry:		Grass/vegetation	20%
Brick, dark buff	35%	Snow	70%
Brick, light buff	45%	Paint:	
Brick, red	20%	White	80%
Cement, gray	20%	White enamel	70%
Granite	20%	Wood:	
Limestone	50%	Light birch	40%
Marble, polished	60%	Mahogany	10%
Plaster, white	50%	Oak, dark	10%
Sandstone	30%	Oak, light	30%
Terra-cotta, white	70%	Walnut	10%

*(Approximate (i.e., typical) reflectance values.)

Figure 6.20   **Reflectance of common materials.**

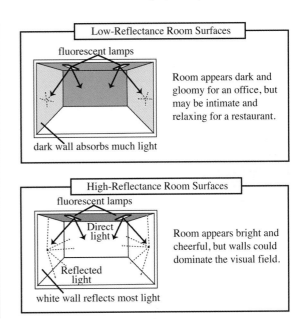

Figure 6.22   **Impact of light reflectance.**

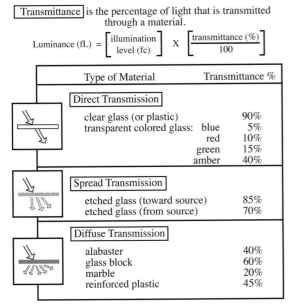

Transmittance is the percentage of light that is transmitted through a material.

$$\text{Luminance (fL)} = \left[\begin{array}{c}\text{illumination}\\\text{level (fc)}\end{array}\right] \times \left[\frac{\text{transmittance (\%)}}{100}\right]$$

Type of Material	Transmittance %
Direct Transmission	
clear glass (or plastic)	90%
transparent colored glass: blue	5%
red	10%
green	15%
amber	40%
Spread Transmission	
etched glass (toward source)	85%
etched glass (from source)	70%
Diffuse Transmission	
alabaster	40%
glass block	60%
marble	20%
reinforced plastic	45%

Figure 6.21   **Transmittance of light.**

this case the obstruction is a molecule that contains chromaphores. For example, inks and dyes contain chromaphores. According to Lambert's Law of Absorption, for materials in which no internal scattering of light occurs, the amount of light transmitted decreases exponentially with the concentration of dye molecules, the thickness of the material, and a constant that describes the characteristics of the chromaphore of the dye molecule.[17]

As shown in Figure 6.22, the reflectances of the surfaces in a room can greatly influence the ambient atmosphere conveyed by the appearance of the room. Ceiling and wall surfaces with a low Reflectance Factor tend to give a room a darker appearance, which might provide a desirably intimate environment for a restaurant, but an undesirably gloomy environment for a classroom or office space.

6.7 The visual field and adaptation level

As discussed earlier, our eyes measure brightness differences and not absolute light levels. Therefore, lighting design in buildings involves largely the control of brightness contrasts.

As can be seen in Figure 6.23, contrast allows us to recognize the shape of physical objects and can be a determining factor in visual

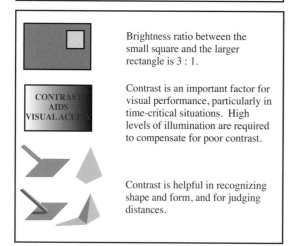

Contrast is created by the difference in brightness (i.e., luminance) of the object being viewed and the immediate surroundings.

Brightness ratio between the small square and the larger rectangle is 3 : 1.

Contrast is an important factor for visual performance, particularly in time-critical situations. High levels of illumination are required to compensate for poor contrast.

Contrast is helpful in recognizing shape and form, and for judging distances.

Figure 6.23 Brightness differences.

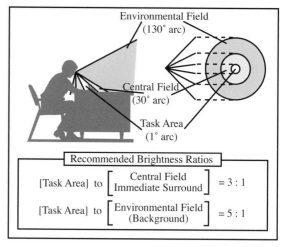

Since human eyes measure brightness differences, the design of the visual field must consider not only task illumination but also the surrounding illumination levels.

Environmental Field (130° arc)

Central Field (30° arc)

Task Area (1° arc)

Recommended Brightness Ratios

[Task Area] to Central Field / Immediate Surround = 3 : 1

[Task Area] to Environmental Field / (Background) = 5 : 1

Figure 6.24 Components of the visual field.

performance. For example, lack of contrast can seriously inhibit our ability to read signs, while excessive contrast in the field of view can cause visual discomfort and in extreme cases actually prevent us from seeing details. Methods that the lighting designer can use to control brightness contrasts include:

- Choice of the types of light sources and their locations in a building space. For example, if most of the light is directed to the ceiling, then this will result in a diffuse illumination within the space, because much of the available light will have been reflected from the ceiling.
- Choice of surface finishes (i.e., materials) in respect to reflection and transmission properties (e.g., translucent, opaque, matt, glossy, etc.), color, and texture.
- Variation of intensity of light from area to area, as well as the spectral distribution of the light source itself.

Broadly speaking, the visual field can be divided into three components (Figure 6.24). The task area, which is the visual focus for detailed activities such as reading and writing, requires the highest level of illumination. However, it is

typically restricted to a very narrow cone that may be no larger than a 1° arc. The immediate surround to the task area (i.e., 30° arc), which is also referred to as the central field, should be less bright than the task area, so that the latter will appear to be highlighted. However, the contrast between these two component fields should not be too great and therefore a 3:1 brightness ratio is normally recommended. Finally, the environmental field, or background illumination, should be the least bright area. Its boundaries are normally circumscribed within a 130° arc, with a recommended brightness ratio of 5:1 to the task area. While these recommended ratios may relate the three component fields to each other to produce a comfortable visual environment, they do not account for the ability of our visual facilities to scale up and down from bright sunlight to minimal nighttime illumination and still maintain the same comfort level.

So what is the mechanism that allows our cognitive system to automatically judge that some part of the visual field is brighter or less bright than another part of the field, and how can we achieve this feat within the enormous range of brightness that our visual facilities are capable of processing? The answer to this question is that our visual facilities will automatically establish an adaptation level in any current lighting environment. This adaptation level is dynamically modified as the average light intensity of the visual environment changes.

The adaptation level serves as a benchmark for comparing the apparent brightness levels of objects or surfaces within the visual field. The word "apparent" is used purposely in this context, because the brightness perceived by the eyes is not a measure of the actual (i.e., objective) light intensity, but simply a relative and subjective comparison with the current adaptation level. For example, with bright sunshine coming directly through a window the shadows within a room will appear very dark. However, if we shield our eyes from the sunlight (i.e., screen the window with our hand), the same shadows will appear much lighter.

The graph shown in Figure 6.25 represents an apparent brightness scale. It allows us to determine the apparent brightness of any surface based on the prevailing adaptation level. For example, a surface with a measured luminance of 10 fL will have an apparent brightness of

about 20 if the adaptation level is 100 fL, and over 140 if the adaptation level should fall to 1 fL.

The notion that what we perceive visually depends not only upon the actual intensity of light (i.e., objective measurement of the amount of light), but also on the state of our visual sensors, conditioned by the current adaptation level, is a fundamental consideration in lighting design. It immediately suggests that the prescription of minimum illumination levels for different tasks is inappropriate unless these are also related to the total amount of light in the entire visual field. A rule-of-thumb measure of the adaptation level is the illumination level of the environmental field or background illumination (Figure 6.24). For this reason the local illumination levels recommended for tasks requiring different degrees of visual acuity, in Figure 6.26, are related in each case to suggested background illumination levels.

The reason why the ratios between the recommended local and background levels are less than the 5:1 discussed earlier (Figure 6.24) for the lower local illumination levels is that at least a minimum amount of background

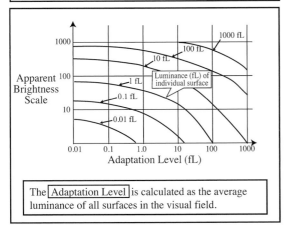

In any visual environment the human eyes adapt to the general brightness level of the space. This Adaptation Level serves as an involuntary reference standard through which that person subjectively perceives the apparent brightness of any individual surface in that space.

The Adaptation Level is calculated as the average luminance of all surfaces in the visual field.

Figure 6.25 The apparent brightness scale.

The required task illumination level depends on the visual intensity of the task and the background illumination (i.e., the Adaptation Level).

Class of Visual Task or Type of Work	Local Illumination (fc)	Background Illumination (fc)
Casual Seeing: corridors, storage areas, etc.	10–15 fc	10–15 fc
Intermittent Tasks: casual reading and writing, cursory inspection, etc.	20–30 fc	10–15 fc
Prolonged Tasks: machine work, office work, prolonged reading and writing.	40–50 fc	15–25 fc
Severe Prolonged Tasks: with small detail and poor contrast.	60–70 fc	20–25 fc
Very Intense Visual Tasks: watch repairs, gauge inspection, etc., medical surgery, etc.	150–300 fc	25–90 fc

Figure 6.26 Typical illumination levels.

illumination is necessary for practical reasons and safety.

The physiological process of light adaptation is very complex and not fully understood at this time. It is certainly much more than the contraction and expansion of the pupils as we make the transition from one level of brightness to another that is much brighter or much less bright. This involuntary reaction is simply a first-level protective mechanism that attempts to shield our eyes from harm. While the eye can adapt to a brightness range in excess of 100 000, it does so at the expense of visual comfort and performance. For example, if we look out of a window to the bright sky on a sunny day and then look back into the room, the interior space will appear gloomy and devoid of details until our eyes have re-adjusted to the much lower brightness of the room. It is important that the lighting designer ensures that the occupants of the building are not subjected to lighting conditions where they have to adapt too quickly over too wide a range of brightness. In this respect, of special concern is the interface between the exterior and the interior that occurs at any external window. Direct view of the sky through a window will expose the eye to a brightness level that could easily be 100 times the adaptation level inside the room. In fact, glare conditions inside buildings occur most commonly at external windows (see Section 6.9).

6.8   Perceptional constancy

Closely related to the phenomena of apparent brightness and adaptation level is our ability to perceive a visual scene the way we know it should be, rather than as it really is. This ability, which is known as perceptional constancy, allows us to perceive an object with little change even though the actual image on our retina may have changed considerably owing to a different viewing angle, a different orientation of the object, or a change in the ambient lighting conditions. Research suggests that there are several factors involved in this complex visual capability. Certainly experience and context are two of those factors. Research studies, involving the very small number of persons who have had their sight restored after being blind from birth or early infancy due to cataracts, showed that these persons were unable to see their environment accurately. For example, they had difficulties with complex images such as faces. This was probably due to the fact that the neurons and synapses in the visual areas of the brain had received little (if any) stimulation during their life. With respect to the role of context, our visual experience creates in our memory an expectation of what a certain object or scene should look like. Conversely, this same preconditioned expectation can be misleading as, for example, in some cases of eyewitness police reports.

Perceptional constancy will manifest itself in several ways. Three of these manifestations are of particular interest to the lighting designer.

- *Lightness Constancy* is our ability to judge the lightness of a surface to be the same, even though the illumination level has changed. If we take a sheet of white paper into a windowless room fitted with artificial lights and a dimming device, then the paper will appear to be white whether we have the lights on full (e.g., providing an illumination level of 100 footcandles) or dimmed down to just a few footcandles. The reason appears to be that the eye is more concerned about the relative amount of light reflected by the paper in relationship to other objects in the room, than with the actual amount of light reflected. The fact that the ratio of reflected light between two surfaces remains the same under different illumination levels can be proven by the following example. Assume a sheet of white paper with a large gray square on it.

reflectance of white paper area = 90% (or 0.90)
reflectance of gray square area = 30% (or 0.30)

If the illumination level is 200 fc, then:

ratio of light reflected from the two surfaces
$$= (200 \times 0.90) / (200 \times 0.30) = \tfrac{1}{3}$$

If the illumination level is only 10 fc, then:

ratio of light reflected from the two surfaces
$$= (10 \times 0.90)/(10 \times 0.30) = \tfrac{1}{3}$$

- *Color Constancy* is our ability to perceive the color of an object to be the same even though the lighting conditions may have changed. In a room with a very brightly colored red wall, the light reflected from the wall onto a white ceiling will give it a distinct pink hue. If we look at the ceiling facing the red wall (i.e., with the red wall in our visual field) then the ceiling will appear to be white. However, if we look at the ceiling facing away from the red wall then we will easily detect the slight pinkishness of the ceiling.
- *Shape Constancy* is our ability to continue to perceive the actual shape of an object, although by virtue of the view angle the shape of the object on the retina is distorted. For example, if we hold a book vertically in front of our eyes we see its shape to be rectangular. Now if we tilt the top edge of the book away from us then we will still perceive the shape of the book to be rectangular, although the image of the book on the retina will be a trapezoid. It appears that shape constancy occurs because our visual facilities take depth into consideration.

Perceptional constancy is of course by no means foolproof. Many experiments can be performed to demonstrate the failings of, for example, our lightness constancy capabilities under particular conditions. Four such conditions are shown in Figures 6.27, 6.28, 6.29, and 6.30.[18]

Figure 6.27 shows the well-known simultaneous contrast effect. The two smaller squares are precisely the same shade of gray, yet the one surrounded by the large black square appears to be a lighter shade of gray than the one surrounded by the large light gray square. Variations of the Koffka ring illusion (Figure 6.28) show how changes in spatial configuration can elude our lightness-constancy capabilities. The gray ring at the top left of Figure 6.28 appears to be of a uniform shade of gray. When the ring is split into two parts vertically, either

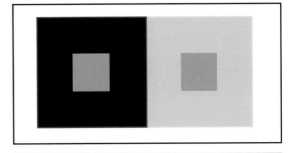

The human eye must be able to judge the relative impact of luminance and reflectance to recognize a gray surface whether viewed in bright sunshine or in the shade. This ability is referred to as Lightness Constancy.

Our Lightness Constancy capabilities are not foolproof. The same gray square appears lighter or darker depending on the surround.

Figure 6.27   Simultaneous contrast effect.

Horizontal division of the visual stimulus into two parts or vertical relative relocation can also fool our Lightness Constancy capabilities.

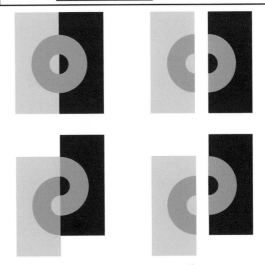

Figure 6.28   Spatial configuration effect.

moving the two parts of the ring apart horizontally or sliding them vertically causes one half of the ring to appear darker than the other half.

Figure 6.29 demonstrates that the simultaneous contrast effect shown in Figure 6.27 can be

Lightness Constancy capabilities are slightly enhanced by articulation (i.e., the number of distinct surfaces or patches within a region).

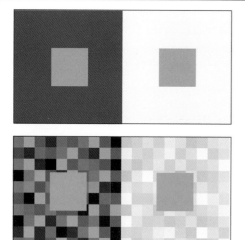

Figure 6.29   Anchoring within a framework.

The gray rectangles on the left side should appear darker than those on the right side, however, the long white border and short black border on the left side reverses the illusion.

Figure 6.30   The T-junction illusion.

enhanced if the surround is broken up into many different areas. This is referred to as the anchoring phenomenon, which is produced by an articulated surround. In Figure 6.30, the horizontal gray strips are all the same shade of gray. We would expect the left strips to appear darker than the right ones. However, the right strips

appear distinctly darker than the left ones. This reversal of the normal visual illusion has been explained in terms of the T-junction effect. According to this explanation, patches straddling the stem of a T are grouped together and the cross-bar of the T serves as a boundary.

It appears that our visual facilities process information on at least three levels. Low-level vision occurs in the retina and appears to include light adaptation. High-level vision occurs within the brain and is said to involve cognitive processes that are based on knowledge about objects, materials, and scenes. In between these two levels there is mid-level vision, which is a fuzzy area that may deal with the effects of surfaces, contours, and groupings.

6.9   The nature of glare

Whenever the variations of brightness in the visual field are too great, the brightest area will become a source of glare. Glare appears to be the result of an over-excitation of the visual receptors in the retina. If the brightness ratio is very large, than the glare conditions will actually impair our ability to see any details immediately surrounding the glare area. This form of glare is appropriately referred to as Disability Glare. Less severe brightness ratios will cause discomfort and may lead to undesirable physiological responses such as a headache, but will not affect our visual performance directly. These kinds of glare conditions are commonly characterized as *Discomfort Glare*.

As shown in Figure 6.31, there are fundamentally two kinds of Disability Glare. Our visual functions will be impaired under *direct glare* conditions when there is a direct line of sight between our eyes and an area of excessive brightness, such as a bright artificial light source without a shade, or a window through which we can see the bright sky. The brightness ratios of 3:1 (between the task area and the immediate surround) and 5:1 (between the task area and the background) suggested earlier in Figure 6.24 are well below the glare threshold. Brightness ratios in excess of 20:1 should gener-

Glare is caused by excessive brightness in the visual field and depending on the degree may produce discomfort or visual disability.

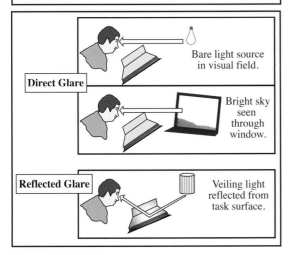

Direct Glare

Bare light source in visual field.

Bright sky seen through window.

Reflected Glare

Veiling light reflected from task surface.

Figure 6.31   Direct glare and reflected glare.

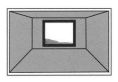

The Problem:

Bright sky seen through window becomes a source of Disability Glare.

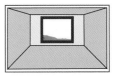

Solution Approach (A):

Raise illumination level around window by increasing artificial lighting.
[Increases energy consumption.]

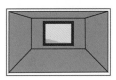

Solution Approach (B):

Block view of sky by means of shading devices or blinds.
[Reduces daylight availability.]

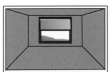

Solution Approach (C):

Use special anti-glare or tinted glass to reduce the brightness of the window.
[Reduces daylight penetration.]

Figure 6.32   Glare mitigation approaches.

ally be avoided in buildings, and ratios of 40:1 and above are guaranteed to produce glare conditions.

Disability Glare may also occur when a bright source of light is indirectly reflected from a shiny surface into our eyes. For example, the light from a well-shaded lamp may be reflected from the glossy pages of a book into the eyes of the reader. This situation produces a veiling condition in the task area and may occur even if the light source is not excessively bright. Fortunately, changing the position of the reflecting task area and/or the eyes relative to the light source easily rectifies such reflected glare situations. Normally, we would simply tilt the book slightly to overcome a reflected glare condition while reading. However, reflected glare is sufficiently prevalent for it to influence the choice of paper for newspapers, magazines and most books.

With the exception of reflected glare, Disability Glare is typically not caused by artificial light sources, since electric lamps rarely generate sufficient light flux to produce brightness ratios in excess of 20:1. However, a common source of Disability Glare is the view of a portion

of a bright sky seen through a window. In the absence of adequate foresight by the designer, this situation can occur when a window is placed in the end-wall of a long corridor. Particular care must be taken to avoid this problem in multi-story hotels, apartments, and dormitories. Walking toward such a misplaced window the surround of the window will appear almost black, since the eyes are unable to adjust to the excessive brightness difference between the bright sky and the relatively dim interior lighting of the corridor.

While the corridor situation described above is an extreme example, this type of direct glare can occur in any room with an external window that provides a view of the sky and therefore warrants further discussion.

As shown in Figure 6.32, there are essentially three viable approaches for mitigating such Disability Glare conditions caused by the interface between the interior and exterior lighting conditions. Since glare is caused by excessive brightness differences, any efforts to mitigate direct glare conditions should be focused on reducing the brightness ratio. This can of course be achieved in two ways: by either decreasing the higher level or increasing the lower level of the brightness levels in the visual field. Raising the interior illumination level near the window will increase the consumption of energy and may therefore not be a viable solution in climatic regions that are blessed with plenty of sunshine and mostly clear skies. However, in parts of the world where skies are typically overcast this solution approach is not uncommon. It leads to the apparently paradoxical situation where the artificial lighting requirements during daytime may be greater than at night.

The more common approach to mitigating direct glare conditions at windows is to reduce the brightness of the window. Unfortunately, this approach inevitably also reduces the amount of daylight available in the room. Design strategies include exterior shading devices, interior blinds, and special tinted or anti-glare glass. The advantage of internal blinds, such as Venetian blinds, is that they are adjustable both with respect to the angle of the blades and the degree to which they cover the window.

While Disability Glare actually impairs our immediate visual performance, the effects of Discomfort Glare are annoying, with milder physiological consequences if exposure continues over many hours. Discomfort glare occurs quite frequently in artificially lit building spaces if light sources are inadequately shielded. The degree of glare is primarily related to the location and type of light source, the nature of the task, and the luminance of the surrounding visual field. Specifically, Discomfort Glare is governed by:

- *The luminance of the glare source.* The size of the glare source, normally an artificial light source in the form of a lamp, is also a factor. If the light flux is spread over a larger surface area, then this will tend to increase the brightness of the immediate surround, thereby mitigating glare conditions.
- *The general background illumination level.* This may be quantified as the Adaptation Level discussed earlier, which is defined as the average luminance of all surfaces in the visual field. It may be calculated by measuring the luminance of each surface and mul-

tiplying this measurement by the area of the surface. The sum of the resulting values divided by the total surface area is the Adaptation Level expressed in foot Lambert (fL) units (see Figure 6.25).
- *The location of the glare source relative to the observer.* If the offending light source is located directly in the line of vision, it will be much more annoying than if it is just visible through the corner of the eyes.
- *The luminance of the immediate surround of the glare source.* Raising the brightness of the surround will decrease the brightness ratio. A simple measure such as a highly reflective finish (e.g., a white ceiling) may be quite effective in reducing the severity of the glare condition.

It is apparent from the foregoing discussion of glare conditions that the reduction of glare requires a reduction in the brightness ratio seen by the eyes. What the reader may have found to be surprising, and even counterintuitive, is that we can mitigate excessively bright conditions by adding more light. The fact is that our visual performance is affected less by actual objectively measured illumination levels than by the perception of these illumination levels as brightness differences. If we further take into consideration that the eye can detect an enormous range of luminances (i.e., from 0.0001 fL to over 100 000 fL: see Figure 6.17), then it is perhaps less surprising that the addition of light can be as effective as the reduction of light in reducing glare conditions. This can be demonstrated experimentally as shown by the Constant Glare Curve in Figure 6.33, which traces the influence of raising the background luminance on glare conditions.

The non-linear slope of the Constant Glare Curve in Figure 6.33 provides some insight into the nature of glare. We notice that, for the same glare conditions, raising the luminance of the background (i.e., raising the Adaptation Level) is much more effective at lower luminance levels of the glare source than at higher levels. In other words, as our eyes become exposed to more and more light, our ability to prevent glare by proportionally increasing the surround

A common approach to the mitigation of glare conditions is to increase the brightness of the background, particularly the immediate surround of the glare source.

Relationship between glare source and background for constant glare conditions.

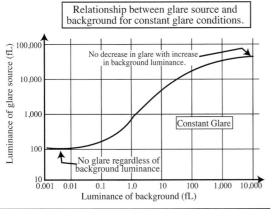

As the brightness of the immediate surround is continuously increased, glare discomfort first decreases and then increases again as the immediate surround becomes part of the glare source.

Figure 6.33   **The constant glare curve.**

The Glare Index was devised in England (1950s) to provide a measure of the subjective perception of brightness ratios in buildings.

$$\text{Discomfort Glare Constant (DGC)} = \dfrac{\left[\begin{array}{c}\text{luminance of}\\\text{glare source}\end{array}\right]^{1.8} \text{X} \left[\begin{array}{c}\text{area of}\\\text{glare source}\end{array}\right]^{0.8}}{\left[\text{background Adaptation Level}\right]}$$

Glare Index (GI) = 10 $\log_{10}$ [Discomfort Glare Constant (DGC)]

Viewer Judgment	DGC	GI	Types of Activity	GI (maximum)
just intolerable	600	28	general offices	19
just uncomfortable	150	22	drawing offices	16
just acceptable	35	16	classrooms	16
just imperceptible	8	10	fine detail tasks	10

Figure 6.34   **The glare index.**

and background luminances becomes less effective. Finally, at some point any further increase in the luminance of the surround simply increases the effective area of the glare source (i.e., the surround becomes part of the glare source).

The concept of a Glare Index was proposed in England during the 1950s (Figure 6.34) for the quantification of Discomfort Glare conditions. Based on subjective human assessments, an empirical formula was derived for the calculation of a Discomfort Glare Constant (DGC) as a function of the luminance of the glare source, the area of the glare source, and the Adaptation Level. The Glare Index (GI) was then established as a logarithmic equivalent of the DGC:

Glare Index (GI) = 10 log10

[Discomfort Glare Constant (DGC)]   [6.5]

It is important to note that the Glare Index applies only to Discomfort Glare conditions and not to Disability Glare. An indication of this limited applicability is given by the viewer judgments, which range from only "just intolerable" to "just imperceptible" and do not take into account the ability to see details. Nevertheless, the Glare Index does provide sound design guidelines by recommending acceptable brightness ratios for different types of activities.

Endnotes

1. Galileo Galilei (1564–1642) was not the inventor of the telescope, but he did improve the magnification of the instrument from four to about nine. However, his major contributions relate to his interpretation of what he was able to observe through the telescope, and his application of mathematics to the laws of motion.
2. Ole Roemer (1644–1710) was also an ingenious builder of precision instruments such as the *transit*, which is a telescope devised to observe stars as they cross the meridian and used for determining time.
3. Isaac Newton (1643–1727) laid the foundations for differential and integral calculus several years before its independent discovery by Leibniz. Utilizing differentiation, he was able to unify under one mathematical umbrella the solutions to many problems that hitherto had been approached through several largely unrelated techniques.
4. There are two types of wave forms: namely, *longitudinal* and *transverse*. In longitudinal wave motion the particles of the medium through which the wave travels are physically displaced in the direction of the wave motion. However, the particles do not travel with the wave, but rather

oscillate back and forth about their mean positions as the wave progresses through the medium. In transverse waves, for example when we create a wave in a horizontally stretched rope, the up-and-down movement of the rope is transverse to the direction of the wave along the rope. Again, the material that makes up the rope does not travel with the wave, but moves up and down (vertically) as the wave moves (horizontally) along the rope.

5. Michael Faraday (1791–1867) discovered that a suspended magnet will revolve around a current-bearing wire, and inferred from these experiments that magnetism is a circular force. He also invented the dynamo and discovered electro-magnetic induction.

6. A Polaroid filter is made of special material with long-chain molecules aligned in the same direction. If these molecules are aligned vertically, then the filter will block the vertical waves and allow the horizontal waves to pass through. In other words, the vertical waves are absorbed by the vertically aligned long-chain molecules.

7. When light of a particular color (i.e., frequency) illuminates a metal surface, then electrons are emitted at a particular velocity. Increasing the intensity of light increases the number of ejected electrons, but not the velocity. At the same time, different-colored lights of the same intensity cause electrons to be ejected with different velocities. This is referred to as the *photoelectric effect*.

8. The laws of Newtonian physics break down at the microscopic subatomic level of electrons, protons, neutrons, and quarks. For example, electrons do not rotate around a nucleus like planets rotate around a sun. Instead they follow the very different laws of quantum physics, such as Heisenberg's Uncertainty Principle. This law states that the more we know about one attribute of the current state of a subatomic particle, the less we know about another attribute. Therefore, if we are 70 percent sure of the velocity of an electron, we can be only 30 percent certain of its position at any given point in time. Quantum physics is derived from the term *quantum*, which is the smallest package of energy that an electron can absorb or give off as it changes its energy level.

9. Experimental results only fairly recently (1965) confirmed that there are three types of cones with different color sensitivities. These correspond approximately to red-, green-, and blue-sensitive

receptors. The green- and red-sensitive cones are grouped closely within the fovea area, while the blue-sensitive cones are found mostly in the para-fovea area. About 65 percent of the cones are red-sensitive, about 33 percent are green-sensitive and only about 2 percent are blue-sensitive.

10. The light emitted by a single candle is about 12 lumen. In comparison, the light emitted by a 100-watt incandescent (i.e., filament) lamp is about 1000 lumen.

11. A solid angle is measured in *steridians* and is somewhat like an inverted circular pyramid or cone. The solid angle of the entire surface of a sphere is equal to 4π steridians.

12. The units of illumination, lumen/square foot and footcandle, are numerically equal (i.e., $20\,\text{lm}/\text{SF} = 20\,\text{fc}$).

13. The Inverse Square Law applies only to a point source. For a line source, the illumination decreases simply by the linear distance (i.e., luminous intensity divided by distance from the line source), and for an area source the illumination is approximately equal to the luminous intensity.

14. Known previously as Imperial units of measurement, which were used throughout the British Commonwealth until these countries adopted the metric system of units in the 1960s and 1970s. Today (2010), the US is the only remaining major country that has not adopted the metric system.

15. The reflectance curve of a material provides the percent reflectance at each wavelength.

16. Named after the eighteenth-century scientist Johann Lambert (1728–1777), who discovered several laws relating to the transmission of light. For example: Lambert's Law of Absorption that defines the exponential decrease of light passing through an absorbing medium of uniform transparency; and, Lambert's Cosine Law, which states that the brightness of a diffusely radiating plane surface is proportional to the cosine of the angle formed by the line of sight and the normal to the surface.

17. The fundamental characteristic of the chromaphore is called the *extinction factor* and is a property of the molecular structure of the dye.

18. From: Adelson, E. H. (2000) *Lightness Perception and Lightness Illusions*, in M. Gazzaniga (ed.) *The New Cognitive Neurosciences*, 2nd edn. MIT Press, Cambridge, MA, pp. 339–51.

7 Daylight Design Principles

In these times of genuine concern about the shortage, cost, and pollution penalty associated with most fossil fuel sources of energy, we are becoming increasingly aware of those forms of natural energy that can be readily utilized without the need for any modification. Among these, daylight should be counted as one of the most generous gifts of nature.

Although the sun is the primary source of daylight, the atmosphere surrounding the Earth diffuses its light and therefore the whole sky becomes a secondary source of light. For several reasons direct sunlight is not normally considered to be a suitable source of daylight in buildings. First, it is very intense, ranging from 6000 to 12000 footcandles, and therefore cannot be used directly for task illumination. Second, it is so much brighter than the ambient environmental luminance (i.e., Adaptation Level), both inside and external to buildings, that it can easily become a source of severe glare (i.e., Disability Glare). Third, it is associated with considerable heat energy and although this may be desirable for the heating of building spaces by natural means, it is an undesirable characteristic in respect to lighting. Accordingly, daylight design is not based on direct sunlight but on secondary light from the sky, which is defined as a luminous hemisphere with the observer's horizon plane as its base.

However, this does not mean that direct sunlight should necessarily be completely excluded from building interiors. Carefully controlled beams of sunlight can add a highly desirable degree of movement, directional highlighting, variety, and excitement to a space. This is particularly true for corridors and similar circulation spaces, where the occupants are mostly transitory and not engaged in detailed visual tasks. Even in spaces where the occupants are seated in relatively fixed locations undertaking reading and writing tasks, movable window shades and blinds may provide sufficient control for the intermittent penetration of direct sunlight.

7.1 Variability of daylight

It is an important characteristic of daylight illumination that it varies constantly during each day and from day to day. The horizontal illumination on a photoelectric cell exposed on the roof of a building but shaded from direct sunlight can vary widely, depending not only on the time of day but also on the degree of cloud cover (if any). A clear sky will be brightest near the sun, and since the sun moves from sunrise to sunset the brightness distribution of the sky will change correspondingly. On the other hand, in the north-western part of Europe the sky is mostly covered by clouds and therefore the overcast sky becomes the principal source of daylight. The influence of dispersed clouds in the sky can be readily seen in the typical daily illumination curves shown in Figure 7.1.

The upper curve depicts the hourly distribution of light that we would expect on a clear day, with perhaps a few isolated cloud whisks producing minor fluctuations. However, the situation will be quite different as soon as major cloud formations appear in the sky. The lower

Building Science: Concepts and Application. Jens Pohl.
© 2011 John Wiley & Sons, Ltd.
Published 2011 by John Wiley & Sons, Ltd.

It is a characteristic of daylight illumination that it varies continuously during each day and from day to day.

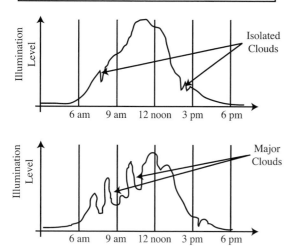

Figure 7.1 Variability of daylight.

Daylight penetration through side windows decreases disproportionally with increased distance from the window.

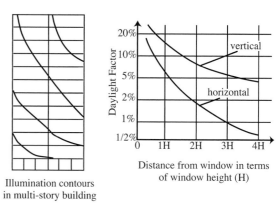

Figure 7.2 Daylight penetration constraints.

curve of Figure 7.1 indicates the significant variations in daylight availability that will occur abruptly as soon as a large cloud either hides the sun or the bright blue sky. In a few seconds the available daylight might be reduced by as much as 30 to 50 percent.

What is also clearly seen in Figure 7.1 is that apart from the influence of clouds, the daily daylight distribution follows a slightly skewed Normal Distribution Curve.[1] The reducing illumination levels in the afternoon occur at a slightly slower rate than the progressively increasing illumination levels during the morning hours.

Since daylight is largely unpredictable, it was argued in the US – prior to the recognition of an increasing energy shortage and cost in the early 1970s – that the internal building environment should be lit artificially to ensure good seeing conditions at all times. At the same time, it was also recognized that apart from any energy conservation considerations, the characteristic variability of daylight might be desirable on psychological grounds.

Whether or not it is possible to light a building adequately by daylight will depend on the circumstances, although for a normal high-rise, city building the answer is normally in the negative. In these buildings lighting conditions are likely to be poor on the lower floors (Figure 7.2) and in deep rooms.

The reduction in daylight as we move further away from the window is by no means linear. For example, as shown by the graph in Figure 7.2, the difference in illumination level on a horizontal surface at points that are one and two window head-heights distant from a side window may be more than 60 percent.

7.2 Quality of daylight and color

As discussed previously in Chapter 6, we often speak of light in terms of the *visible spectrum*, indicating that light consists of a number of wavelengths of electromagnetic radiation. These wavelengths range in color from violet through indigo, blue, green, yellow, and orange to red. If all of these wavelengths are present then we perceive colorless light. However, should the same light beam fall onto a surface that absorbs some wavelengths more than others, then this surface will appear colored to the observer. In other words, the color of a surface is governed by the selective absorption properties of that surface. Some surfaces reflect all wavelengths in the visible spectrum equally and will therefore appear white, grey, or black (i.e., colorless) to the observer.

The electromagnetic spectrum of daylight varies with the condition of the sky and the direct influence of the sun. The bright blue color of a clear sky is in stark contrast to the grayish appearance of an overcast sky. Direct sunlight, on the other hand, is much warmer in appearance than either a clear or overcast sky. The color spectrum of any light source, whether natural or artificial, is often expressed in terms of its *color* temperature,[2] which defines the distribution of electromagnetic wavelengths emitted by the light source. In other words, as explained in the footnote below, color temperature is a measure of the color composition of a light source and has nothing whatsoever to do with the operating temperature of that light source.

Through our eyes we perceive color as light and therefore evaluate its properties subjectively. The fact that adjectives are used to describe different colors emphasizes the difficulty of attempting to specify color in technical terms. Although the description "apple-green" does not represent the precise specification of a particular color, it nevertheless conveys a more meaningful picture than "Munsell 5GY". It might be argued that since light is contained within a narrow band of the electromagnetic spectrum, it follows that color can be accurately specified by wavelength. However, wavelength does not take into account the brightness or luminance of the light source and the purity or saturation (i.e., the extent of dilution with white light) of the color. For the complete specification of a color we require values for the following three color characteristics:

- the dominant wavelength, referred to as the *hue* of the color;
- the luminance or brightness, referred to as the *value* of the color;
- the degree of saturation or *chroma* of the color.

Over the years a number of different methods of color specification have been developed to meet different requirements. For colored surfaces it is normal practice to specify the color in relationship to its appearance or rendition under a specified light source. Such a system was devised by Albert Munsell (1858–1918), an American artist, in 1915. The Munsell Color Atlas applies to colored surfaces only. Each color is specified in terms of:

- *Value*, which is a measure of the degree of dilution with white. The range between black (0) and white (10) includes nine grades of gray. Accordingly, if a colored pigment is mixed with a neutral base, the *value* from 0 to 10 will indicate the whiteness of the base.
- *Hue* describes the actual color, such as red, yellow, and so on, of the surface. For each *hue* there is an example of increasing purity.
- *Chroma* measures the intensity or saturation of the color. The *hue circle* contains the *hues* at maximum *chroma*.

By reference to Figure 7.3, a color specified as "R5/2" is a red with a *value* of 5 and a *chroma* of 2, while "R3/2" would be a darker red, and

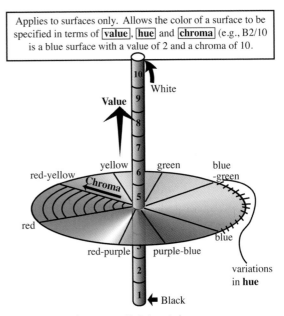

Figure 7.3 The Munsell Color Atlas.

"R5/l0" would be a much stronger red. Although the Munsell system cannot be applied to light sources, it conveniently provides an approximate indication of the percentage light reflectance of a surface based on the *value* of the color.

approximate light reflectance =

[color *value* × (color *value* − 1)]%   **[7.1]**

Accordingly, "R5/2", "R4/2", and "R3/2" have light reflectances of approximately 20, 12, and 6 percent, respectively.

In 1931 the Commission Internationale de l'Eclairage (CIE) agreed upon a system of color notation to provide a common basis for all color-Dh. 7, measuring instruments (Figure 7.4). The system is based on the color-matching characteristics of the average eye. To establish adequate subjective test data, a number of observers were asked to make a series of color matches using a colorimeter (Figure 7.5). The instrument is very similar to the photometer described in Section 7.4.

However, whereas the photometer requires the observer to match two patches of light, colo-

rimeters are used to match two patches of color. While one part of a divided surface is illuminated by the source of light under investigation, the other part of the surface is exposed simultaneously to three standard sources. One source is red, another blue, and the third green. By adjusting the relative intensities of these colored light sources, the observer is able to match the two light patches until they look exactly alike.

While this seems quite straightforward, there are in fact two complicating factors that require further explanation. The first of these deals with the notion that two identical visual stimuli may have different color spectrums. In the above colorimeter example, even though the two colored light patches may look alike they are highly unlikely to have the same spectral composition. Even the same observer could produce matching colored light patches with different spectral compositions for the same source patch. In other words, different spectral compositions can produce identical color stimuli as perceived by the eyes. This phenomenon is referred to as *metamerism* and forms the basis of all color reproduction techniques.

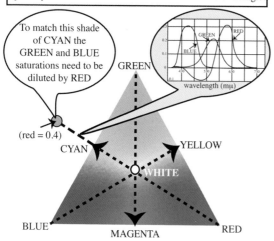

Figure 7.4   The CIE Color Notation.

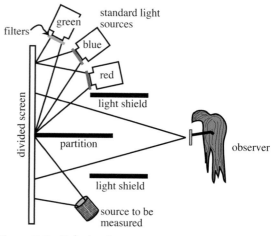

Figure 7.5   Colorimeter.

The second factor is demonstrated in Figure 7.4, which shows the color triangle formed by the three primary colors: red, green, and blue. Let us assume that each of the primary colors is produced by a white light source fitted with a filter appropriate to its color. Further, the intensity of each of the light sources is adjusted so that it reduces uniformly to zero at the opposite boundary of the triangle. The sides of the triangle represent the greatest saturation that can be produced by the primary color lights for each of the color hues. For example, the cyan hue located in the center of the left side of the triangle is composed of 50 percent green plus 50 percent blue plus 0 percent red. However, the human eye can identify saturations of cyan that lie outside the boundary of the triangle. These shades of cyan can be produced only by diluting the saturation levels of green and blue with red. Therefore, the particular shade of cyan shown by the point outside the left edge of the triangle in Figure 7.4 will require the subtraction of red from the other two primary colors (i.e., green and blue). In other words, not all of the colors that can be perceived by the human eye can be created by the simple addition of the three primary colors within the color triangle.[3]

Based on a large number of subjective tests using the colorimeter technique, the CIE *chromaticity diagram* shown in Figure 7.6 has been produced.

It avoids the problem of negative values through the adoption of three supersaturated primary colors. This allows any color within the chromaticity diagram to be specified as a mixture of these three notional primary colors (i.e., X, Y, and Z).[4] The actual values of X, Y, and Z that uniquely describe a particular visually perceivable hue are referred to as the *tristimulus* values. It follows that different combinations of light waves that result in the same set of tristimulus will be indistinguishable by the human eye.

7.3   How much daylight is available?

Owing to variability, lack of control, and the difficulty of achieving high illumination levels

The full range of colors visible to the eye can be represented by the CIE Chromacity Chart in terms of the color coordinates X and Y (i.e., saturation and hue) plus the Z value (i.e., brightness or luminance).

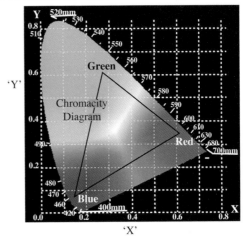

Figure 7.6   CIE Chromacity Diagram.

in local areas, daylight alone cannot normally provide satisfactory illumination levels for tasks involving higher degrees of visual acuity. Generally speaking, it will therefore be the function of daylight to provide general illumination levels compatible with the task to be performed in the building environment, on the understanding that artificial light sources will be available to provide local task illumination if and when required.

However, the concept of adequate lighting incorporates more than just sufficient light. Obviously the visual field must be free from glare and the light must come from the correct direction. Accordingly, the major daylighting concern is how to admit sufficient light for comfortable vision, without the presence of glare. This problem is a very complex one, not only owing to the variation in brightness of the sky, but owing also to the necessity for the designer to balance natural lighting with heat insulation and the capital and operating costs of artificial light installations.

The amount of light received inside a building must be related to the light available externally, to form a reasonable basis for daylight design.

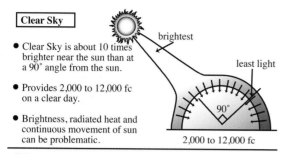

Clear Sky

- Clear Sky is about 10 times brighter near the sun than at a 90° angle from the sun.
- Provides 2,000 to 12,000 fc on a clear day.
- Brightness, radiated heat and continuous movement of sun can be problematic.

brightest

least light

90°

2,000 to 12,000 fc

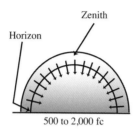

Overcast Sky

- Overcast Sky is about 3 times brighter at the zenith than at the horizon.
- Provides 500 to 2,000 fc depending on cloud cover
- Mathematically defined as an international standard (CIE Standard Overcast Sky).

Zenith

Horizon

500 to 2,000 fc

Figure 7.7   Idealized sky conditions.

There are essentially two common measures of the natural light available from the sky, namely:

1 The *uniform brightness sky*, which applies to the dry, sunny regions of the world where a clear atmosphere is prevalent. In such regions the clear, blue sky has a fairly even brightness distribution over most of the sky, except for the sun and its immediate surround (Figure 7.7).

This local area, which moves from east to west each day at the rate of approximately 15° per hour, is about 10 times as bright as the remainder of the sky. The following empirical relationship has been proposed for the outdoor illumination (E_H) on a horizontal surface from the sun and the whole *clear sky*:

$$E_H = A\,[1750 \times (\sin(a))^{0.5}]$$
$$+ B\,[13200 \times \sin(a) \times 10^{-0.1m}]\,fc \quad [7.2]$$

where:

    a = altitude of the sun
    m = air mass (or cosec(a))
$10^{-0.1m}$ = transmission factor of atmosphere.

In equation [7.2] the first term represents the contribution to the total illumination (E) provided by the sky, and the second term represents the contribution provided by the sun. The substitution of appropriate values for the constants A and B allows equation [7.2] to be adapted to different sky conditions (i.e., conditions other than *clear sky* conditions), as follows:

$A = 0.89$ and $B = 0.35$: for thin film of clouds

$A = 0.54$ and $B = 0.26$: for clouded sky

$A = 1.02$ and $B = 0.08$: for light, white clouds and clear sun

For a *clouded sky*, the values of 0.46 for A and 0.26 for B allow equation [7.2] to be contracted to the much simpler form (sun altitude a measured in degrees):

$$E_H = 52(a) \quad [7.3]$$

Krochmann (1963) proposed a slightly more elaborate empirical relationship to account for the influence of the sun under overcast sky conditions:

$$E_H = 30 + [1950 \times \sin(a)] \quad [7.4]$$

Taking into account these various proposals, it has been suggested (Lynes, 1968) that the illumination (E_H) on a horizontal surface out of doors should be based on the following relationships:

temperate climates where overcast skies predominate: equation [7.4]

hot, dry climates where clear skies predominate: equation [7.2]

temperate climates generally: equation [7.3][5]

The horizontal illumination values (E_H) obtained by equations [7.2] and [7.4] are not very different; however, equation [7.3] produces increasingly larger values for higher sun altitudes, as shown below.

Sun altitude	Clear sky (7.2)	Overcast sky (7.4)	Mean sky (7.3)
10°	500 fc	370 fc	530 fc
20°	750 fc	700 fc	1060 fc
30°	900 fc	1005 fc	1590 fc
40°	1100 fc	1280 fc	2120 fc
50°	1200 fc	1520 fc	2640 fc
60°	1300 fc	1720 fc	3180 fc
70°	1380 fc	1860 fc	3710 fc
80°	1450 fc	1950 fc	4240 fc

It may appear surprising that the *mean sky* illumination exceeds the illumination for both cloudless and overcast conditions. The reason is that the brightest portions of the sky are usually the sunlit edges of white clouds, which would not normally exist under *clear sky* and *overcast sky* conditions.

2 The *standard overcast sky*, which applies to maritime, cloudy, temperate regions where the sky is mostly overcast. This sky condition was internationally standardized by the Commission Internationale de L'Eclairage (CIE) in 1955. While it is not of uniform brightness, its luminance is symmetrically distributed from the zenith to be about one-third less bright at the horizon (Figure 7.8).

The CIE Standard Overcast Sky was adopted by the Commission Internationale de L'Eclairage in 1955.

- The sky luminance distribution from the zenith to the horizon depends on the altitude (a) of the particular patch of sky being viewed, as follows:

$$\text{Luminance at altitude (a)} = \frac{\begin{bmatrix} \text{luminance} \\ \text{at zenith} \end{bmatrix} \times \begin{bmatrix} 1 + 2 \sin a \end{bmatrix}}{3} \quad \text{(fL)}$$

- The illumination level provided by the whole overcast sky on a horizontal surface on Earth, is given by:

$$\text{illumination level} = 0.78 \begin{bmatrix} \text{luminance} \\ \text{at zenith} \end{bmatrix} \quad \text{(fc)}$$

Figure 7.8   **CIE Standard Overcast Sky.**

The natural light available at any point in the building environment must be based on a particular value of the external illumination. Owing to the continuous variation of daylight it is necessary to resort to a statistical analysis and determine probability curves relating to the external illumination levels available for portions of the working day. This information, based on continuous measurements of daylight levels over a number of years, is now available for most major cities. It is common practice to assume that the daylight should be adequate for the greater part of the normal working day (i.e., 8 am to 4 pm) and this is normally considered to be around 85 percent of daytime working hours.

The CIE Standard Overcast Sky increases in brightness from the horizon to the zenith, so that the luminance at the zenith is about three times that at the horizon. The actual gradation of luminance from zenith to horizon is expressed by the equation:

$$L_a = L_z / (1 + 2 \sin(a)) \qquad [7.5]$$

where:

L_a = luminance at an altitude of a° above the horizon

L_z = luminance at the zenith.

Thus at the horizon, where the altitude is zero (i.e., a° = 0 and therefore sin (a) = 1):

$$L_0 = L_z / 3 \qquad [7.6]$$

It has been found in practice that although the total illumination provided by an overcast sky in different parts of the world may vary widely, the luminance distribution given by equation [7.5] is reasonably constant. Also, the author has found – based on a large number of measurements of daylight conditions in actual buildings undertaken by architecture students at Cal Poly, San Luis Obispo – that even for the clear sky conditions prevalent in the California Central Coast region the CIE Standard Overcast Sky correlated better with actual lighting conditions than the Uniform Brightness Sky.[6]

To ensure adequate natural light inside buildings it is the usual procedure to design on the basis of an assumed overcast sky. Any point in a room that is remote from windows will be directly in line with a section of the sky near the horizon, and will therefore receive least light when the sky is clouded.

7.4   Measurement of daylight

There are two basic types of instrument used to measure light: namely, visual and photoelectric meters. Visual instruments of photometry, such as the photometer shown in Figure 7.9, rely on the subjective comparison of two patches of light, one of which can be controlled to match the other.

Normally the standard light source and the light source to be measured enter the central chamber of the photometer from opposite directions, illuminating the two surfaces of a central dividing partition. The observer is able to see both of these illuminated surfaces simultaneously through mirrors, and adjust the distance of the standard light source from the partition until the two patches of light match in brightness.

The use of a photometer is not recommended for building designers who are only from time to time involved in the measurement of light levels. Proper application of this kind of visual instrument requires skill and experience. The difficulties encountered in the design of the required control luminance patch, the constant need for calibration, and individual differences in sensitivity to light of different wavelengths, may lead to unreliable readings in unskilled hands.

Photoelectric cells convert light into electricity and therefore measure the current or voltage generated by the incident light radiation.

By far the most common choice for both daylight and artificial light measurements is the selenium photoelectric cell or light meter (Figure 7.10), in which incident light is converted directly into electrical energy without the need for an additional, external source of electricity. The selenium cell consists simply of a crystalline selenium plate sandwiched between a metal plate acting as cathode and a metal contact ring anode. This assembly is normally encased in a non-conductive housing and soldered rather than clamped, to avoid damage to the

A photoelectric instrument that measures the electric current or voltage generated by the light incident on a selenium plate.

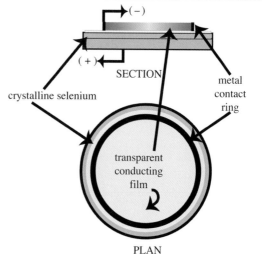

A visual instrument that requires the operator to subjectively adjust a standard light source to match the light source to be measured.

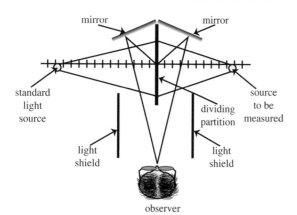

Figure 7.9   **Photometer.**

Figure 7.10   **Photoelectric light meter.**

sensitive selenium plate. Unfortunately, selenium cells tend to *drift*, owing to a decrease in response during the first few minutes of exposure to light. Accordingly, readings should not be recorded until the cell has been illuminated for about ten minutes.

7.5 Model analysis

Before the availability of computers, model analysis was a very popular method for exploring the daylight design of buildings. A scale model can be constructed rather inexpensively and fairly quickly out of cardboard. Therefore, even today with the availability of sophisticated computer programs that can render the lighting conditions of building interiors, model analysis is still considered a useful design tool for at least the subjective investigation of the proposed lighting conditions of interior spaces.

It has been proven conclusively that the distribution of illumination inside a scale model is identical with that found in a full-size building, provided that the absorption of all surfaces in the model is precisely that of the original building and the luminance of all sources is accurately reproduced. Accordingly, scale models of buildings may be exposed either to the luminance of the outdoor sky or more conveniently to an electrically controlled artificial sky dome.

An *artificial sky dome* of the type shown in Figure 7.11 consists of a reflecting enclosure lit by a series of electric lamps, which may be adjusted to simulate any particular outdoor illumination level. An alternative to the artificial sky dome is a square box lined with flat mirrors, referred to as a *mirror-box artificial sky* (Figure 7.12).

The roof of the mirror sky consists of an opal acrylic sheet illuminated from above by a carefully distributed set of fluorescent lamps. Three principal criteria govern the design of either type of artificial sky:

- a luminous overhead surface to represent the sky. It is desirable for the luminous distribution of this surface to be adjustable;

Highly reflective internal surface of dome is illuminated by lamps located at the base of the dome. A movable artificial sun can add a significant level of sophistication.

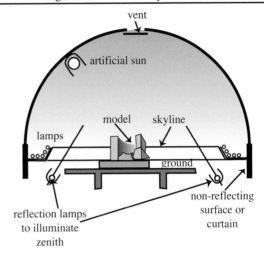

Figure 7.11 Artificial sky dome.

Internal walls are lined with mirrors to ensure that the horizon is at eye level within the model but at an infinite distance. Illuminated from the top by artificial light sources, the light is diffused by a translucent opal acrylic sheet.

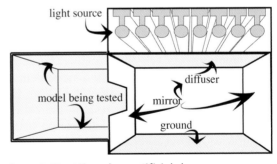

Figure 7.12 Mirror-box artificial sky.

- a ground surface of known reflectance;
- a correctly located horizon in relationship to the model. In the case of the artificial sky dome the model is placed in the center under the dome, and therefore the boundary of the

dome on the base platform satisfies the horizon criterion. For the mirror box artificial sky, the mirrors that line the internal walls produce an infinite number of inter-reflections, which ensure that the image of the horizon is always at the eye-level of the observer inside the box (and at an infinite distance from the observer).

In the dome-shaped artificial sky the white and highly reflective internal surface of the dome is illuminated from below by a series of lamps. Normally these lamps are positioned around the internal perimeter of the dome on moveable panels. Slight changes in the luminance distribution of the dome surface may be obtained by tilting the perimeter light panels vertically. However, the upper limit of illumination that may be achieved is severely limited, owing to problems of heat dissipation and ventilation. Although this is not necessarily a significant disadvantage when concerned with the measurement of *daylight factors* (see Section 7.6), it does prevent the use of this type of artificial sky for subjective studies of glare and visual comfort conditions. For these explorations the mirror box artificial sky is more useful, because it is capable of producing much higher levels of illumination.

7.6   The daylight factor concept

The amount of daylight available outdoors varies hour by hour owing to the movement of the sun, and sometimes even minute by minute under intermittent cloud conditions. If, in addition, we take into account that our eyes measure brightness differences and not absolute illumination levels, then it really does not make sense to design the daylight conditions inside a building in terms of specific illumination levels. An alternative and more useful approach is to determine the proportion of the ambient external daylight that should be available at particular locations inside a given building space. These considerations led to the acceptance of the concept of a *daylight factor*, which expresses

The The Daylight Factor expresses the illumination available on a horizontal surface inside a building as a percentage of the illumination provided by the whole sky on a horizontal surface located outside the building.

$$\text{Daylight Factor} = \frac{100 \left[\begin{array}{c} \text{indoor illumination} \\ \text{on a horizontal surface} \end{array}\right]}{\left[\begin{array}{c} \text{outdoor illumination from whole sky} \\ \text{on a horizontal surface} \end{array}\right]} (\%)$$

Daylight Factor is useful for ...

- Determining the distribution of daylight from area to area within a building.
- Comparing different window layouts.
- Comparing the availability of daylight in different buildings.
- Comparing the availability of daylight at a particular point at different times.

Figure 7.13   The Daylight factor concept.

the daylight available inside a building as a percentage of the daylight concurrently available out of doors. Specifically, the Daylight Factor assumes that the daylight available from the sky may be measured by the total illumination (E_H) received on a horizontal plane from the whole sky (Figure 7.13).

Therefore, the Daylight Factor (DF) is given by:

DF = [(indoor illumination at a point)/

(external illumination from sky)]×100 %

If E_P is the illumination at a point indoors and E_H is the simultaneous external illumination from the whole sky, then:

$$\text{DF} = 100\,[E_P\,/\,E_H]\,(\%) \qquad [7.7]$$

As a guide to the amount of natural light available in the interior spaces of a building, the Daylight Factor has the advantage of relative constancy. Although there may be wide fluctuations in the outdoor illumination level, the ratio of outdoor to indoor illumination will remain constant as long as the distribution of sky luminance remains static. Unfortunately, due to direct sunshine or isolated clouds the distribution of sky luminance will vary in practice.

Nevertheless, the Daylight Factor remains a very useful and popular method for investigating:

- the distribution of daylight from area to area within a building;
- the comparison of various window layouts;
- the comparison of the availability of daylight in different buildings;
- the comparison of measurements taken at different times in the same or different building spaces.

The determination of the Daylight Factor at a particular point in a space is normally undertaken in three stages, although in the case of an open site this can be reduced to two stages. First, we calculate the direct light from the sky, referred to as the *sky component*. This is followed by the calculation of the *externally reflected component*. However, this component exists only if external obstructions such as buildings are visible through the window. On the other hand, if external obstructions block out the entire view of the sky, then there will be no *sky component*. Finally, the many inter-reflections that will occur among the surfaces in the space are calculated as an *internally reflected component*. This component is always present because it will be produced by either the Sky Component or the Externally Reflected Component, or both.

Accordingly, as shown in Figure 7.14, the total Daylight Factor at any point inside a building will incorporate up to three components:

- the Sky Component (SC), due to light received directly at the point under consideration from that section of the sky that is visible through the window;
- the Externally Reflected Component (ERC), due to light reflected from external objects, such as buildings, visible through the window;
- the Internally Reflected Component (IRC), due to light received by reflection from surfaces within the building.

While the Externally Reflected Component will not occur in the case of an open site, it is also true that in the case of densely grouped, high-rise buildings in urban areas the Sky Component

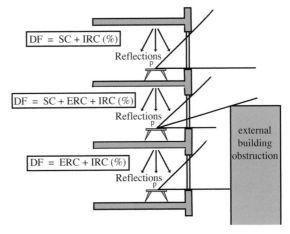

Figure 7.14 **Daylight factor components.**

may not occur on the lower floors, particularly at points remote from windows.

7.6.1 Sky component (SC)

For an idealized, uniform sky and unglazed openings, the Sky Component is equal to a measure of the luminance of a uniformly bright sky, referred to as the *sky factor*. Although the Sky Factor has little direct practical value, since sky luminance is not uniform, it can be calculated very accurately and has therefore considerable application in the settling of legal disputes.

For purposes of building design, the Sky Component takes into account both a non-uniform sky luminance and transmission losses in the window glazing. In the case of predominantly clear sky conditions it can be calculated by adjusting the idealized, numerical value of the Sky Factor for variations in sky luminance (R_L) and the transmission loss of clear glass (T_G), as follows:

$$SC = (\text{Sky Factor}) \times R_L \times T_G \ (\%) \qquad [7.8]$$

Alternatively, R_L may also be described as the sky brightness ratio. In this case it is defined as the average brightness of the section of the sky seen through the window, divided by the average brightness of the whole sky. The Sky Factor therefore takes into account the brightness of the altitude of the sky visible through the window. Sky luminance factors (R_L) for average altitude angles of portions of the sky visible through a window are given below.

Altitude angle	R_L	Altitude angle	R_L
0°	0.50	50°	1.09
10°	0.58	60°	1.17
20°	0.72	70°	1.24
30°	0.86	80°	1.27
40°	0.98	90°	1.28

The transmission loss (T_G) for clear glass is about 10 percent at normal angles. However, this percentage will increase at high incident angles and adjustments will have to be made in those special cases. The following light transmission ranges for common types of glass used in buildings are normally applied in Daylight Factor calculations:

Glass type	Light transmission
Clear glass (single-glazed units)	90–92%
Clear glass (double-glazed units)	56–76%
Clear plate and tempered glass	90–92%
Heat-absorbing glass	40–75%
Glare-reducing glass	12–68%
Low-E glass (double-glazed units)	70–73%
Low-E glass (triple-glazed units)	55–64%
Glass blocks	81–85%
Frosted glass	63–76%
Patterned glass	52–92%

The British Research Station (BRS) has published a very convenient set of Sky Component (SC) tables (Table 7.1 and Figures 7.15 and 7.16) for the CIE Standard Overcast Sky that are based on simple geometric ratios.

These ratios take into account the geometry of a side window in respect to its distance,

height, and horizontal displacement from the point (P) at which the Daylight Factor is to be determined.

$$H / D = [\text{window head height above "P"}]$$
$$/ [\text{distance of "P" from window}] \quad [7.9]$$

$$W / D = [\text{window width to one side of "P"}] /$$
$$[\text{distance of "P" from window}]$$
$$[7.10]$$

The distance (D) of point (P) from the window is measured as the perpendicular distance from the window wall.

Four different cases of the application of the BRS Sky Component (SC) table are shown in Figures 7.17 to 7.20 below.

Case (1) in Figure 7.17 is the simplest case, in which point (P) is at windowsill height and located symmetrically on the center line of the window. Therefore, H is equal to the height of the head of the window above sill level (i.e., 6FT), while the perpendicular distance between point (P) and the window wall D is 8FT. Since the total width of the window is 15FT and point (P) is located exactly opposite the center of the window, W is 7.5FT. Accordingly the ratios H/D and W/D are equal to 0.75 and 0.94, respectively. By extrapolating between H/D ratios of 0.7 and 0.8 in Table 7.1, these ratios generate a Sky Component (SC) of approximately 2.5 percent. However, that accounts for the daylight provided by only half of the window. Since point (P) is located on the center line of the window, the daylight provided by the entire window will be twice the value obtained for either side, or 5 percent in this case.

In case (2), shown in Figure 7.18, point (P) is still on the center line of the window, but 1FT above sill level. This changes the H/D ratio to 5/8 or 0.63, while the W/D ratio remains at 0.94. The portion of the window below the plane of point (P) is typically ignored, because an observer stationed at point (P) would normally not be able to see any portion of the sky through that lower portion of the window.[7]

Case (3) in Figure 7.19 illustrates a situation where point (P) is located below the window-

Table 7.1 The BRS Sky Component SC tables for the CIE Standard Overcast Sky.

Angle of obstruction

H/D	0.1	0.2	0.3	0.4	0.6	0.8	1.0	1.2	1.4	1.6	1.8	2.0	3.0	∞	Angle of obstruction
∞	1.3	2.5	3.7	4.9	6.9	8.4	9.6	10.7	11.6	12.2	12.6	13.0	14.2	15.0	90°
5.0	1.2	2.4	3.7	4.8	6.8	8.3	9.4	10.5	11.1	11.7	12.3	12.7	13.7	14.2	79°
4.0	1.2	2.4	3.6	4.7	6.7	8.2	9.2	10.3	10.9	11.4	12.0	12.4	13.3	13.7	76°
3.5	1.2	2.4	3.6	4.6	6.6	8.0	9.0	10.1	10.6	11.1	11.8	12.2	12.9	12.9	74°
3.0	1.2	2.3	3.5	4.5	6.4	7.8	8.7	9.8	10.2	10.7	11.3	11.7	12.4	12.7	72°
2.8	1.1	2.3	3.4	4.5	6.3	7.6	8.6	9.6	10.0	10.5	11.1	11.4	12.0	12.3	70°
2.6	1.1	2.2	3.4	4.4	6.2	7.5	8.4	9.3	9.8	10.2	10.8	11.1	11.7	11.9	69°
2.4	1.1	2.2	3.3	4.3	6.0	7.3	8.1	9.1	9.5	10.0	10.4	10.7	11.2	11.5	67°
2.2	1.1	2.1	3.2	4.1	5.8	7.0	7.9	8.7	9.1	9.6	10.0	10.2	10.7	10.9	66°
2.0	1.0	2.0	3.1	4.0	5.6	6.7	7.5	8.3	8.7	9.1	9.5	9.7	10.0	10.3	63°
1.9	1.0	2.0	3.0	3.9	5.4	6.5	7.3	8.1	8.5	8.8	9.2	9.4	9.7	9.9	62°
1.8	0.97	1.9	2.9	3.8	5.3	6.3	7.1	7.8	8.2	8.5	8.8	9.0	9.3	9.5	61°
1.7	0.94	1.8	2.8	3.6	5.1	6.1	6.8	7.5	7.8	8.2	8.5	8.6	8.9	9.1	60°
1.6	0.90	1.7	2.7	3.5	4.9	5.8	6.5	7.2	7.5	7.8	8.1	8.2	8.5	8.6	58°
1.5	0.86	1.6	2.6	3.3	4.6	5.6	6.2	6.8	7.1	7.4	7.6	7.8	8.0	8.1	56°
1.4	0.82	1.5	2.4	3.2	4.4	5.2	5.9	6.4	6.7	7.0	7.2	7.3	7.5	7.6	54°
1.3	0.77	1.4	2.3	2.9	4.1	4.9	5.5	5.9	6.2	6.4	6.6	6.7	6.9	7.0	52°
1.2	0.71	1.3	2.1	2.7	3.8	4.5	5.0	5.4	5.7	5.9	6.0	6.1	6.2	6.3	50°
1.1	0.65	1.1	1.9	2.5	3.4	4.1	4.6	4.9	5.1	5.3	5.4	5.4	5.6	5.7	48°
1.0	0.57	0.99	1.7	2.2	3.0	3.6	4.0	4.3	4.5	4.6	4.7	4.7	4.8	5.0	45°
0.9	0.50	0.83	1.5	1.9	2.6	3.1	3.4	3.7	3.8	3.9	4.0	4.0	4.1	4.2	42°
0.8	0.42	0.68	1.2	1.6	2.2	2.6	2.9	3.1	3.2	3.3	3.3	3.3	3.4	3.4	39°
0.7	0.33	0.53	0.97	1.3	1.7	2.1	2.3	2.5	2.5	2.6	2.6	2.6	2.7	2.8	35°
0.6	0.24	0.39	0.74	0.98	1.3	1.6	1.8	1.9	1.9	2.0	2.0	2.0	2.1	2.1	31°
0.5	0.16	0.25	0.52	0.70	0.97	1.10	1.3	1.4	1.4	1.4	1.4	1.5	1.5	1.5	27°
0.4	0.10	0.14	0.34	0.45	0.62	0.75	0.89	0.92	0.95	0.95	0.96	0.96	0.97	0.98	22°
0.3	0.06	0.06	0.18	0.26	0.34	0.42	0.47	0.49	0.50	0.50	0.51	0.51	0.52	0.53	17°
0.2	0.03	0.02	0.09	0.11	0.14	0.20	0.21	0.22	0.22	0.22	0.22	0.23	0.23	0.24	11°
0.1	0.01	0.02	0.02	0.03	0.04	0.05	0.05	0.06	0.06	0.06	0.06	0.07	0.07	0.08	6°
0	0.1	0.2	0.3	0.4	0.6	0.8	1.0	1.2	1.4	1.6	1.8	2.0	3.0	∞	0°

Ratio (W/D) = Width of window to one side of normal/distance from window
(Ratio H/D = Height of window head above working plane/distance from window)

The British Research Station (BRS) has published simplified Sky Component (SC) tables based on simple geometric relationships.

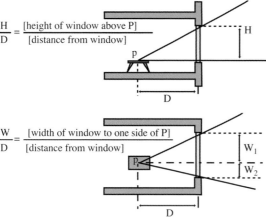

$$\frac{H}{D} = \frac{[\text{height of window above P}]}{[\text{distance from window}]}$$

$$\frac{W}{D} = \frac{[\text{width of window to one side of P}]}{[\text{distance from window}]}$$

Figure 7.15   BRS Sky Factor table parameters.

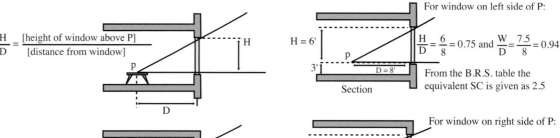

Case (1): Reference plane at windowsill level and reference point (P) on center line of window.

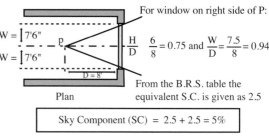

For window on left side of P:

$H = 6'$ $\frac{H}{D} = \frac{6}{8} = 0.75$ and $\frac{W}{D} = \frac{7.5}{8} = 0.94$

From the B.R.S. table the equivalent SC is given as 2.5

Section

For window on right side of P:

$W = 7'6"$ $\frac{H}{D}$ $\frac{6}{8} = 0.75$ and $\frac{W}{D} = \frac{7.5}{8} = 0.94$

$W = 7'6"$

From the B.R.S. table the equivalent S.C. is given as 2.5

Plan

Sky Component (SC) = 2.5 + 2.5 = 5%

Figure 7.17   Case (1) – reference point at windowsill level.

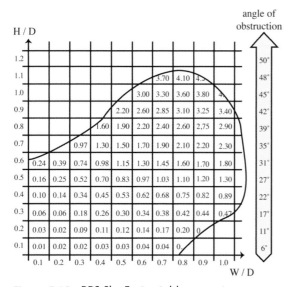

Figure 7.16   BRS Sky Factor table excerpt.

Case (2): Reference plane above sill level and reference point (P) on center line of window.

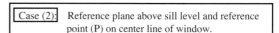

For window on left side of P:

$H = 5'$ $\frac{H}{D} = \frac{5}{8} = 0.63$ and $\frac{W}{D} = \frac{7.5}{8} = 0.94$

From the B.R.S. table the equivalent SC is given as 1.8

Section

*(PS: The portion of the window below the reference plane is ignored.)

For window on right side of P:

$W = 7'6"$ $\frac{H}{D}$ $\frac{5}{8} = 0.63$ and $\frac{W}{D} = \frac{7.5}{8} = 0.94$

$W = 7'6"$

From the B.R.S. table the equivalent S.C. is given as 1.8

Plan

Sky Component (SC) = 1.8 + 1.8 = 3.6%

Figure 7.18   Case (2) – reference point above windowsill level.

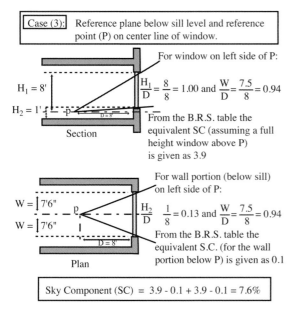

Figure 7.19   Case (3) – reference point below windowsill level.

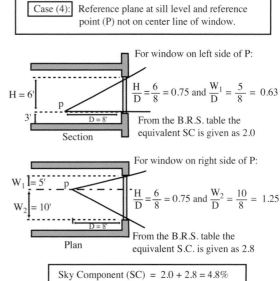

Figure 7.20   Case (4) – reference point not on center line of window.

sill. The determination of the Sky Component (SC) in this case requires us to proceed in two stages. First, we calculate the H_1/D ratio for a hypothetical window that extends from the actual window head down to the plane of point (P). In other words, we temporarily assume that the windowsill is located at the same height above floor level as point (P). Then we calculate the H_2/D ratio for the portion of the hypothetical window that extends from the actual window-sill down to the plane of point (P). The true Sky Component (SC) is found by subtracting the SC given by Table 7.1 for the H_2/D ratio from the SC given by Table 7.1 for the H_1/D ratio (i.e., 3.9% − 0.1% = 3.8%). Again, since point (P) lies on the center line of the window, this SC value is doubled to account for the two sides of the window (i.e., 3.8% + 3.8% = 7.6%).

Case (4) shown in Figure 7.20 is actually more typical than the other three cases, because the point at which the Sky Component (SC) is to be determined is seldom on the center line of a window. Under these circumstances the SC value has to be calculated separately for each side of the window. In Figure 7.20, with point (P) at windowsill height, the H/D ratio for either

side of the window is 6/8 or 0.75. The W_1/D ratio is 5/8 or 0.63, since the width of the window extending from the perpendicular line that point (P) subtends to the window to the left side of point (P) is 5FT. From Table 7.1 we extrapolate the SC value for this portion of the window to be approximately 2.0.

However, the width of the portion of the window on the right side of the perpendicular line between point (P) and the window is 10FT. Therefore the W_2/D ratio for this portion of the window is 10/8 or 1.25. Using this ratio together with the H/D ratio of 0.75 (which applies to both sides of the window) to look up Table 7.1, we obtain an SC value of approximately 2.8. Therefore, the Sky Component (SC) for case (4) is 4.8% (i.e., 2.0% + 2.8%).

In a more extreme case, where the location of the window is so far to one side of point (P) that the perpendicular line subtended by point (P) to the window wall does not lie within the width of the window, the Sky Component (SC) is also calculated in two steps. For example, let us assume that the window in Figure 7.20 (i.e., case (4)) is replaced with a much narrower 4FT-wide window located 6FT to the right of point

(P). In other words, the perpendicular line from point (P) to the window wall is now 6FT to the left of the window. Relative to point (P), the Sky Component (SC) of this window is calculated by subtracting the SC value of a hypothetical window that extends from the perpendicular subtended by point (P) to the left side of the actual window to another hypothetical window that extends from the same perpendicular to the right side of the actual window. The first W_1/D ratio is 6/8 or 0.75, and the second W_2/D ratio is 10/8 or 1.25. With a H/D ratio of 6/8 or 0.75, which applies to both of these hypothetical window configurations, the SC values (from Table 7.1) are approximately 2.2 and 2.9, respectively. Therefore, the Sky Component (SC) of this 4FT wide window is 0.7% (i.e., 2.9% − 2.2%). The low SC value is due to the fact that the window is located far to the right of point (P) and therefore provides little daylight exposure to point (P).

7.6.2   Externally reflected component (ERC)

Part of the view through the window may be obstructed by buildings that are visible because they reflect light toward the observer. Therefore, they may be treated as a secondary sky of much lower luminance. In practice, since a precise calculation is difficult, the luminance of the obstructed portion of the sky is assumed to be between 10 and 20 percent of the sky component, unadjusted for variations in sky luminance.

$$ERC = (\text{Sky Factor}) \times B_R \ (\%) \qquad [7.11]$$

where:

ERC = Externally Reflected Component
   B_R = ratio of brightness of obstruction to average brightness of sky (usually 0.2).

For the window configuration shown in Figure 7.21 (i.e., $W/D = 10/10$ or 1.0) and an angle of obstruction of 17°, the SC value provided by Table 7.1 is 0.47. If the luminance of the visible surface of the obstructing building is 20 percent of the luminance of the sky (i.e., B_R is equal to 0.2), then this SC value is adjusted to 0.09 (i.e.,

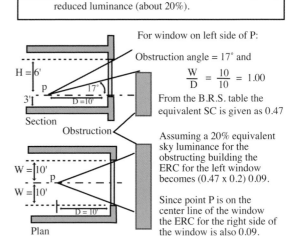

Figure 7.21   Externally reflected component.

0.47 × 0.2). Since point (P) is located on the center line of the window, the Sky Component (SC) is equal to the sum of the SC values for each portion of the window, namely 0.2% (i.e., 0.09% + 0.09% = 0.2%).

7.6.3   Internally reflected component (IRC)

The calculation of the effect of the internal reflections is very much complicated by the differences in reflection factors of the normally dull floor and light-colored ceiling and walls. It is unfortunate that since the highest-quality daylight is directed downward from the sky, it will be first reflected by the floor, the lower sections of the walls, and the work plane. Lesser-quality daylight that is reflected into a room from external obstructions is directed upward, and will therefore be reflected for a second time by the typically more brightly colored ceiling and upper sections of the walls. This suggests that the Internally Reflected Component (IRC) is likely to be a small fraction of the total Daylight Factor when there is a substantial Sky Component (SC). In fact, in practice it has been found that under those conditions the IRC value is seldom greater than 10 percent of the Daylight Factor. In situations where the SC value is rela-

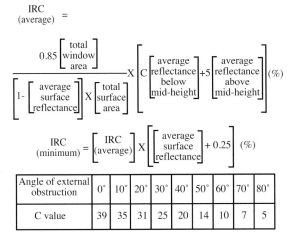

IRC:	The calculation of the IRC takes into account that the lower part of a building space normally has darker surface finishes than the upper part.

$$\text{IRC}_{(average)} =$$

$$\frac{0.85 \begin{bmatrix} \text{total} \\ \text{window} \\ \text{area} \end{bmatrix}}{\left[1 - \begin{bmatrix} \text{average} \\ \text{surface} \\ \text{reflectance} \end{bmatrix}\right] X \begin{bmatrix} \text{total} \\ \text{surface} \\ \text{area} \end{bmatrix}} X \left[C \begin{bmatrix} \text{average} \\ \text{reflectance} \\ \text{below} \\ \text{mid-height} \end{bmatrix} + 5 \begin{bmatrix} \text{average} \\ \text{reflectance} \\ \text{above} \\ \text{mid-height} \end{bmatrix} \right] (\%)$$

$$\text{IRC}_{(minimum)} = \begin{bmatrix} \text{IRC} \\ (average) \end{bmatrix} X \left[\begin{bmatrix} \text{average} \\ \text{surface} \\ \text{reflectance} \end{bmatrix} + 0.25 \right] (\%)$$

Angle of external obstruction	0°	10°	20°	30°	40°	50°	60°	70°	80°
C value	39	35	31	25	20	14	10	7	5

Figure 7.22 Internally reflected component.

tively small, the contribution of the IRC will be proportionally greater, although the overall Daylight Factor will be much smaller.

Although a number of calculation techniques had been developed in the past, these were largely replaced by a simplified method for estimating the average (IRC_{AVE}) and minimum (IRC_{MIN}) values of the Internally Reflected Component (Figure 7.22) proposed by the British Research Station (BRS) in 1954 (Hopkinson et al., 1966).

This method draws a distinction between the reflectivity of the surfaces of the upper and lower portions of a room, as follows:

$$\mathbf{IRC_{AVE} = 0.85 x A_G / [A_S (1 - R_T)] \times}$$
$$\mathbf{[C (R_{FW}) + 5 (R_{CW})] (\%)} \quad \mathbf{[7.12]}$$

where:

IRC_{AVE} = average Internally Reflected Component
A_G = total window area
A_S = total area of walls, floor and ceiling
R_T = average reflectance of all surfaces
C = factor dependent on angle of obstruction (see Figure 7.22)
R_{FW} = average reflectance of floor and walls below mid-height
R_{CW} = average reflectance of ceiling and walls above mid-height.

The minimum Internally Reflected Component (IRC_{MIN}) is then derived as a function of the relative reflectivity of the internal surfaces of the space under consideration.

$$\mathbf{IRC_{MIN} = IRC_{AVE} [R_T + 0.25] (\%)} \quad \mathbf{[7.13]}$$

As an example of the calculation of both the average and minimum Internally Reflected Component, we will consider a room that is 10FT wide, 20FT long, and 8FT high. It has a complete window wall at one end (i.e., 10FT by 8FT) and no windows in the other three walls.

Step (1): Calculate the total area of walls, floor and ceiling (A_S):

$$\text{ceiling area} = 200\text{SF (i.e., } 10 \times 20 = 200)$$
$$\text{floor area} = 200\text{SF (i.e., } 10 \times 20 = 200)$$
$$\text{wall area} = 480\text{SF (i.e., } 2(10 \times 8)$$
$$+ 2(20 \times 8) = 480)$$
$$\text{total surface area} = 880\text{SF (i.e., } 200 + 200$$
$$+ 480 = 880)$$

Step (2): Calculate the total window area (A_G):

$$\text{total window area} = 80\text{SF (i.e., } 10 \times 8 = 80)$$

Step (3): Calculate the average reflectance of all surfaces (R_T), if:

$$\text{solid wall reflectance} = 40\% \text{ (i.e., } 400$$
$$\times 0.4 = 160)$$
$$\text{ceiling reflectance} = 80\% \text{ (i.e., } 200$$
$$\times 0.8 = 160)$$
$$\text{floor reflectance} = 20\% \text{ (i.e., } 200$$
$$\times 0.2 = 40)$$
$$\text{window glass reflectance} = 10\% \text{ (i.e., } 80$$
$$\times 0.1 = 8)$$
$$\text{average surface reflectance} = 0.42 \text{ (i.e., } [160$$
$$+ 160 + 40 + 8] / 880)$$

Step (4): Calculate the average reflectances below and above mid-height:

$$\text{reflectance below mid-height} = 0.28 \text{ (i.e., } [80$$
$$+ 40 + 4] / 440)$$
$$\text{reflectance above mid-height} = 0.55 \text{ (i.e., } [80$$
$$+ 160 + 4] / 440)$$

Step (5): Calculate the average Internally Reflected Component (IRC$_{AVE}$):

$$IRC_{AVE} = [0.85 \times 80]/[(1-0.42) \times 880]$$
$$\times [(39 \times 0.28) + (5 \times 0.55)]$$
$$= \mathbf{1.8\%}$$

Step (6): Calculate the minimum Internally Reflected Component (IRC$_{MIN}$):

$$IRC_{MIN} = [1.8 \times (0.42 + 0.25)]$$
$$= \mathbf{1.2\%}$$

The individual values calculated for the three components (i.e., SC, ERC, and IRC) are summated and then adjusted for a further loss in light transmission due to deposits of dust and grime on the window glazing. The allowance to be made for dirty windows depends on the locality and the cleaning cycle. The following typical correction factors may be applied:

Locality	Occupancy	Factor
Outer suburban area	Clean	0.9
	Dirty	0.7
Built-up residential area	Clean	0.8
	Dirty	0.6
Built-up industrial area	Clean	0.7
	Dirty	0.5

While the BRS Sky Component tables (Table 7.1) take into account the light-transmission loss through normal window glass, an additional adjustment will be necessary in the case of special glass with greatly reduced light-transmission properties (e.g., heat-absorbing glass or low-E glass in triple-glazed units). Finally, if gross window dimensions were used in the calculation of *H/D* and *W/D* ratios for the determination of SC and ERC values, then these values should be modified to allow for the area taken up by the window frame. The typical *frame* factors shown in Figure 7.23 should be applied with caution.

The proportion of frame area to total window area is not only dependent on the frame mate-

The calculated Daylight Factor must be adjusted for glazing, window frames and dirty windows. (The BRS table takes into account the light transmission loss of normal window glass.)

Glass	Glass Type	Factor
	Heat Absorbing glass	0.7
	Glass blocks	0.9
	Wired glass	0.9
	Frosted glass	0.8
	Double glazed windows	0.8

Frame	Window Frame Material	Factor
	Wood (openable windows)	0.65
	Wood (fixed windows)	0.75
	Steel window frames	0.85
	Aluminum window frames	0.80

Dirt	Locality	Occupancy	Factor
	Rural suburban	clean	0.9
		dirty	0.7
	Urban residential	clean	0.8
		dirty	0.6
	Industrial area	clean	0.7
		dirty	0.5

Figure 7.23   Daylight factor adjustments.

rial as suggested in Figure 7.23, but also on the overall size of the window. For example, in the case of large, fixed windows the proportional area of the window frame may be negligible.

7.7 Glare from daylight

Direct, reflected, and diffuse sunlight are the most common causes of glare from windows. In these cases the contrast between the luminance of the window and the surrounding surfaces may be sufficiently pronounced to produce conditions varying from noticeable visual stress to disability glare and the impairment of vision. Basically, there are four possible remedies available to ameliorate such glare conditions:

• Raising the level of illumination in the vicinity of the windows by means of supplementary, artificial lighting installations. While this remedy is often used in regions where overcast skies are prevalent, it tends to be uneconomical in regions where clear sky conditions are predominant. In the latter case the amount of artificial light that is required to mitigate the glare condition may not be compatible with the energy conservation objectives of the design solution.

- Blocking direct sunlight or reducing the section of the sky visible through the windows by means of blinds, curtains, fins, louvers, or canopies. In the northern hemisphere this is a relatively simple matter if the main windows face south (or north in the southern hemisphere). On the other hand, east and west elevations may require adjustable vertical sunshading devices, which tend to be expensive in respect to both initial acquisition cost and maintenance requirements.
- The use of roof lights. As shown in Figure 7.24, various configurations with and without the provision of sun shading are available. The principal limitation of roof lights is that they are applicable only to single-story buildings (or the top floor of multi-story buildings).
- The use of special anti-glare or low-transmission glass in combination with light-colored interior surfaces, especially on the window wall, to increase the luminance of the building environment. It should be noted, however, that the application of low-transmission glass will result in a substantial reduction in the amount of natural light

available inside the building, while the contrast in brightness between the window and surrounding surfaces is little affected. Further, it is well to remember that one of the main functions of a window is to provide a view. Depending on the exterior brightness and light transmission, these special glasses will, at times, behave like mirrors and therefore interfere with the transparency of the window.

Endnotes

1. The Normal Distribution Curve is a statistical measure of the degree of variation within a related set (i.e., population) of data. A steep curve indicates that most of the data values are clustered around the mean (i.e., average) value, which is located at the center of the curve, while a flatter curve indicates a wider distribution. The precise distribution characteristics of any particular population can be calculated mathematically as Standard Deviations from the mean. Setting the area under the Normal Distribution Curve to be equal to 1 (i.e., 100 percent of the population), the mean plus or minus one Standard Deviation represents 68 percent of the population and the mean plus or minus 2 Standard Deviations represents 94 percent of the population. Mathematical adjustments are made in calculating the Standard Deviations of Normal Distribution Curves that are slightly skewed, such as in the case of the typical daily daylight distribution shown in Figure 7.1 above.
2. Contrary to its name, color temperature is not related to the operating temperature of a light source. Instead, it is related to the spectral distribution of radiation that is emitted by a full radiator (i.e., a black body) when it is heated to different temperatures. These temperatures are measured in degrees Kelvin (K) and referred to as color temperatures. Accordingly, the spectral distribution of an overcast sky is approximately equivalent to the spectral distribution of a black body heated to 6400 K. Similarly, the color temperature of direct sunlight and a clear blue sky are approximately 5500 K and 11 500 K, respectively.
3. Since computer monitors rely on an additive mixture of the three primary colors (and are therefore commonly referred to as RGB monitors), they cannot accurately represent many of the colors in

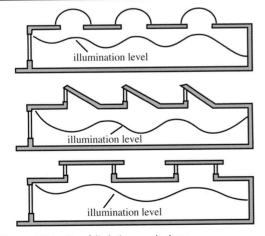

While daylight penetration from side windows is normally inadequate in areas more than 15 FT from the window wall, roof openings can provide fairly uniform daylighting over unlimited areas.

illumination level

illumination level

illumination level

Figure 7.24   Roof lighting variations.

the chromaticity diagram. The black-line triangle shown in Figure 7.6 provides an indication of the restricted color range that applies to an average RGB monitor.

4. The CIE supersaturated primary colors do not actually exist. In other words, they are notional mathematical constructs that lie outside the boundaries of the chromaticity diagram. Constructed as a right-angled triangle, which circumscribes the chromaticity diagram, the two sides of the triangle that form the 90° angle also represent the *x*- and *y*-axes of the CIE chromaticity diagram.

5. Actually a slightly modified form of equation [7.3] (i.e., 53(a) instead of 52(a)) was suggested. However, the difference between 53(a) and 52(a) is barely 2 percent.

6. Over a period of several years (1973–1978), small groups of students were required to undertake a class assignment in which they chose any interior space on campus, measured actual light levels at nine equidistant points within the space at approximately 9 am, 12 noon, and 4 pm on successive days, and then compared these measurements with predicted values generated by a computer program. The computer program was capable of calculating two sets of illumination levels at user-specified grid-intersection points. One set was based on a Uniform Brightness Sky and the other set was based on the CIE Standard Overcast Sky. Except for spaces with windows facing due west, the calculated values that were based on overcast sky conditions invariably correlated significantly better with the actual measurements than the estimates that were based on uniform clear sky conditions.

7. While this is certainly true for the Sky Component (SC), there may be instances when a highly reflective surface at ground level outside the window (e.g., water or the shiny roof surface of a neighboring building that is located just below the windowsill level) may reflect light through the lower part of the window. In this rather unusual case the portion below the windowsill level would not be ignored, but calculated as an Externally Reflected Component (ERC). As we will see later in this section, the ERC is calculated as a Sky Component with reduced luminance (i.e., normally 20 percent).

8 Artificial Lighting

It is highly unlikely that daylight alone can satisfy all of the lighting requirements in a building. Certainly at night there will be a need for artificial light. Also, even during daytime periods when there might be an abundance of external daylight there is likely to be a need for supplementary task illumination. This need for supplementary artificial light occurs in particular in office buildings, where deeper rooms cannot be adequately served by windows in side walls. However, notwithstanding these reasons for some form of artificial lighting, the application of good building design practices leading to the exploitation of daylighting opportunities is of paramount importance (Figure 8.1).

Artificial light is only the last consideration in a three-tier design approach that commences with the layout of the floor plan, careful consideration of the orientation and shape of spaces, selection of the finishes of the larger surfaces such as ceiling and walls, and then seeks ways of introducing daylight in desirable quantities.

Today, electric light sources constitute the main form of artificial light, although the conversion of electricity into light is by no means efficient. As shown in Figure 8.2, only 7 percent of the output produced by a standard filament (i.e., incandescent) lamp is in the form of light, while 93 percent is heat energy.

Even fluorescent lamps produce almost twice as much heat as the sun. The situation is exacerbated by the fact that the more efficient electric light sources such as mercury and sodium lamps are mostly unusable because of poor color-rendition properties.

The problems encountered in artificial lighting are often not the same as those encountered in natural lighting. Since both the luminance and location of the lighting installation are easily controlled, it is not a question of providing sufficient light, but one of optimizing the visual environment in relation to the discrimination of form, color rendition, work performance, physical comfort, and the emotional well-being of the occupant.

8.1 Definition of terms

In the design of artificial lighting installations we will be encountering some notions and units of measurement that are derived directly from concepts in the field of physics. One of these units of measurement is the *kilowatt hour* (KWH). Although this is a metric unit, it is used internationally as a measure of electric-energy consumption.

In reference to Figure 8.3, work is performed when a force is applied over some distance. Power is then defined as the amount of work that is performed per unit time and measured in the metric system in *watt* (W).[1] Since energy is equal to the amount of power exerted over time, it follows that the metric unit of electric power is the *kilowatt hour*.

To fully appreciate the principles of discharge lamps we need to understand the fundamental relationship that exists between the terms electric current, potential difference, and resistance

Building Science: Concepts and Application. Jens Pohl.
© 2011 John Wiley & Sons, Ltd.
Published 2011 by John Wiley & Sons, Ltd.

Artificial (i.e., electric) light is not the total solution for the lighting of building interiors, but only the third tier in a three-tier design approach.

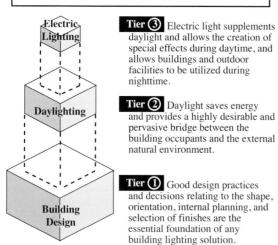

Tier ③ Electric light supplements daylight and allows the creation of special effects during daytime, and allows buildings and outdoor facilities to be utilized during nighttime.

Tier ② Daylight saves energy and provides a highly desirable and pervasive bridge between the building occupants and the external natural environment.

Tier ① Good design practices and decisions relating to the shape, orientation, internal planning, and selection of finishes are the essential foundation of any building lighting solution.

Figure 8.1   Lighting design approach.

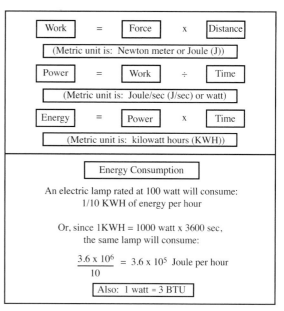

Figure 8.3   Units of electric power and energy.

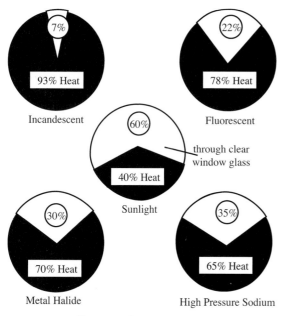

Figure 8.2   Efficiency of light sources.

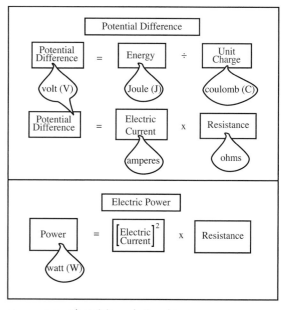

Figure 8.4   Electricity relationships.

(Figure 8.4). In the physics domain of static electricity, the *energy* in *joules* (J) produced by an electric field is equal to the product of the *potential difference* in *volts* (V) and *unit charge* in *coulombs* (C). However, for an electric current flowing through a conducting material the *potential difference* (volts) is given by the product of the *current* (amperes) and the *resistance* (ohms).

As shown in the lower part of Figure 8.4, *electric power* (watts) can also be expressed as the product of the square of the *current* (amperes) and the *resistance* (ohms).

The relationship between *potential difference, current,* and *resistance* is important in artificial lighting because of the prominent role played by discharge lamps in all interior lighting installations today. These lamps require a high potential difference between two poles to initiate an electric discharge, and then a much lower potential difference to maintain the light-producing discharge during the continued operation of the lamp. The variation in potential difference is easily produced with the aid of an electric transformer that produces the desired potential difference by first increasing and then throttling back the electric current.

The concept of *color temperature* was explained in some detail previously in Chapter 7. It will therefore suffice here to only briefly reiterate that the term *color temperature* is used to describe the color spectrum emitted by a light source. The reason why the color spectrum is expressed in terms of a temperature is because in this way it can be compared to the emission characteristics of a *black body* when it is heated. Although a black body is an idealized concept in physics that does not actually exist, it is most useful because it allows the spectrum of wavelengths that is emitted at different temperatures to be mathematically calculated. The fact that *color temperature* is unrelated to the operating temperature of a light source is evident in the table of the *color temperature* of different natural and artificial light sources shown in Figure 8.5. An overcast sky, which is quite cool, has a color temperature of 7000 K, while an incandescent lamp, which is too hot to touch, has a color temperature of only 2500 K.

The term *efficacy* is used to describe energy efficiency in terms of the light flux produced (lumen) per electric power (watt) consumed. The unit of efficacy is therefore *lumen/watt* (lm/W).

As indicated in Figure 8.5, higher-wattage lamps have a higher efficacy than lower-wattage lamps. Therefore, a 200-watt lamp provides significantly more light than four 50-watt lamps. Also, there exists a theoretical maximum effi-

Color Temperature			
Color temperature (K) describes the color of a light source based on its radiation spectrum, and is not a measure of its operating temperature.			
candlelight	1900 K	incandescent light	2500 K
overcast sky	7000 K	incandescent-halogen	3500 K
north light	8000 K	fluorescent	3500 to 6500 K

Efficacy
Efficacy is a measure of the energy efficiency of a light source in terms of ⌈lumen⌉ of light produced per ⌈watt⌉ of electricity consumed.

- Higher wattage lamps have a higher efficacy than lower wattage lamps (e.g., a 100 watt lamp provides significantly more light than two 50 watt lamps).

- The theoretical maximum efficacy of white light is about 200 lm/w. For yellow-green light (550 mμ) it is about 680 lm/w.

Figure 8.5 Color temperature and efficacy.

cacy for light, depending on the spectral distribution. It is about 200 lm/W for white light and over 600 lm/W for yellow-green light, owing to the greater sensitivity of the eye to the 550 mμ wavelength.

Finally, we need to be familiar with the terms that are used to describe the artificial light fixture itself (Figure 8.6).

The term *luminaire* applies to an entire fixture, which includes one or more *lamps* (i.e., the actual light source), the accessories that are required to hold and operate the lamp, and any device that is used to control the distribution of light such as a lampshade. As mentioned previously, discharge lamps require an electrical transformer capable of generating the initial potential difference that is required to initiate the discharge of ions between the anode and cathode of the lamp. This transformer is referred to as *ballast*.

8.2 Creation of light artificially

Let us for a moment reconsider the principle of *black-body* radiation discussed earlier in connection with color temperature (see also Chapter 1,

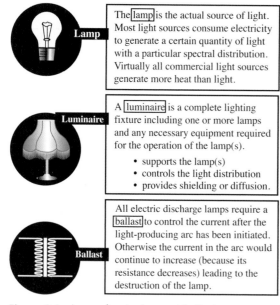

The <u>lamp</u> is the actual source of light. Most light sources consume electricity to generate a certain quantity of light with a particular spectral distribution. Virtually all commercial light sources generate more heat than light.

A <u>luminaire</u> is a complete lighting fixture including one or more lamps and any necessary equipment required for the operation of the lamp(s).

• supports the lamp(s)
• controls the light distribution
• provides shielding or diffusion.

All electric discharge lamps require a <u>ballast</u> to control the current after the light-producing arc has been initiated. Otherwise the current in the arc would continue to increase (because its resistance decreases) leading to the destruction of the lamp.

Figure 8.6   Lamp, luminaire, and ballast.

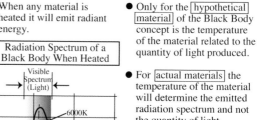

Historically the development of artificial light sources has centered on raising a material (e.g., a thin wire) to incandescence.

• When any material is heated it will emit radiant energy.

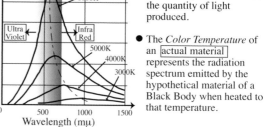

• Only for the <u>hypothetical material</u> of the Black Body concept is the temperature of the material related to the quantity of light produced.

• For <u>actual materials</u> the temperature of the material will determine the emitted radiation spectrum and not the quantity of light produced.

• The *Color Temperature* of an <u>actual material</u> represents the radiation spectrum emitted by the hypothetical material of a Black Body when heated to that temperature.

Figure 8.7   Black-body radiation spectrum.

Section 1.3.5). A black body consists of an ideal material that absorbs all electromagnetic radiation, including light, falling upon it. If this idealized black body is heated, it will emit radiation of a wavelength directly related to the temperature of the body. The quantity of radiation produced is not the same at all wavelengths, but rather the radiation spectrum resembles a skewed Normal Distribution Curve, with the peak of the curve moving to the left as the temperature of the black body increases.

Figure 8.7 shows the distribution of power in the spectrum of a black-body radiator. Not only are the curves for higher temperatures always above the curves for lower temperatures, but also the peaks (i.e., maxima) of the curves are displaced toward the shorter wavelengths as the temperature is increased.

However, while it is clearly shown in Figure 8.7 that a black body would produce a maximum amount of light if it were to be heated to 6000 K, this does not mean that any other material heated to that temperature will produce a maximum amount of light – or any light at all, for that matter. We must remember that a black body is an idealized material that does not actu-

ally exist. It must be stressed again that the operating temperature of a lamp is distinct from its color temperature. In other words, an artificial light source operating at a temperature of 100°F may produce much more light than one operating at a temperature of 200°F.[2] A black-body radiator simply provides a convenient standard for comparing the radiation spectrum emitted by a lamp (i.e., the color-rendition characteristics of the lamp).

The principal artificial light sources used in buildings today are electrical in nature. They fall into two distinct categories: namely, incandescent lamps and discharge lamps (Figure 8.8).

While there are only two kinds of incandescent lamp, there are several types of discharge lamp, subject to the environment within which the electrical discharge takes place. If we are to compare these different artificial light sources, it is necessary to establish some criteria by which the characteristics of a light source may be assessed. Cost, color, and utility would appear to provide the essential elements for such a comparison.

Capital costs and operating costs are determined by the luminous efficiency or efficacy

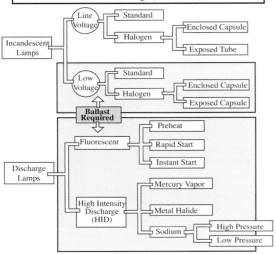

Today, artificial light sources generate visible radiation electrically either through incandescence or through an electrical discharge (i.e., an arc).

Figure 8.8   Artificial light sources.

As shown in Figure 8.9, the lifespan of different kinds of lamp varies greatly, with discharge lamps exceeding the lifespan of incandescent lamps by a factor of 5 to 10. Within the discharge category, with the exception of metal-halide lamps, the High Intensity Discharge (HID) lamps typically have by far the longest lifespan. However, the ability to operate for long periods before failure is not the only measure of efficiency. The useful life of a lamp is governed also by the capacity of the lamp to maintain its initial luminous efficiency over its lifespan. As will be seen later in Figures 8.18 and 8.21, the *depreciation* of lamps varies from an average of about 15 percent to a high of 30 percent in the case of some metal-halide lamps.

The color rendering properties of a lamp are normally considered to be more important than the actual color of the source. Since the appearance of a colored surface exposed to a light source is governed primarily by the spectral distribution of the light emitted, the radiation spectrum will serve as a useful guide to the color-rendering properties of a lamp. It is unfortunate that in addition to the fact that more than 60 percent of the energy output of all electric light sources is heat and not light (Figure 8.2), the more efficient lamps have the poorest color-rendition properties.

Finally, the utility or practical convenience of a lamp is governed by a number of physical and operational characteristics such as its size, shape, wattage range, and need for auxiliary equipment.

8.2.1   Incandescent (filament) lamps

In these lamps a fine tungsten wire, referred to as the filament, is raised to incandescence by the passage of an electric current. With a *color temperature* of around 3200K, over 90 percent of the radiation is in the infrared region (Figure 8.10).

Evaporation of the filament results in the familiar blackening of the bulb and ultimately causes the tungsten wire to break. Tungsten is normally chosen for the filament material because of its high melting point and slow rate of evaporation. Since higher operating

The life span of discharge lamps is typically five to ten times longer than incandescent lamps.

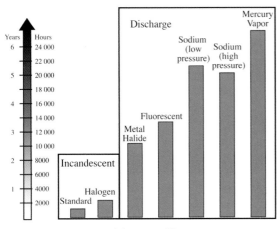

Figure 8.9   Average lifespan of lamps.

(i.e., lumen per watt of power consumed), the lumen maintenance (i.e., lumen output during the operational life cycle), the initial capital cost of the lamp installed in a luminaire, and the useful life of the lamp.

In incandescent lamps a fine tungsten coiled wire (i.e., filament) is raised to incandescence by the passage of an electric current.

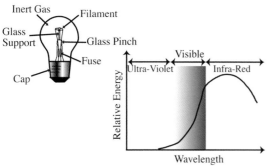

● Operating temperature limited to about 3000K due to rate of evaporation of tungsten.

● Only 7% of the emitted radiation is in the visible range (remainder is emitted as heat).

Figure 8.10   The incandescent (filament) lamp.

The operating temperature of an incandescent lamp is very much a compromise between lifespan and efficiency, based on the relationship:

$$\left[\begin{array}{c}\text{lifespan}\\\text{of lamp}\end{array}\right] = \dfrac{1}{\left[\text{luminous efficiency}\right]^6}$$

The use of halogen gas inside the bulb results in a regenerative cycle that doubles the lifespan of an incandescent lamp to about 2000 hours.

① Tungsten particles boil off filament and move toward bulb wall.

② Halogen vapor circulates as convection currents are set up at temperatures above 500°F.

③ Halogen vapor combines with tungsten particles to form tungsten halide.

④ Near the hot filament the tungsten halide dissociates and redeposits tungsten particles onto the filament.

Figure 8.11   The halogen regenerative cycle.

temperatures will produce greater efficiency in incandescent lamps, it is to be expected that higher-wattage units with thicker filaments will be more efficient than lower-wattage lamps. In fact, a single 100-watt filament lamp will be some 5 lm/W (i.e., 30 percent) more efficient than two 50-watt lamps. Accordingly, the design operating temperature of a filament lamp will be very much a compromise between lifespan and efficiency, based on the following approximate relationship:

lifespan of lamp = 1 / (luminous efficiency)^6
  (HRS)   **[8.1]**

Fortunately, the rate of evaporation of the tungsten filament can be reduced by raising the vapor pressure of the gas in the lamp. Most commonly the gas used is a mixture of argon and nitrogen, although it has been shown that halogen gas (i.e., iodine, chlorine, bromine, or fluorine) will set up a regenerative cycle (Figure 8.11).

In tungsten–halogen lamps the evaporated tungsten associates with the halogen to form tungsten-halide vapor, which dissociates when diffused back to the hot filament, thereby rede-

positing tungsten on the filament. This regenerative cycle enables the filament to operate at slightly higher temperatures, with a resulting increase in efficiency and a service life of up to 2000 hours and little fall-off in lumen maintenance.

There are two further problems associated with the large amount of radiation emitted by filament lamps in the infrared region of the spectrum (Figure 8.10). Not only is up to 93 percent of the input energy wasted for purposes of lighting, but the resultant heat radiation may substantially increase the temperature of the building environment, in particular when very high levels of illumination (e.g., hospital operating theaters) are required. Furthermore, since the color-rendering properties of a lamp are very much affected by its spectral distribution, incandescent lamps will tend to soften the appearance of colored surfaces by virtue of their predominant infrared radiation. Even though the color-rendering characteristics of these lamps are by no means true, or similar to daylight, they are commonly accepted as being pleasant and flattering.

From a more general versatility point of view, incandescent lamps are convenient to

The design of the luminaire of an incandescent downlight can greatly improve the performance of the lamp.

 A standard non-reflective opaque lamp shade may trap (i.e., absorb) more than 50% of the light emitted by the lamp.

 A more focused light beam within a reflective (R) lamp shade (aluminum coating) will direct more light onto the task area.

 An ellipsoidal reflector (ER) lamp is the most efficient choice for a downlight. A 75 watt ER-lamp will provide as much task illumination as a 150 watt R-lamp.

Figure 8.12   Luminaire considerations.

use because they provide instantaneous light, require no auxiliary equipment, and are available in a very large range of wattages, shapes, and sizes.

As shown in Figure 8.12, the choice of luminaire can greatly influence the ultimate light output of an incandescent lamp. This is particularly true for *direct lighting* fixtures (Figure 8.25) in which virtually all of the light is directed downward. The strategies commonly used by the manufacturers of such light fixtures to minimize the absorption of light by the inside surface of the lampshade include: a highly reflective metal surface finish (e.g., aluminum coating); a more focused light beam, produced by a lamp unit with its own encapsulated reflective surround; and, an ellipsoidal reflector (ER) lamp that utilizes a lens to produce a sharply defined parallel light beam.

8.2.2   Discharge lamps

In all discharge lamps light is produced by the passage of an electric current through a gas or vapor (Figure 8.13). High Intensity Discharge

In all ☐ discharge lamps ☐ light is produced by the passage of an electric current through a gas or vapor. The light is produced by the ionized gas.

● Essentially, an arc is set up between two electrodes at opposite ends of the lamp.

● A ballast is required to initially produce a high potential difference between the two electrodes to initiate the discharge.

● Once the arc has been started the ballast must choke back the current to maintain the arc.

● The efficacy and lifespan of discharge lamps are far superior to incandescent lamps (i.e., 4:1 and 10:1, respectively).

Figure 8.13   Discharge lamp principles.

In all ☐ high intensity discharge lamps ☐ the light is emitted from a small arc tube inside a protective outer bulb.

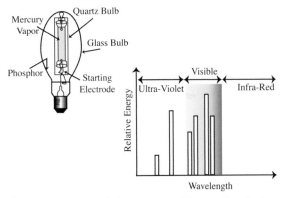

● Non-continuous radiation spectrum with strong lines in the ultra-violet, blue-green and yellow regions.

● Absence of red radiation is responsible for poor color rendition characteristics.

Figure 8.14   High-intensity discharge lamps.

(HID) lamps, such as the high-pressure mercury vapor lamp (Figure 8.14), consist essentially of an arc tube with electrodes at both ends, containing a small quantity of mercury in combination with a low-pressure rare gas such as argon.

It is the function of the rare gas to facilitate initiation of the discharge. However, the presence of the rare gas will serve little purpose unless a very large potential difference is first created electrically. For this reason the mercury vapor lamp, like all discharge lamps, requires a choke circuit and incorporates its own starting electrode.

Although there are several types of discharge lamp that are basically distinguished by their operating pressure, in all of them a discharge is initiated in the filling gas accompanied by a low brightness glow. In other words, it may take some time for the lamp to attain its full light-generation capacity. For example, in the case of the high-pressure mercury lamp, as the mercury vapor pressure builds up a narrow, bright arc develops over a period of several minutes along the center of the arc tube. As shown in Figure 8.14, the emitted radiation spectrum displays strong lines in the ultraviolet region, while distribution in the visible region comprises separate lines in the blue-green and yellow wavelengths. The lack of red radiation is responsible for the poor color rendition, but at the same time allows a higher luminous efficiency.

The color-rendition characteristics of the high-pressure mercury lamp can be improved in two ways: first, by coating the inside surface of the bulb with a phosphor such as magnesium fluorogermanate or yttrium vanadate (the phosphor coating is capable of reradiating some of the ultraviolet wavelengths into the visible range); and second, by adding metal halides into the discharge tube (through the introduction of metallic vapors such as iridium iodide). In the latter case, while the resulting metal-halide lamp displays a continuous radiation spectrum in the visible range, it is by no means evenly distributed (Figure 8.15).

Although the color rendition properties of the high-pressure mercury lamp in the uncorrected form may be acceptable for exterior lighting and some high-bay industrial applications, this lamp is normally not considered for interior lighting. The metal-halide lamp, on the other hand, is much more acceptable for external and for high-bay interior lighting.

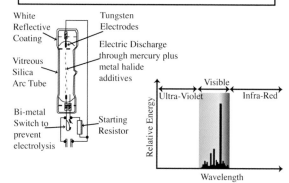

The metal halide lamp is a color-corrected form of the high pressure mercury lamp through the use of metallic vapors (e.g., iridium iodide).

● Increased light output (i.e. efficacy) and smaller size than high pressure mercury lamps.

● Restriction on the position in which the lamp may be operated (i.e., burned).

Figure 8.15   The metal-halide lamp.

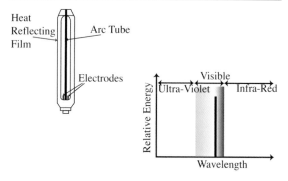

The low pressure sodium lamp has general electrical and operating characteristics similar to those of the high pressure mercury lamp.

● Most limiting feature is the unique yellow radiation, which produces very poor color rendition.

● Very efficient light source with an efficacy of up to 180 lm/w.

Figure 8.16   The low-pressure sodium lamp.

The low-pressure sodium lamp (Figure 8.16) is a very efficient light source capable of producing up to 150 lm/W.

Since it is also a discharge lamp, it has general electrical and operating characteristics similar to those of the mercury lamp. The most limiting feature of the sodium lamp is its unique yellow radiation, which is responsible for high luminous efficiency but very poor color rendition. This is most unfortunate, since the sodium lamp has the highest efficacy of all currently available electric light sources. For this reason it is understandable that considerable efforts have been made by manufacturers to improve the color-rendition performance of the sodium lamp.

It was found that the color-rendition properties of the sodium lamp can be improved by operating the lamp at above atmospheric pressure. However, the ability to do so has been restricted in the past by the lack of an enclosure capable of containing the hot, chemically active sodium. This problem has now been overcome by the development of crystalline alumina. Accordingly, high-pressure sodium lamps with crystalline alumina enclosures produce white light at a reduced efficiency of about 110 lm/W (Figure 8.17).

Application of this modified sodium lamp is found in outdoor street lighting and to a lesser extent in the lighting of high-bay industrial interiors.

A comparison of mercury vapor, metal-halide, and high-pressure sodium lamps (Figure 8.18) indicates that all three of these high-intensity discharge lamps require a ballast to produce the high potential difference that is required to produce the initial discharge. While the lifespan of the metal-halide lamp is over 10 000 hours, it is less than half that of the other two lamps at more than twice the capital cost.

8.2.3 Fluorescent lamps

The fluorescent lamp basically utilizes a low-pressure mercury discharge. At the low operating pressure (i.e., approximately 0.00015 psi) more than 95 percent of the radiation emitted is outside the visible spectrum in the ultraviolet region (Figure 8.19). Some 25 percent of this ultraviolet radiation is reradiated into the visible range by a fluorescent powder (i.e., phosphor) coating on the inside of the enclosing tube.

The major difference between the light from a fluorescent lamp and from a high-pressure mercury lamp is that the former produces a continuous spectrum. Furthermore, the color-rendition properties of the fluorescent lamp

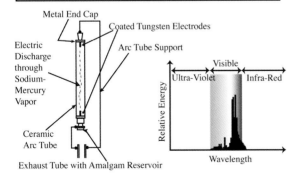

Figure 8.17 The high-pressure sodium lamp.

	Mercury Vapor	Metal Halide	High Pressure Sodium
Efficacy	25 to 50 lm/w	65 to 100 lm/w	40 to 140 lm/w
Lifespan	24 000 (+) hrs	10 000 (+) hrs	20 000 (+) hrs
Depreciation	10 to 15%	10 to 30%	10 to 15%
Cost (2004)*	$7.50/1000 lm	$12.50/1000 lm	$5.50/1000 lm
Color Temp.	3900K	3200 to 5000K	1900 to 2800K
Accessories	ballast	ballast	ballast
Wattages	40 to 1500 w (250–400 w most common)	175 to 1500 w	50 to 1000 w

*(Based on 100 watt lamp (approximate, 2004).)

Figure 8.18 Comparison of mercury vapor, metal-halide, and high-pressure sodium lamps.

In fluorescent lamps a low pressure mercury discharge produces mostly (i.e., 95%) ultra-violet radiation, which is partly (i.e., 25%) reradiated into the visible range through a phosphor coating on the inside of the tube.

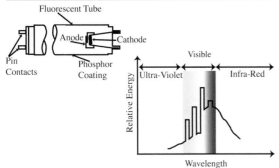

- The emitted radiation spectrum can be partly controlled by the consistency of the phosphor film.

- Commonly tubular, ranging in diameter from 5/8 inch (T5) to 2-1.8 inch (T-17), and up to 8 FT in length.

Figure 8.19 The fluorescent lamp.

Fluorescent Lamps are available in a wide range with varying color rendition properties.

Lamp Designation	Color of Emitted Light	Color Rendition Characteristics	
"Daylight"	blue-white	FAIR:	unflattering to skin and warm tones
"Cool White"	white with blue tint	GOOD:	blends with daylight
"Warm White"	yellow-white	FAIR:	blends well with light from filament lamps
"Soft White"	white with pink tint	GOOD:	enhances warm tones and flattering to skin
"Cool Deluxe"	white	EXCELLENT:	best color rendition available
"Warm Deluxe"	white	GOOD:	creates warm atmosphere and flattering to skin
"Natural White"	white with pink tint	EXCELLENT:	very good color rendition in warm atmosphere
"White"	white with yellow tint	FAIR:	may be used interchangeably with "warm white" or "cool white"

Figure 8.20 Color-rendition properties of fluorescent lamps.

can be partly controlled by the precise consistency of the phosphor film. This has resulted in a range of fluorescent lamps being commercially produced for different lighting purposes (Figure 8.20).

Since fluorescent lamps are discharge lamps, they require a ballast to provide a high starting voltage (i.e., potential difference) to initiate the discharge. The switch circuit is one of the simplest and most reliable circuits, even though it suffers from the disadvantage of a small time delay before starting. In the transformer circuit this disadvantage has been eliminated at a slightly increased cost.

Since the emission of short-wave radiation (i.e., ultraviolet) is related to the vapor pressure inside the lamp, which in turn is affected by the ambient temperature, it is understandable that the light output of a fluorescent lamp will vary with the surface temperature of the tube. A fall-off in light will occur in excessively hot (e.g., 20 percent at 140°F) or cold temperatures. In cold stores it is normal practice to enclose fluorescent tubes in larger acrylic casings for insulation purposes. Apart from this, ambient temperature will affect the starting condition, although a switch start circuit tends to overcome most of the problems. A more serious limitation of fluorescent lamps is the restricted wattage range commercially available (i.e., typically 40, 80, and 125 watt). Lower-wattage lamps tend to have reduced luminous efficiency, while 200 watt represents a practical upper limit at this stage of the technical development of fluorescent lamps.

In recent years, owing to an increasing need and desire for energy conservation, many incandescent lamps have been replaced with fluorescent lamps. This has been a relatively simple matter in the case of public and commercial office buildings where the length of fluorescent tubes did not present an obstacle for the background illumination provided by ceiling and cornice lighting. However, a similar replacement of incandescent lamps in desk lamps had to wait for the development of compact fluorescent lamps. In these lamps the traditional long tube has been literally folded into an assembly of multiple smaller diameter short tubes that can readily fit into a normal incandescent light fixture.

Figure 8.21 clearly shows the superior performance of both types of fluorescent lamps

	Incandescent Lamp	Fluorescent Tubular	Fluorescent Compact
Efficacy	17 to 38 lm/w	40 to 90 lm/w	26 to 61 lm/w
Lifespan	1000 to 2000 hrs	13 000 hrs	10 000 hrs
Depreciation	10 to 20%	10 to 15%	10 to 15%
Cost (2004)*	$2.00/1000 lm	$1.50/1000 lm	$11.00/1000 lm
Color Temp.	2100 to 3300K	2500 to 7500K	2700 to 5000K
Accessories	none	ballast	ballast
Wattages	wide range	limited	limited
*(Based on 100 watt lamp (approximate, 2004).)			

Figure 8.21 Comparison of incandescent and fluorescent lamps.

Chemoluminescence can be produced by the interaction of certain chemicals without the presence of electricity. Used mostly in flares. Also available as a glass vial in a plastic tube that provides a light green glow for about three hours when the tube is bent to break the vial.

Electroluminescence produces light when phosphor is excited directly by pulsating electromagnetic field. Electroluminescent lamps are available as thin sheets on flexible or rigid backings. They provide very little light, but have a high efficacy and long life span.

sealant   electrode
reflecting layer
dielectric film
transparent contact
glass

Fiber Optic Bundles are capable of transmitting light. Each strand is surrounded by a coating of transparent material with a reflective index lower than the fiber core, to prevent light leakage. The fibers conduct light by a process of internal reflection.

Figure 8.22 Other potential light sources.

over the incandescent lamp in respect to efficacy and lifespan. The only advantages of the incandescent lamp are its simplified operating environment (i.e., neither a ballast nor any special electrical circuit is required) and its very wide range of wattages. However, the initial acquisition cost of the compact fluorescent lamp is still more than five times the cost of an incandescent lamp, and almost eight times the cost of an equivalent fluorescent tube.

8.2.4 Other light sources

Although light sources based on the discharge principle are likely to retain their dominant position in the marketplace for some time to come, there are other sources of light with varying application potential (Figure 8.22).

Foremost among these are electroluminescent lamps. While fluorescent lamps produce light indirectly through the excitation of phosphors, electroluminescent sources produce light directly from electrical energy produced by an applied voltage. Although present applications of electroluminescent lamps in the form of

Light-Emitting Diodes (LED) are still limited, they show great promise for the future in terms of lifespan (over 40 000 hours) and efficacies in the vicinity of 100 lm/W (see Chapter 12, Section 12.5.4).

Neon lamps, which are used extensively in advertising, consist of an evacuated glass tube filled with ionized neon gas. By means of a transformer capable of increasing the normal 115-volt input voltage to around 8000 volts, an electric current is passed through the ionized gas in the tube. The essentially red light produced in this manner may be changed in several ways: by varying the gas pressure; by mixing the neon gas with helium; or by using colored glass tubing. The efficiency of the neon lamp is rather low, in the region of 5 lm/W.

Will industry be able to make more headway in harnessing the light produced by chemical reactions? Currently the exploitation of chemoluminescence is limited to flares and glass vials in plastic tubes that provide a green glow for a few hours when the tube is bent to break the vial.

Fiber-optic bundles are capable of transmitting light with a somewhat limited efficiency by a process of internal reflection. This would potentially allow the transmission of direct sunlight or perhaps some high-intensity artificial light source (e.g., laser light) to be transmitted through ducts into building spaces. Some assemblies of this type that transmit direct sunlight into windowless interior spaces have been commercially available for several years. However, to date they have not found widespread application.

Color adaptation, although not as prominent a factor in lighting design as the adaptation to brightness, is nevertheless a condition that needs to be taken into account in the design of artificial lighting installations. Specifically, there are two factors to consider:

Different kinds of artificial light source may vary widely in respect to their color-rendition characteristics. For example, the low-pressure sodium lamp reduces all colors to shades of gray-brown; the mercury vapor lamp will overemphasize yellow and convert red to brown; while the incandescent lamp will brighten yellow, orange, and red and therefore tend to dull blue and green.

The perception of color is very much related to the background color and luminance. For example, if an entire wall is covered with a particular color, the eye will adapt and the color will seem less saturated. A pink carpet in a room with pink walls will be less prominent, or perhaps less offensive, than if the walls have been painted white or cream.

Although the human eye will make a considerable effort to adapt to the color-rendition characteristics of a particular artificial light source, it cannot compensate for serious deficiencies in the radiated spectrum. Accordingly, the success of an artificial lighting installation may be gauged in part at least by its ability to provide satisfactory perception of the surface colors in the space. One practical lesson to be learned from this is that any color scheme for a building space should be chosen under the light source by which it will normally be seen, and, if possible, under the same background conditions.

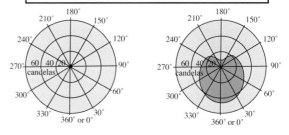

Polar diagrams provide a convenient graphical representation of the luminous intensity of a light source or luminaire.

- Provides a quantitative measure of the luminous intensity in any direction in one plane.

- Provides qualitative information about the characteristics of a luminaire.

- Does not show us whether one luminaire produces more light than another.

Figure 8.23   Polar diagrams.

8.3   Functions of the luminaire

Since light travels in straight lines, it is possible to specify light distribution in terms of intensity and direction alone. Polar diagrams provide a means of presenting graphically, in terms of polar coordinates, the luminous intensity distribution of a given light source or luminaire.

As shown in Figure 8.23, the luminaire is considered to be at the point of intersection of radial lines normally representing directions in the vertical plane. Concentric circles provide a scale of luminous intensity expressed in candelas.

On this grid of intersecting radial lines and concentric circles the luminous intensities of a particular luminaire are plotted in each direction. The resultant polar curve represents the intensity distribution in the plane under consideration. If the distribution is symmetrical about a vertical axis, as is the case with incandescent installations, one diagram will be representative of the distribution in all vertical planes. In the case of fluorescent luminaires the polar diagrams in other planes will be required for full information, although often one average curve will suffice.

The information that can be obtained from a polar diagram is twofold. First, it provides numerical values of the luminous intensity in any direction on one plane. Second, it provides much qualitative information about the properties of a luminaire. By viewing a polar diagram we can differentiate at a glance between various types of luminaires such as direct, indirect, and so on. However, we cannot determine from the polar diagram whether one luminaire produces more light flux (i.e., lumen) than another, because the flux emitted in a given direction is not directly proportional to the intensity in that direction. Accordingly, the area enclosed by a particular polar curve does not provide any indication of the amount of luminous flux emitted by that light source. It simply indicates the distribution of the light emitted.

As discussed previously in Section 8.1, a luminaire is defined as a complete, fixed or portable lighting unit including one or more lamps and any associated equipment required for its operation. However, it does not include any permanent parts of a building such as a ceiling or structural element. There are basically three functions that a luminaire must perform:

- It must support and possibly protect the lamp. In the case of some artificial light sources, such as for example metal-halide lamps (Figure 8.15), the luminaire must hold the lamp in a particular operating position.
- It must control the distribution of light from the lamp by directing the light flux where it is required.
- It must provide some form of control over the luminance of the source in order to prevent glare. This control may be in the form of shielding or diffusion.

Since glare is caused mainly by the existence of a direct line of vision between the observer and a source of high luminance, it is normal practice to restrict or limit luminance in the immediate visual field. For this reason artificial lighting codes will prescribe shielding angles and a

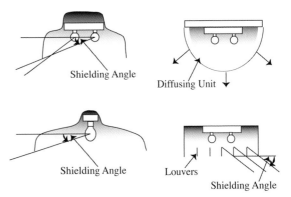

The two principal functions of a luminaire are to distribute the light emitted by a lamp and to shield the light source from the line of sight of the viewer.

Shielding Angle

Diffusing Unit

Shielding Angle

Louvers

Shielding Angle

Figure 8.24 **Shielding the eyes.**

maximum luminance. While for most industrial installations it will be possible to provide adequate shielding by means of metal troughs, in the case of fluorescent units containing more than one tube, troughs would need to be excessively deep and therefore louvers are used. In the latter case the calculation of the shielding angle is based solely on the geometry of the louver grid (Figure 8.24).

The addition of louvers will naturally tend to constrict the light distribution, resulting in the need for closer spacing of luminaires generally. Sometimes the louver blades themselves will constitute a source of glare. This may be due to over-brightness of the source, or a high reflectance blade finish, or both. In either of these cases it is normally sufficient to darken or otherwise reduce the reflectance of the louver blades.

A wide variety of luminaires are commercially available for the lighting designer to choose from (Figure 8.28). They are essentially distinguished by the proportion of light that they direct downward to the work plane and upward to the ceiling. The greater the proportion of light aimed upward and then reflected downward by the ceiling, the more diffuse the lighting environment will be. If most of the light

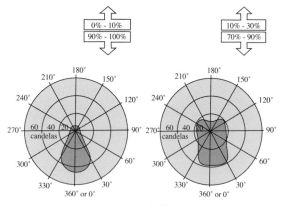

Figure 8.25   Direct and semi-direct luminaires.

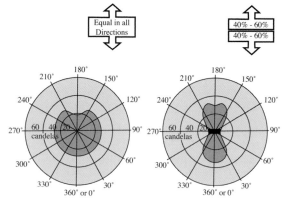

Figure 8.26   Diffuse and direct–indirect luminaires.

is directed downward, then shadows will be distinct, accentuating the three-dimensional nature of the objects in the building space.

Direct luminaire: Practically all of the light is directed downward, resulting in a low vertical surface illumination (Figure 8.25).

Direct luminaires are normally used for individually controlled task lighting, in combination with a general background lighting system.

Semi-Direct luminaire: Similar to the direct–indirect system, although the ceiling light component is small. Therefore the room will lack diffuseness, possibly resulting in annoying shadows if the number of fixtures per ceiling area is small (Figure 8.25).

Diffuse luminaire: The diffuse system provides light approximately equally in all directions (Figure 8.26). The distance between the luminaire and the ceiling should be sufficient to avoid excessive ceiling brightness.

Direct–Indirect luminaire: Provides approximately equal distribution of light upward and downward (Figure 8.26).

Can be a very successful lighting system, owing to the fact that it provides a bright ceiling and yet provides up to 50 percent direct lighting. Accordingly, there is little likelihood of any problems arising due to brightness differences between the background and the task area.

Semi-Indirect luminaire: Similar to the indirect system, except that the shade is translucent, thus allowing about one-third of the light to fall directly into the room (Figure 8.27). Nevertheless, the ceiling remains the main radiating source.

Indirect luminaire: Nearly all the light output is directed to the ceiling and upper walls of the room (Figure 8.27). The ceiling and upper wall sections in effect become a secondary light source, and if these surfaces have similar reflections, then the room illumination will be diffuse and devoid of shadows.

When recessed luminaires are used the ceiling will receive reflected light only, and will therefore tend to be the darkest part of the room. The resultant brightness ratio between the luminaire and ceiling is likely to be high and therefore unsatisfactory in any but the smallest rooms, where the general illumination level is expected to be high if the wall and ceiling sur-

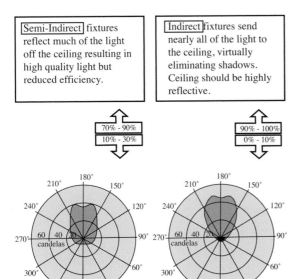

Semi-Indirect fixtures reflect much of the light off the ceiling resulting in high quality light but reduced efficiency.

70% - 90%
10% - 30%

Indirect fixtures send nearly all of the light to the ceiling, virtually eliminating shadows. Ceiling should be highly reflective.

90% - 100%
0% - 10%

Figure 8.27 Semi-indirect and indirect luminaires.

Luminaire Classification	Typical Distribution		Luminaire Features and Application
	Upward	Downward	
DIRECT	0%	100%	Closed top metal reflector or recessed trough for task lighting.
SEMI-DIRECT	20%	80%	Metal reflector with large slots at the top or diffuser type fluorescent fixtures.
DIFFUSE	Equal in all directions		Opal glass enclosed diffuser for incandescent lamps.
DIRECT-INDIRECT	50%	50%	Opaque cylindrical shade with open ends.
SEMI-INDIRECT	80%	20%	Incandescent and fluorescent units with open top and diffuse underside.
INDIRECT	100%	0%	Coves and cornices or suspended fixtures with open tops and closed undersides.

Figure 8.28 Comparative analysis of luminaires.

faces are light-colored. To achieve a comfortable brightness balance in building interiors it is common practice to limit brightness ratios between areas of unequal illumination level. As discussed previously in Section 6.6, maximum brightness ratios are suggested as follows:

Ratio of task to surround	3:1
Ratio of task to remote background	5:1
Ratio of luminaire to surround	15:1
Maximum brightness ratio anywhere	35:1

It is therefore implied that an artificially lit interior will incorporate either general or local lighting, or more often than not both of those. General lighting schemes are designed to provide uniform illumination (often of a diffuse nature) over a hypothetical horizontal plane extending throughout the entire space. This may be achieved by a pattern of ceiling fittings or a continuous luminous ceiling. Local lighting, on the other hand, is intended to provide high levels of illumination over relatively small areas, such as workbenches and machinery. Luminaires for local lighting are best located immediately above the work plane with the light directed to the task area.

8.4 Light fixtures

Apart from the boundless variety of commercially available, mostly stand-alone luminaires (Figure 8.28) that are either directly connected to the electrical wiring of the building and operated through a remote switch (e.g., a ceiling-mounted diffuse luminaire), or fitted with an electrical cord that can be conveniently plugged into an electrical receptacle (e.g., a desk lamp), there are a number of more or less built-in light fixtures. These fixtures typically form part of the building itself and are normally neither portable nor removable without at least some minor form of renovation or reconstruction.

Coves are normally located along part or the entire length of a wall, just under the ceiling, as shown in the top section of Figure 8.29. Since virtually all of the light that they produce is reflected from the ceiling, the quality of light will be diffuse and the brighter ceiling will endow the room with a feeling of spaciousness.

Coffers are typically recessed into the ceiling (mid section of Figure 8.29), and could be categorized as artificial skylights.

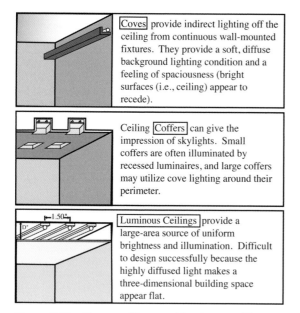

Figure 8.29   Coves, coffers, and luminous ceilings.

Coves provide indirect lighting off the ceiling from continuous wall-mounted fixtures. They provide a soft, diffuse background lighting condition and a feeling of spaciousness (bright surfaces (i.e., ceiling) appear to recede).

Ceiling Coffers can give the impression of skylights. Small coffers are often illuminated by recessed luminaires, and large coffers may utilize cove lighting around their perimeter.

Luminous Ceilings provide a large-area source of uniform brightness and illumination. Difficult to design successfully because the highly diffused light makes a three-dimensional building space appear flat.

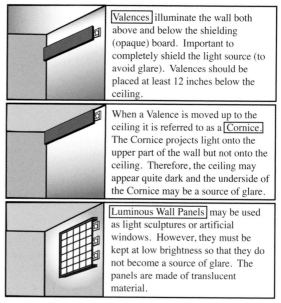

Figure 8.30   Valences, cornices, and luminous wall panels.

Valences illuminate the wall both above and below the shielding (opaque) board. Important to completely shield the light source (to avoid glare). Valences should be placed at least 12 inches below the ceiling.

When a Valence is moved up to the ceiling it is referred to as a Cornice. The Cornice projects light onto the upper part of the wall but not onto the ceiling. Therefore, the ceiling may appear quite dark and the underside of the Cornice may be a source of glare.

Luminous Wall Panels may be used as light sculptures or artificial windows. However, they must be kept at low brightness so that they do not become a source of glare. The panels are made of translucent material.

However, because of the limitations of artificial light sources the light produced is of course far less intense than a normal skylight, particularly under clear sky conditions. Therefore, whereas a single skylight is usually sufficient to light an entire room during daytime hours, several coffers would be required to provide adequate light during nighttime.

Luminous Ceilings (bottom section of Figure 8.29) have become less popular in recent times, owing to the need for energy conservation. Also, the diffuse nature of the light produced by a luminous ceiling tends to create a somewhat drab environment that is devoid of shadows unless other directional sources of light are added.

Valences are similar to coves, but with one major difference. Like coves they normally run along the entire length of a wall; however, they are located a foot or two below the ceiling and open both at the top and at the bottom (top section of Figure 8.30). This means that they are able to reflect light both from the ceiling and the upper part of the wall. While the resultant light distribution is still quite diffuse, the reflecting surfaces extend from the ceiling to the upper portions of the wall(s), thereby accentuating to a greater degree than coves the three-dimensional character of the room.

Cornices are formed by moving a valence board directly to the ceiling, as shown in the mid section of Figure 8.30. As a result, reflected light is received only from the upper portions of the wall(s). With the ceiling more or less in darkness cornice lighting can produce an intimate environment that might be suitable for a restaurant or, in combination with direct-indirect luminaires, for a lounge or waiting area (e.g., in a health facility).

Luminous Wall Panels are sometimes used in windowless spaces to provide an impression of window light (bottom section of Figure 8.30). Care must be taken to avoid glare conditions by keeping the brightness of the wall panel low. This is particularly important because a luminous wall panel is in the direct line of sight of the occupants of the space.

8.5 The lumen method of lighting design

The lumen method of artificial lighting design provides a means of calculating the average illumination on a horizontal plane over the whole interior from a known lighting installation or, alternatively, the number and wattage of lamps required to provide a specified level of average illumination. In either case, the direct and reflected components of light are taken into account for the particular room dimensions, reflectance, and type of luminaire. Calculations are very much simplified by the use of tables, and the method is in general applied to lighting installations employing approximately, symmetrically disposed overhead lighting units.

Fundamental to the lumen method of design is the concept of Coefficient of Utilization (CU), which is defined as:

CU = [total flux on work plane (F_P)] / [total

flux emitted by lamps (F_L)]   [8.2]

Normally, only a portion of the flux emitted by the lamps reaches the work plane, and therefore the Coefficient of Utilization is always less than unity. Light flux is lost by obstructions and absorption due to walls and ceiling.

The numerical value of the Coefficient of Utilization for any particular lighting installation will depend on the following factors (Figure 8.31):

Type and efficiency of the luminaire: The more light flux that is directed to the work plane, the higher will be the value of the Coefficient of Utilization.

Reflectivity of room surfaces: The reflectivity of finishes is expressed in terms of a percentage reflection factor.

Mounting height of luminaire: The proportion of flux absorbed by the walls will depend mostly on the mounting height and the room dimensions. Increases in mounting height will tend to decrease the coefficient of utilization.

Based on the concept of Coefficient of Utilization (CU) the Lumen Method provides a means of calculating the number and wattage of lamps required to produce a specified level of average illumination.

$$\text{Coefficient of Utilization (CU)} = \frac{\left[\begin{array}{c}\text{total flux on work plane} \\ (F_P)\end{array}\right]}{\left[\begin{array}{c}\text{total flux emitted} \\ \text{by lamps } (F_L)\end{array}\right]}$$

Due to obstructions and light absorption by walls and ceiling the CU is always less than unity. The actual value of the CU depends on:

● Type and efficiency of luminaires.

● Reflectivity of room surfaces.

● Mounting height of luminaires.

Figure 8.31 Coefficient of utilization (CU).

Tables of Coefficients of Utilization (CU) normally take into account the type of luminaire, the reflectivity of the room surfaces, the mounting height, and the room dimensions. Both mounting height (H FT) and room proportions (i.e., room length (L FT) and room width (W FT)) are embraced by the concept of Room Index (RI), in the following manner (Figure 8.32):

$$\text{RI} = \frac{[(\text{room length}) \times (\text{room width})]}{[(\text{mounting height above work plane}) \times (\text{room length} + \text{room width})]}$$

[8.3]

Having obtained the Room Index, the Coefficient of Utilization is obtained from tables (such as Table 8.1) for the appropriate type of luminaire and room surface-reflection factors. To look up the Coefficient of Utilization in Table 8.1, we find the appropriate luminaire with the closest Light Output Ratio (LOR) in the left column. The corresponding CU value is given by the correct combination of the Room Index value and the ceiling and wall reflectances.

The CU value is dependent on: type of luminaire; room surface reflectivities; and, the Room Index (RI):

$$RI = \frac{[\text{room length (FT)}] \times [\text{room width (FT)}]}{\left[\begin{array}{c}\text{mounting height}\\\text{above workplane (FT)}\end{array}\right] \times \left(\left[\begin{array}{c}\text{room}\\\text{length}\end{array}\right] + \left[\begin{array}{c}\text{room}\\\text{width}\end{array}\right]\right)}$$

$$CU = F_P / F_L$$

where: F_P = [workplane illum. (E)] x [workplane area (A)]

therefore: $E = F_P / A$ (fc)

and: F_L = [number of lamps (N)] x [flux of lamps (f_L)]

therefore: $N = F_L / f_L$

$$\text{Illumination on workplane (E)} = \frac{CU \times N \times f_L}{A} \times \left[\begin{array}{c}\text{maintenance}\\\text{factor}\end{array}\right] \text{ fc}$$

$$\text{Number of lamps (N)} = \frac{E \times A}{CU \times f_L} \times \frac{1}{\left[\begin{array}{c}\text{maintenance}\\\text{factor}\end{array}\right]}$$

Figure 8.32   Room index (RI).

The numerical value of the Coefficient of Utilization is then applied as follows:

CU = [total flux on work plane (F_P)] / [total flux emitted by lamps (F_L)]   [8.2]

F_P = [illumination on work plane (E)] × [area of work plane (A)]   [8.4]

F_L = [number of lamps (N)] × [flux emittedby one lamp (F_L)]   [8.5]

Combining equations [8.2], [8.4], and [8.5] and incorporating a maintenance factor (M), we obtain:

E = [CU × N × F_L × M] / A (lm/SF or fc)   [8.6]

Alternatively, if the illumination on the work plane (E) is specified, equation [8.6] may be rewritten in terms of the number of lamps (N) required, as follows:

N = [E × A] / [CU × F_L × M]   [8.7]

An example of the application of equation [8.6] is shown in Figures 8.33 and 8.34.

As a second example, we will calculate the average illumination level on a 3FT high work plane, which would be obtained from 24 twin 40W fluorescent lamps each emitting 2600 lm of light flux and ceiling mounted in 24 louvered luminaires. The room has dimensions of 60FT long (L), 25FT wide (W), and 9FT high (H), with light-colored walls and ceiling. We will assume a maintenance factor (M) of 0.8.

Step 1: Calculate the Room Index (RI) according to equation (8.3):

RI = L × W / H (L + W)

RI = $[60 \times 25] / [(9-3) \times (60+25)] = 3$ (approx.)

Step 2: Find the coefficient of utilization (CU) from Table 8.1, if the reflection factors for the ceiling and walls are 70% and 30%, respectively.

CU = 0.45 (approx.)

Step 3: Calculate the average illumination level on the work plane (E) if the flux per single lamp is 2600 lm and the maintenance factor (M) is 0.8, using equation [8.6]:

E = [CU × N × F_L × M] / A (lm/SF or fc)

E = $[0.45 \times (24 \times 2) \times 2600 \times 0.8] / (60 \times 25)$ lm/SF or fc

E = 30 lm/SF or fc

Two separate examples of the reverse calculation are shown in Figures 8.35 and 8.36, and below. In the case of the example (below) we will determine the number of triple 40W tubular fluorescent lamps required to provide an average illumination (E) of 25 fc at desk level in an architectural drawing office 40FT long (L), 20FT wide (W) and 10FT high (H). A suspended pan-shaped fitting will be used, partly open-top and louvered beneath. Assume the reflection factor of the ceiling to be 50 percent and of the walls 10 percent. The light flux produced by a single lamp is 2600 lm and the maintenance factor (M) is 0.85.

Table 8.1 Typical coefficient of utilization table.

Description of fitting, and typical downward light output ratio (%)	Basic downward LOR (%)	Reflection factor (%)						
		Ceiling	70		50		30		0
		Walls	50	10	50	10	50	10	0
		Room index	Coefficient of utilization						
250 W reflectorized mercury lamp (100). (fitting for color-corrected mercury lamp)	100	0.6	0.54	0.44	0.53	0.44	0.52	0.44	0.43
		0.8	0.65	0.55	0.64	0.55	0.63	0.55	0.54
		1.0	0.71	0.60	0.70	0.60	0.68	0.60	0.59
		1.25	0.77	0.64	0.76	0.66	0.76	0.66	0.65
		1.5	0.82	0.72	0.81	0.71	0.80	0.71	0.70
		2.0	0.90	0.80	0.87	0.79	0.86	0.78	0.76
		2.5	0.93	0.84	0.90	0.83	0.90	0.82	0.80
		3.0	0.96	0.88	0.93	0.87	0.92	0.85	0.83
		4.0	0.98	0.92	0.96	0.91	0.94	0.89	0.87
		5.0	1.00	0.96	0.99	0.94	0.96	0.92	0.90
Enamel slotted trough, louvred (45–55) Shallow ceiling-mounted louvre panel (40–50)… Louvred recessed (module) fitting (40–50)… (fittings for fluorescent lamps)	50	0.6	0.27	0.22	0.26	0.22	0.26	0.22	0.20
		0.8	0.32	0.27	0.32	0.27	0.31	0.27	0.25
		1.0	0.35	0.30	0.35	0.30	0.34	0.30	0.29
		1.25	0.38	0.32	0.38	0.33	0.38	0.33	0.32
		1.5	0.41	0.36	0.40	0.35	0.40	0.35	0.34
		2.0	0.45	0.40	0.43	0.39	0.43	0.39	0.38
		2.5	0.47	0.42	0.45	0.41	0.45	0.41	0.40
		3.0	0.48	0.44	0.46	0.43	0.46	0.42	0.41
		4.0	0.49	0.46	0.48	0.45	0.47	0.44	0.43
		5.0	0.50	0.48	0.49	0.47	0.48	0.46	0.45
Suspended pan-shaped fitting, partly open top, louvred beneath (50) … (fitting for fluorescent lamp)	50	0.6	0.32	0.24	0.30	0.24	0.29	0.23	0.21
		0.8	0.39	0.31	0.36	0.29	0.35	0.29	0.27
		1.0	0.43	0.35	0.40	0.34	0.38	0.32	0.30
		1.25	0.47	0.39	0.44	0.38	0.42	0.35	0.32
		1.5	0.51	0.43	0.47	0.41	0.44	0.38	0.35
		2.0	0.56	0.49	0.51	0.46	0.47	0.42	0.38
		2.5	0.58	0.52	0.53	0.49	0.49	0.44	0.40
		3.0	0.60	0.55	0.55	0.51	0.51	0.46	0.41
		4.0	0.63	0.58	0.57	0.54	0.52	0.48	0.43
		5.0	0.64	0.60	0.59	0.56	0.53	0.50	0.45
Open-end enamel trough (75–85) … Closed-end enamel trough (56–83) … Standard dispersive Industrial Reflector (77) (fitting for filament or fluorescent lamps)		0.6	0.36	0.28	0.35	0.28	0.35	0.28	0.27
		0.8	0.45	0.37	0.44	0.37	0.44	0.37	0.36
		1.0	0.49	0.40	0.49	0.40	0.48	0.40	0.39
		1.25	0.55	0.46	0.53	0.45	0.52	0.45	0.43
		1.5	0.58	0.49	0.57	0.49	0.55	0.49	0.48
		2.0	0.64	0.55	0.61	0.55	0.60	0.54	0.52
		2.5	0.68	0.60	0.65	0.59	0.64	0.58	0.56
		3.0	0.70	0.62	0.67	0.61	0.65	0.61	0.59
		4.0	0.73	0.67	0.70	0.65	0.67	0.64	0.62
		5.0	0.75	0.69	0.73	0.67	0.70	0.67	0.65

What is the average illumination level on a 3 FT high workplane in a 30 FT by 25 FT room with an 8 FT ceiling height and 12 twin ceiling mounted 40 watt fluorescent lamps, each emitting 2600 lumens? Assume a maintenance factor of 0.8 and light colored surfaces.

RI = Room Index   L = length of room (FT)
W = width of room (FT)   N = number of lamps
H = mounting height above work plane (FT)
CU= Coefficient of Utilization f_L = flux per single lamp (lm)
A = area of work plane (SF)   M = maintenance factor
E = illumination level on work plane (fc)

- Step A: Calculate the Room Index (RI):

$$RI = \frac{L \times W}{H(L+W)} = \frac{30 \times 25}{(8-3) \times (30+25)} = 2.7$$

- Step B: From tables the CU for ceiling and wall reflection factors of 70% and 50%, respectively is found to be 0.47.

- Step C: Calculate the illumination level (E fc):

$$E = \frac{CU \times N \times f_L \times M}{A} = \frac{0.47 \times (12 \times 2) \times 2600 \times 0.8}{(30 \times 25)} = 31 \ fc$$

Figure 8.33   Calculation of the average illumination level (E Lm/SF or Fc).

How many twin 40 watt fluorescent lamps are required to provide an average illumination level of 20 fc at desk height in an office 40 FT by 20 FT and 9 FT high? Ceiling mounted louvered luminaires and ceiling and wall reflectances of 50% and 50%, respectively, are assumed.

RI = Room Index   L = length of room (FT)
W = width of room (FT)   N = number of lamps
H = mounting height above work plane (FT)
CU= Coefficient of Utilization f_L = flux per single lamp (lm)
A = area of work plane (SF)   M = maintenance factor
E = illumination level on work plane (fc)

- Step A: Calculate the Room Index (RI):

$$RI = \frac{L \times W}{H(L+W)} = \frac{40 \times 20}{(9-3) \times (40+20)} = 2.2$$

- Step B: From tables the CU for ceiling and wall reflection factors of 50% and 50%, respectively is found to be 0.43.

- Step C: Calculate the number of lamps assuming 2600 lm per lamp and a maintenance factor of 0.9:

$$N = \frac{E \times A}{CU \times f_L \times M} = \frac{20 \times 40 \times 20}{0.43 \times (2600 \times 2) \times 0.9} = 8$$

Figure 8.35   Number of lamps required for a given illumination level.

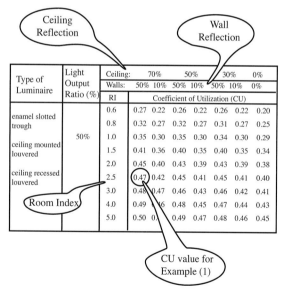

Figure 8.34   Looking up the CU value for the example shown in Figure 8.33.

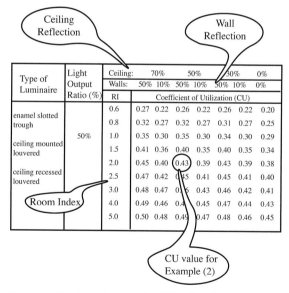

Figure 8.36   Looking up the CU value for the example shown in Figure 8.35.

Step 1: Calculate the Room Index (RI) according to equation [8.3]:

$$RI = L \times W / H(L+W)$$
$$RI = [40 \times 20]/[(10-3)\times(40+20)]$$
$$= 1.9 \ (approx.)$$

Step 2: Find the coefficient of utilization (CU) in Table 8.1 if the reflection factors for the ceiling and walls are 50% and 10%, respectively.

$$CU = 0.46 \ (approx.)$$

Step 3: Given that the flux (E) per single lamp is 2600 lm and incorporating a maintenance factor (M) of 0.85, find the number of triple 40W units required. Apply equation [8.7]:

$$N = [E \times A] / [CU \times F_L \times M]$$

$$N = [25 \times (40 \times 20) / [0.46 \times 2600 \times 0.85]$$

$$N = 20 \text{ single lamps (or 7 triple 40W units)}$$

8.6 The room cavity ratio

Some state and national building energy standards, such as California Title 24, utilize the concept of Room Cavity Ratio (RCR) as a metric for determining the allowable artificial lighting load in building spaces. Typically, a floor plan is divided into *areas*, then the RCR is calculated for each *area*, and finally either the maximum allowable wattage per square foot (W/SF), or the illumination level in lumen per square foot (lm/SF) or footcandles (fc), is provided from a table.

An *area* is normally defined in terms of its perimeter enclosure. – for example, any space with 75 percent or more of its perimeter defined by either solid or transparent floor-to-ceiling partitions or walls. The RCR of such an *area* is then calculated with equation [8.8]:

$$RCR = \frac{5\,[(\text{light fixture height above task surface}) \times (\text{area length} + \text{area width})]}{[(\text{area length}) \times (\text{area width})]}$$

[8.8]

Maximum wattage (or illumination) allowances will be higher for larger RCR values. For example, the allowable wattage for the spray-booth *area* of an aircraft manufacturing plant may be 2.4 W/SF if the RCR is less or equal to 5, and 3.4 W/SF if the RCR is greater than 5.

8.7 The PSALI concept

The Permanent Supplementary Artificial Lighting of Interiors (PSALI) concept was developed in England in the 1950s for the purpose of sup-plementing daylight with artificial light in those building spaces where the daylight level is inadequate. Particularly, in the case of multi-story buildings there is a tendency for ceiling heights to be low and rooms to be deep, so that the maximum number of floors can be accommodated within a minimum building height. Moreover, large windows are likely to lead to conditions of sky-glare and excessive heat transfer.

At the time, and this was well before energy became scarce and prohibitively expensive, it was argued on purely economic grounds that there were benefits to be found in omitting windows altogether. However, even though a number of fairly successful windowless buildings were built, the counterargument – that windows are a significant factor in contributing to the physical and psychological well-being of the building occupants – generally prevailed.

The underlying research into the optimum means of integrating natural and artificial light was conducted by the British Research Establishment. One of the basic assumptions of the PSALI concept that grew out of this research is the notion that daylight should remain the dominant feature of a building interior, unless the particular occupancy specifically requires the exclusion of daylight (e.g., some museums and certain medical facilities). Accordingly, PSALI systems are designed on the principle that artificial lighting should provide adequate illumination levels where natural light is inadequate and should mitigate the appearance of gloom in those parts of a building space that are remote from external windows.

As a rule of thumb, the artificial lighting level (E_{PSALI}) that is required in support of a PSALI installation may be related to the average value of the Daylight Factor ($DF_{average}$) in the room under consideration, as follows:[3]

$$E_{PSALI} = [\pi \times DF_{average} \times (\text{external illumination level})] / 10 \text{ (lm/SF or fc)}$$

[8.9]

It is suggested that the section of the room where this PSALI lighting is required may be confined to the area where the Daylight Factor is 20 percent or less of that near the window.

Unfortunately, the above relationship cannot be applied universally. In regions where clear skies are predominant the sky luminance will differ markedly with orientation, while the overall luminance range is normally very wide. For example, the range between an overcast and bright sky in England is from about 500 fL to 4000 fL, while in parts of California the range is likely to extend from 800 fL to 8000 fL. It is therefore apparent that PSALI installations will tend to be very expensive in terms of energy usage and therefore uneconomical in regions where bright skies are a normal occurrence.

Light fittings for PSALI installations are very often of the laylight[4] type, louvered to avoid glare, and some 4FT wide, running along the length of the room with the back edge about 3FT from the inner wall. It has been suggested that the luminance of such laylights should not exceed 200 fL, so as to avoid discomfort glare conditions.

Since the artificial illumination level of a PSALI installation will invariably be higher during the day than at night, it follows that the level of lighting should be reduced as the daylight fades. This may be achieved by either providing two separate installations, or by providing some means of switching out a percentage of the total light sources as necessary. It is also important to consider the color-rendition properties of the artificial light sources. The PSALI installation should provide light near to the color of daylight, while the nighttime light should preferably be of a warmer color. In fact, it is generally recognized that the lower the level of illumination, the warmer the color of the artificial light source should be.

Endnotes

1. It is of interest to note that one *watt* of power is equivalent to about 3 BTU of heat in the American system of units.
2. t should also be noted that the operating temperature of a lamp is measured in °F or °C, while its color temperature is measured in K.
3. In the original form of equation [8.9] the PSALI illumination level is calculated as a function of the *sky luminance* (measured in foot Lambert (fL) or candela/SF) and not the *external illumination level* as shown above. However, for a luminous hemisphere the illumination level at the center of the hemisphere is numerically equal to the luminance of the hemisphere.
4. A laylight may be described as a large area light source recessed into the ceiling.

9 The Nature of Sound

Noise is fast becoming one of the more serious pollutants of our environment. At the same time, controlled sound is one of the most important means of communication, as well as providing a medium for enjoyment, relaxation, and emotional fulfillment.

In recent years, the level of sensitivity of the average building user has greatly increased, so that both the control of unwanted sound (or noise) and the enhancement of speech and music have become important objectives in building design. Unfortunately, the line between noise and desirable sound cannot always be clearly defined. A sound such as might be produced by a new motor-bike can be at the same time ecstasy to its teenage owner and most objectionable to his next-door neighbor. The acoustical design of a building cannot therefore be based wholly on the objective measurement of sound, but is also greatly influenced by the mental state and expectations of its occupants.

9.1 What is sound?

Sound is the result of vibrations caused by a source that emits pressure fluctuations on a spherical front. The form of the vibrations is cyclic, with a compression and a rarefaction completing one cycle (Figure 9.1). Furthermore, these vibrations are in the form of longitudinal waves and will therefore require some type of medium (i.e., solid, liquid, or gas) to travel through.

For example, let us consider the sound generated by the vibration of a guitar string. There will be a region of relative compression where the wave front or vibration is carried onto neighboring particles, followed by a rarefaction in the same region as the particles return to their former equilibrium positions. Accordingly, sound waves are propagated not by the mass movement of the medium, but by the progressive, elastic vibration of the particles of the medium about their mean positions. The particles themselves oscillate about their normal positions (Figure 9.2), setting other particles into similar oscillating motion as they collide with their neighbors.

This kind of oscillating motion is very similar to the motion of a pendulum and is referred to in physics as Simple Harmonic Motion.

As shown in Figure 9.3, the distance between two adjacent centers of compression (or centers of rarefaction) is defined as the wavelength (λ FT), while the rate at which the vibrations occur is called the frequency (f cycles per second (cps) or hertz). The wavelength and frequency of sound are related, so that high-frequency sounds have a short wavelength and low-frequency sounds have a long wavelength. The frequency range to which the human ear responds is about 30 cps to 20 000 cps, corresponding to wavelengths in the vicinity of 37 FT to 0.02 FT or ¼ IN, respectively.

The velocity of sound in a medium is directly proportional to the modulus of elasticity for solid materials or the bulk modulus for liquids and gases, and inversely proportional to the density of the medium. Therefore, the velocity

Building Science: Concepts and Application. Jens Pohl.
© 2011 John Wiley & Sons, Ltd.
Published 2011 by John Wiley & Sons, Ltd.

Sound is a physical force in the form of a vibration produced by a source that emits pressure fluctuations.

- Sound vibrations move through a medium as longitudinal waves without the mass movement of the medium.

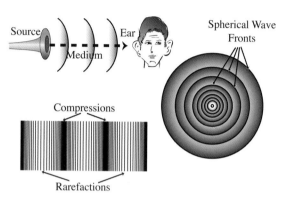

- Sound waves are propagated by the progressive elastic vibration of the particles of the medium about their mean positions (i.e., in Simple Harmonic Motion).

Figure 9.1   Sound as wave motion.

The distance between two adjacent centers of compression or rarefactions is the | wavelength | of a sound.

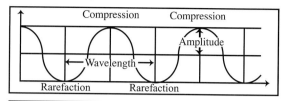

The velocity of sound in a medium is directly proportional to the modulus of elasticity (or bulk modulus for liquids and gases) and inversely proportional to the density of the medium.

Medium Type	Mod. of Elasticity	Density	Velocity of Sound
air (at 68°F)	19 psi	0.075 LB/CF	1 126 FT/sec (768 mph)
air (at 86°F)	19 psi	0.075 LB/CF	1 164 FT/sec (794 mph)
water	246 500 psi	62 LB/CF	4 600 FT/sec (3,136 mph)
steel	28 000 000 psi	490 LB/CF	16 400 FT/sec (11,182 mph)

Figure 9.3   Wavelength and velocity of sound.

In longitudinal wave motion each vibrating particle in the medium moves only an infinitesimal distance about its normal position. As it oscillates in Simple Harmonic Motion it collides with adjacent particles and causes them to vibrate likewise. In this way the sound vibration moves through the medium as a succession of compressions and rarefactions of vibrating particles.

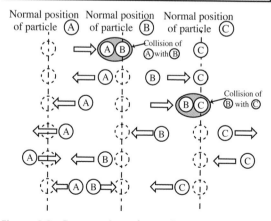

Figure 9.2   Propagation of sound.

of sound will differ according to the medium and in the case of a gaseous medium also somewhat slightly with the temperature of the gas (Figure 9.3), as follows:

velocity of sound in air (at 68°F)
$$= 1126 \text{ FT} / \sec \text{ or } \quad 768 \text{ mph}$$

velocity of sound in air (at 86°F)
$$= 1164 \text{ FT} / \sec \text{ or } \quad 794 \text{ mph}$$

velocity of sound in water
$$= 4600 \text{ FT} / \sec \text{ or } \quad 3136 \text{ mph}$$

velocity of sound in mild steel
$$= 16 400 \text{ FT} / \sec \text{ or } \quad 11 182 \text{ mph}$$

This has implications for the control of noise in buildings, particularly in respect to mechanical equipment such as the large fans and cooling equipment used in air-conditioning systems. The noise vibrations generated by this kind of equipment will be transmitted at 12 times the speed of airborne noise through the structural frame of the building, unless precautions are taken to isolate the equipment by means of damping devices.

Sound vibrations may be classified into three general groups:

| periodic | aperiodic | broad band |

Periodic sound repeats itself consistently, such as a pure tone (one frequency) or a set of the same combination of tones that are periodically repeated.

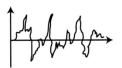

Aperiodic sound such as an explosion or hammering typically is impulsive in nature and consists of a complex set of frequencies.

Broad band sound (also referred to as white noise) consists of many frequencies at similar intensities (e.g., hissing sound made by the release of air or steam that is under pressure).

Figure 9.4   Types of sound vibration.

For convenience, sound vibrations may be classified (Figure 9.4) into the three general groups of *periodic*, *aperiodic*, and *broad-band* sound.

- Periodic sound includes both simple tones of one frequency and complex tones of more than one frequency that are repeated over regular intervals. Examples include the ticking of a clock, the regular beat of a drum, the sound produced by an idling car engine, or the chime of a door bell.
- Aperiodic sound is impulsive in nature and typically produced by a single action such as hammer blows, falling objects, slamming of a door, or an explosion. Such impulsive sounds typically involve a complex combination of frequencies at different intensities.
- Broad-band sound, also referred to as *white noise*, consists of many frequencies all of which are at approximately the same intensity. Typical examples include the rapid discharge of air from a car tire, the venting of steam from a pressure vessel, or the background sound in a large commercial aircraft produced by a combination of engine noise,

the air-conditioning plant, and the movement of the plane's fuselage through the external air.

For each of these groups of sound vibrations the essential parameters are provided by intensity, frequency composition, and time distribution. The sources of sound that are of immediate concern to the environmental designer are related to the natural environment (e.g., thunder, water flow, and air movement), the artificial mechanical environment (e.g., traffic and industrial processes) and the various methods of communication (e.g., speech, music, radio, and television).

9.2   Objective units of sound measurement

Although the pressures generated by vibrations are very small, the ear is able to respond to a very large range of these pressures. From physics we know that pressure is produced by the action of a force on an area.[1] In the study of acoustics this pressure or intensity is referred to as the amount of sound power either falling on or passing through a particular area. Since the unit of power in the metric system of units is the *watt,* it follows that sound intensity can be objectively measured in *watt per square meter* (w/m^2). The range of sound intensities that the human ear is sensitive to is enormous. Experiments have been conducted to show that we can just detect a sound intensity of 10^{-12} watt/m^2 and that our ears start to hurt when we are subjected to a sound intensity of around 10 watt/m^2.

Alternatively, sound can also be measured directly in terms of pressure. The unit of pressure in the metric system of units is the *pascal* (Pa) and expressed in this unit the threshold of hearing and the threshold of pain are equal to 0.00002 Pa and 200 Pa, respectively. Owing to this enormous range of audibility, neither sound intensity expressed in watt/m^2 nor sound pressure expressed in Pa is a practical and useful measure of the volume of a sound. Imagine a sound-meter scale with 10^{13} divisions.

Prior to the availability of electronic calculators, logarithm tables provided a simplified method for the multiplication and division of large numbers.

- Any number can be expressed in standard scientific form as a power of 10.

e.g., $1000 = 10^3$ or $0.0001 = 10^{-4}$ or $892.3 = 8.923 \times 10^2$

- Using 10 as a convenient base, the logarithm ($\log_{10}$) of any number is the exponent of that number expressed as a power of 10.

e.g., $\log_{10}(0.01) = \log_{10}(10^{-2}) = -2$
$\log_{10}(10.0) = \log_{10}(10^1) = 1$
$\log_{10}(100) = \log_{10}(10^2) = 2$

- Logarithm tables simplify calculation as follows:

i.e., $A \times B = \log_{10}(A) + \log_{10}(B)$
$A \div B = \log_{10}(A) - \log_{10}(B)$
$\log_{10}(A^n) = n \log_{10}(A)$

Figure 9.5 The logarithmic scale.

The human ear is sensitive to a very large range of pressures or sound intensities. This can be reduced to a more manageable logarithmic scale of Sound Pressure Level (SPL) or Sound Intensity Level (SIL).

- In the Metric system the unit of pressure is Pascal (Pa) and the reference sound pressure (i.e., threshold of hearing) is 0.00002 Pa:

$$SPL = 20\log_{10}\left[\frac{P}{0.00002}\right] (dB)$$

- Also, the unit of power is the watt. Since sound intensity is sound power falling on unit area it follows that the unit of sound intensity is watt/square meter (w/m^2). The reference sound intensity (i.e., threshold of hearing) is 10^{-12} w/m^2:

$$SIL = 10\log_{10}\left[\frac{I}{10^{-12}}\right] (dB)$$

Figure 9.6 Sound pressure level (SPL).

However, once again mathematics comes to the rescue. A very wide numerical range can be conveniently reduced to a much smaller proportional range by applying the concept of logarithms. Expressed logarithmically as powers of 10, the number 10 is equivalent to the logarithmic value of 1, 100 becomes 2, 1000 becomes 3, and so on (Figure 9.5).

Therefore, a sound pressure or sound intensity range of 10^{13} becomes a logarithmic range of just 13. The logarithmic equivalent of sound pressure and sound intensity is referred to as Sound Pressure Level (SPL). The decibel (dB) was chosen as the unit of SPL.[2]

The SPL of any sound can be calculated as a logarithmic ratio based on the threshold of hearing, expressed either in terms of sound pressure (10^{-5} Pa) or sound intensity (10^{-12} watt/m^2), as shown in equations [9.1] and [9.2] below (and Figure 9.6).

$$SPL = 20 \log_{10} P / P_O (dB) \quad [9.1]$$

Thus if the ambient sound pressure at any point in a room is 0.002 Pa, then the corresponding SPL can be calculated by applying equation [9.1] as follows: $20 \log_{10}(0.002 / 0.00002)$ is equal to $20 \log_{10}(100)$ is equal to 40 dB.

Similarly, the Sound Intensity Level (SIL) can be calculated as a logarithmic ratio of any ambient sound intensity compared with the threshold of hearing sound intensity of 10^{-12} watt/m^2.

$$SIL = 10 \log_{10} I / I_O (dB) \quad [9.2]$$

We often refer to human hearing as perception on a logarithmic scale. As can be seen in Figures 9.7 and 9.8, the perception of loudness corresponds more realistically to a logarithmic scale.

The difference in SPL between a quiet office and a busy or noisy office is just 20 dB. The smallest difference in SPL that is just perceptible is 3 dB, while we require a difference of at least 5 dB for the change in loudness to be clearly noticeable.

The reader may well ask: What is the difference between SPL and SIL? In the field of building acoustics they are considered to be numerically equal.[3] For example, if a sound pressure of 0.2 Pa is equal to a sound intensity of 0.0001 watt/m^2, then the following calculations using equations [9.1] and [9.2] will show that they both produce the same SPL of 80 dB.

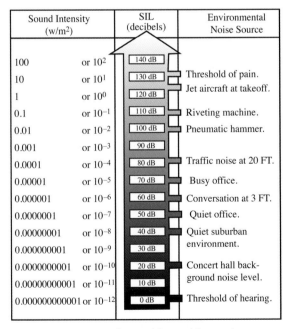

Figure 9.7 **Range of sound pressures and equivalent sound pressure levels (SPL).**

Sound Intensity (w/m²)		SIL (decibels)	Environmental Noise Source
100	or 10^2	140 dB	
10	or 10^1	130 dB	Threshold of pain.
1	or 10^0	120 dB	Jet aircraft at takeoff.
0.1	or 10^{-1}	110 dB	Riveting machine.
0.01	or 10^{-2}	100 dB	Pneumatic hammer.
0.001	or 10^{-3}	90 dB	
0.0001	or 10^{-4}	80 dB	Traffic noise at 20 FT.
0.00001	or 10^{-5}	70 dB	Busy office.
0.000001	or 10^{-6}	60 dB	Conversation at 3 FT.
0.0000001	or 10^{-7}	50 dB	Quiet office.
0.00000001	or 10^{-8}	40 dB	Quiet suburban environment.
0.000000001	or 10^{-9}	30 dB	
0.0000000001	or 10^{-10}	20 dB	Concert hall background noise level.
0.00000000001	or 10^{-11}	10 dB	
0.000000000001	or 10^{-12}	0 dB	Threshold of hearing.

Figure 9.8 **Range of sound intensities and equivalent sound intensity levels (SIL).**

$$SPL = 20 \log_{10} P / P_O \text{ (dB)}$$
$$= 20 \log_{10}[0.2 / 0.00002]$$
$$= 20 \log_{10}[10\,000] = 20\,(4) = \mathbf{80\,dB} \qquad \textbf{[9.1]}$$

$$SIL = 10 \log_{10} I / I_O \text{ (dB)}$$
$$= 10 \log_{10}[0.0001 / 10^{-12}]$$
$$= 10 \log_{10}[100\,000\,000] = 10\,(8) = \mathbf{80\,dB} \textbf{ [9.2]}$$

The fact is that it is much easier to measure sound pressure than sound intensity, using a microphone. Such meters are relatively simple to construct and calibrate. Of course, they produce readings in SPL by automatically converting the measured sound pressure into its logarithmic equivalent dB value.

9.3 Addition, deletion, and reduction of sound pressure levels

When two sounds of equal or unequal intensities are added, the effective sound pressure leve1 is not simply the sum of the two individual sound pressure levels. This is because the decibel scale is a logarithmic scale, and the calculation of a combined sound pressure level therefore requires the individual sound pressure levels to be converted to sound pressures before they can be added. After addition, the effective sound pressure is converted back to an equivalent sound pressure level in decibels. Accordingly, the addition of two sounds of SPLs L_1 and L_2, with corresponding sound intensities of SILs I_1 and I_2 occurring together, will proceed as follows:

$$L_1 = 10 \log (I_1 / I_O)$$
$$I_1 / I_O = \text{antilog } (0.1\,L_1)$$
$$I_1 = I_O \,[\text{antilog } (0.1\,L_1)]$$

and similarly

$$I_2 = I_O \,[\text{antilog } (0.1\,L_2)]$$

Therefore the composite SPL L, is given by:

$$L = 10 \log (I_1 + I_2) / I_O$$
$$\mathbf{L = 10 \log\,[\text{antilog}\,(0.1\,L_1) + \text{antilog}\,(0.1\,L_2)]\,(dB)}$$
$$\textbf{[9.3]}$$

Since the decibel scale is a logarithmic scale, the effective SPL of two sounds is NOT the arithmetic sum of the individual SPLs.

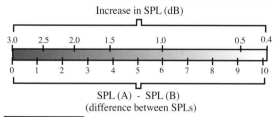

Rules of Thumb:

- The sum of two equal SPLs is 3 dB higher than the separate SPLs (e.g., 50dB + 50dB = 53dB).

- If two unequal SPLs are about 5dB apart then the sum is approximately 1dB higher than the louder source (e.g., 50dB + 55dB = 56dB).

- If two unequal SPLs are more than 9dB apart then their sum is approximately equal to the louder source (e.g., 50dB + 60dB = 60dB).

Figure 9.9 Addition of two SPLs.

Multiple SPLs can be added by successively adding two SPLs. For example, three SPLs of 40dB, 40dB and 60dB produce:
$$SPL(40 + 40) = 40 + 3 = 43dB$$
$$SPL(43 + 60) = 60 + 0 = 60dB$$

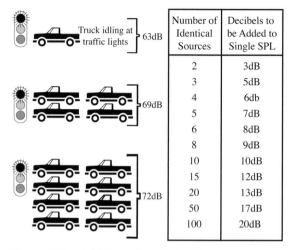

Number of Identical Sources	Decibels to be Added to Single SPL
2	3dB
3	5dB
4	6db
5	7dB
6	8dB
8	9dB
10	10dB
15	12dB
20	13dB
50	17dB
100	20dB

Figure 9.10 Addition of multiple SPLs.

As a rule of thumb, the scale shown in Figure 9.9 indicates that the sum of two equal SPLs is always 3 dB higher than the separate levels.[4] In the case of unequal sound pressure levels, we may adopt the general rule that if one level is more than 9 dB higher than another, the sum may simply be taken as the larger of the separate values (e.g., for two levels of 40 dB and 50 dB the sum is 50.4 dB, which is close enough to 50 dB).

As shown in Figure 9.10, the addition of multiple SPLs can proceed in pairs. Alternatively, the simple table shown in Figure 9.10 can be used. Therefore the combined SPL produced by 20 trucks, each emitting 80 dB, would be 93 dB (i.e., 80 + 13 = 93 dB).

The deletion of SPLs can be dealt with by reversing the steps for addition. However, this task is greatly simplified by reference to the following two tables:

We can see from Table 9.1 that a change in SPL of 3 dB is only just perceptible. The following example will illustrate the importance of this experimentally verified finding. Let us assume that there are four automatic riveting

Table 9.1 Perception of SPL changes.

Human perception of change in SPLs	
Change in SPL (dB)	Human perception
1 dB	Imperceptible
3 dB	Just perceptible
5 dB	Clearly noticeable
10 dB	Major change

machines located in close proximity in a particular part of a factory. The ambient SPL in that part of the factory, mostly produced by these four machines, is 89 dB. Although all four of the riveting machines are of the same type, one is an older model and consequently generates more noise than the other three machines. According to recent sound measurements, each of the new models generates 75 dB, while the old model generates 87 dB. Is it warranted, on the basis of noise reduction alone, to replace the older riveting machine with a new model? The difference between the SPL generated

Table 9.2 Deletion of sound sources.

Difference in dB between total SPL and source to be deleted	Reduction in dB of the total SPL due to the deletion
1 dB	7 dB
2 dB	4 dB
3 dB	3 dB
4 to 5 dB	2 dB
6 to 9 dB	1 dB

by the old machine and the ambient SPL is 2 dB (i.e., 89 dB – 87 dB). From Table 9.2 we see that the removal of the older model would decrease the overall SPL by 4 dB to 85 dB. According to Table 9.1, that would be a perceptible reduction in the overall SPL and therefore worthwhile.[5]

By how much a given sound is reduced over distance depends on whether the sound is produced by a *point source*, a *line source*, or an *area source*. In the case of a point source the precise reduction in SPL at a distance of D FT from a known source can be calculated on a proportional basis as follows. If SPL_1 is the sound pressure level at a distance of D_1 FT from the source, then the sound pressure level SPL_2 at a distance of D_2 FT from the source is given by:

$$SPL_2 = SPL_1 - 20 \log_{10} [D_2 / D_1] \text{ (dB)} \quad [9.4]$$

Using equation 9.4 we can, for example, calculate the SPL at 10 FT, 20 FT, and 40 FT from the source, if the SPL is 90 dB at a distance of 1 FT from the source.

$$SPL_{10} = 90 - 20 \log_{10} [10/1] = 90 - 20 [1.0] = 70 \text{ dB}$$
$$SPL_{20} = 90 - 20 \log_{10} [20/1] = 90 - 20 [1.3] = 64 \text{ dB}$$
$$SPL_{40} = 90 - 20 \log_{10} [40/1] = 90 - 20 [1.6] = 58 \text{ dB}$$

Or, what would be the SPL at 10 FT from the source, if the SPL of 90 dB had been recorded at a distance of 2 FT from the source?

$$SPL_{10} = 90 - 20 \log_{10} [10/2] = 90 - 20 [0.7] = 76 \text{ dB}$$

From a practical point of view, definitions of a *point source* and a *line source* are provided in Figure 9.11. As a rule of thumb (Figure 9.12) the SPL of a point source is reduced by about 6 dB

The reduction of sound over distance depends on whether we are dealing with a point source or a line source.

Point Source:

● Must have its largest dimension smaller than 1/5th of the distance from the source (e.g., a 6 FT source would be a Point Source at any distance greater than 30 FT).

● Obeys the inverse square law, which means that the sound intensity (not the SIL or SPL) is reduced by the square of the distance from the source.

Line Source:

● Any sound source larger than 1/5th of the distance from the source, or a moving source such as an aircraft, train or automobile.

● Loses approximately half of its sound intensity (not SIL or SPL) for each doubling of distance from the source.

Figure 9.11   Reduction of sound in the environment.

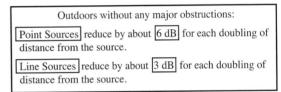

Outdoors without any major obstructions:

Point Sources reduce by about 6 dB for each doubling of distance from the source.

Line Sources reduce by about 3 dB for each doubling of distance from the source.

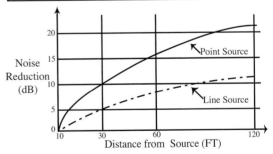

Area Sources have little sound reduction at distances up to 1/3rd of their shorter dimension. This increases to about 3 dB for each doubling of distance between 1/3rd of their shorter and 1/3rd of their longer dimension, and about 6 dB for each doubling of distance beyond.

Figure 9.12   Comparison of point, line, and area sound sources.

with each doubling of distance and, in the case of a line source such as a traveling car, by about 3 dB for each doubling of distance.

In comparison, an *area source* experiences little sound reduction at distances of up to one-third of its shorter dimension. However, this increases to about 3 dB for distances between one-third of the shorter dimension to one-third of the longer dimension, and to about 6 dB for each doubling of distance beyond.

9.4   The concept of octave bands

As briefly mentioned previously in Section 9.1, the human ear is sensitive to a very wide range of frequencies, ranging from around 30 Hz to 20 000 Hz. Within this range the perception of approximately equal changes in frequency is based on the ratio between two frequencies and not on the arithmetic difference between them. In other words, the perceived difference between two sounds of frequencies 100 Hz and 200 Hz is not the same as our perception of the difference between 200 Hz and 300 Hz, or between 400 Hz and 500 Hz. In each of these cases we would judge the differences in frequency to be significantly less than the arithmetic difference. However, we would judge the frequency interval between 200 Hz and 400 Hz to be about the same as that between 100 Hz and 200 Hz, and likewise between 400 Hz and 800 Hz, and so on. For this reason architectural acoustics has borrowed the concept of *octave bands* from the field of music.

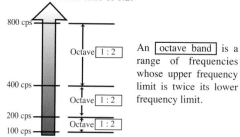

The human ear's perception of the interval between two frequencies is based on their ratio and not on the arithmetic difference between them.

● For frequency intervals to be perceived as being equal they must be in the same ratio. For example, a person would judge the frequency difference between 1000 cps and 2000 cps to be the same as between 4000 cps and 8000 cps because both intervals are in the ratio of 1:2.

An octave band is a range of frequencies whose upper frequency limit is twice its lower frequency limit.

● When equal interval sensations of a stimulus are governed by a certain constant ratio then the perception of this stimulus follows a logarithmic scale. The human perception of most acoustic stimuli follows a logarithmic scale.

Figure 9.13   The concept of octave bands.

As shown in Figure 9.13, an *octave band*, or simply an *octave*, is defined as a range of frequencies whose upper limit is twice its lower limit.

Since frequencies below 50 Hz and above 10 000 Hz are rarely of any consequence in buildings, the range of 44 Hz to 11 307 Hz has been divided into eight frequency bands (Figure 9.14), as follows:

At times when a more detailed sound analysis is called for, such as in the determination of building material properties or the explora-

low frequencies:	44 to 89	mid-frequency = $[44 \times 89]^{\frac{1}{2}}$	= 62.6 or 63 Hz
	89 to 177	mid-frequency = $[89 \times 177]^{\frac{1}{2}}$	= 125.5 or 125 Hz
middle frequencies:	177 to 354	mid-frequency = $[177 \times 354]^{\frac{1}{2}}$	= 250.3 or 250 Hz
	354 to 707	mid-frequency = $[354 \times 707]^{\frac{1}{2}}$	= 500.3 or 500 Hz
	707 to 1414	mid-frequency = $[707 \times 1414]^{\frac{1}{2}}$	= 999,8 or 1000 Hz
high frequencies:	1414 to 2827	mid-frequency = $[1414 \times 2827]^{\frac{1}{2}}$	= 1999.3 or 2000 Hz
	2827 to 5654	mid-frequency = $[2827 \times 5654]^{\frac{1}{2}}$	= 3998.0 or 4000 Hz
	5654 to 11 307	mid-frequency = $[5654 \times 11307]^{\frac{1}{2}}$	= 7995.6 or 8000 Hz

The center frequency of an octave is not the arithmetic average between the upper and lower limit, because the bandwidths of successive octaves are not equal.

- The center frequency of an octave band is obtained by geometrically averaging the upper and lower frequency limits, as follows:

$$\text{Center Frequency} = \sqrt{\left[\text{Lower Frequency}\right] \times \left[\text{Higher Frequency}\right]}$$

For example, the center frequency of an octave band ranging from 200 cps to 400 cps is calculated to be:

$$\sqrt{200 \times 400} = 283 \text{ cps (approx.)}$$

- In building acoustics we use eight octaves between 44 cps and 11 300 cps.

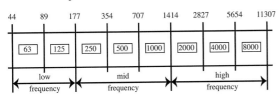

Figure 9.14   Center frequency of an octave.

Approximately 75% of sound energy in speech is contained in vowels (the low frequency component of speech) but the consonants (the high frequency component of speech) provide most of the intelligibility.

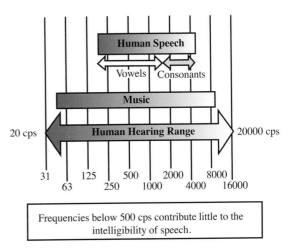

Frequencies below 500 cps contribute little to the intelligibility of speech.

Figure 9.15   Human speech.

tion of room acoustics, a more finely grained one-third octave band analysis may be performed. However, in the same way that the mid-frequency of an octave band is not the arithmetic mean between the lower and upper boundary frequencies, the mid-frequency of a third-octave band cannot be determined by simple arithmetic. If we know the mid-frequency of a particular octave band, such as 63 Hz for the first octave band (i.e., 44 to 89 Hz), then the mid-frequencies of its three one-third octave bands are calculated as follows:

mid-frequency of first third-octave band
$$= 62.6 \div 2^{1/3} = 62.6 \div 1.26 = 49.7 \text{ or } 50 \text{ Hz}$$

mid-frequency of second third-octave band
$$= 62.6 \text{ or } 63 \text{ Hz}$$

mid-frequency of third third-octave band
$$= 62.6 \times 2^{1/3} = 62.6 \times 1.26 = 78.9 \text{ or } 80 \text{ Hz}$$

It is interesting to note that virtually all of the sound energy in speech is contained within the five octave bands that extend from 177 Hz

to 5654 Hz, with close to three-quarters of that sound energy being provided by vowels (Figure 9.15).

However, it is the relatively high-frequency consonants that are largely responsible for the intelligibility of speech. It is interesting to compare this with the frequency range of some common musical instruments (Figure 9.16).

9.5 Subjective units of sound measurement

The perception of sound, like the perception of heat and light, is a subjective mechanism, and it is therefore necessary to relate the objective measurements of vibration (i.e., sound pressure, SPL, sound intensity, and SIL) with the ability of the human ear to distinguish and measure the resulting audible sound.

The situation is complicated by the fact that the human ear not only varies in its response to high and low sound pressure differences, but

Pitch is the subjective measure of the perception of sound frequency. Low frequency sound is often described as boomy and high frequency as screechy.

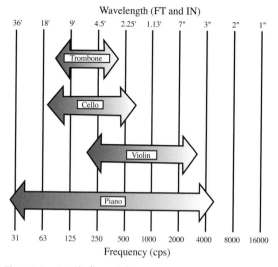

Figure 9.16 **Pitch and frequency.**

The human ear is less sensitive at high frequencies and much less sensitive at low frequencies. Therefore a subjective scale has been established to relate perceived loudness in phons to objective SPL in decibels. At a frequency of 1000 cps decibels and phons are numerically equal.

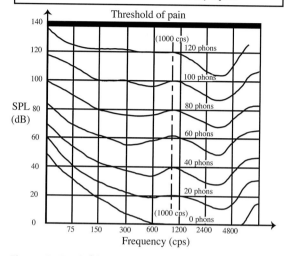

Figure 9.17 Subjective loudness (phon).

also to frequency. For example, if notes of 50 Hz and 1000 Hz frequencies are played alternately at a sound pressure level of 40 dB, then the higher-frequency note will appear to be louder. The greatest sensitivity of the ear occurs at approximately 4000 Hz, but this falls off quite sharply for higher and lower frequencies. It is therefore to be expected that the threshold of hearing has different SPL values at different frequencies, because the perceived loudness of a sound depends on both its SPL and frequency. At higher SPLs (e.g., above 100 dB) the sensitivity of the ear is much more evenly distributed, with the result that the threshold of pain tends to be fairly constant at about 130 dB to 140 dB for the audible frequency range. To allow for this subjective characteristic of the hearing mechanism, a scale of equal loudness levels has been devised (Figure 9.17). A pure tone of 1000 Hz frequency has been adopted as a reference standard and a sound pressure of 0.00002 Pa (i.e., 0 dB SPL) chosen as the zero level of a loudness scale of units called the *phon* scale. Since 1000 Hz serves as the reference frequency, SPLs

in *decibels* and subjective loudness levels in *phon* are identical at that frequency.

It can be seen in Figure 9.17 that for the 40-phon contour, a pure tone of 100 Hz at an SPL of 52 dB will appear equally loud as a tone of 4000 Hz, at 30 dB. However, the phon scale does not provide information in regard to the manner in which persons normally rate one sound with another. At times, it would be convenient to be able to specify one sound as being twice or three times as loud as another. The *sone* scale has been devised to achieve this aim, by rating the loudness of sounds in a linear manner. It was suggested that since a loudness level of about 40 phon normally exists in quiet environments, this loudness level be equivalent to one sone. Accordingly, a noise which is twice as loud would be 2 sone or 49 phon. On the basis that there exists sufficient correlation between the phon scale and the intuitive judgments of large groups of people, it has been agreed internationally that a doubling of sound will produce approximately a 10-phon increase in loudness (Figure 9.18).[6]

Since the phon scale does not provide a convenient way of rating the loudness of sounds, the ⬚sone⬚ scale was devised to indicate whether one sound is half as loud or twice as loud (and so on) as another, in a linear manner.

- A loudness level of 40 phons was chosen to be equivalent to 1 sone, since the background loudness in most environments is greater than 40 phons.

- A doubling of sound intensity from 40 phons to 49 phons is equivalent to 2 sones.

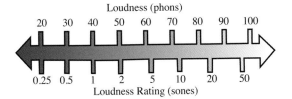

Loudness (phons)
20 30 40 50 60 70 80 90 100

0.25 0.5 1 2 5 10 20 50
Loudness Rating (sones)

- Strictly speaking the above phons to sones conversion scale applies to pure tones only. The rating of broad band sound consisting of a number of frequencies is a much more complex matter.

Figure 9.18 **Subjective loudness (phon).**

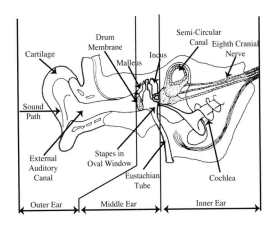

- Placement of two ears on opposite sides of the head allows the direction of sound to be detected (through the slight time delay and difference in loudness).

- The middle ear incorporates a transducing mechanism that converts sound vibrations in air from the outer ear to sound vibrations in liquid in the inner ear.

Figure 9.19 **The anatomy of the ear and the biological hearing mechanism.**

9.6 How do we hear sound?

The structure of the human ear has adapted over millions of years to receive and transmit to the brain those vibrations that constitute the hearing stimulus. Sound pressures set the ear drum (Figure 9.19) in vibration and this movement is transmitted by a system of levers to the inner ear where nerves are stimulated.

It is therefore apparent that the ear incorporates an effective transducing mechanism (i.e., the middle ear) for transferring the vibration of air (i.e., the outer ear) to the fluid system surrounding the hair cells of the hearing nerve (i.e., the inner ear). Owing to its particular shape, the outer ear matches over a wide range of frequencies the impedance of the ear drum on the external air.

As shown by the mechanical simulation of the hearing mechanism depicted in Figure 9.20, the middle ear changes by multiple lever action the relatively large movements of the ear drum to smaller movements of greater force, more suitable for activating the fluid system of the

inner ear. This transducing mechanism is necessary because a gas such as air is compressible and a liquid is not. The sound vibrations transmitted through air represent a relatively small force acting over a relatively large distance. This has to be converted in the middle ear to a relatively large force acting over a very small distance.

The perception of the sound occurs by means of hair cells embedded along the basilar membrane, which transversely divides the spiral wound cochlea bone (Figure 9.20).

Although it is known that the basilar membrane is able to discriminate between frequencies, this innate capability is thought to be insufficiently accurate to explain the extremely high degree of frequency discrimination achieved by a person.[7] We must, therefore, assume that the brain interprets the electrical impulses that flow from the nerve endings of the hair cells.

Hearing sensitivity, particularly at the higher frequencies, diminishes with age even in healthy persons. This aging condition is referred to as presbycusis and can reduce the sensitivity of

The perception of sound occurs in the inner ear by means of hair cells embedded in the basilar membrane, which is wound around the cochlea (shell-like bone).

Schematic Representation of Ear

Sound Path
ear drum
hammer, anvil and stirrup bones
stapedius muscle
basilar membrane (stretched out)
hair cells

| Outer Ear | Middle Ear | Inner Ear |

- The outer ear is shaped to enhance the reception of sound pressure in air.

- The liquid vibrations are sensed by the hair cells of the basilar membrane and transmitted as signals by the auditory nerve to the brain.

- The large vibrations of the ear drum are transmitted by lever action of the hammer, anvil and stirrup bones into smaller vibrations of greater force in the liquid of the inner ear.

Figure 9.20 Mechanical simulation of the human hearing mechanism.

the human ear to frequencies below 5000 Hz. However, long-term and repeated exposure to noise levels above 90 dB are known to cause permanent hearing damage regardless of age, a condition referred to as sociocusis.

9.7 Hearing conservation in the environment

Whereas it has been clearly demonstrated on the basis of statistical data that an adverse thermal building environment will have a detrimental effect on its occupants, no such definitive large scale studies appear to have been conducted with respect to the impact of noise on the productivity of building occupants. However, there is a great deal of medical evidence that directly links high-level noise to hearing loss (Figure 9.21). Attempts have been made to classify the possible effects of noise on man into main groups (Figure 9.22).

Research has indicated that for relatively short periods of time (i.e., 1 to 2 hours), persons

Hearing is easily damaged by exposure to very high SPLs over a short period of time or elevated SPLs over an extended period of time.

Short Term Exposure (120 (+) dB):

Can cause abrupt physical damage to the middle ear. For example, rupture of the tympanic membrane at about 160 dB and permanent damage to the cochlea accompanied by pain, nausea, nystagmus (i.e., shifting of the visual field) and loss of orientation at SPLs above 135 dB.

Long Term Exposure (90 (+) dB):

Can cause gradual physical damage over a period of months or years to the hair cells in the basilar membrane. Persons working in noisy environments (e.g., factories, aircraft servicing areas in airports, and dancehalls) are particularly susceptible to hearing loss.

Figure 9.21 Physical hearing damage.

The subjective impact of noise on mental and motor behavior may be categorized as interference with activities and disturbance of attitudes.

Interference with Activities:
Even slightly elevated noise levels may interfere with activities such as speech communication (above 50 dB), working, reading, relaxing, convalescing, and sleeping.

Disturbance of Attitudes:
Annoyance is caused in particular by higher frequency sound and noise that the listener considers to be unnecessary. A noisy environment can certainly accentuate nervous stress and disorders, particularly if associated with a fear of economic and status loss.

Figure 9.22 Subjective considerations.

undertaking tasks requiring a high degree of concentration do not appear to be significantly affected by moderately high background noise levels involving indistinguishable or musical sound. Nevertheless, it is certainly true that very high noise levels, and in particular certain types of noise, will cause annoyance and, after lengthy exposure, permanent hearing damage. Attempts have been made to classify the possible effects of noise on man into main groups. Foremost among these are the effects on anatomical structures and principal physiological processes, such as the vibration of bodily structures, damage to the middle ear (i.e., rupture of the tympanic membrane at an SPL of about 160 dB), temporary or permanent damage to the cochlea, and pain due to SPLs in excess of 135 dB, which may also be accompanied by nausea and apparent shifting of the visual field (i.e., nystagmus) or loss of orientation. Less clearly defined are the subjective effects on mental and motor behavior, which may be categorized as follows:

Category A – Physical impact leading to interference with the following kinds of activity
- Speech communication (usually above 50 dB);
- Working (depending on the kind of work performed);
- Relaxing;
- Sleeping (usually above 35 dB);
- Reading;
- Convalescing;
- Traveling.

Category B – Physiological impact leading to the disturbance of attitudes
- Annoyance (typically caused by unwanted or unnecessary noise);
- Fear of bodily injury or economic and social loss of status;
- Accentuation of nervous stress and disorders.

In recent years experience has shown that the construction of new or the extension of existing public complexes that produce a great deal of noise (e.g., regional airports and sporting complexes) near residential neighborhoods, can lead to severe public reaction. It has become apparent that blatant disregard of the acoustic aspects of city and regional planning considerations may lead to time-consuming and costly political action, if the provocation is directed at a sufficiently wide sector of the population. Such examples have been related in particular to the large-scale expansion of existing airports. The public response tends to escalate in stages with increasing severity, as follows:

Stage 1: Attempts to provide noise barrier or buffer.
Stage 2: Leaving or avoiding the noise field.
Stage 3: Action against the party blamed for the noise, progressing in stages:
- discussion within localized groups;
- complaints to local authorities;
- complaints to State and National authorities;
- public demonstrations;
- threats of legal action;
- vigorous legal action.
Stage 4: Illegal actions such as sabotage.

It is incumbent on architects and environmental planners to take into account the external and internal sound environments throughout the design process, in an effort to avoid the likely occurrence of noise interference with the activities of building occupants. Desirable sound environments fall into two main categories; namely, those that satisfy existing laws, and those that enable the full enjoyment of work, recreation, and sleep. Over the past several decades an increasing number of national, state, and local government authorities have adopted zoning ordinances in an attempt to shield the public from noisy environments. These ordinances typically specify performance standards for industrial and vehicular traffic noise sources and require measurements to be made at the boundaries of industrial areas and where highways intrude on residential neighborhoods. While the World Health Organization is concerned with all threats to health and efficiency, the International Standards Organization (ISO) and the International Electrotechnical Commission (IEC) deal respectively with criteria for hearing conservation, annoyance and speech communication, and with instrumentation.

One of the foremost design aims should be to provide noise levels that will promote efficiency and safety, while maintaining good relationships among neighboring communities. The fact that sound that is annoying to one person may be highly desirable to another (e.g., music) further complicates the achievement of this elusive aim. Over recent years three parameters have been established for desirable sound environments.

- *Hearing conservation:* Protection from physical damage.
- *Satisfactory communication:* Sufficiently low speech interference level.
- *Comfort and enjoyment:* Uninhibited concentration, relaxation, and sleep.

Early studies of the relationship between deafness and noise were aimed at the prediction of the average hearing loss to be expected after a certain exposure time to a specific noise environment. The resultant range of hearing loss was found to vary widely, depending on the individual susceptibility to hearing damage of the subject. This led to the establishment of Damage Risk Criteria based on critical noise levels likely to cause the onset of hearing damage in average ears. However, since it is not possible to gauge accurately the threshold of noise-induced deafness of an individual until some permanent hearing loss has occurred, this approach has now been largely superseded by the formulation of Hearing Conservation Criteria.

In general, Hearing Conservation Criteria allow SPLs that are some 10 dB below the Damage Risk Criteria. Investigations in several countries have shown that about 85 dB in the critical octave frequency bands between 300 Hz and 4800 Hz should be chosen as an upper limit necessary for the protection of persons whose hearing is susceptible to damage. In environments where higher noise levels are likely to occur, it will be necessary to provide the occupants with some form of hearing protection. There is some evidence to suggest that the duration of exposure is also a significant factor. It is generally accepted that a reduction of expo-

sure by 50 percent would allow the Hearing Conservation Level to be raised by some 3 dB.

The precise measurement of noise-induced deafness is somewhat complicated by the natural loss of sensitivity of the ear that occurs with increasing age. This phenomenon is described in medical terms as presbycusis and is symptomized in particular by the loss of sensitivity at higher frequencies. Some years ago, when television first became available in Australia, a number of manufacturers received an inordinate number of complaints from customers who had purchased television sets. In each case these complaints were traced back to the alleged presence of a high-frequency background sound that allegedly originated from the set and disturbed the viewer. The manufacturers were puzzled that these complaints came almost exclusively from young people, and that their service inspectors consistently reported that they were unable to detect the offending sound. After a certain amount of confusion it was found that the complaints had been justified in as much as the frequency and SPL of the reported sound placed it in a range affected by presbycusis.

One of the most common detrimental effects of noise is interference with communication. The requirements for unimpeded speech communication are related to the frequency components and dynamic properties of speech, as well as the background noise level. Research has been undertaken to study the contribution to intelligibility of small sections of the speech spectrum and the masking effect of background noise, as a means of predicting the effectiveness of communication in a given environment. These studies have shown that the intelligibility of normal conversation is reduced whenever the sound pressure level of speech is less than 10 dB above the level of ambient, broad-band, background noise. If we assume the ordinary speaking voice to reach a level of about 60 dB at a distance of 3 FT, then it is apparent that the background noise level in any room to be useful for discussions should not exceed 50 dB.

During the 1950s the procedure for predicting the effectiveness of communication in the office environment was considerably simplified

Table 9.3   Maximum background noise levels (i.e., SIL) for reliable speech communication.

Distance between speaker and listener	Normal	Speaker's voice level		
		Raised	Loud	Shouting
1 FT	66 dB	72 dB	78 dB	84 dB
2 FT	60 dB	66 dB	72 dB	78 dB
4 FT	54 dB	60 dB	66 dB	72 dB
6 FT	50 dB	56 dB	62 dB	68 dB
12 FT	44 dB	50 dB	56 dB	62 dB
24 FT	38 dB	44 dB	50 dB	56 dB

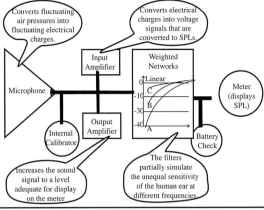

The instrument for noise measurement is the Sound Level Meter, consisting of a microphone, input and output amplifiers calibrated in decibels, and weighted networks (i.e., filters).

Converts fluctuating air pressures into fluctuating electrical charges.

Converts electrical charges into voltage signals that are converted to SPLs.

Microphone

Input Amplifier

Weighted Networks

Meter (displays SPL)

Internal Calibrator

Output Amplifier

Battery Check

Increases the sound signal to a level adequate for display on the meter

The filters partially simulate the unequal sensitivity of the human ear at different frequencies.

By international agreement sound measurements are recommended to be taken with the A weighted network and are designated as dBA.

Figure 9.23   Sound-level meter components.

by the notion of Speech Interference Levels (SIL).[8] The SIL is the average in decibels (dB) of the SPLs in the three octave bands 600–1200 Hz, 1200–2400 Hz, and 2400–4800 Hz. On the basis of questionnaire-rating studies the well-known American acoustics pioneer Leo Beranek found that, although SILs are a necessary measure of satisfactory speech communication, there are some noises for which the loudness level (LL) must also be considered. He therefore devised a set of Noise Criteria (NC) curves to relate SILs and LLs on the assumption that the noise is continuous (Beranek, 1960). He recommended the following maximum background noise levels (i.e., SIL) to allow reliable speech communication at the distances indicated (Table 9.3).

9.8   Sound-measurement instruments

Precise measuring instruments are required for the comparison of sound levels taken at different places and different times. The basic instrument of noise measurement is the Sound-Level Meter, consisting of a microphone, amplifier with attenuators calibrated in decibels, a meter calibrated in decibels for reading the amplifier output, and weighted networks (Figure 9.23).

Performance standards for Sound-Level Meters are typically established in individual countries, generally based on recommendations compiled by the International Electrotechnical Commission (IEC, 1961).

Most modern Sound-Level Meters use transistor circuits with large amounts of feedback and temperature compensation to stabilize performance. The transistor amplifier has the significant advantages of low weight, negligible heat output, and small power consumption. High-quality Sound-Level Meters, referred to as Precision Sound-Level Meters, normally incorporate a convenient electrical system for calibrating the amplifier gain and a calibrated control for adjusting this gain to suit microphones of varying sensitivity.

Sound-Level Meters also incorporate a number of filter networks that modify the overall frequency response of the instrument to approximately simulate the response of the human ear. The selection of any network is controlled by a switch that usually provides a choice of three filter networks (i.e., A, B, and C). Precision Sound-Level Meters have a linear network (L_m) without filters, in addition to the three filter networks. This fourth network provides a linear (flat) frequency response for use in conjunction with analyzers and recorders.

The degree of rating and tolerance at each frequency of these weighting networks are specified by national standards according to

Weighting networks that proportionally reduce the measured SPL at low frequencies (to compensate for the lower sensitivity of the human ear) are provided in a SLM.

Weighting Network A [dBA]: Is essentially an inversion of the 40 phon equal loudness contour. It is intended for low SPL noise and has been adopted as the international standard for all SPL measurements.

Weighting Network B [dBB]: Is essentially an inversion of the 70 phon equal loudness contour, originally proposed for mid-range frequencies. It has been largely abandoned in recent years.

Weighting Network C [dBC]: Is essentially an inversion of the 100 phon equal loudness contour. It was intended for very loud low frequency sound, but has also been largely abandoned in favor of the dBA weighting network.

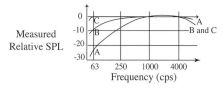

Figure 9.24   The weighting networks.

A SLM may have a digital (e.g., LED) or analog (i.e., moving needle indicator) display. However, all SLMs are provided with a fast (1/8 sec.) and slow (1 sec) response speed mode, and at least an A and C weighting network.

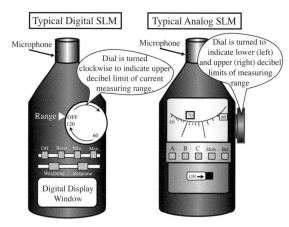

Figure 9.25   Typical sound-level meters.

recommendations of the IEC. With C-weighting, the response is practically unaltered in the region of 60 Hz to 4000 Hz. However, at 31.5 Hz the response is −3 dB, which represents a halving of the input. B-weighting is virtually unmodified between 300 Hz and 5000 Hz, while the A-network is unmodified between 1000 Hz and 2000 Hz only (Figure 9.24).

For medium noise levels, the ear responds approximately in accordance with the B-network, while for low levels the A-network should be used, and for traffic noise the C-network is the closest simulation. It follows that if the appropriate weighting network is used, the reading will be approximately in *phon* (i.e., a measure of loudness). On the recommendation of the IEC most measurements are now taken with an A-weighting and therefore designated as dBA, irrespective of the noise level.

Sound-Level Meters incorporate a calibrated attenuator in the form of a switch calibrated in 10 dB steps and synchronized to provide a reading of the sound field in conjunction with a display meter. A typical implementation of this switch mechanism is shown in Figure 9.25.

It is important to check the validity of the attenuator switch at regular intervals and measure the signal-to-noise ratio in all positions. The display meter is normally calibrated from −6 to +10 dB. Simple addition of the display meter reading to the attenuator switch calibration provides the SPL measurement.

Naturally, the microphone is the vital component of a Sound-Level Meter, since it converts the ambient sound energy into electrical energy. The condenser, crystal, and dynamic microphones are most commonly used for sound measurement. Each suffers from some defect in performance, and it is therefore necessary to investigate a number of critical characteristics before a selection can be made for any particular noise-measurement situation. The physical size of a microphone is directly related to its frequency response. Especially when the microphone faces a high-frequency sound source, pressure build-up across its face can give rise to inordinately high readings. Some Sound-Level Meters are designed to be used in a manner that will allow the sound field to pass across the diaphragm of the microphone, so that a flat response is obtained. The same flat response may be achieved for sound coming from any direction, by using a small microphone. Other factors that lead to poor frequency response include resonance of air cavities, or critical components such as diaphragms and microphone shapes that in themselves disturb the sound field.

The difference between the highest level at which a microphone will operate without distortion and the electrical noise that is generated within its various circuits is defined as the dynamic range. Since microphones are easily damaged by inadvertent exposure to high-level sound fields, it is also important to know the upper safe limit of exposure.

Crystal microphones were commonly used in conjunction with Sound-Level Meters before the development of high-quality condenser microphones. A common type of crystal material is ammonium dihydrogen phosphate (ADP), which has a low specific output but is operative for temperatures up to 257°F. These two properties do not conflict, because a material of low sensitivity is useful only in high-energy sound fields, with their attendant heat. Some less expensive Sound Level Meters have hearing-aid type Rochelle-salt microphones with rather poor humidity and temperature characteristics (upper limit of about 113°F, which can be easily reached during field noise measurements). A further type of crystal microphone commonly in use with Sound-Level Meters is the PZT microphone. The letters PZT refer to lead zirconate titanate ceramic, which has good high-temperature characteristics (up to 212°F).

Dynamic microphones, sometimes referred to as moving-coil microphones, operate on the principle that a coil of wire mounted behind a diaphragm induces a voltage as it moves in the annular space of a magnetic system. By virtue of its design the dynamic microphone will normally assume larger dimensions than its condenser or crystal counterparts, and it is therefore likely that its frequency response will be affected by pressure buildup at frequencies normally encountered in sound measurements. For this reason high-quality dynamic microphones employ controlled damping behind the dia-

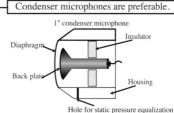

Figure 9.26   The condenser microphone.

phragm to level the response characteristics. Although inherently low electrical impedance makes these microphones suitable for use on long extension cables, they have two shortcomings. They are susceptible to induced stray electrical noise, and to the attraction of metallic dust particles.

Condenser microphones (Figure 9.26) consist basically of a thin metallic, pressure-sensitive diaphragm stretched in front of an insulating metal disc. They are high-quality, stable microphones now normally prescribed for Sound-Level Meters. Since the choice of a particular Sound-Level Meter follows directly from the selection of the most suitable microphone system, a comparison of the performance characteristics of condenser, crystal, and dynamic microphones is provided in the bottom half of Figure 9.26 in respect to the following characteristics: sensitivity; frequency response; linearity; dynamic range; stability, ruggedness; and, physical size.

Sound Analysis with Sound Analyzers: Experience with Sound-Level Meters has shown that overall decibel readings do not provide a true indication of how the measured sound will be perceived by human ears, even when weighting networks are used. For example, a Sound-Level Meter adds noise levels according to the objective rule that a doubling of the source adds 3 dB to the ambient noise level, while the ear may add complex sound levels of equal intensity (subjectively) and recognize an increase of 6 phon or more. It is therefore common practice to analyze sound measurements into their component frequencies before accurate predictions of subjective response are made. The most commonly used type of Sound Analyzer divides the sound spectrum into eight bands of center frequencies (i.e., 63, 126, 250, 500, 1000, 2000, 4000, and 8000 Hz).

Most Sound-Level Meters have provisions for attaching a Sound Analyzer directly to the body of the Sound Level Meter. In fact, often the Sound Analyzer is designed to draw its electrical power from the power source (i.e., batteries) of the Sound Level Meter.

Calibration, Testing, and Measurement: Calibration and testing are an essential aspect of dependable sound measurement. Standards based on IEC recommendations as a rule require periodic testing of a considerable number of characteristics, including overtaxing, influence of temperature, relative humidity, as well as electrical and magnetic fields, which are determined either by the assembly as a whole or its individual components. Most of these characteristics will be similar for instruments of the same type, and it is therefore convenient to divide calibration tests for Sound-Level Meters into two categories: namely, type tests and individual tests. These were defined by the German DIN 45633 Standard (DIN 1966) in 1966, as follows:

Type Tests:

1 Influence of static pressure.
2 Testing of dynamic characteristics in all measurement ranges and for all weighting-networks.
3 Influence of mechanical vibration.
4 Influence of magnetic and electrostatic fields.
5 Temperature range.

6 Influence of relative humidity.
7 Overtaxing.
8 Effect of externally connected circuits or instruments.
9 Directional properties.
10 Difference between the weighting-network ratings for diffuse sound fields and plane, propagating waves (for a number of frequencies).
11 Influence of large sound fields.

Individual Tests:

1 The ratings of the weighting networks in open sound fields.
2 Dynamic characteristics of the indicator mechanism.
3 Effective-value registration.
4 Graduation of the scale of the indicator mechanism.
5 Accuracy of the overall-measuring-range switch.
6 Absolute value of the reference frequency.
7 Inherent noise level of the instrument.

In the case of Precision Sound-Level Meters, which are used for very accurate acoustical analyses and legal disputes, it is normal practice to calibrate the Precision Sound-Level Meter before every use and at frequent intervals during any one period of use. The +3 dB level on the display meter is recommended as a reference calibration level, since it represents the average of the range most often used during measuring. When coupled to a tape recorder, the meter reading and attenuator settings should be stated, so that the analyzing equipment can be adjusted to the same setting during replay. If these calibration and testing instructions are closely adhered to, then the quality of the instrument alone will determine the error incurred in measurements of the ambient noise level.

Sound-Level Meters are commonly used to measure widely varying sound fields under changing conditions and for different purposes. The noise levels under investigation will differ in frequency spectrum and may originate from more than one source. Measurements may be taken in the open or between reflecting walls, in a reverberation room or anechoic chamber.[9] The purpose of the measurements may be, for example, to: estimate the danger of hearing damage; to assess the effectiveness of acoustic remedies; to compare building materials or systems of construction; or to control legally prescribed maximum noise levels. In every case the method of measurement must suit the problem, since the mode of application could have considerable influence on the final interpretation of the test results.

During the actual reading of the instrument scale the observer must be positioned in such a way that he or she does not noticeably disturb the sound field in the vicinity of the microphone. The avoidance of interference due to reflections from the observer is of particular importance for the measurement of pure tones and narrow-band noise. This requirement will generally be satisfied if the observer is at least 4 FT distant from the microphone at one side of a tripod-mounted Sound-Level Meter. The German standard DIN 45633 recommends an optimum distance of 3 meters (i.e., 10 FT) between the microphone and the observer. This would normally require the microphone to be connected to the Sound-Level Meter by means of an extension cord.

In the particular case of sound-insulation measurements, if a constant noise source of 90 dBA exists on one side of a partition and the Sound-Level Meter reading on the A-network is 50 dBA on the other side, then the insulation provided by the partition is calculated to be 40 dBA (i.e., $90 - 50 = 40$ dBA). This is naturally on the assumption that the background noise level on the Sound-Level Meter side of the partition is less than about 40 dBA (which can be neglected because 40 dBA + 50 dBA = 50 dBA). Measurements on both sides of the partition should be taken for at least three distances from the partition and the average calculated. This procedure will tend to avoid the possibility that the microphone may have been influenced by reflections, standing waves, or interference patterns.

Endnotes

1. Expressed in more technical terms, pressure is equal to force per unit area.
2. The decibel unit is named after Alexander Graham Bell (1847–1922), the inventor of the telephone.
3. Strictly speaking, from the point of view of a physicist they are not exactly equal.
4. This is readily verified as follows: if $L_1 = L_2 = 40$ dB, then $L_{1+2} = 10 \log_{10} (10\,000 + 10\,000) = 43$ dB.
5. It should be noted that according to Figure 9.10, the addition of the fourth car will increase the combined SPL generated by four cars by 1 dB (i.e., from 5 dB for three equal sound sources to 6 dB for four equal sound sources) to 81 dB.
6. In comparison, a doubling of sound energy produces only a 3 dB increase in SPL, which is the objective equivalent of loudness in phon (see Section 9.3).
7. The German physicist Zwicker (1961) has been able to identify some 24 critical sections of the basilar membrane with individual frequency perception characteristics.
8. Unfortunately, the acronym for Speech Interference Level (SIL) is identical to the acronym for Sound Intensity Level (SIL) referred to previously in Section 9.2. However, this should not cause too much confusion since SPL is mostly used in preference to Sound Intensity Level in the field of building acoustics.
9. Reverberation rooms and anechoic chambers are special acoustic laboratories designed to produce maximum reflection or absorption, respectively. Accordingly, in a reverberation room all of the surfaces are acoustically hard surfaces to maximize the inter-reflection of sound within the room, while in an anechoic chamber the walls and ceiling are typically sprayed with a highly sound-absorbing finish such as a porous plastic foam. A similar type of treatment is applied to the floor of an anechoic chamber, with the addition of a wire mesh screen on top to support light pedestrian traffic.

10 Room Acoustics

Sound behaves very much like light in several respects, even though the wavelength of sound is several orders of magnitude longer than the wavelength of light. As we saw in the previous chapter, the wavelength of sound ranges from about ¼ IN to 37 FT, compared with less than one ten-thousandth of an inch for light (see Chapter Six).[1] Sound can bend around obstructions and if the obstruction is very much smaller than the wavelength of the sound, then there may be virtually no acoustic shadow on the other side of the obstruction.

In a simplified manner, the path of sound in an enclosed space can be simulated with light rays emanating from a point source. Even though the light rays cannot reproduce the spherical progression of sound, they do provide an accurate indication of how the sound waves will be reflected from surfaces in their path. While this kind of model analysis falls far short of a comprehensive representation of the acoustic environment that is likely to be experienced in the space, it does provide valuable information at a relatively low level of effort. The required model can be constructed out of inexpensive cardboard and a commonly available laser pointer can be used as a light source.

Building designers may resort to this kind of model analysis because the bounding surfaces of an interior space have a profound influence on the quality of sound in that enclosed space. For this reason, before we can explore the acoustics of building spaces for speech and music we must digress briefly to consider the principles of sound reflection and diffraction.

10.1 Reflection and diffraction of sound

When a sound wave strikes the boundary surface of an enclosed space part of the sound energy is reflected back into the space, part is transmitted through the boundary, and part is absorbed by conversion to heat within the material (Figure 10.1).

This relationship between reflected, transmitted, and absorbed sound is very conveniently expressed in terms of numerical coefficients as either percentages or fractions (i.e., decimal values) of one whole, as follows:

Reflection = (reflected sound energy)/
Coefficient (ρ)   (incident sound energy)

Absorption = (absorbed sound energy)/
Coefficient (α)   (incident sound energy)

Transmission = (transmitted sound energy)/
Coefficient (τ)   (incident sound energy)

However, the Absorption Coefficient is often considered to include the Transmission Coefficient when we are concerned simply with the proportion of sound that remains in the space. Under these circumstances the distinction between absorption and transmission is of little consequence. Similarly, when we are concerned with the transmission of noise from one space to another we typically do not distinguish between reflected and absorbed sound, since

Building Science: Concepts and Application. Jens Pohl.
© 2011 John Wiley & Sons, Ltd.
Published 2011 by John Wiley & Sons, Ltd.

When sound waves are reflected from a surface the angle of incidence is equal to the angle of reflection. In this respect sound waves behave the same way as light rays.

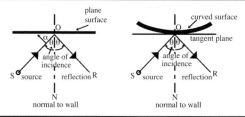

The Reflection Coefficient is the fraction of the total incident sound that is reflected (always less than 1.0).

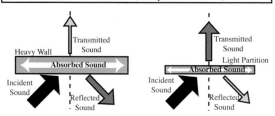

Figure 10.1   Reflection of sound.

neither of these reaches the external side of the noise barrier.

The property of a boundary that exerts most influence on its sound reflection, absorption, and transmission characteristics is the density of the material that the boundary is composed of. This statement requires further discussion. As explained in the previous chapter, sound is a physical force that generates pressure. Therefore, the transmission of sound from one side of a barrier, such as a wall, to the other side requires the actual movement (i.e., vibration) of the wall. In other words, the pressure created by the sound waves on the internal side of the wall creates a force that causes the wall to deflect slightly. This deflection, however slight, will produce sound waves on the other side of the wall. Successive sound waves produce successive deflections, so that the wall starts to vibrate. Under most sound conditions experienced in buildings this vibration is so slight that it cannot be seen. However, quite often it can be felt when the wall is touched lightly with one hand and the sound source has low frequency,

such as a truck passing by. Naturally, the heavier the wall the more sound energy will be required to set it into vibration.

There are of course other factors involved. For example, the stiffness (i.e., rigidity) of the wall also plays a role. A stiff wall is set in vibration more easily than a pliable wall, which will tend to dampen the mechanical reaction to the incident sound waves through its sluggishness. These and other factors involved in the transmission of sound through a barrier are discussed in more detail in the next chapter.

What is perhaps less intuitively obvious is why a heavy wall can be expected to have a lower coefficient of absorption. The reason is that a dense material is also less porous and this reduces the ability of sound waves to penetrate into the material and set air pockets within the material into vibration, thereby converting some of their mechanical energy into heat energy owing to friction. As a result, since a heavy wall transmits less sound and absorbs less sound, a greater proportion of the incident sound is reflected.

When sound is reflected from a hard, smooth surface the law of reflection, which also applies to light, is closely obeyed. Typical reflection patterns for plane and curved walls are shown in Figure 10.1. In the case of a curved wall the reflection occurs as if a tangent plane exists at the point where the incident sound ray (i.e., wave) meets the wall.

If the surface is irregular, as shown in Figure 10.2, then the degree to which the reflections are diffused depends on the relationship between the size of the irregularities and the wavelength of the incident sound. As a rule of thumb, the amount of diffusion will be significant if the wavelength of the incident sound is less than four times the radius of curvature of the protrusions.

If the surface is not a continuous boundary but takes the form of a reflecting panel or shield that is placed in the path of the incident sound, then the behavior of the sound depends very much on its wavelength. If the dimensions of the panel are not several times larger than the wavelength, then much of the sound will tend

Sound may be diffused by reflection if the reflecting surface has an irregular surface and the dimensions of the irregularities are greater than 1/4 of the wavelength of the incident sound.

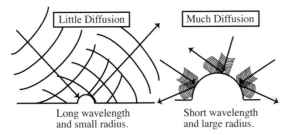

Long wavelength and small radius.   Short wavelength and large radius.

● Diffusion of sound at side walls of a hall is preferable to absorption for speech and music.

● Effective diffusion will require irregularities with a wide range of dimensions to accommodate different frequencies (i.e., wavelengths).

Figure 10.2   Reflection on irregular surfaces.

The ability of sound waves to bend around an obstacle is referred to as diffraction. Long wavelength sound has greater 'bending' capabilities than short wavelength sound.

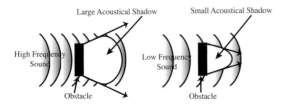

 If the obstacle is small in relation to the wavelength (e.g., half the size of the sound wave) of the sound then much of the sound will 'bend' around the obstacle with virtually no acoustical shadow being produced.

Figure 10.3   Acoustical shadows.

to bend or *diffract* around the obstacle in its path (Figure 10.3).

In this respect the behavior of sound appears to be quite different from the interaction of light with an obstacle; however, in reality that is not true. It is simply a matter of scale. Owing to the

much shorter wavelength of light (see the discussion at the beginning of this chapter), the physical dimensions of any surface that might be encountered in a building will be several orders of magnitude larger.

In halls for speech and music reflecting panels are often used to improve and control the quality of the acoustic environment. To be effective the dimensions of these panels must be at least five times larger than the wavelength of the sound to be reflected. As an example let us consider a lecture hall. What are the minimum dimensions of a suspended panel designed to reflect to the front section of the audience the typically mid-frequency speech sounds produced by the lecturer?

$$\text{mid-frequency} = 500 \text{ to } 2000 \text{ cps}$$
$$\text{wavelength of sound} = [(\text{speed of sound}) / (\text{frequency of sound})]$$
$$\text{speed of sound in air} = 1100 \text{ FT/sec}$$
$$\text{wavelength at } 500 \text{ cps} = [1100 / 500] = 2.2 \text{ FT}$$
$$\text{wavelength at } 2000 \text{ cps} = [1100 / 2000] = 0.6 \text{ FT}$$

Therefore, to effectively reflect sound waves at the lower end of the mid-frequency range (i.e., 500 cps), the dimensions of the panel need to be at least 11 FT by 11 FT.

Conversely, the acoustical shadow that will be produced behind a large reflecting surface may be highly undesirable or very useful, depending on the circumstances. In the case of an auditorium the acoustic shadow that is likely to occur under deep balconies must be avoided by the designer, because of its unfavorable effect on the listening conditions of that section of the audience. In the case of halls for music, involving a much wider range of wavelengths, the situation is exacerbated because low-frequency sound is able to penetrate more deeply under balconies than high-frequency sound. Therefore, there is an additional danger that the audience positions under a deep balcony will receive an unbalanced frequency spectrum.

A useful application of the acoustic shadow phenomenon is the construction of walls along freeways to shield adjacent communities from

When sound passes through an opening the sound waves tend to bend around the edges of the opening, thereby extending the optical zone (sound waves do not always travel in a straight line like light) with a diffracted zone.

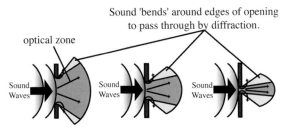

Sound 'bends' around edges of opening to pass through by diffraction.

optical zone

Sound Waves

Sound Waves

Sound Waves

With decreasing opening size an increasingly larger proportion of sound passes through by diffraction.

The acoustical transparency of an opening is always greater than the optical transparency.

The acoustical transparency increases with increasing wavelength (i.e., decreasing frequency).

Figure 10.4   **Diffraction around openings.**

vehicular traffic noise. Unfortunately, much of the noise produced by trucks and fast-moving cars tends to be in the low-frequency range between 100 and 300 cps (i.e., from 11 FT down to 3.7 FT). Therefore, an effective traffic noise barrier needs to be quite high, making it a rather costly proposition. It needs to be able to resist substantial horizontal forces due to wind,[2] and possibly earthquakes if located in a seismic region.

Sound is also subject to diffraction when it passes through a small opening (Figure 10.4). The proportion of the transmitted sound that passes through the opening by diffraction increases with both decreasing frequency and decreasing size of the opening. In other words, for low-frequency sound and small openings almost all of the sound is transmitted by diffraction (i.e., it bends around the edge of the opening). Consequently, the amount of sound that is transmitted through a small opening is always greater than what would seem possible based on the visual appearance of the opening. In technical terms, the sum total of sound passing through a small opening is made up of

two components: namely, the optical zone component; and the diffraction zone component.

10.2   Absorption of sound

Although a small amount of sound is absorbed during its passage through air by the friction of oscillating molecules, this absorption is negligible at low frequencies (i.e., frequencies less than 1000 cps), and quite small even at higher frequencies. In halls for speech and music the absorption of the audience is usually the largest single factor, due mainly to the absorption provided by clothing. Accordingly, the acoustic conditions in an auditorium will change significantly in relation to the number of people present and their location. This problem has been largely overcome in modern auditoria and concert halls by the use of highly absorbent seating, with each individual seat providing, ideally, the same absorption whether occupied by a person or not.

There remains then for consideration the absorption that inevitably takes place whenever sound waves strike the wall surfaces of a room. The surface on which the sound impinges may move slightly owing to air pressure changes, or if it is porous, air may penetrate to some depth. In either case energy will be expended and this naturally causes a reduction of sound energy. As a result, the reflected sound wave is bound to be weaker than the incident wave, and the degree of absorption will depend on the Absorption Coefficient (α) of the surface. The latter provides a simple numerical scale that relates the incident sound energy to the sound energy absorbed by the surface. Perfect reflection and complete absorption (e.g., an open window) are rated on this scale as zero and unity, respectively. While the Absorption Coefficient varies with the angle of incidence of the sound waves, in practice it normally suffices to state the average value taken over all angles (Figure 10.5).

The unit of sound absorption is the *sabin* named after the American acoustician Wallace Sabine (1869–1919). As discussed earlier in this

Construction and/or Material	125 cps	500 cps	2000 cps
Walls:			
clay bricks (glazed)	0.03	0.03	0.05
clay bricks (painted)	0.01	0.02	0.02
concrete (painted)	0.10	0.06	0.09
gypsum board (1/2") (on two sides of studs)	0.27	0.05	0.03
glass window	0.35	0.18	0.07
Floors:			
wood floor on joists	0.15	0.10	0.06
wood parquet on concrete	0.04	0.07	0.06
concrete or terrazzo	0.01	0.01	0.02
linoleum on concrete	0.02	0.03	0.03
carpet (heavy) on concrete	0.05	0.14	0.60
Miscellaneous:			
water surface (pool)	0.01	0.01	0.02
curtain fabric (10 oz.)	0.03	0.11	0.24
curtain fabric (18 oz.)	0.14	0.55	0.70
metal roof deck	0.40	0.15	0.04
wood roof deck	0.24	0.14	0.13
glass pane (1/4" or thicker)	0.15	0.04	0.02

Figure 10.5   Absorption coefficients.

If the surface area of a wall (i.e., any surface) is 80 SF and the Absorption Coefficient is 0.25 at 125 cps then the sound absorption provided by that wall is 20 sabins (i.e., 80 x 0.25) at a frequency of 125 cps.

Example: The Sound Absorption Coefficients in a large conference room measuring 20 FT (length) by 15 FT (width) by 8 FT (height) are:

Surface Material	Location	125 cps	500 cps	2000 cps
clay bricks (painted)	walls	0.01	0.02	0.02
carpet (1/4" pile)	floor	0.04	0.15	0.50
pegboard (1/4" over 4" fiberglass)	ceiling	0.80	1.00	0.38

What is the total sound absorption in the empty room?

wall area = 2(20 x 8) + 2(15 x 8) = 560 SF
wall sound absorption = 560 x 0.01 = 5.6 sabins at 125 cps
floor area = 20 x 15 = 300 SF
floor sound absorption = 300 x 0.04 = 12.0 sabins at 125 cps
ceiling area = 20 x 15 = 300 SF
ceiling sound absorption = 300 x 0.80 = 240.0 sabins at 125 cps

Total sound absorption (125 cps) = 5.6 + 12.0 + 240.0   = 257.6 sabins.
Total sound absorption (500 cps) = 11.2 + 45.0 + 300.0 = 356.2 sabins.
Total sound absorption (2000 cps) = 11.2 + 150.0 + 114.0 = 275.2 sabins.

Figure 10.6   Absorption of a wall surface.

chapter, the *Sound Absorption Coefficient* is a measure of the proportion of incident sound that is absorbed by a surface expressed as a decimal number (so that perfect absorption is equal to 1.0).

Figure 10.6 shows a calculated example of the total sound absorption in *sabins* provided by a conference room with acoustically *hard* (i.e., reflective) wall surfaces, a carpeted floor, and an acoustic ceiling.

Two additional measures of sound absorption are commonly used:

Noise Reduction Coefficient = The average of the Sound Absorption Coefficients at the four frequencies of 250 cps, 500 cps, 1000 cps, and 2000 cps.

For example, a material with Sound Absorption Coefficients of 0.31 (at 250 cps), 0.52 (at 500 cps), 0.83 (at 1000 cps), and 0.91 (at 2000 cps) will have the following Noise Reduction Coefficient (NRC):

$$NRC = [(0.31 + 0.52 + 0.83 + 0.91) / 4] = 0.65$$

Average Absorption Coefficient = Total absorption of all surfaces in a room (i.e., area times Absorption Coefficient divided by the total surface area).

The well-known *conservation of energy* principle in physics tells us that energy cannot be simply lost. Therefore the absorption of sound must involve the conversion of sound energy to one or more other forms of energy. Fundamentally, sound-absorbing mechanisms and devices are divided into three categories: porous absorbers, panel absorbers, and volume absorbers.

In *Porous Absorbers* incident sound waves force the air in the pores of a material to vibrate producing friction, which converts sound energy into heat energy. When soft materials such as carpet or heavy fabric are exposed to sound waves the air contained in the pores of the material is set into motion, causing the transformation of some sound energy into heat energy. However, if the porous surface of the material is covered with paint or a plastic membrane, then the absorption may be seriously affected and it is therefore normal practice to choose materials with a natural finish.

In *Panel Absorbers* incident sound waves set a solid panel mounted in front of an air space into vibration. The mechanical action of the panel, dampened by the air pocket, absorbs the sound energy. Examples include the diaphragmatic action of airtight membranes such as paper, oilcloth, and plywood panels, which are mounted at some distance from a solid wall. The incident sound waves will cause the membrane and the air in the cavity behind it to vibrate, thereby dissipating sound energy. While the absorption will be a maximum whenever the vibrating panel is in resonance, it may also be increased by filling the air cavity with a resilient material.

In *Volume Absorbers* incident sound waves acting through a small opening set a contained volume of air into vibration. The vibration of air inside the container and the surging of the air through the small opening convert sound energy into heat energy.

10.2.1   Porous absorbers

It follows from the table of common building materials shown in Figure 10.5 that rough, soft, porous, and light materials absorb most sound, while smooth, hard, dense, and heavy materials absorb least. We may therefore generalize that the structure of the material, as well as the surface finish, will affect the degree of absorption. In this respect a distinction can be drawn between *rigid* porous surfaces and *flexible* porous surfaces. Porous surfaces that are rigid may be characterized by the following three properties:

- Porosity, which is a measure of the amount of air-filled space in the material.
- Flow resistance, which is best described as the resistance of the material to the direct passage of air. If P_1 and P_2 are the air pressures on the two opposite sides of a material, then the flow resistance F_R is given by:

$$F_R = [(\text{flow velocity}) \times (P_1 - P_2)$$
$$/(\text{thickness of material})] \qquad [10.1]$$

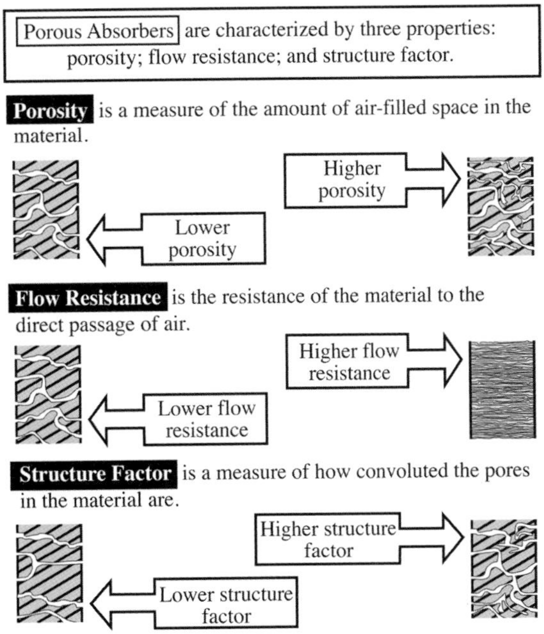

Figure 10.7   Porous absorbers in theory.

(where the *flow velocity* is assumed to be in the direction of P_1 to P_2.)

- Structure factor, which provides a measure of the amount of air-filled space in sealed pores, cul-de-sac pores, or the equivalent. Accordingly, a material in which all pores run straight through from one side to the other would have a very low structure factor of around one.

Illustrations of these interrelated properties are contained in Figure 10.7, while Figure 10.8 describes some typical practical applications. Flow resistance is of considerable importance and warrants some further explanation. When sound travels through air, not only is some sound energy dissipated (i.e., absorbed), but the sound also experiences a very small characteristic impedance as it furnishes the forces required to alternately squeeze and accelerate the air molecules during its motion. Owing to the general principle of conservation of energy, the energy stored during the application of these forces will be regained in the next half cycle of wave motion. If the sound waves reach the end of one medium, then part of the

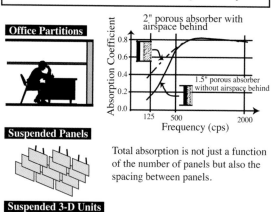

Porous Absorbers consisting of fiberglass or mineral wool with a protective fabric wrapping are commonly used in low height office partitions and as wall or ceiling mounted panels.

Office Partitions

2" porous absorber with airspace behind

1.5" porous absorber without airspace behind

Suspended Panels

Total absorption is not just a function of the number of panels but also the spacing between panels.

Suspended 3-D Units

Each unit provides a certain amount of absorption at a particular frequency.

Figure 10.8 **Porous absorbers in practice.**

sound energy will continue in the second medium while the remainder is reflected back into the first medium. Depending on the compatibility of the characteristic impedances of the two media, either a large or small fraction of the total incident sound energy will continue to travel through the second medium. Naturally, if there is a large difference between the characteristic impedances of the two media, most of the energy is likely to be reflected. This explains the deleterious effect on absorption that a thin surface layer of paint will have on a porous material. The paint will tend to seal the pores, thereby increasing the flow resistance of the surface with the result that more sound energy will be reflected.

Flexible porous surfaces fall into two categories. If the material has a low flow resistance (i.e., the pores penetrate through from one surface to another), it will have properties very similar to those of *rigid* porous materials, although by virtue of its flexibility the material will tend to move under the pressure of the incident sound waves. This movement will tend to increase the effective density of the porous material, as well as improve its absorptive

capacity due to energy losses. On the other hand, in the case of a *flexible* porous material containing sealed pores (e.g., plastic foams) the flow resistance will be much higher and the absorption due to elastic movement is likely to dominate.

Impervious surfaces, whether rigidly mounted or not, will normally allow a fair amount of vibration under the action of sound pressures. This vibration will be a maximum when the frequency of the incident sound waves is the same as the natural frequency of the surface. Under these conditions the amplitude of the vibration will be reinforced and the amount of sound energy dissipated (i.e., absorbed) will be correspondingly large. This phenomenon is referred to as *resonance* and will be discussed in more detail in the following section.

In summary, a good *porous absorber* is a material with many interconnected and continuous open pores. Such pores will produce a great deal of friction as the air, set into vibration by the incident sound waves, pumps back and force within the material. Accordingly:

- Only open-cell materials are good *porous absorbers*. Plastic foams such as expanded polyurethane, which are excellent thermal insulators, are poor sound absorbers due to their closed cell structure.
- Open-cell plastic foams, such as melamine and polyester, are good sound absorbers owing to their interconnected cell structure.
- General building construction advantages of open-cell plastic foams include light weight, fiber-free composition, and moldability. Disadvantages include their combustibility and the emission of toxic fumes during a fire.
- The Absorption Coefficient of a *porous absorber* typically increases with thickness. This is mainly due to the increased volume of air that can be set into vibration, thereby facilitating the dissipation of sound energy as heat.

10.2.2 Panel absorbers

We have mentioned previously the ability of materials to be set in motion by incident sound waves. Naturally, the resultant elastic vibration will cause a certain amount of sound energy to be dissipated. Although the velocity of sound in air is constant for all frequencies, the velocity of vibration that a sound wave may produce in a material will vary with the frequency of the sound. It follows that at some particular frequency the velocity of the sound wave in air will be identical to the velocity of the resultant vibration of the incident surface. At this critical frequency, the transfer of sound energy from air to surface is most efficient and the absorption is likely to be very high. This condition is referred to as *resonance* and for a *panel absorber* the largest amount of absorption will occur for frequencies where the vibrating panel is in resonance. In architecture, the entire structure of a high-rise building, an individual room subjected to standing waves,[3] or a *panel absorber*, are all examples of situations where *resonance* can play a critical role.

The resonance frequency (f_{RES}) of a *panel absorber* is a function of the mass of the panel (LB/SF) and the depth of the air space (IN) between the panel and the construction element on which it is mounted (e.g., a wall). It can be calculated as follows:

$$f_{RES} = [170/((\text{panel mass}) \times (\text{air space depth}))^{1/2}] \text{ cps} \quad [10.2]$$

Since *panel absorbers* have a relatively low Absorption Coefficient, they are rarely used in buildings to absorb noise at the source, such as in the mechanical spaces. However, they are used to considerable advantage in halls for speech and music, where the amount of sound that must be absorbed is less of a concern then considerations related to sound quality and visual appearance. Since the air that is contained between the back of the panel surface and the wall acts as a damping device – much like mattress springs would if the panel were to be attached to the wall by such metal springs – it follows that the amount of absorption provided can be fine-tuned in at least two ways (Figure 10.9).

First, the placement of fiberglass or mineral wool in the cavity will increase the Absorption Coefficient by virtue of the increase in damping.

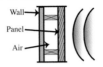

| Panel Absorbers | absorb sound energy by mechanical action through 'damping' forces. Damping is provided by the air behind the panel, the edge fixing of the panel, and the resistance to bending vibrations of the panel itself.

The incident sound waves set the panel into vibration, thereby converting sound energy into mechanical energy.

The vibrating panel sets the air behind it into vibration. The vibrating air acts much like a spring, absorbing energy as it dampens the vibration of the panel.

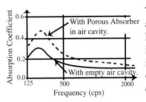

The Absorption Coefficient of a Panel Absorber increases if a Porous Absorber is placed inside the air cavity. This increases the damping effect of the air by increasing the effective viscosity of the air.

Figure 10.9   Mechanical action of a panel absorber.

Second, the depth of the air space behind the panel will influence the resonant frequency of a panel absorber. A relatively thin cushion of air will result in a stiffer spring action, while a thicker cushion of air will produce a more pliable spring action. Applying equation [10.2], we can see by inspection that combinations of large panel mass and deep air cavity will lead to lower resonant frequencies. However, even at resonant frequencies the Absorption Coefficient provided by a panel absorber rarely exceeds 0.3, unless it is made of a very inelastic (i.e., limp) material such as thin lead sheeting.

10.2.3   Acoustic ceilings

The sound-absorption properties of a typical suspended acoustical tile ceiling combine the characteristics of porous absorbers and panel absorbers. An acoustical tile, whether it has regularly spaced holes or is textured in some way, is essentially a rigid board (i.e., a panel) made of a porous material. From this point of view it has the characteristics of a porous absorber. However, since acoustical tiles are usually suspended from a structural frame below the floor above or below the roof, with a large air cavity in between, they also have the properties of a panel absorber.

Manufacturers normally quote the absorption characteristics of acoustical tiles in terms of the Noise Reduction Coefficient discussed at the beginning of Section 10.2. This is an average value, since the Noise Reduction Coefficient is based on four frequencies within the range of 250 to 2000 Hz or cps (i.e., 250, 500, 1000, and 2000 cps).

10.2.4 Volume absorbers

A further category of absorption is provided by perforated or slotted panels backed by porous materials, according to the Helmholtz principle. Absorption devices based on this principle are commonly referred to as volume absorbers.

As shown in Figure 10.10, the incident sound waves are forced through a narrow opening into a larger space containing air. The latter is set into vibration if the natural period of vibration in this space is the same as the frequency

of the particular sound. We might say that the air in the space has its own resonance, and when the sound wave emerges from the aperture it is forced to vibrate. This causes air to surge in and out of the aperture, resulting in the absorption of sound energy due to friction.

$$f_{RES} = [(2165 \times \text{area of neck})/((\text{neck volume})$$
$$\times (\text{air space volume}))^{1/2}]\,\text{cps} \qquad [10.3]$$

It is normal practice to further impede the movement of the vibrating air by the addition of some porous material to the neck, or by loosely filling the air space with fibrous material. This brings us to an interesting point: namely, resonators can also act as stores for energy rather than just dissipaters. This phenomenon, which occurs when the viscosity of air in the aperture is sufficiently large, has been developed by Parkin and Morgan (1965) as a means of prolonging the reverberation time for frequency groups in the Royal Festival Hall, London.

The most common application of volume absorbers in buildings is in the form of walls constructed with slotted hollow concrete blocks, also referred to as *acoustical blocks* (Figures 10.11 and 10.12).

Owing to the thickness of the wall of the concrete block, the slotted opening becomes the neck of a Helmholtz resonator, while the hollow portion of the block serves as the large air space. The addition of a *septum* inside the larger air space, as shown in Figure 10.11, essentially creates two resonant frequencies. The rear cavity will absorb the lower-frequency sound and the front cavity will absorb the higher-frequency sound.

10.3 Speech communication

In an enclosed space, sound originating from a source will spread out on the surface of a sphere of continually increasing diameter until some part of this surface reaches the enclosing shell, where some of the sound is absorbed or transmitted and the remaining portion is reflected according to simple geometrical rules. In quick

---

A | Volume Absorber | consists of a neck-type opening connecting a larger volume of air to the room environment (like a bottle). The incident sound waves set the air in the neck into vibration, which in turn activates the air in the larger volume.

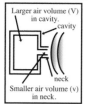

Larger air volume (V) in cavity.

Smaller air volume (v) in neck.

As the air in the neck churns backward and forward it converts some of the incident sound energy into friction and then heat. The oscillations in the neck peak at the resonance frequency (f_R) of the Volume Absorber, which can be calculated as follows:

$$f_R = \cfrac{2165 \left[\begin{array}{c}\text{cross-sectional}\\\text{area of neck}\end{array}\right]}{\sqrt{\left[\begin{array}{c}\text{Volume}\\\text{of neck}\end{array}\right] \times \left[\begin{array}{c}\text{Volume}\\\text{of cavity}\end{array}\right]}} \quad \text{(cps)}$$

Example:

What is the resonance frequency (f_R) of a Volume Absorber with a neck that measures 2 in. by 2 in. by 4 in. (length) and a cavity that is a 12 in. cube?

area of neck = 2 x 2 = 4 SI
volume of neck = 2 x 2 x 4 = 16 CI
volume of cavity = 12 x 12 x 12 = 1728 CI

$$f_R = \frac{2165 \times 4}{\sqrt{16 \times 1728}} = 52 \text{ cps}$$

Figure 10.10 Volume absorber or Helmholtz resonator.

The absorption of a Volume Absorber is a maximum at its resonance frequency, which is usually in the low frequency range.

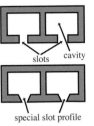

slots   cavity

special slot profile

metal septum

porous material
(e.g., fiberglass)

- The most commonly used Volume Absorber is a special concrete block unit with two slots (i.e., neck) and sealed on three sides (i.e., cavity).

- Changing the width, height and profile of the slots provides some limited control over the resonance frequency of the Volume Absorber (typically no more than an octave).

- The placement of a metal divider (i.e., septum) in each cavity improves the higher frequency absorption (i.e., low frequency sound will pass through the septum, while high frequency sound will activate the air in the front portion of the cavity only). The septum essentially creates two resonance frequencies.

- Addition of porous material (e.g., fiberglass or mineral wool) to the slot and/or cavity will further increase the sound absorption capabilities.

Figure 10.11 **Different configurations of a concrete block absorption unit.**

Volume Absorbers are also referred to as volume resonators and Helmholtz resonators. They absorb sound energy by friction in the narrow opening (i.e., neck or slot) and by the damping provided by the air in the cavity.

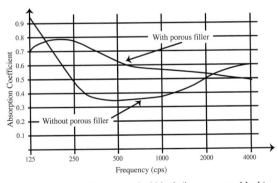

Test results for an 8 inch acoustical block (i.e., concrete block) clearly indicate both the increased absorption in the mid-frequency region and the broadening of the absorption in the low frequency range that can be achieved with a metal septum and porous filler.

Figure 10.12 **Role of resonance in a volume absorber.**

succession, this remaining portion of the sound is inter-reflected from surface to surface within the enclosed space. During each reflection the sound energy is reduced by absorption and transmission until eventually all of the energy is dissipated. During this process of sound decay, the occupants of the space will receive some of the sound directly and some indirectly by reflection. It is logical that the listeners will hear the direct sound only once, while reflections will reach them from various directions for a period of time that is largely determined by the Absorption Coefficients of the reflecting surfaces.

Although there appears to be little change in the loudness of a sound as its direction changes, the listener can distinguish among sounds that arrive from different directions. As discussed previously, the brain is able to correlate the separate signals from each ear on a selective time-delay basis. This phenomenon is an integral part of the appreciation of sound, a fact that is simply demonstrated by blocking one ear for short periods of time when exposed to music in a fairly reverberant space. Reverberation is here defined as the acoustic sensation that is produced by the slow decay of sound. Naturally, if the enclosed space is influenced by extraneous background noise, the weaker reflections will not be heard and listening may become more difficult. The listening process may also be hindered by excess reverberation within the enclosed space. If we assume that about 10 speech sounds are produced each second during normal speech, it is apparent that excessive reverberation (i.e., the prolonged inter-reflection of each speech sound) will tend to interfere with each new speech sound. Accordingly, it is very important that the listener should receive as much sound as possible within the first few milliseconds (e.g., 30 to 50 milliseconds). This has led to the prominent development of Reverberation Time into a major acoustical criterion (see Section 10.4 later).

10.3.1 Speech interference level

Experience has shown that unwanted sound (i.e., noisiness) rather than sound intensity (i.e., loudness) is the major cause of annoyance. Noisiness seems to increase at a greater rate than loudness, whenever the pitch of a sound is raised or the complexity of the spectrum is increased. Furthermore, the reaction to noisiness is time-dependent. It has been demonstrated that annoyance levels are higher if unwanted sound persists beyond 200 milliseconds. Owing to the fact that individuals vary in their reaction to noise, we are forced to assess these subjective reactions on a statistical basis.

In regard to interference with speech or music, it has been found that individual variation is not great and it is therefore possible to predict with reasonable accuracy the effect of ambient noise. However, when it is a question of annoyance, we are unfortunately faced with a wide range of responses. Nevertheless, it is highly desirable – and indeed possible – to make some estimate of the response of a group of persons to a particular background noise level.

The criterion of Speech Interference Level is widely used to specify the permissible levels of background noise that will not interfere with speech communication. Background noise will increase our threshold of hearing and as a result we may be able to distinguish only a few of the sounds necessary for satisfactory speech intelligibility. The energy of the various speech sounds is distributed over a frequency range of below 100 cps to above 10 000 cps. Fortunately, a complete frequency range is not required for reliable intelligibility, and it can be shown that a high percentage of the information in speech is contained in the frequency range from 200 cps to 6000 cps. Indeed, measurement and calculation may be simplified even further by using a three-octave band analysis. The bands normally chosen are 600–1200 cps, 1200–2400 cps, and 2400–4800 cps. The average of the sound levels in these three bands is described as the Speech Interference Level.

However, it should be pointed out that Speech Interference Levels were developed as a simplification of the more complex method of assessing articulation (ANSI, 1969, 1989). Early researchers in this field measured the intelligi-

bility ratio using syllables, words, and sentences. A speaker would constitute a source and communicate a predetermined list of sounds, while a number of listeners would attempt to write down the sounds as they heard them. The intelligibility ratio was then defined as the percentage of syllables correctly recognized by the listeners. Word and sentence intelligibility can be measured similarly, although in these cases scores are likely to be higher because of the inherent redundancies of normal speech.

10.3.2 Background noise

The concept of Speech Interference Level (abbreviated to SIL in Tables 10.1, 10.2, and 10.5, and in Figure 10.13) was briefly discussed previously, in Section 9.7.

Table 10.1   Maximum background noise levels (i.e., SIL) for reliable speech communication (according to Beranek).

Distance between speaker and listener	Speaker's voice level			
	Normal	Raised	Loud	Shouting
1 FT	66 dB	72 dB	78 dB	84 dB
2 FT	60 dB	66 dB	72 dB	78 dB
4 FT	54 dB	60 dB	66 dB	72 dB
6 FT	50 dB	56 dB	62 dB	68 dB
12 FT	44 dB	50 dB	56 dB	62 dB
24 FT	38 dB	44 dB	50 dB	56 dB

Table 10.2   Maximum background noise levels (i.e., SIL) for reliable speech communication (according to Furrer).

Noise criteria curve (NCA)	Maximum speech intelligibility distance	
	Normal voice	Raised voice
40 NCA	23 FT	40 FT
45 NCA	13 FT	25 FT
50 NCA	7 FT	12 FT
55 NCA	4 FT	7 FT
60 NCA	2 FT	4 FT

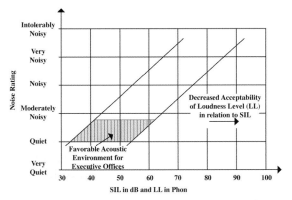

Figure 10.13   The relationship between SIL and LL (acording to Beranek).

For convenience, Table 9.3 is reproduced hereunder as Table 10.1. This table lists the Speech Interference Levels that barely allow reliable conversation at the distances and noise levels indicated. The values listed in Table 10.1 are based on average male speakers and average listeners, and will thus involve some variations due to individual differences. This variation has been estimated to be of the order of 10 dBA. While it is mainly noise in the three octave bands (i.e., 600–1200, 1200–2400, and 2400–4800 cps) that will interfere with speech, noise at lower frequencies will also interfere if it is sufficiently loud (Houtgast and Steeneken, 1984; Steeneken and Houtgast, 1985).

Experience in office environments has shown that communicating persons (i.e., speakers and listeners) are keenly aware of the deleterious effect of background noise on speech intelligibility. Beranek found that a large percentage of office workers communicate *often* to *very often*, and that the Speech Interference Level for continuous noise should therefore not exceed 40 dB. Furthermore, office staff seem to desire a Loudness Level (LL) that does not exceed the Speech Interference Level by more than 22 phons (Figure 10.13). It appears therefore that the objective measure of Speech Interference Level is in some cases inadequate and that the subjective LL should be also taken into account.

Accordingly, in 1956 Beranek proposed Noise Criteria Curves (NC or NCA[4]) as a design crite-

rion for the specification of maximum permissible or desirable background noise levels in various occupancies (Beranek, 1960). It is assumed that the background noise is nearly steady. For intermittent noise, short-duration loud noise may be permitted to exceed the sound pressure levels indicated by these curves without creating undue interference with speech communication. Since this type of specification is possible only in conjunction with a complete frequency analysis of the background noise, the Noise Criteria Curves are plotted on a chart of eight octave bands. The measured octave band levels for each of the eight octaves are plotted on the chart and the corresponding NC value is noted. The noise is then rated according to the highest NC value in any band.

This led Beranek to propose the following NC ranges for the maximum background noise levels in various types of office space.

NC-20 to NC-30: Executive offices and large conference rooms (50 persons) that require a *very quiet* environment for clear communication at some distance.

NC-30 to NC-35: Private and semi-private offices, reception rooms, and small conference rooms (20 persons) that require a *quiet* environment to facilitate communication in a normal voice at a distance of 10 to 30 FT (e.g., around a 15 FT table).

NC-35 to NC-40: Medium-sized offices and industrial business offices in which communication in a normal voice at a distance of 6 to 12 FT around an 8 FT table should be possible.

NC-40 to NC-50: Large engineering, banking, lobbies, and waiting rooms in which communication in a normal voice at a distance of 3 to 6 FT around a 5 FT table should be possible.

NC-50 to NC-55: Unsatisfactory for conferences of more than two or three persons, since satisfactory speech communication in a normal voice is restricted to a distance of about 2 FT.

Above NC-55: A *very noisy* environment that is not recommended for any office space.

Noise measurements made for the purpose of judging the acceptability of the noise in an office environment in comparison with these suggested criteria should be made with the office in normal operation, but with no one talking at the particular work station or conference table where the noise is being measured. The equivalent background noise in an unoccupied office space should be between 5 and 10 NC units lower.

Beranek's recommendations for maximum allowable background noise levels have been generally followed to the present day, even though individual acoustic engineers may have presented their own suggestions in slightly different forms. For example, on the basis of the NCA version of the NC curves the Swiss acoustic engineer Willi Furrer (1964) recommended the noise ratings for speech intelligibility shown in Table 10.2.

The English acoustic engineers Parkin and Humphreys (1958) proposed four criteria for permissible noise levels in rooms used for speech and music. Even though they decided to present their recommendations on the basis of octave bands, the relationship to Noise Criteria Curves and therefore the influence of Beranek is evident. These maximum recommended noise levels (Table 10.3) refer to intruding noise, assumed to be of a meaningless nature. Criterion A is fairly close to the threshold of hearing for

continuous noise and applies to situations where almost complete silence is required (e.g., concert halls). Criterion B may be accepted as a compromise if Criterion A is unattainable and also applies to broadcasting studios, opera houses, and larger theaters. Criterion C applies to classrooms, music rooms, conference rooms, and assembly halls, while Criterion D refers to courtrooms and churches.

10.3.3 Masking sound principles

Masking is concerned with the effect of one noise on another. It is a common experience to have one sound completely drowned out when another, louder noise occurs. For example, during the early hours of the evening the normal domestic refrigerator motor may not be heard, because of the usual background noise level occurring at that time. However, late at night when there is much less background noise, the motor noise of the same refrigerator will become relatively louder and possibly annoying. Actually the noise level produced by the motor is the same in the two instances; however, the apparent noise level is louder at night because there is less background or masking noise present. Similarly, speech that may be perfectly intelligible in a relatively quiet sound environment will become less intelligible as the background noise level becomes louder until, ultimately, complete masking will take place. While it is possible to determine directly the amount of noise reduction (i.e., attenuation) required of a particular wall separating a noisy and quiet sound environment, this applies only when there is no other noise in the receiving room. Obviously, if there is some other noise present, then the intruding noise will be partially masked. It is therefore possible to influence the Speech Interference Level of a particular acoustic environment through an artificially produced *sound blanket* (i.e., background sound).

The masking of one tone by another was described in the early 1900s by Wegel and Lane (1924). It was observed that the masking of one pure tone by another is most apparent when the two tones are of approximately the

Table 10.3 Maximum background noise levels for various occupancies recommended by Parkin and Humphreys.

Frequency (octave band in cps or Hz)	Criterion			
	A	B	C	D
37 to 75 cps	53	54	57	60
75 to 150 cps	38	43	47	51
150 to 300 cps	28	35	39	43
300 to 600 cps	18	28	32	37
600 to 1200 cps	12	23	28	32
1200 to 2400 cps	11	20	25	30
2400 to 4800 cps	10	17	22	28
4800 to 9600 cps	22	22	22	27

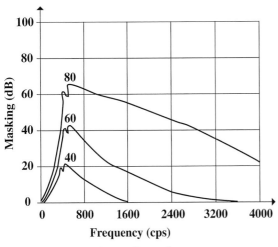

Figure 10.14   Masking effect of a pure tone.

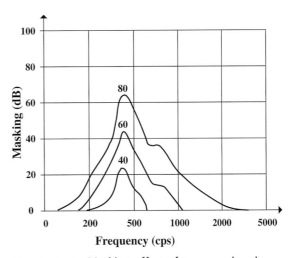

Figure 10.15   Masking effect of a narrow band.

same frequency. On the basis of their experiments dealing with monaural listening, Wegel and Lane made certain predictions as to the manner in which pure tones will mask speech communication. The typical masking effect of a pure tone at a frequency of 400 cps is shown in Figure 10.14.

The number on each curve refers to the sound level above the level of the masking tone. On studying these curves, it is readily appreciated that the masking effect of a pure tone is greatest near the frequency of the total component, falling off steeply on either side. As a means of comparison, curves of masking versus frequency for masking by a narrow band are shown in Figure 10.15, based on the research of Egan and Hake (1950). Clearly, these curves are quite similar to the curves shown in Figure 10.14 apart from the elimination of the sharp dips, which are known to be caused by beats.

In 1959 Bryan and Parbrook (1959, 1960) published results of their own experiments on masking sound and compared these with the earlier publications of Egan and Hake (1950) and Wegel and Lane (1924). By interpolating the shift in the masked threshold for the harmonics of a masking tone of frequency 400 cps, they found some divergence between the results of these two research groups. Not only are the slopes of the masking curves different, but

there is also a discrepancy of some 15 dB in the masking threshold. Bryan and Parbrook's experimental results are generally in good agreement with those of Egan and Hake.

Hempstock (in Jones et al., 1967) draws attention to the *critical band* principle, which may be applied when the masking stimulus is less than 50 dB above the threshold of audibility. The *critical band* is here defined as the width of a band of uniform noise that contains the same power as a tone at its masked threshold. By masking a pure tone with noise of increasing bandwidth, while keeping the central frequency of this noise similar to that of the pure tone, it is possible to determine variations in the degree of masking. However, a stage is reached at which the degree of masking remains unaltered with any further increase in bandwidth. Hence a critical bandwidth may be found for the specific frequency of the pure tone being masked.

10.3.4   Artificial sound blankets

Experience has shown that high levels of intruding noise can result in substantial physiological stress in the occupants of a building space. However, it must be recognized that the resultant stress situation can be amplified or reduced by the state of mind, motivation, occupation, and degree of familiarization of each individual person (Carr, 1967; Stevens, 1951). Further, it is necessary to distinguish between continuous steady-state noise, continuous variable noise, and random impulsive noise. As long as the level is not too high (e.g., below 80 dB), continuous steady-state sound appears to be able to be tolerated by most persons for prolonged periods without a negative psychological impact. For example, aircraft passengers can communicate quite comfortably with adjacent passengers in the presence of an ambient steady-state noise level of 75 dBA to 80 dBA. Also, background noise levels of 55 dBA to 60 dBA may be quite acceptable in general office areas under most conditions.

The annoyance generated by intruding sound is a complicated, subjective issue. Broadly speaking, it has been found that the degree of annoyance produced is more closely related to the nature of the noise and its relationship with everyday experience, rather than the Loudness Level. The noise produced by a dentist's drill is a lucid illustration of this supposition.

In hot-humid climates, a serious conflict arises between thermal and acoustical comfort requirements in buildings that are not air-conditioned. Open windows of substantial size are essential for uninterrupted cross-ventilation. The intruding noise level may not be sufficiently high to completely mask speech communication, yet can cause considerable reduction in the intelligibility of telephone conversations. Faced with this situation, Australian acoustic consultants Carr and Wilkinson (see Carr, 1967) developed a customized window unit with three specific features designed to mitigate both the thermal and acoustic environment within the building (Figure 10.16).

First, double glazing reduces the intruding noise level. Second, continuous and controlled air movement is provided by a tangential fan assembly, and third, the mechanical operation of the fan provides steady-state masking sound. To validate the design of their window unit, Carr and Wilkinson measured the noise level in an executive office, exposed to external traffic noise, before and after installation of the window unit (Figure 10.17).

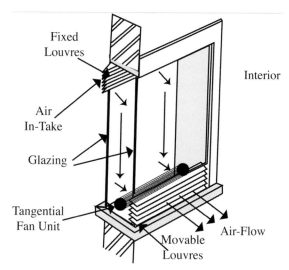

Figure 10.16 Window-fan masking unit (after Carr and Wilkinson).

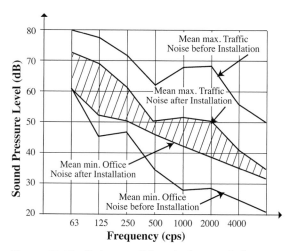

Figure 10.17 Noise conditions before and after installation of window fan unit.

They found that the fan provided a broadband masking sound equivalent to approximately NC 40, and described the spectrum of this masking sound as nondescript and tolerable. Although extraneous traffic noise was still audible, it was not considered to be disturbing or annoying by the occupant of the office.

From a more general point of view, artificial sound blankets in office spaces would normally have two objectives. First, to provide speech privacy in those places and at times when discussions are likely to deal with confidential business or personnel matters, and second, to reduce the degree of annoyance produced by intruding noise. However, in principle, it may be argued that the introduction of additional noise into an environment that already suffers from noise pollution should be avoided. Therefore, the application of masking sound is normally reserved for situations where orthodox methods of sound insulation are likely to be very expensive or inadequate. In these situations, the sound-conditioning system provides a diffuse, nondescript background sound free from any distinctly annoying tones, tuned to provide the maximum masking effect at the lowest possible volume. It is common practice to gradually increase the volume from entrance foyer to main office and provide for similar adjustments in various sections of the office space (Pickwell, 1970).

10.3.5   Open-plan school buildings

During the 1950s there was considerable interest in the application of artificial masking sound systems to overcome inherent speech interference problems in open-plan building designs. In particular, masking sound was seen as a means of achieving an acceptable level of acoustic privacy in open-plan school buildings. We will examine this proposition in some detail.

One of the objectives of the designer of an educational building complex, such as a school, is to arrange the internal spaces in a manner that will allow the curriculum to be effectively developed and delivered. Within the total enclosed space, it will therefore be necessary to arrange a number of smaller group areas, each intended to develop a subsection of the curriculum at specific times. The most skillful division into group areas will be that which allows full use of every space for the greatest part of each day. However, because of the importance of maintaining favorable hearing conditions at all times in learning situations, acoustics has long been considered a fundamental environmental factor essential to the efficient functioning of school buildings.

Traditional practices for the design of school buildings called for the architect to separately plan the acoustical environment of classrooms individually. Under these circumstances it is possible to meet the speech privacy requirements of each classroom through sound insulation. The background noise levels in unoccupied schoolrooms can be held to a range of 35 to 40 dBA for ordinary classrooms and as low as 25 dBA for language rooms, music rooms, and special classrooms (Knudsen and Harris, 1962). To achieve these low background noise levels the architect has to rely heavily on:

- *Building layout:* Special attention must be paid to site planning in relationship to external noise centers. Adequate siting, grading, and landscaping may contribute considerably to noise attenuation. Similarly, within the school building, classrooms can be arranged in a manner that will minimize the sound insulation requirements.
- *Noise insulation:* By avoiding direct air-paths and applying proven noise-reduction solutions such as massive wall construction, internal background noise could be held to stringent levels such as 40 dBA for speech communication rooms and 45 dBA for music rooms (Knudsen and Harris, 1962; Doelle, 1965).

However, these building design and construction measures are not compatible with the notion of open-plan school buildings – a notion that desires spaces to be integrated into visually undivided large units without permanent enclosures and continuing through curtains, folding doors, glazed screens, or other forms of removable partitioning. In other words, the realization of open-plan design objectives presents the architect with acoustical problems of severe complexity. Every school activity is a potential noise source. During the 1950s and 1960s a small number of open-plan school buildings were constructed in the US. Even though these schools were judged to be reasonably acceptable from a noise-control point of view, such

School area	Mean noise level	Extreme noise level
Laboratories	70 to 75 dB	85 dB
Recitation areas	60 to 65 dB	75 dB
Activity areas	65 to 70 dB	90 dB
Individual instruction	50 to 55 dB	70 dB
Band practice	70 to 75 dB	95 dB
Group singing practice	65 to 70 dB	85 dB
Indoor play areas	80 to 85 dB	95 dB
Cafeteria	75 to 80 dB	90 dB
Outdoor playgrounds	75 to 80 dB	85 dB
External street traffic	80 to 85 dB	105 dB

school designs have not been favored in more recent years. The reasons may be more related to a need for standard modular classroom units to meet the demands of rapid expansion within economic constraints, than to the failure of open-plan concepts due to lack of noise control.

The noise levels listed in Table 10.4 serve as a guide to the average and extreme intensity ranges that may be expected in typical school building spaces (Caudill, 1954).

Movable partitions are intrinsically poor sound attenuators and any endeavor to increase their sound attenuation performance is accompanied by a substantial cost factor. Furthermore, when large spaces are subdivided into temporary cells, we must allow for pedestrian access and ventilation openings, thus creating direct air-paths and thereby nullifying a high percentage of expensive insulation treatment. The general noise levels within a school building that are listed in Table 10.4 may be broken down into three main noise groups (Knudsen and Harris, 1962), as follows:

- *Speech noise*, characterized primarily by the three-octave frequency band ranging from 600 to 4800 cps.
- *Impact noise*, consisting mostly of low-frequency sound generated by footsteps, foot shuffling, scraping of furniture, and dropping of objects.
- *Mechanical noise*, generated by mechanical and electrical services, and external vehicular traffic.

If we assume a continuous masking sound to have a spectrum typical of school activities, then in relation to the level of the masking noise the threshold of audibility will be raised by proportional amounts for each octave band. For example, suppose a noise of 70 dBA in the 600 to 1200 cps octave band is to be reduced to practical inaudibility in an adjoining room. In the absence of any masking in the second room, the required reduction will be about 59 dBA to 11 dBA (where 11 dBA is the threshold of hearing). However, if a masking noise level of y dBA in the 600 to 1200 cps octave band is present in the second room, the amount by which the threshold of audibility is raised in this octave band may be calculated as x dBA. The numerical value of x is dependent on the spectrum and level. For example, if y is equal to 35 dBA, then the threshold of audibility will be raised to about:

$$11 \text{ dBA} + 35 \text{ dBA} = 46 \text{ dBA}$$

The required sound attenuation of the wall separating the two adjoining rooms is likewise reduced to approximately 23 dBA.

In the absence of any objective measure available to determine the annoyance caused by noise, Ingerslev (among others) suggested a criterion based on *acceptable noise levels* (Ingerslev, 1952). This criterion assumes the existence of a background noise level due to occupancy. In an area where approximately 20 to 30 students are present, the background noise level (while no special activity is taking place) due to movement, breathing, and so on, will be approximately 50 dB (or 48 dBA). It is further suggested by Ingerslev that noise of a level 20 dB (or 18 dBA) below the background noise level will be inaudible if the two noise levels have the same spectrum. Accordingly, in reference to the previous example, intruding noise from an adjoining area is unlikely to cause any annoyance if its level is 30 dBA or less.

These conditions may be further illustrated by reference to Figure 10.18, where one large school space is subdivided into a number of smaller group-activity areas.

Allowing for the various activities specified to take place in areas A, B, C, D, and E, the noise level that will intrude into anyone of these areas

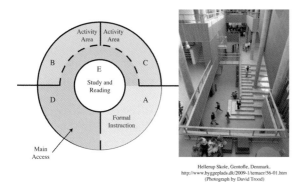

Hellerup Skole, Gentofte, Denmark.
http://www.byggeplads.dk/2009-1/temaer/56-01.htm
(Photograph by David Trood)

Figure 10.18   Conceptual layout of an open-plan
school.

may be designated as x dBA. At the same time, the background noise level due to occupants seated within this same area may be designated as y dBA. Therefore, for the intruding noise level x dBA to be practically inaudible (or at least not annoying):

x dBA must be less then or equal to

$$[y \text{ dBA} - 20 \text{ dBA}] \qquad [10.4]$$

By superimposing a masking noise level of z dBA, the overall noise level will be only slightly increased.[5] If m dBA is the actual masking noise level due to the combination of y and z dBA, then equation [10.4] can be rewritten in terms of m dBA as follows:

$$m \text{ dBA} = x \text{ dBA} + 20 \text{ dBA} \qquad [10.5]$$

In equation [10.5], x dBA is the intruding noise level and m dBA is the total masking noise level caused by the combined presence of the noise levels due to occupancy and masking sound. This general relationship provides a simplified basis for the determination of the superimposed (artificial) masking noise level z dBA, with the limitation that the total masking level m dBA must be of a sufficiently low level so as not to interfere with speech communication. In this respect it must be emphasized that the numerical value of m that is calculated with equation [10.5] is such that the intruding noise will be inaudible in relation to the total masking sound level. However, normally it would not be considered necessary to follow the stringent requirement of *inaudibility* in practice.

Taking into account the tolerable Speech Interference Levels listed in Table 10.1, the following maximum acceptable masking noise levels (m dBA) are suggested for typical instruction and study areas in schools:

Individual instruction	50 dBA
Small-group instruction	45 dBA
Group activity	50 dBA
Library and reading	40 dBA

These levels are considerably in excess of the background noise levels recommended for orthodox classrooms in non-open-plan school buildings (e.g., 25 dB by Doelle (1965), 35 dB by Knudsen and Harris (1962), and 30 dB by Beranek (1962)). In defense of this apparent diversion from accepted standards, at least two pertinent arguments may be presented. First, the standards stated by these authors are related to non-open-plan principles of school design, where requirements and methods of sound control follow a very different pattern. Second, studies conducted during the past 50 years have generally included the suggestion that there are three basic teaching spaces, namely: large-group instruction, small-group instruction, and individual study. It can be argued that the acoustical environment required in each of these spaces is determined by the number of students involved and the activities being performed. In an endeavor to be more precise on this issue, Table 10.5 provides a more detailed interpretation of those arguments.

The presence of an artificially produced sound blanket will no doubt substantially decrease the sphere of interaction of sound radiated from two or more noise sources. Yet it is equally true that if the masking noise level is too high, then the whole purpose of its presence will be defeated, since it is likely to cause annoyance of its own accord. Noise reduction at the source will allow the total masking noise level to be kept down to a minimum. In the case of school buildings designed according to open-plan principles, where heavy partitions are not feasible in most locations, noise reduction at the source will be limited to the treatment of walls, ceilings, and floors with sound-absorbing material.

Table 10.5 Suggested maximum SIL values for open-plan schools employing masking sound.

Maximum SIL	Communication environment	School area
30 dB	Very quiet room suitable for lecturing and music involving large groups of students.	Large hall Auditorium
35 dB	Quiet room with normal voice communication up to 30 FT possible.	Library Reading room
40 dB	Satisfactory for discussions involving up to 12 students. Normal voice communication up to 12 FT possible.	Interview room Staffroom
45 dB	Normal voice communication up to 6 FT and raised voice communication up to 12 FT.	Small group instruction
50 dB	Satisfactory for discussions involving up to 6 students.	Individual study and instruction
55 dB	Unsatisfactory for discussions involving more than 4 students. Normal voice communication up to 3 FT and raised voice communication up to 6 FT.	Laboratory Art studio

10.4 Halls for speech and music

The design of larger halls (i.e., auditoria) for speech and music is a complex undertaking. It requires the designer to balance several factors that influence the clarity of speech and the quality of music, respectively. Both the direct sound and the sound that reaches the audience after it has been reflected from the enclosing surfaces of the hall need to be considered. However, the reflected sound must reach the listener within a critical time window, otherwise it may interfere with the next direct sound instead of reinforcing the previous direct sound from which the reflections originated.

Sound travels about 55 FT in 0.05 sec, a time interval that the human ear can barely detect. Therefore, for perfect sound reinforcement the first reflection or echo should reach the listener within 0.05 sec of the direct sound. Also, all subsequent reflections of the same direct sound should be sufficiently weak (i.e., much lower SPL than the direct sound) so as not to be audible above the next direct sound. This time-based relationship between a direct sound and its first reinforcing reflection can be expressed in a simple geometric equation that governs the dimensions of a hall in which the communicating sound is not reinforced by electronic means (see also Figure 10.21 later). If x is the direct distance (FT) between the sound source and the listener, y is the distance (FT) between the sound source and the reflecting surface, and z is the distance (FT) between the reflecting surface and the listener, then:

$$x + y - z \leq 55 \text{ (FT)} \qquad [10.6]$$

The limit suggested by equation [10.6] may be extended in practice, depending on the loss of intelligibility that might be tolerated or even desirable. For example, in the case of a church where speech is likely to be slow and well articulated this upper limit could be extended to 60 FT. Also, the blending of one sound into the next sound may be called for in the case of romantic music.

To obtain good sound reinforcement for speech communication, reflections should preferably come from two directions so that any directional effect is either eliminated or very much reduced. Furthermore, if wall- or ceiling-mounted reflectors are used to provide this reinforcement it is important that they should be of large enough dimensions. As discussed previously in Section 10.1, to be effective the length and width dimensions of the reflecting surface should be five times the wavelength of the sound. In the case of speech this would suggest that the walls of the hall should be at least 11 FT high (i.e., the wavelength for a sound frequency of 500 cps is 2.2 FT, and 5 times 2.2 FT is equal to 11 FT).

When sound waves travel through air, energy is absorbed as the air particles (i.e. molecules) bump into each other. The amount of absorption depends on the relative humidity, but is very small at frequencies below 2000 cps and above 10,000 cps.

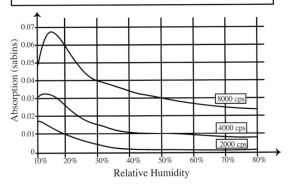

Due to air absorption thunder 'cracks' when heard up close and 'rumbles' from a distance. The high frequencies are absorbed by the air.

Figure 10.19   Sound absorption in air.

Due to the many factors involved, audience Absorption Coefficients apply only to average conditions.

Type of Seats (occupied and unoccupied)	Frequency (cps)					
	125	250	500	1000	2000	4000
Occupied Seats:						
heavily upholstered	0.76	0.83	0.88	0.91	0.91	0.89
medium upholstered	0.68	0.75	0.82	0.85	0.86	0.86
lightly upholstered	0.56	0.68	0.79	0.83	0.86	0.86
Empty Seats:						
heavily upholstered	0.72	0.79	0.83	0.84	0.83	0.79
medium upholstered	0.56	0.64	0.70	0.72	0.68	0.62
lightly upholstered	0.35	0.45	0.57	0.61	0.59	0.55

Approximate Absorption Coefficients (per SF of seating)

Figure 10.20   Absorption due to audience (according to Beranek, 1966).

10.4.1   Audience absorption

Sound is absorbed not only by any surface in its path, but also by any medium through which it travels. As discussed in Chapter 9, when sound travels through air it sets the air molecules into harmonic motion very much like a pendulum. The propagation of the sound wave through the air medium is then made possible by the progressive movement of these molecules as they bump into the next molecules in line. Naturally, this uses up some energy.

As shown in Figure 10.19, the amount of energy dissipated is very small, particularly at frequencies below 2000 cps and above 10 000 cps under normal relative humidity conditions (i.e., above 40 percent).

By far the largest contributor to absorption in an auditorium is the audience: as much as 75 percent for concert halls. That stands to reason when we consider that the audience represents an appreciable portion of the exposed surface area of a hall (usually close to 25 percent) and the clothing worn by each person is composed of soft, semi-porous material with multiple folds and creases. Two alternative methods are commonly used to quantify audience absorption: per audience seat; or per square foot of floor area covered by the audience. The area method is normally preferred. Using this method the sound absorption at a particular frequency is calculated by multiplying the applicable Absorption Coefficient by the area occupied by the audience seats (Figure 10.20).

Several factors influence audience absorption, including the type of upholstery, the kind of clothing worn by the audience, and the slope (if any) of the floor. Experiments have shown that at shallow angles of incidence (i.e., when the sound waves graze an absorbing surface such as clothing) the absorption is higher. Accordingly, the effectiveness of sound absorption decreases as the angle of incidence of the sound waves approaches 90°, meaning that the audience absorption is higher in a hall with a relatively flat floor.

10.4.2   Psycho-acoustic considerations

The establishment of acoustical criteria arose basically out of the need to relate the physical

In a well-designed auditorium each audience position should receive direct sound and a strong first reflection within 50 milliseconds.

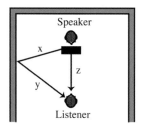

Since sound travels approximately 55 FT in 50 msec the following simple equation holds for the design of an auditorium:

$$X + Y - Z \leq 55 \text{ FT}$$ ..①

- The reflected sound can come from side walls or the ceiling, but not from the rear wall (time delay would be too long).

- Rectangular or fan-shaped halls are likely to provide the best sound conditions.

- The ideal limit of 55 FT in equation ① is often extended to 65 FT in practice.

Figure 10.21   Auditorium size limits.

The ability of the human ears to integrate identical sounds that follow each other within 40 milliseconds was discovered by Helmut Haas through experiments with a large number of listeners.

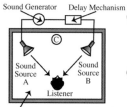

Anechoic Chamber (in which all surfaces provide total sound absorption, and therefore there are no sound reflections).

① If there is no time delay and sounds A and B are at the same SPL then the listener perceives one sound coming from C.

② If sound B is delayed by up to 40 msec and the SPL of B is less than 10 dB above A then the listener perceives one sound coming from A.

③ If the SPL of the delayed sound B is 3 dB below sound A then the maximum integration time increases to 80 msec.

④ A similar sound that is heard separately from the earlier sound is called an echo. Echoes are disturbing because they interfere with the intelligibility of speech.

Figure 10.22   The Haas effect.

measurement of sound to the subjective perception of sound, in an effort to protect persons from noises that are potentially harmful or annoying and to optimize the enjoyment of sounds (e.g., music) produced for entertainment purposes.

The acoustic performance of an auditorium (Figure 10.21) – particularly one used primarily for musical entertainment, such as a concert hall – is naturally a function of the auditory perception and mental processes of the individual members of the audience. These aspects fall under the subject matter area of psychoacoustics and include the following:

- The average adult under 40 years of age is conscious of sounds ranging in frequency from about 30 cps (i.e., wavelength of 37 FT) to 15 000 cps (i.e., wavelength of 1 IN), if the sound pressure level is sufficiently high. Persons above this age tend to be less sensitive to higher frequencies (i.e., the SPL may need to be raised by 10 dB or more for the higher frequencies to be heard).
- The change in frequency of a pure tone that can be barely detected by a person will depend on the frequency of the tone. At low frequencies smaller changes in frequency can be detected (i.e., about 0.3 percent), while below 20 dB the ear loses its ability to detect changes in frequency altogether.
- Similarly, the ability to detect a change in loudness depends on both the frequency and SPL. The maximum sensitivity to a change in sound pressure level occurs at a frequency of around 4000 cps, when a change of only 0.5 dB can be detected.
- If two similar sounds from different sources are separated in time by less than 35 milliseconds they will appear to the listener to be coming from the source of the first sound. This is known as the Haas effect (Figure 10.22).
- If a sound is followed by an identical sound more than 50 msec later, intelligibility is reduced. This would correspond to a difference in path length between a direct and a reflected sound of more than 55 FT.
- When a sound undergoes a continuous change for more than 0.8 sec a listener will find it difficult to ascertain the precise nature of the change.

- Tones that are of very short duration (i.e., less than 10 msec) are perceived simply as clicks without any apparent pitch.[6] On the other hand, if a note lasts longer than 100 msec there tends to be no improvement in pitch quality.
- After 0.5 sec a tone attains a maximum loudness. Beyond this point time fatigue occurs, with the result that the tone appears less loud.
- It appears that a tone becomes less distinct after a duration of 0.15 sec. At the same time SPLs in excess of 90 dB tend to overload the ear and produce distortion.

10.4.3   The concept of reverberation time

In a previous section we discussed at length the ability of surfaces to absorb and reflect incident sound. It is logical that in a room successive reflections from the bounding surfaces will continuously reduce the sound energy until the sound can no longer be heard (Figure 10.23).

Toward the end of the nineteenth century Wallace Sabine established a measure of the rate of decay of sound in a finite room. This measure, which is referred to as *Reverberation*

Time, relates the total absorption in the room (A sabins) to the volume of the space (V CF) for a sound decay of 60 dB in the following formula:

$$\textbf{Reverberation Time (RT)} = [(k \times V)/A]\textbf{ (sec)}$$
$$\textbf{[10.7]}$$

Therefore, if a sound of 90 dB is created in a previously quiet room, then the time taken for this sound to die down to 30 dB after the source has ceased is the Reverberation Time of that room. In equation 10.7:

k = a constant (0.05 if volume V and area A are in CF and FT-sabin, respectively; or 0.16 if V and A are in metric units (i.e., cm and m-sabin)).

A = the total absorption in sabins, which is found by multiplying each individual area by its Absorption Coefficient and summating these into one numerical value:

$A = \Sigma\,(\alpha \times a)$

where: α are the Absorption Coefficients corresponding to the individual surface areas a.

Reverberation Time provides a measure of the liveliness or noise sensitivity of a room. A correct Reverberation Time will ensure that sounds do not persist in a room to an extent that would interfere with intelligibility. For a given room volume, a short Reverberation Time corresponds to high absorption power, while a long Reverberation Time corresponds to small (total) absorption power. Since the total intensity of the reverberant sound produced by a continuous source is inversely proportional to the total absorption, a 50 percent reduction in Reverberation Time will require a doubling of the total absorption power, and hence the reverberant sound level will be decreased by 3 dB.

During the twentieth century, Reverberation Time emerged as an important acoustic criterion not only for speech communication, but also for concert halls. Although there has been some disagreement regarding the relative significance of auditorium size and type of performance in determining an optimum Reverberation Time in any given situation, it is still generally agreed that Reverberation Time

The persistence (i.e., reverberation due to successive reflections) of sound in a room after the source has ceased is governed by the amount of absorption in the room.

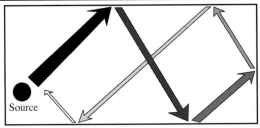

As the sound energy diminishes the inter-reflections within the room become weaker and weaker.

Sound is absorbed to varying degrees by:

- Each surface (e.g., wall, ceiling, floor) that the sound impinges on.
- The occupants of the room (particularly through their clothing).
- The air in the room.

Figure 10.23   Impact of absorption on reverberation in a hall.

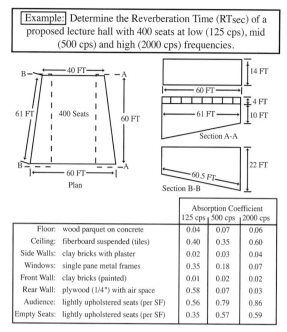

| Example: | Determine the Reverberation Time (RTsec) of a proposed lecture hall with 400 seats at low (125 cps), mid (500 cps) and high (2000 cps) frequencies. |

		Absorption Coefficient		
		125 cps	500 cps	2000 cps
Floor:	wood parquet on concrete	0.04	0.07	0.06
Ceiling:	fiberboard suspended (tiles)	0.40	0.35	0.60
Side Walls:	clay bricks with plaster	0.02	0.03	0.04
Windows:	single pane metal frames	0.35	0.18	0.07
Front Wall:	clay bricks (painted)	0.01	0.02	0.02
Rear Wall:	plywood (1/4") with air space	0.58	0.07	0.03
Audience:	lightly upholstered seats (per SF)	0.56	0.79	0.86
Empty Seats:	lightly upholstered seats (per SF)	0.35	0.57	0.59

Figure 10.24   Reverberation time calculation example.

is a critical parameter in the design of halls for speech and music.

Example: Calculate the Reverberation Time of a proposed lecture room with the surface finishes stipulated in Figure 10.24.

We begin by calculating the approximate area of each surface that has a different finish and therefore also a different Absorption Coefficient:

$$a_{floor} = [60 \times (40 + 60)/2] \qquad = 3000 \text{ SF}$$

$$a_{ceiling} = [60.5 \times (40 + 60)/2] \qquad = 3025 \text{ SF}$$

$$a_{side\ walls} = [2 \times (61 \times (14 + 22)/2)] = 2196 \text{ SF}$$

$$a_{windows} = [61 \times 4] \qquad = 244 \text{ SF}$$

$$a_{front\ wall} = [40 \times 22] \qquad = 88$$

$$a_{rear\ wall} = [60 \times 14] \qquad = 840 \text{ SF 0 SF}$$

$$a_{audience} = 2100 \text{ SF (assume 70}$$
$$\text{percent of floor area)}$$

To calculate the total absorption in the lecture hall for any given frequency, we simply multiply the area of each surface by the corresponding Absorption Coefficient. Therefore, at a frequency of 125 cps:

$$\begin{aligned} A_{125} = &[(3000 \times 0.04) + (3025 \times 0.40) + \\ &(2196 \times 0.02) + (244 \times 0.35) + \\ &(880 \times 0.01) + (840 \times 0.58) + \\ &(2100 \times 0.56)] \\ = &\ 3131 \text{ (FT-sabin)} \end{aligned}$$

Similarly, the total absorption for frequencies of 500 cps and 2000 cps can be calculated as follows:

$$\begin{aligned} A_{500} = &[(3000 \times 0.07) + (3025 \times 0.35) + \\ &(2196 \times 0.03) + (244 \times 0.18) + \\ &(880 \times 0.02) + (840 \times 0.07) + \\ &(2100 \times 0.79)] \\ = &\ 3115 \text{ (FT-sabin)} \end{aligned}$$

$$\begin{aligned} A_{2000} = &[(3000 \times 0.06) + (3025 \times 0.60) + \\ &(2196 \times 0.04) + (244 \times 0.07) + \\ &(880 \times 0.02) + (840 \times 0.03) + \\ &(2100 \times 0.86)] \\ = &\ 3949 \text{ (FT-sabin)} \end{aligned}$$

Next, it is necessary to calculate the volume of the lecture hall:

$$V = [(40 + 60)/2 \times (14 + 22)/2 \times 60] = 54\,000 \text{ CF}$$

It is now possible to determine the actual Reverberation Time (RT) for each of the three frequencies by substituting the appropriate values for total absorption into equation [10.7]:

$$RT_{125} = [(0.05 \times 54000)/3131] = 0.86 \text{ sec}$$
$$RT_{500} = [(0.05 \times 54000)/3115] = 0.87 \text{ sec}$$
$$RT_{2000} = [(0.05 \times 54000)/3949] = 0.68 \text{ sec}$$

The optimum reverberation time is based on the volume and function of the hall. In this case, around 0.8 sec should ensure adequate speech intelligibility. The average Reverberation Time for the three frequencies should be within 10 percent of the optimum value (in this case the average Reverberation Time is 0.80 sec). A slightly higher Reverberation Time for the 125 cps frequency band is desirable.

If the absorption of the floor is relatively small, then the shading due to the audience may be conveniently neglected. Otherwise the absorption of the floor surface may be reduced by 40 percent at 500 cps. It must be noted that the Reverberation Times calculated above all assume a capacity audience. A closer examination of the Absorption Coefficients listed in Figure 10.24 for occupied and empty seats shows that these vary considerably. As might be expected, they are consistently lower for the empty seats (i.e., 62 percent lower at 125 cps, 72 percent at 500 cps, and 69 percent at 2000 cps). For the sake of comparison the Reverberation Times of the half empty lecture hall are calculated to be:

$$RT_{125} = [(0.05 \times 54000) / 2921 = 0.92 \text{ sec}$$
$$RT_{500} = [(0.05 \times 54000) / 2884] = 0.94 \text{ sec}$$
$$RT_{2000} = [(0.05 \times 54000) / 3676] = 0.73 \text{ sec}$$

Furrer (1964) has demonstrated the significance of audience absorption by means of acoustical tests conducted in the Musiksaal at Basel in Switzerland.

From the graphs shown in Figure 10.25 it appears that prior to renovation, at a frequency of 1000 cps, the reverberation time of the empty hall with wooden seats was some three times longer than when fully occupied. At the same time, the provision of upholstery produced a

> Since the audience contributes greatly to the total sound absorption in a hall, ideally the sound absorption of a seat should be the same whether occupied or not.
> No such seat has been produced to date.

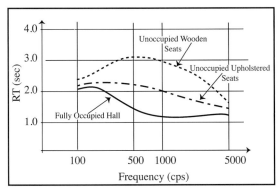

(Reverberation Times for wooden and upholstered seating with and without audience in the Musiksaal Town Casino at Basel (Switzerland) used by Johann Sebastian Bach (1685-1750).)

Figure 10.25 Impact of absorption on reverberation time.

significantly shorter reverberation time for the empty hall. The dependence of reverberation time on audience absorption suggests a need to allow for variable audiences. This can be at least partly achieved by ensuring that each individual unoccupied seat provides approximately the same absorption as a seated person. The desired effect may be further increased by perforating the underside of the seats (i.e., the underside would provide maximum absorption when the seat is empty, if the seats are collapsible).

Strictly speaking, the concept of Reverberation Time proposed by Sabine is based on assumptions that are unlikely to be achieved in practice. These assumptions include: uniform intensity of sound throughout the hall, and equally absorbent surfaces and reflections at all angles. Nevertheless, the agreement between theory and practice has been generally considered to be satisfactory.

10.4.4 Concert halls

For the evaluation of musical perception, it is of particular interest to refer to existing concert halls for at least two reasons. First, since there are a substantial number of halls well known for their superior acoustics, and second, because some halls are known to have played an important part in the history of music. In the past there have been strong ties between individual composers and particular halls. The relationship that is known to have existed between Johann Sebastian Bach (1685–1750) and St. Thomas Church in Leipzig, Germany is but one example.

According to surveys the Reverberation Time of concert halls that are known to have good acoustics is close to 1.8 sec (Parkin et al., 1952; Beranek, 1962, 1966). For example:

Beethoven Halle, Bonn (Germany)	1.8	sec
Symphony Hall, Boston (US)	1.8	sec
Musiksaal, Basel (Switzerland)	1.7	sec

On the basis of systematic investigations it has been generally agreed that the optimum reverberation time for average and large halls (i.e., 70 000 CF to 485 000 CF) is independent of the

A good Reverberation Time (RT) for speech intelligibility in a hall is usually around 1 sec. For music the RT may be closer to 2 sec., depending on the type of music (longest for church music).

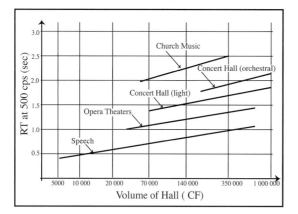

The larger the volume of a hall the longer the distance traveled by the direct and reflected sound.

Figure 10.26   Reverberation times for different kinds of hall.

volume. However, this does not invalidate the notion that large halls require a slightly longer Reverberation Time (Figure 10.26).

At the same time Kuhl and Kath (1963) suggested optimum reverberation times of 1.5 sec for classical and modern music (e.g., Mozart and Stravinsky), and 2.1 sec for romantic music (e.g., Brahms).

Discussions among acoustic engineers questioning the adequacy of Reverberation Time as the principal design criterion for concert halls appear to have started in the 1930s. In an effort to define acoustical conditions more precisely, further criteria were proposed by Wente (1935), Mason and Moir (1941), Somerville (1951), Meyer (1954), Somerville and Head (1957), and Nickson and Muncey (1964). Since then it has become common practice for acoustic consultants to take into account a small number of criteria in the design of concert halls. These now generally include the following:

- The correct Reverberation Time for each frequency. Ideally, all frequencies should decay at the same exponential rate. However, since the lower frequencies appear to be softer, it has been proposed that a longer Reverberation Time is permissible at the lower frequencies (i.e., 15 percent at 250 cps and 30 percent at 125 cps). Nevertheless there must be no sudden change in slope of the decay curve.

- Speech requires a relatively short Reverberation Time from 0.5 sec for small rooms to 1.0 sec for larger halls. Music requires a longer Reverberation Time ranging from 1.6 sec to over 2 sec for very large halls (Figure 10.26).

- For music the *Bass Ratio* should be between 1.1 and 1.25 for longer Reverberation Times (i.e., greater than 1.8 sec) and between 1.1 and 1.45 for lower Reverberation Times (i.e., less than 1.8 sec).[7]

- Walls, ceiling and overhead reflectors (if any) are required to be in such a geometrical arrangement that each audience position receives one substantial echo within 35 milliseconds of the direct sound. All reflections that arrive at the listener within this period are often referred to as the *first reflection*.

- Avoidance of sound-reflecting, concave surfaces that could lead to sound concentrations or undesirable echoes.

- Exclusion of all external noise by adequate insulation. This may require rather expensive systems of discontinuous construction. If a concert hall is located close to an airport or directly below a regular flight path, sound attenuation in excess of 70 dB may be required for all external walls. Double and triple wall and ceiling constructions are common practice for broadcasting and television studios (Kuhl and Kath, 1963). At the same time care must be taken to avoid ventilation noise, because the amount of low-frequency sound generated by air flow within ducts increases exponentially with increasing air speed.[8] Accordingly, it is desirable to control the speed of air in the ventilation ducts before consideration is given to the insertion of noise attenuators in the duct network.

- The acoustical performance of a concert hall should be adjustable to allow some degree of fine tuning for variable audience size and type of music.

Unfortunately, there exists no definable or measurable criterion for the intelligibility of music. The matter is further complicated by the fact that we are concerned with the subjective assessment of not just one, but three groups of persons, namely: the audience, the conductor, and the musicians. It is normal for the listener in the audience to attribute any minor acoustical faults to the musicians or the conductor, and not to the auditorium. Moreover the listener is often conditioned to stereophonic sound reproduction and expects to be treated to the same or better quality in the concert hall. While compact discs usually provide a crisp and clear reproduction, the concert hall will tend toward warmth and richness. This might not always be appreciated.

Beranek (1962) suggested a method of rating the acoustics of concert halls. Each hall is given a rating on a scale subdivided into 100 arbitrary units and incorporating eight desirable aspects (Table 10.6). These qualities are based primarily on Reverberation Time in relationship to the type of music to be played. Adjustments were necessary for opera, where the required speech clarity leads to a somewhat shorter Reverberation Time. Beranek used this method to rate the acoustics of a considerable number of halls in several countries, taking into account the opinions of musicians, conductors, and knowledgeable members of the audience. The following elaboration in respect to some of the criteria in Table 10.6 may be helpful:

Diffusion: Sound diffusion is preferable to sound absorption for side walls. Good diffusing surfaces are rough surfaces with many recesses. However, the roughness must be in the order of magnitude of the wavelengths to be reflected (i.e., to be diffused). Therefore, recesses of 3 FT to 10 FT will be required for music. Rear walls could be corrugated if they are concave. Also, absorption treatment is commonly applied to rear walls, because reflections from rear walls will arrive too late for useful sound reinforcement.

Surface material: Wood paneling is a poor reflector of sound at low frequencies; however, plaster and gypsum board is good if thick enough (i.e., two or more layers of ½ IN sheeting). Where absorption treatment is applied, the absorbing material must be effective over a wide range of frequencies.

Orchestra layout: Ideally, all instruments and singers should be grouped within a 20 FT radius to avoid *time delay* problems. In churches the choir should be in one group and somewhat elevated in respect to the congregation. The ceiling height above the choir should be at least 20 FT to avoid *reflection* problems. To the conductor it is of importance that the musicians should be able to play their instruments without any special effort. Ideally, the conductor should perceive the music on identical terms with the audience. It is essential that the musicians should not be disturbed by any extraneous

Table 10.6   Framework for rating concert halls (according to Beranek, 1962).

Desirable aspect or quality	Maximum score	Optimum feature to score maximum points
Intimacy	40	One reflection within 20 milliseconds
Liveliness	15	Correct reverberation time
Warmth	15	Correct reverberation time at low and middle frequencies
Loudness of direct sound	10	No more than 60 FT from conductor to listener in mid-hall
Loudness of reflected sound	6	Reverberation time is approximately equal to $3 \times 10^{-6} \times volume$ (sec)
Diffusion	4	Coffered ceiling
Balance and blend	6	Correct orchestra layout
Ensemble	4	A performer can hear all others

or audience noise. At the same time the musicians would like to hear the orchestra and themselves as a balanced unit.

Dimensions: As discussed previously, the size of an auditorium without electronic sound reinforcement is governed by the requirement that every audience position should receive a strong *first reflection* within 50 milliseconds of the direct sound (i.e., $x + y - z \leq$ 65 FT, and ideally 55 FT). The volume per seat should be as small as practical (i.e., 100 to 130 CF per seat) and the ceiling height should be one-third to two-thirds of the width dimension (two-thids for smaller halls).

In regard to the most desirable physical shape of a concert hall, there are basically three shapes that come under consideration, namely: rectangular, fan-shaped, and horseshoe. Of these, the rectangular shape seems to hold the most potential. The main disadvantage of the fan-shaped hall is that the rear wall and balcony front are normally curved, thereby producing a serious risk of echoes. The rectangular hall is free from this risk and in addition has the advantage of strong cross-reflection between parallel walls, which may lead to added *fullness* of sound.

It is an essential property of a good concert hall ceiling that it should produce an equal distribution of sound. There are therefore serious objections to sharply curved shells. The Sydney Opera House is a prominent example of the problems that can arise when a particular roof shape is selected for other than acoustical reasons.

10.4.5 The Sydney Opera House

The Sydney Opera House, designed by the Danish architect Jørn Utzon, is often described as one of the eight *wonders of the world*. This description is based more on its external architectural expression than its acoustical excellence, although the performance of its principal concert hall has received the approval of such renowned acoustic experts as Beranek (Beranek, 2004). Located on the Bennelong peninsula, which juts out into Sydney's picturesque harbor,

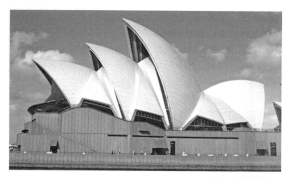

Figure 10.27   Sydney Opera House.

the gleaming concrete shells of the Opera House present a memorable view that has become an international icon for both the city of Sydney and Australia as a whole (Figure 10.27).

Today the Sydney Opera House complex consists of five halls, as follows:

Concert Hall – with 2679 seats, is the principal auditorium for concerts and contains the world's largest mechanical tracker-action organ with over 10 000 pipes.

Opera Theater – with 1547 seats, is the main auditorium for opera and ballet performances.

Drama Theater – with 544 seats, was not part of Utzon's original design.

Studio Theater – with 364 seats, also was not part of Utzon's original design.

Playhouse – with 398 seats, was added long after the completion of the original construction in 1999.

What makes this imposing building complex particularly interesting from a design point of view is the apparent conflict between its exciting structural solution and the requirements of good acoustic performance, as discussed previously in this chapter. The internal concave curvature of the concrete shells would lead to sound concentrations in the audience if these surfaces were allowed to serve as the primary reflecting elements. At face value it would appear that this potential problem could be fairly easily overcome by reflecting the direct sound before it can reach the curved shell walls. It would seem that this could be accomplished by means of suspended reflecting panels. However, as was discussed in Sections 10.1 and 10.4, for such panels to be effective they would need to be at least five times as large (in each dimension) as the wavelength of the incident sound. Therefore, for effective low-frequency sound reflection the panels would need to be quite large (with dimensions greater than 20 FT by 20 FT for frequencies below 250 cps) and consequently very heavy. For adequate structural integrity, a suspended plywood panel of that size would probably require an effective thickness of 2 IN (e.g., ⅞ IN plywood sheets on either side of a timber frame), with a corresponding weight of around 12 LB/SF or over 2 ton for a 400 SF reflector panel.

Unfortunately, the suspension of such a relatively heavy object from a lightweight shell structure presents a formidable structural problem. Thin concrete shells obtain their structural integrity from double curvature and continuity. For example, it is virtually impossible to crush a whole egg in the palm of one hand. This is because the load is applied evenly over the surface of the egg and, even though the eggshell is very thin, it can support a substantial distributed load. However, the same eggshell can be easily pierced with a pointed object such as a knitting needle. In other words, thin concrete shells are surprisingly strong in supporting evenly distributed loads, but very weak in supporting concentrated loads such as those represented by a heavy suspended plywood panel.

The solution to this dilemma in the case of the Sydney Opera House was to build another enclosure for the concert and opera halls within the external concrete shell perimeter (Figure 10.28).

This solution was welcome for another nonstructural reason. The location of the Opera House in the Sydney Harbor exposed it to the unusually high sound levels generated by foghorns that warn ships of approaching danger. It would be incongruous and unacceptable to have a particularly quiet portion of a concert performance suddenly interrupted by the excruciating sound of a foghorn. The wide air cavity between the external concrete shells

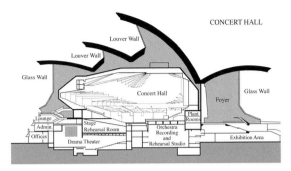

Figure 10.28 Sectional view of the main concert hall (Sydney Opera House).

and the internal enclosures of the halls provided the means for applying the necessary noise insulation.

Throughout history, significant public building projects have often been the subject of a great deal of controversy and political intrigue. The Sydney Opera House project has been no exception in this regard (Flyvbjerg, 2005). Planning for an opera house in Sydney essentially began in the late 1940s, with recognition of the need for a more suitable venue for large theatrical productions than was at that time provided by the Sydney Town Hall. In 1954 the advocates for a new building gained the support of the state governor, who authorized an international architectural competition. The renowned American architect Eero Saarinen served as a prominent member of the selection committee. It is rumored that at the time the committee commenced the task of evaluating the 233 entries, Saarinen was not able to travel to Australia because of other commitments. So as not to delay the evaluation process, he asked the committee to go ahead and reduce the competition entries to a small number of the best designs. He would then assist the committee with the selection of the winning entry as soon as he was able to come to Sydney.

When Saarinen eventually joined the committee he was apparently not satisfied with the selections made by the committee and asked to see all of the 233 entries. He was particularly impressed by the submission of the Danish architect Jørn Utzon, which had not been

Occupancy	125 cps	250 cps	500 cps	1000 cps	2000 cps
Unoccupied	2.45	2.46	2.45	2.55	2.60
Occupied	2.10	2.20	2.10	2.30	2.20

Table 10.7 Measured reverberation times (sec) of the Sydney Opera House.

included in the committee's selection of finalists. Saarinen persuaded the committee that if they wanted Sydney to have a landmark Opera House, then this innovative design of sail-like concrete shells would serve magnificently. The committee accepted his recommendation and in 1955 announced the Utzon design as the winning entry. Subsequently, Jørn Utzon arrived in Australia in 1957 to take up residence in Sydney and complete the final design drawings and commence construction.

The initial cost estimate for the design and construction of the Opera House was (AU) $7 million. However, this was a political cost estimate based on what the current state government felt to be acceptable to the public, rather than a true estimate of actual costs. The correspondingly dubious construction time for the entire project was announced as five years, with a targeted completion date of January 1963. In fact, the final cost was (AU) $102 million and the Sydney Opera House was formally completed 10 years after that original deadline, in October 1973. From the very start the building became an icon of controversy, with various public groups in strong opposition or support of the entire venture. Increasing cost estimates, as well as design and construction delays, fueled the controversy. With a change of state government in 1965, the relationship between architect and client deteriorated to the point where the government refused to honor a progress payment of architectural fees; Utzon consequently resigned and returned to Denmark in 1966 (Duek-Cohen, 1967; Baume, 1967). Thereafter, the design and construction of the Opera House was completed by a government appointed triad of three Australian architects[9] (Hall, 1973; Drew, 2000).

The significant changes to the design after the resignation of Utzon were related to the interior design and finishes, the addition of the Drama and Studio Theaters, the structural solution of the expansive glass walls at the front of the shells, and the enclosure of the podium down to the water level. Apart from the addition of the two theaters, which completely changed the layout of the floor plan, Utzon's entire interior acoustic design concept was replaced by a different solution, which includes 21 very large, torus-shaped, circular acrylic reflectors that are suspended from an enormous circular ceiling some 82 FT above the stage. Vernon Jordan of the German firm V. L. and N. V. Jordan served as the acoustical consultant (Jordan, 1973). The measured Reverberation Times of the Concert Hall recorded after the completion of construction are just over 2 sec (Table 10.7).

It is interesting to note that owing to the unusually high ceiling, the volume per audience seat is also much higher than the 100 to 130 CF/seat normally recommended. For this hall it is 324 CF/seat.

Endnotes

1. The wavelength of the visible portion of the electromagnetic spectrum (i.e., light) extends from about 450 to 750 millimicrons, which is equivalent to a range of 0.00011 to 0.00019 IN.
2. The horizontal force is given by the formula: Force = [(wind speed)^2/400]. Therefore, a wind speed of 50 mph will produce a horizontal force of more than 6 LB/SF. For a 30 FT high wall this equates to nearly 200 LB/FT.
3. Standing waves can occur between two parallel walls in a building space when the distance between these walls is some exact multiple of the wavelength of the ambient sound. Accordingly, the walls of rectangular rooms for music are typically slightly offset from 90°. For a detailed treatment of standing waves see Mehta et al., 1999 (pp. 383–392) and Louden, 1971 (pp. 101–104).

4. NC curves are based on the linear measure of Sound Pressure Level (SPL), while NCA curves are based on the A-weighted scale that makes some allowance for the reduced sensitivity of the human ear at lower sound frequencies. (see Section 9.8).

5. The reader will remember that SPLs in decibels cannot be added by simple arithmetic. The addition of two equal SPLs produces an increase in SPL of approximately 3 dB.

6. Pitch is the subjectively perceived frequency of a sound. The actual objectively measured frequency may differ owing to overtones in the sound.

7. The Bass Ratio is a ratio of Reverberation Times (RT) as follows:

$$(RT_{125} + RT_{250})/(RT_{500} + RT_{1000}).$$

8. It can be shown that the acoustic power of low-frequency noise varies as the sixth power of the air velocity.

9. The New South Wales Government appointed Peter Hall as principal design architect, David Littlemore as construction supervisor, Lionel Todd as chief of documentation, and E. H. Farmer ex officio in his capacity as the State Architect of New South Wales, Australia.

11 Noise Control and Insulation

The control of noise in the external environment and inside buildings is at least as important to the quality of life as the design of building spaces for the enjoyment of music and the promotion of good speech communication conditions. So what is *noise* as opposed to sound? By definition any sound that is annoying, distracting and generally unwanted is commonly referred to as noise. The term *unwanted* appears to be of particular significance in determining whether a particular sound is perceived to be tolerable or annoying. For example, persons are usually not annoyed by noise originating from their own activities, but may be greatly annoyed if a similar noise is produced by the apparently unnecessary activities of others.

11.1 Noise control by legislation

In the years following World War II the average noise level in highly industrialized countries grew at an alarming rate. During the period from 1935 to 1955, Knudsen (1955) estimated a yearly increase in the average noise level of one decibel, which indicates an approximate doubling of loudness in about one decade. To counteract this trend many local, state, and national government authorities around the world felt compelled to take some action. As a first step, particularly at the national level, the responsible government agencies recognized the need for an assessment of the nature and extent of the problem. This led to the funding of several research studies and field surveys aimed at providing a basis for legislation to control the creation and mitigation of noise (Aldersey-Williams, 1960; Piess et al., 1962; Karplus and Bonvallet, 1953; HMSO, 1963).

In the built environment we are normally concerned not with noise sources that may produce permanent damage to the hearing mechanism, but with the more complicated and less precise aspects of annoyance. It is now generally recognized that:

- Persons are unlikely to be annoyed by noise originating from their own activities.
- It is possible for individuals to become accustomed to certain noises.
- Annoyance is a function of the sound pressure level, as well as the frequency spectrum of the noise.
- There are some noises (e.g., such as those that produce fear or that disturb sleep) to which persons are unable to adapt even after prolonged exposure (Nickson, 1966).

The matter is further complicated by the highly subjective nature of individual reactions to noise. Not only do individuals exhibit different tolerances and conditioning abilities, but their reactions also vary with the particular circumstances. At times it is indeed difficult to assess whether the reaction produced has been activated by physiological or psychological stimuli.

Unexpected impulsive sounds may increase the pulse rate and cause muscular contractions. Accordingly, on the basis of the definition of health stipulated by the World Health Organization, namely, "… *health is a state of complete*

Building Science: Concepts and Application. Jens Pohl.
© 2011 John Wiley & Sons, Ltd.
Published 2011 by John Wiley & Sons, Ltd.

physical, mental and social well-being, and not merely an absence of disease and infirmity", it must be accepted that noise can constitute a health hazard even though there may be no risk of actual physical hearing damage.

Outdoor noise sources can be generally divided into three main groups: namely, industrial, residential, and traffic noise. Of these residential and in particular traffic noise seem to constitute the major source of annoyance, since interference from industrial noise has now been largely eliminated by the implementation of town planning legislation. However, one aspect of industrial noise has gained importance in recent years, and that is noise from building construction sites in urban areas. Most large multi-story buildings have construction periods exceeding 12 months and generate a great deal of noise at least during the first half of this period, while site works and the erection of the structural frame are in progress.

Most of the noise produced in residential areas is due to traffic and activities, such as children at play, motor mowers, radios, and television. The interference of noise produced by tenants in multi-unit dwellings is of particular concern. For this reason building codes in most countries stipulate minimum sound transmission loss values for party walls between adjacent apartments and condominiums.

In respect to external noise sources, the approach to legislation is based on the control of maximum noise levels. This applies in particular to vehicular traffic noise although, as can be seen in Figure 11.1, there is some variation between countries, and even between states in the US.

For example, the difference between California and New York is 9 dB, which constitutes a doubling of loudness. The recommendations made by the Ministry of Transport in England, based on the Wilson Report (HMSO, 1963) are generally more stringent. In Europe, prior to the formation of the European Economic Union, the situation was similarly disjointed, with each country progressively drawing up its own requirements and methods of measurement, covering one or more types of vehicles. Today,

Type of External Noise Source	Maximum SPL	Distance from Source	US State or Country
Diesel-powered tractors, trucks and buses.	95 dBA	25 FT	California
Motorcycles.	90 dBA	25 FT	California
Regular passenger cars and sports vehicles.	85 dBA	25 FT	California
All vehicles travelling at more than 35 mph.	94 dBA	25 FT	New York
All new vehicles with more than two wheels.	85 dBA	17 FT	England
New motorcycles and other mechanically propelled two-wheeled vehicles.	90 dBA	17 FT	England

Figure 11.1   Legislated maximum noise levels.

the EEU has established standards in virtually all fields, including noise control, that must be observed by its members.

11.2   Airborne and solid-borne sound

The attenuation of sound in air varies directly with the frequency of the sound and inversely with the relative humidity of the air. For example, an attenuation constant of up to 9 dB per 100 FT may be obtained for a sound of 10 000 cps frequency under ambient atmospheric conditions, if the relative humidity is 20 percent. Similarly, sound is refracted by both temperature and wind gradients, giving rise to so-called *shadow zones*. These may be created when a blanket of air at high temperature is located near the surface of the ground, or upwind from a sound source, particularly if the topography is sufficiently rough to reduce the wind velocity near the surface of the ground. Unfortunately, the converse also applies downwind from a noise source, or in the case of a temperature inversion. Under these conditions, the noise

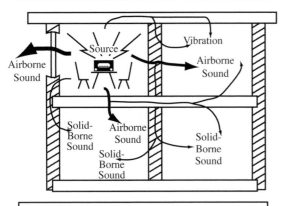

Most of the noise in buildings is due to airborne sound such as speech, music, fans, motors, aircraft, and automobiles.

Solid-borne sound is produced by sources that act directly on the structure of a building such as footsteps, banging of doors, and traffic noise transmitted through the footings of the building.

Figure 11.2 Transmission of airborne and solid-borne noise through a building.

that would normally disperse into the atmosphere is refracted back toward the ground. It is therefore apparent that whenever noise measurements are taken externally over long distances, the weather conditions should be accurately recorded and considered during the analysis of the test results.

In the case of buildings, as shown in Figure 11.2, an airborne sound may travel directly to the ear of a listener, or it may be instrumental in setting up vibrations in the surrounding structure and partitions, which will in turn create compression waves in the surrounding air. Since sound waves in air can be transmitted with little loss of intensity along apparently insignificant paths, such as keyholes, ventilation grills, badly fitted door jambs, it is essential that sound barriers should be impervious and carefully sealed at the perimeter to eliminate *flanking paths*. With particularly intense sounds it is sometimes possible to physically feel the vibration of a partition, and it is therefore not difficult to understand that this movement of the partition will act on the surrounding air in

exactly the same manner as a loudspeaker. Accordingly, for airborne sound insulation to be effective, it will be necessary to reduce the ability of an insulating partition to be set in vibration by incident sound waves.

Solid-borne sound is produced by sources that act directly on the structure of a building, in the form of impacts or vibrations. Impact sources include footsteps, scraping of furniture, and slamming of doors, while vibration sources include traffic noise transmitted through the footings of a building and machinery such as air-conditioning compressors and fans. All of these are transmitted through and from the structure. In fact, the presence of solid-borne sound may sometimes be detected by listening with one ear pressed tightly against a wall or floor surface. For example, in dense urban areas such as New York or London the vibrations generated by a subway train traveling at some speed well below the ground may be felt throughout the structure of the buildings above its path. Broadly speaking, solid-borne sound insulation will rely on methods of dampening the impact of objects (e.g., carpets effectively dampen the impact of footsteps and moving furniture) and reducing or isolating the vibration of the source (e.g., flexible mountings).

11.3 Airborne noise insulation

Airborne noise may be reduced by the use of absorption, by means of effective insulation barriers, or by a combination of both of these. Since the degree of interference of noise with voice communication is closely related to the relative sound pressure levels of the interfering noise and the background noise level due to occupancy, it might be expected that sound reduction at the source by means of absorption would constitute a viable method of airborne noise insulation. Unfortunately, the only instance where absorption alone will be an economical proposition is found in large offices where there are many noise sources and the occupants are scattered over a large area. Even here it is rare to achieve a reduction in airborne noise in excess of 6 dB (Lawrence, 1968). However, in the case of marginal noise problems affecting speech communication this improvement may be adequate.

In Chapter 10 (Section 10.1) we discussed the relationships that exist among the Coefficients of Absorption (α), Transmission (r), and Reflection (ρ). In all cases a value of 1 indicates complete effectiveness (i.e., full absorption, transmission, and reflection), while a value of 0 implies total ineffectiveness (e.g., an open window is presumed to provide full absorption and absolutely no insulation or reflection. Since values of the Transmission Coefficient (r) for common building elements such as walls and floors tend to be very small (i.e., between 10^{-2} and 10^{-8}) and therefore rather awkward to use, the sound-insulation capabilities of a barrier are normally measured on a logarithmic scale in terms of Transmission Loss (TL) values.

Transmission Loss (TL) = 10 log (1 / r)   [11.1]

If we know the Transmission Coefficient of a material, then we can calculate the theoretical TL value. For example, a ¼ IN thick glass window pane has a Transmission Coefficient of 0.00078 (i.e., 7.8×10^{-4}). Therefore, applying equation [11.1] the TL value becomes:

$$\text{Transmission Loss (TL)} = 10\log(1/0.00078)$$
$$= 10\log(1,282) = 31 \text{ dB}$$

Similarly, we can extrapolate equation [11.1] to calculate the Transmission Coefficient that will result in a given TL value. For example, a desired TL of 30 dB should give us a required TL value that is very close to that of the ¼ IN thick glass pane used in the previous calculation.

$$30 = 10\log(1/r)$$
$$\log(1/r) = 30/10$$
$$(1/r) = 10^3$$
$$r = 10^{-3} = 0.001 \text{ (which is close to 0.00078)}$$

Why is a good sound-absorption material not also a good sound-insulation material? If, for example, a material has an Absorption Coefficient of 0.95 at a particular frequency (i.e., at that frequency 95 percent of the sound will be absorbed), then surely 95 percent of the sound will also not be transmitted. Let us test this hypothesis. If 95 percent of the sound is absorbed, then the Transmission Coefficient for this material at that frequency is:

$$\text{Transmission Coefficient (r)} = (1 - 0.95)$$
$$= 0.05 \text{ (or } 5 \times 10^{-2})$$

Substituting in equation [11.1], we obtain:

$$\text{Transmission Loss (TL)} = 10\log(1/0.05)$$
$$= 10\log(20) = 13 \text{ dB}$$

The reason why the hypothesis is wrong is because the Absorption Coefficient (α) is a linear measure, while the Transmission Coefficient (r) is a logarithmic measure. For a more practical example, let us consider heavy curtain fabric (18 oz), shown in Table 10.5 (Chapter 10) to have an Absorption Coefficient of 0.55 at a frequency of 500 cps. The Transmission Coefficient at that frequency is:

$$\text{Transmission Coefficient (r)} = (1 - 0.55)$$
$$= 0.45 \text{ (or } 4.5 \times 10^{-1})$$

Substituting in equation [11.1], we obtain:

$$\text{Transmission Loss (TL)} = 10\log(1/0.45)$$
$$= 10\log(2.2) = 3.4 \text{ dB}$$

These two examples foreshadow another important principle of sound insulation that will be discussed in more detail later. A good sound barrier must be devoid of air paths, because air is a good conductor of sound. This is incompatible with the characteristics of a sound-absorption material that depends on porosity in the form of open air pockets and cul-de-sac pores for its absorption capabilities (i.e., to convert sound vibration through friction into heat).

Before delving into sound insulation in more detail the reader should be aware that airborne sound can be significantly reinforced by solid components.

As shown in Figure 11.3, the sound produced by a tuning fork is greatly amplified when the tuning fork is placed on a solid element such as a table. In a similar manner the strings of a

An airborne sound source may be amplified when it sets a solid element into vibration.

Tuning fork is much louder when placed on a table, which vibrates in unison with the tuning fork.

The sound produced by a guitar is greatly magnified by the wooden body acting as a sounding board.

Explanation:

The amplification occurs because of the efficient conversion of vibrational energy into sound energy, if the dimensions of the vibrating element are at least of the same order of magnitude as the wavelength of the sound.

(A tuning fork and a guitar string are much smaller than the wavelength of the sound they produce. Therefore, the addition of the table or the wooden body of the guitar amplifies the sound through their larger size.)

Figure 11.3   The sound-board effect created by placing a tuning fork on a table.

violin or guitar would produce little sound without the wooden body of the instrument acting as a sounding board. However, for the sounding board to be effective it must be of at least the same order of magnitude as the wavelength of the sound produced by the strings. Therefore, at least up to a point, the larger the table the louder will be the sound produced by the interaction of the relatively small tuning fork with the much larger table.

11.3.1   Single-leaf panels and the Mass Law

Although most space dividers in buildings, such as walls and floors, are composed of several materials that are applied in layers (e.g., an external timber wall constructed of a sheet of drywall on the inside and a sheet of stucco on the outside of a timber frame), we will first consider the sound-insulation characteristics of single-layer panels. Such a single-leaf panel obeys what is commonly referred to as the *Mass Law*. To facilitate mathematical analysis it is assumed that a single-leaf panel consists of many connected parts that move largely inde-

pendently of each other when the panel is set in motion (i.e., vibration) by an incident sound wave. This is, of course, very much an idealized model of the vibration of the panel. In reality the movements of these theoretical parts of the panel are not at all independent of each other. It stands to reason that the stiffer the panel, the more each part will be impacted by the movement of its neighbors. However, it has been verified by means of physical tests that the TL of a single-leaf panel increases in direct logarithmic proportion to its surface mass (i.e., mass per SF) and the frequency (f) of the sound to which it is exposed.

In the case of building construction the surface mass of a component such as a wall is governed by the density (d LB/CF) and thickness (t FT) of the material. Therefore, the Mass Law may be stated as follows:

Transmission Loss (TL)
$$= 20 \log (d \times t \times f) - C \,(dB) \qquad [11.2]$$

where C is a constant and equal to 33 in the American system of units, and 47 in the metric system of units (i.e., with d in kg/m^3 and t in m).

Applying equation [11.2] to an 8 IN thick concrete wall with a density of 150 LB/CF, exposed to a sound with a frequency of 500 cps, we obtain:

$$TL_{500} = 20 \log [150 \times (8/12) \times 500] - 33$$
$$TL_{500} = 20 \log [50000] - 33$$
$$TL_{500} = 20 \, (4.7) - 33 = 94 - 33 = 61 \text{ dB}$$

The direct logarithmic relationship between density, thickness, and frequency in equation [11.2] leads to an interesting and useful conclusion: Doubling of any one of these three quantities has the same numerical impact on the value of TL. In each case, it will result in an increase in the value of TL by the exact amount of "20 log (2)", which is equal to 6. Therefore, as shown in Figures 11.4, 11.5, and 11.6, each doubling of the thickness, frequency or density of a single-leaf panel will increase its theoretical noise insulation (i.e., Transmission Loss value) by 6 dB.

For an idealized single-leaf panel doubling of the thickness of the panel will increase the TL value by 6 dB.

$$TL = 20\log_{10} [\text{ (frequency)} \times \text{(density)} \times \text{(thickness)}] - 33 \text{ (dB)}$$

For a concrete panel with a density of 150 LB/CF and a sound frequency of 1000 cps:

Concrete Panel	Thickness	Frequency	Transmission Loss Calculation	TL
(25 LB/SF)	2 in.	1000 cps	$20\log_{10} (1000 \times 150 \times 2/12) - 33$	55 dB
(50 LB/SF)	4 in.	1000 cps	$20\log_{10} (1000 \times 150 \times 4/12) - 33$	61 dB
(75 LB/SF)	6 in.	1000 cps	$20\log_{10} (1000 \times 150 \times 6/12) - 33$	65 dB

Figure 11.4 Effect of thickness on a single-leaf panel.

For an idealized single-leaf panel doubling of the frequency of the sound will increase the TL value by 6 dB.

$$TL = 20\log_{10} [\text{ (frequency)} \times \text{(density)} \times \text{(thickness)}] - 33 \text{ (dB)}$$

For a concrete panel with a density of 150 LB/CF and a thickness of 4 in.:

Concrete Panel	Thickness	Frequency	Transmission Loss Calculation	TL
(50 LB/SF)	4 in.	500 cps	$20\log_{10} (500 \times 150 \times 4/12) - 33$	55 dB
(50 LB/SF)	4 in.	1000 cps	$20\log_{10} (1000 \times 150 \times 4/12) - 33$	61 dB
(50 LB/SF)	4 in.	2000 cps	$20\log_{10} (2000 \times 150 \times 4/12) - 33$	67 dB

Figure 11.5 Effect of frequency on a single-leaf panel.

For an idealized single-leaf panel doubling of the mass (i.e., density) of the panel will increase the TL value by 6 dB.

$$TL = 20\log_{10} [\text{ (frequency)} \times \text{(density)} \times \text{(thickness)}] - 33 \text{ (dB)}$$

For a sound frequency of 4000 cps and three 1/2 in. thick panels made of corkboard (35 LB/CF), plywood (70 LB/CF) and gypsum (140 LB/CF).

Panel Type	Thickness	Frequency	Transmission Loss Calculation	TL
(1 LB/SF)	1/2 in.	4000 cps	$20\log_{10} (4000 \times 35 \times 1/24) - 33$	42 dB
(3 LB/SF)	1/2 in.	4000 cps	$20\log_{10} (4000 \times 70 \times 1/24) - 33$	48 dB
(6 LB/SF)	1/2 in.	4000 cps	$20\log_{10} (4000 \times 140 \times 1/24) - 33$	54 dB

Figure 11.6 Effect of mass on a single-leaf panel.

However, as discussed previously, the Mass Law makes assumptions that are only partly realized in practice. While surface mass is certainly the most important factor that determines the sound insulation provided by a single-leaf panel, other factors such as stiffness, boundary conditions, and the angle of incidence of the sound will influence the degree to which the theoretical TL value predicted by the Mass Law is realized in practice.

Figure 11.7 shows schematically the significant increase in TL that will result from measures such as cutting grooves in the surface of a panel, aimed at reducing the overall stiffness of the panel. Similarly, but to a lesser extent, the damping that will be provided by the manner in which the panel is fixed at the boundary will also affect its stiffness. In addition, the actual sound insulation provided is also dependent on the angle of incidence of the noise. In practice, wave fronts of sound generally arrive over a range of angles from 0° to 80°, which is referred to as field incidence, while the Mass Law assumes that the sound waves are incident at

The Mass Law assumes that the particles in a panel oscillate independently of each other (i.e., that the panel has no stiffness) similar to molecules in air. In fact, all solid materials have some stiffness, and the stiffer the panel the lower its TL.

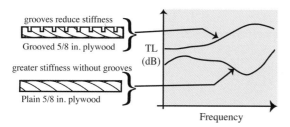

In practice, the TL of a single-leaf panel is a function of:

- Mass (most important factor)
- Stiffness (elasticity of material)
- Damping (boundary conditions)
- Angle of incidence of the sound

Figure 11.7 **The impact of stiffness on the TL value of a single-leaf panel.**

If a sound barrier contains more than 10% of openings then its overall sound insulation will be no more than 10 dB regardless of the TL value of the solid portion of the barrier.

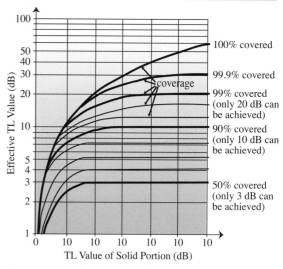

Figure 11.8 **The impact of openings on the TL value of any sound barrier.**

an idealized angle of 90° (i.e., perpendicular) to the panel surface.

Taking these factors into consideration, the theoretical TL value for each doubling of density, thickness, or frequency, reduces by at least 20 percent to 5 dB in practice. If the sound barrier is totally sealed so that there are no direct air paths, then stiffness is the factor that contributes most to this discrepancy between theory and practice.

However, as shown in Figure 11.8, the presence of any direct air paths will drastically reduce the effectiveness of any sound barrier. If a barrier contains more than 10 percent of openings, its overall TL value will be equivalent to no more than about 10 dB, regardless of the insulation value of the solid portion of the barrier. This has become a serious problem in commercial buildings, where it is very difficult to eliminate flanking paths around or over the top of modular partitions. Naturally, continuation of such partitions above the ceiling would interfere with ventilation. A simple method of checking the adequacy of seals around full-height partitions in air-conditioned (or mechan-

ically ventilated) buildings is to close off the return-air duct and measure the reduction in the supply air velocity. In the case of partial enclosures (i.e., partial height partitions), the noise insulation provided is mainly governed by reflecting surfaces nearby. Accordingly, the provision of absorptive material on large, horizontal overhead surfaces will generally ameliorate conditions (Mariner and Park, 1956; Bishop, 1957). In summary, the following guidelines should be kept in mind by the building designer:

- Generally, the heavier a wall the more effective its sound insulation capabilities will be.
- Stiffness reduces the sound-insulation capabilities of a barrier. Lead is the most effective sound-insulation material, because it is very dense and limp at the same time. However, lead is so limp that it cannot support its own weight in most structural configurations. Also it is potentially toxic (e.g., from handling of lead sheets during construction) and expensive. Therefore, it is typically used only as a hidden layer in the highest-quality modular partitions and doors.

- If a sound barrier has an acoustically weak element, then its overall TL value is likely to be close to the TL value of the weak element.
- The smallest air path, such as a badly fitting door or even a large keyhole, will transmit sound to a disproportionate degree directly through the barrier.
- When a sound barrier contains different components such as windows and doors, then the effective TL value of the barrier is *not* directly proportional to the relative areas of the components (as would be the case for thermal insulation). The effective sound insulation of a barrier consisting of two different components can be determined by reference to a table that relates the difference in TL values of the two components to the percentage area of the smaller component (Table 11.1).

The application of Table 11.1 is shown in Figure 11.9, where the overall TL value of a 210 SF wall with a TL value of 45 dB containing a 21 SF door with a TL value of 25 dB, is determined to be 34.5 dB. It is of interest to note that although the area of the door is only 10 percent of the wall area the reduction in the overall TL value is over 23 percent.

Utilizing the graph shown in Figure 11.8, this example is taken one step further in Figure 11.10 where it is assumed that the door has been poorly fitted with a 2 IN gap at the bottom. Even though this direct air path is only 0.3 percent of

the total wall area the impact is quite dramatic, with an additional 25 percent reduction in the overall TL value.

Most manufacturers quote TL values of structural walls and partitions as an average of the reduction in decibels of a diffuse sound field passing through the partition, mounted in a specified manner, for nine frequencies (i.e., 125, 175, 250, 350, 500, 700, 1000, 2000, and 4000 cps).

Example (1): Determine the overall TL value of a wall (10 FT high by 21 FT long) containing a door (7 FT high by 3 FT wide) if the TL of the wall portion is 45 dB and the door is 25 dB.

Step ①: Calculate the door area as a percentage of the total wall area:

$$\left.\begin{array}{l}\text{door area} = 7 \times 3 = 21 \text{ SF} \\ \text{wall area } = 10 \times 21 = 210 \text{ SF}\end{array}\right] \text{— door area} = 10\%$$

Step ②: Determine difference between TL values of wall and door:

$$TL_{wall} - TL_{door} = 45 - 25 = 20 \text{ dB}$$

Step ③: Look up reduction in wall TL value in table:

Difference in TL Values	Area of Smaller Component as Percentage of Total Area							
	50%	20%	10%	5%	2%	1%	0.5%	0.1%
15	12.0	8.5	6.0	4.0	2.0	1.0	1.0	0.0
20	17.0	13.0	(10.5)	8.0	5.0	3.0	2.0	0.5
30	27.0	23.0	20.0	17.0	13.0	10.0	8.0	3.0

Overall TL value of wall = 34.5 dB

Figure 11.9 Sound insulation impact of a well-fitted door.

Table 11.1 Reduction in transmission loss (TL) of an assembly of two components.

Difference in TL values	Area of smaller component as percentage of total area							
	50%	20%	10%	5%	2%	1 %	0.5%	0.1%
5	3.0	1.5	1.0	0.5	0.0	0.0	0.0	0.0
6	4.0	2.0	1.0	0.5	0.0	0.0	0.0	0.0
7	5.0	2.5	1.5	1.0	0.5	0.0	0.0	0.0
8	6.0	3.0	2.0	1.0	0.5	0.0	0.0	0.0
9	6.5	4.0	2.5	1.0	0.5	0.5	0.0	0.0
10	7.5	4.5	3.0	2.0	1.0	0.5	0.0	0.0
15	12.0	8.5	6.0	4.0	2.0	1.0	1.0	0.0
20	17.0	13.0	10.5	8.0	5.0	3.0	2.0	0.5
30	27.0	23.0	20.0	17.0	13.0	10.0	8.0	3.0
40	47.0	33.0	30.0	27.0	23.0	20.0	17.0	10.5

Example (2): What would be the impact on the TL value of the wall if the door were to be poorly fitted with a 2 in. gap between the bottom edge of the door and the floor?

Step ① : Calculate percentage of solid portion of wall (including door):

$$\text{air gap area} = \frac{2}{12} \times 3 = 0.5 \text{ SF}$$

$$\text{wall area} = 10 \times 21 = 210 \text{ SF}$$

$$\text{solid portion of wall} = \frac{209.5}{210} \times \frac{100}{1} = 99.7\%$$

Step ② : Determine the effective TL value of wall from graph:

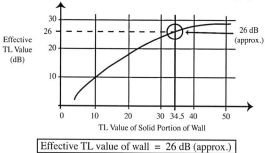

Effective TL value of wall = 26 dB (approx.)

Figure 11.10   Sound insulation impact of a poorly fitted door.

If a sound barrier is forced to vibrate at its natural frequency then the amplitude of the vibrations will be much larger and the TL value of the barrier will be greatly reduced.

● Resonance of building elements such as walls typically occurs at low frequencies.

● The greater the stiffness of the barrier the more sound is transmitted.

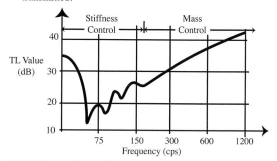

● Stiffness and mass of a sound barrier are opposed to each other, and tend to cancel each other out.

Figure 11.11   Impact of resonance.

These tabulated values are normally based on laboratory tests using very massive side walls and may therefore not be realized in practice (Harris, 1957). In Figure 11.2 are shown two adjacent rooms. Noise created in room A will reach a listener in room B mainly by a direct sound path, but also by a number of indirect sound paths. These secondary paths may decrease the sound insulation of an installed partition by up to 10 dB. Similarly, if transmission loss values are given as the average for a range of frequencies, it is important to ensure that the frequency range is sufficiently wide.

There are two important aspects of the relationship between the mass and sound-transmission loss of a partition that require further explanation.

Resonance: If a barrier is forced to vibrate at its natural frequency, the amplitude of the vibration is likely to be very large. Under these conditions the TL of a partition will be sharply reduced (Figure 11.11).

Resonance occurs often at very low frequencies and is largely controlled by stiff-ness. Although the effects of stiffness and mass both vary with frequency, they are opposed to each other and tend to cancel each other out (Day et al., 1969). It is therefore apparent that the ideal barrier material is one that is heavy, limp, and highly damped.

Coincidence Effect: The incidence of sound pressures on the surface of a barrier will set the barrier in vibration, producing bending waves. Although the velocity of sound in air is constant for all frequencies, the velocity of induced bending waves in solids increases with higher frequencies. Naturally, at some particular frequency, the velocity of bending waves in a given barrier will coincide with the velocity of sound in air. This is known as the *Critical Frequency* and gives rise to a more efficient transmission of sound.

As shown in Figure 11.12, a significant reduction in sound insulation occurs at frequencies above the Critical Frequency, which suggests that for partition walls the Critical Frequency should be as high as possible.

At higher frequencies the bending waves induced by sound in a barrier may approach the velocity of sound and reduce the TL value of the barrier., This is known as the Coincidence Effect.

- The incidence of sound on the surface of a barrier will set the barrier in vibration, producing bending waves.

- The velocity of the bending waves increases with higher frequencies.

- At the Critical Frequency the velocity of the bending waves approaches the velocity of sound resulting in a more efficient transmission of sound through the barrier.

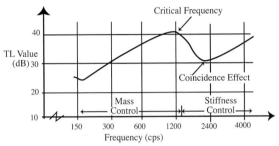

Figure 11.12 The coincidence effect.

The Critical Frequency of a sound barrier is a function of the density, modulus of elasticity, and the thickness of the material. For a given material:

$$\text{Critical Frequency} \propto (1/\text{panel thickness})$$

Therefore, by increasing or decreasing the thickness of a single-leaf panel it is possible to slightly adjust its Critical Frequency upward or downward beyond the frequency range of the transmitted sound. However, reducing the thickness of a panel to increase the Critical Frequency will also reduce the TL value at the lower frequencies. Fortunately, in practice the Coincident Effect is of concern only for relatively thin partitions such as plywood, glass, and gypsum panels.

Another way of reducing the impact of the Coincidence Effect is to increase the damping of a barrier by adding a viscoelastic layer such as mastic, acrylic sheeting, or one or more layers of lead sheeting. A relatively new type of material with superior damping characteristics is *loaded vinyl*, which consists of a polymer mixed with a fairly heavyweight inorganic material

such as calcium carbonate or barium sulfate (ASI, 2007). For similar reasons it would seem that a lead sheet hanging loosely as a curtain would satisfy the requirements of an ideal barrier, because it is very heavy and well damped (i.e., limp). For example, a 1/32 IN thick sheet of lead weighs some 2 LB/SF and has a transmission loss value of 32 dB. Thus a ¼ IN lead sheet weighing 15 LB/SF has a transmission loss value equivalent to a 9 IN thick solid brick wall weighing 105 LB/SF.[1]

11.3.2 Sandwich barriers and multi-leaf walls

As we saw in the previous section, the doubling of thickness of a single-leaf barrier provides only about a 5 dB increase in the TL value. It is therefore more economical to use a multi-leaf barrier consisting of two or more elements. These are also commonly known as "sandwich barriers", and consist of a combination of materials chosen for both structural and acoustical properties. For example, two sheets of relatively high stiffness and strength such as plywood might be combined with a polystyrene core. Since high stiffness is an undesirable property for a sound barrier, the overall stiffness of a sandwich panel can be reduced by selecting a core material with low shear strength. Thus at low frequencies, when the bending waves are large, the core will act as a rigid spacer; while at high frequencies, when the bending waves are short, the low shear strength of the core will effectively reduce the stiffness of the panel (Day et al., 1969).

An alternative approach to a sandwich panel is to separate two single-leaf panels with an air space. The cavity wall or double-leaf partition potentially offers the greatest scope for large noise reduction in building construction. Although in theory it should provide at least twice as much transmission loss as each leaf separately, in the field that is not found to be the case. In other words, if the two leafs are completely decoupled, then the effective TL value should be the sum of the two individual TL values. However, in practice the two leaves of a double-leaf barrier can never be completely decoupled. Even if all direct ties and common footings are eliminated, the transmission loss of a double-leaf barrier still falls short of the predicted value. Normal 2 IN wide cavities, which are very effective for heat-insulation purposes, might provide no more than a 2 dB increase in sound insulation. The following explanation applies.

At low frequencies the air in the cavity loosely couples the two leaves, very much like a coil spring, giving rise to a resonant frequency that is determined by the mass of the leaves and the width of the cavity. Thus, during resonance the transmission-loss value of the barrier is sharply reduced and it is therefore necessary to ensure that the resonant frequency is very low (i.e., below 100 cps). In practice this means that if the two leaves are of low mass, the cavity will need to be fairly wide. At frequencies above the resonant frequency, the insulation of the cavity barrier will increase more rapidly than that of a solid barrier, although at about 250 cps the danger of cavity resonance arises (Day et al., 1969). This problem can be overcome by partly filling the cavity with sound absorbent material, such as fiberglass, flexible plastic foam, or mineral wool. Absorbent cavity infill has been found to be most effective in lightweight construction, with an expected increase in transmission loss of around 5 dB.

From a general point of view the following three categories of sound insulation barrier, based on the amount of sound transmission loss required, need to be considered by building designers:

- *Below 40 dB transmission loss:* The two leaves of a multi-leaf barrier may be connected by common studs or other framing. Although the use of absorbent infill in the cavity is advisable, it could be reduced to a relatively thin blanket.
- *Between 40 and 50 dB transmission loss:* The required degree of transmission loss will require studs to be staggered, so that there is no direct connection between the two leaves. Experience has shown that even the bridging

provided by tie wires in a brick cavity wall may be sufficient to negate the required isolation.
- *Above 50 dB transmission loss:* The method of support of the entire room enclosure (i.e., the perimeter linking) assumes major importance, so that some form of discontinuous construction is normally required.

The sound-transmission loss provided by a single window pane follows the same laws discussed in Section 11.3.1 for single-leaf barriers (i.e., mass and stiffness). However, while the assumption of random incidence of sound is reasonable in the case of an internal wall, it does not apply to external windows. Vehicular traffic and other outdoor noise sources normally produce a predominant angle of incidence. Accordingly, TL values provided by manufacturers for window units are often given for different angles, such as 0° (i.e., normal), 45°, and 70°. Double glazing conforms to the sound-insulation pattern of a cavity partition. Therefore, in order to ensure a low resonance frequency, the small mass of the two sheets of glass will need to be supplemented by a wide cavity (i.e., 9 IN or preferably wider). A further increase in transmission loss of around 5 dB may be obtained in the frequency range of 400 cps to 3200 cps by lining the frame surrounding the cavity with absorbent material.

To calculate the effective sound-transmission loss of a composite wall (e.g., glass and solid) it is necessary to determine the Transmission Coefficient (r) for each section using equation [11.1], as follows:

Transmission Loss (TL) = 10 log (1 / r) [11.1]

Rewriting equation 11.1 in terms of r, we obtain:

$$r = 1 / [antilog (TL / 10)]$$

In the case of a solid, 9 IN, single-leaf brick wall with a TL value of 45 dB and a glazed window unit with a TL value of 25 dB, the Transmission Coefficients for the brick wall (r_w) and the window (r_g) are given by:

$$r_w = 1 / [antilog (4.5)] = 3.2 \times 10^{-5}$$
$$r_g = 1 / [antilog (2.5)] = 3.2 \times 10^{-3}$$

If the areas of the brickwork and window unit are 200 SF and 50 SF, respectively, then the weighted average sound Transmission Coefficient (r_{wg}) of the composite wall is calculated to be:

$$r_{wg} = [200\,(3.2 \times 10^{-5}) + 50\,(3.2 \times 10^{-3})]$$
$$/\,[200 + 50] = 6.7 \times 10^{-4}$$

Hence the TL value of the composite wall is found from equation [11.1] to be:

$$TL = 10\log(1/0.00067) = \mathbf{31.7\,dB}$$

It is therefore apparent that the effective Transmission Loss value of a composite construction is closer to the lowest transmission-loss value of the component elements.

11.3.3 Sound Transmission Class (STC)

Since the Transmission Loss value of a sound-insulation barrier varies with the frequency of the incident sound, an accurate evaluation of the sound-insulation characteristics of a panel will require a detailed TL-frequency analysis. Apart from the effort involved, the results do not readily lend themselves to the comparison of alternative panel constructions. Also, a simple average of the TL over a range of frequencies is likely to be misleading, because it underestimates the impact of the low values.

For this reason the Sound Transmission Class (STC) was introduced to provide a single value that could be used to rate the sound insulation capabilities of a barrier. It is governed by ASTM standard E-90 (ASTM, 1990), which specifies the precise conditions under which a panel must be tested to determine its STC rating.

As shown in Figure 11.13, the test must be performed in two reverberation chambers[2] that are separated by a wall with a large rectangular opening.

The panel to be tested is placed in the opening and the utmost care is taken to carefully seal the perimeter of the panel so that there are no direct air paths between the two reverberation chambers. A noise source of known frequency distribution is generated on one side of the panel, and the transmitted sound is measured on the

The Sound Transmission Class (STC) provides an index (i.e., a single value) to rate the sound insulation capabilities of a barrier.

- Governed by ASTM standard E90, the STC rating of a barrier is established on the basis of sound measurements in a laboratory.

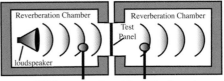

SPL is measured on either side of panel
(in 1/3rd octave bands between 125 cps and 4000 cps)

The measured TL values at each 1/3rd octave band frequency are compared with the standard STC Contour to determine the STC of the panel.

- STC values do not provide any information about decreases in TL at particular frequencies (e.g., due to resonance and Coincidence Effect).
- STC values are limited to the 125 cps - 4,000 cps frequency region (i.e., speech).

Figure 11.13 **Sound transmission class.**

other side. Measurements are recorded at 16 one-third octave bands between 125 cps and 4000 cps and plotted on graph paper, with the TL value on the horizontal axis and the frequency on the vertical axis.

The STC of the panel is then obtained by comparison with a standard *STC contour* (i.e., the *contour* is superimposed on the plotted graph) according to the following procedure. The standard contour, preferably drawn on tracing paper, is then moved up as high as possible by sliding it across the plotted test results until neither of two limits is exceeded:

Limit 1: The sum of the test values that exceed the standard *contour* is not greater than 32 dB.
Limit 2: No test value must exceed the standard *contour* by more than 8 dB.

The STC rating of the panel is then given as the TL value of the plotted test results that corresponds to the STC value at 500 cps on the standard contour. It is simply referred to as a number without the dB unit.

While the STC rating is a very useful measure of the airborne sound-insulation characteristics of a barrier, it nevertheless suffers from two deficiencies. First, it is limited to the range of frequencies between 125 cps and 4000 cps. This range may be exceeded in certain indoor situations where high-pitched noise is encountered. Second, it does not provide any information about the actual shape of the TL-frequency curve and may therefore hide sudden dips in the curve.

11.4   Solid-borne noise insulation

A major acoustical problem confronting architects is the elimination of noise originating through impact on a solid surface, such as footsteps, banging doors, and machinery vibration. The resultant energy is readily transmitted through the structure of the building and large areas can be set in vibration, giving rise to a high degree of radiated airborne noise. Two factors of modern building construction have highlighted this problem: namely, the generally lower background noise levels in air-conditioned buildings, and the use of lighter structures.

11.4.1   Impact Insulation Class (IIC)

While determination of the sound Transmission Loss of a wall is relatively straightforward for airborne noise, the matter is very much more complicated in the case of solid-borne noise, where the energy produced depends on the properties of the impacting force and the solid medium. The procedure that has been adopted internationally utilizes a standardized source of impact energy in the form of a mechanical device.

The solid-borne sound[3] equivalent to the STC rating for airborne sound is the Impact Insulation Class (IIC). According to ASTM guidelines, and similar to the STC test described above, the solid-borne sound insulation is measured by fixing the panel to be tested in an opening between two adjoining rooms. The sound source is provided by a standard tapping machine with five equally spaced hammers, and the frequency range is set lower than the 16 one-third octave bands between 100 cps and

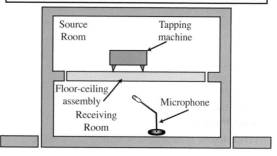

A standard tapping machine (with five hammers) is used to rate the Impact Insulation Class (IIC) of a sound barrier.

The measured TL values at each 1/3rd octave band frequency (100 to 3,150 cps) are compared with the standard IIC Contour to determine the IIC of the floor-ceiling assembly.

● As for STC ratings the IIC ratings are stated simply as numerical values without the unit 'dB'.

● IIC values are highly skewed in favor of low frequencies and therefore do not correlate well with the human perception of sound.

Figure 11.14   Impact insulation class.

3150 cps. The lower frequency range is justified because the kind of noise generated by footsteps and vibrating machinery is normally at lower frequencies.

A typical floor–ceiling testing configuration is shown in Figure 11.14, with the tapping machine mounted above the test panel. The measured sound levels below the test panel are plotted on graph paper and compared with a standard *IIC contour*. Using a similar procedure and applying the same two limits that were described in Section 11.3 for the STC rating, the IIC rating is determined by the TL value of the plotted test results that corresponds to the IIC value at 500 cps on the standard contour. The only two differences in the procedure are that the *IIC contour* is moved vertically down from the top (while the *STC contour* is moved vertically up from the bottom) across the plotted test curve, and the final IIC rating is obtained by subtracting the corresponding TL value on the 500 cps line of the IIC contour from 110 dB. However, just as in the case of the STC rating, the dB unit is also omitted for the IIC rating. The greater the IIC rating, the higher the solid-borne noise insulation that is provided by the barrier.

11.4.2 Methods of solid-borne noise insulation

Methods of solid-borne or structure-borne insulation differ substantially from those of airborne insulation, and it is therefore essential that every effort be made to ascertain whether a disturbing noise originates from an airborne or solid-borne sound source. Although the solution of each individual solid-borne source is unique, there are nevertheless three well-proven general approaches that should be considered:

- the use of resilient floor covering to reduce impact induced vibration;
- the use of isolating, flexible mountings (or anti-vibration pads) for machinery, in conjunction with the provision of limp or spring-loaded connections between all ducts and vibrating machinery;
- the use of discontinuous systems of construction in the form of floating floors and completely isolated multiple walls (Figures 11.15 and 11.16).

The reduction of impact noise from footsteps may be assisted by the use of resilient floor coverings. For example, the increase in IIC that can be obtained by laying a padded carpet on top of a concrete slab is in the vicinity of 60. The increase is less than 10 if the padded carpet is replaced by vinyl tiles. The advantages of carpet are not only high-impact noise insulation and effective noise reduction at the source by absorption, but also psychological. Where floors have been carpeted in schools, the general decrease in impact noise has been accompanied by a softening of the normal institutional atmosphere and a greater concern for appearance and manners by the students. However, it should be noted that apart from increased sound absorption, the carpet has virtually no effect on airborne noise insulation.

Further impact noise insulation may be obtained by discontinuous floor and ceiling constructions. Floors can be constructed in multiple layers with resilient interlays or flexible mountings, so that the surface layer, which receives the impacts, is virtually a floating mass. Many systems of discontinuous floor construction are commonly in use, and some of these are shown schematically in Figures 11.17 and 11.18.

> The increase in structure-borne noise insulation due to a resilient floor covering is far greater for a hard inflexible floor such as a concrete slab, than a more flexible wood floor.

- A resilient floor covering has virtually no effect on airborne noise insulation, except that the carpet will provide some sound absorption.

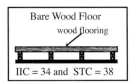 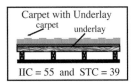

Bare Wood Floor	Carpet with Underlay
IIC = 34 and STC = 38	IIC = 55 and STC = 39

- Approximate expected increase in IIC for different floor coverings.

Floor and Covering	IIC Increase
Carpet and underlay on:	
wood flooring	20
concrete slab	60
Vinyl or rubber on:	
wood flooring	5
concrete slab	7

Figure 11.15 Impact of resilient floor coverings on structure-borne noise insulation.

> A floating floor is a form of discontinuous construction that increases both the structure-borne and airborne noise insulation.

- To be effective the top layer of a floating floor must be separated at all sides from walls and other structural components.

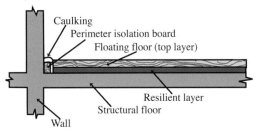

- Floating floors are used where high values of STC (above 50) and IIC (above 50) are required.

- Perimeter isolation is usually provided by fiberglass board or plastic foam.

Figure 11.16 Discontinuous construction at the floor level of buildings.

Either a concrete or a wood structural floor may have a concrete floating floor layer.

- The floating concrete slab is normally 2 to 4 inches thick and reinforced with wire mesh.

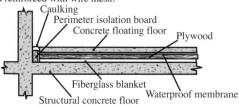

A honeycomb resilient floor board consisting of a cellulosic honeycomb core sandwiched between two layers of fiberglass (5/8 in) is available as an alternative to compressed fiberglass.

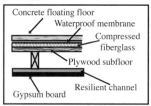

- A concrete floating floor provides the following ratings:
    - On concrete floor structure: IIC = 74 and STC = 62
    - On wood floor structure: IIC = 58 and STC = 60

Figure 11.17   Concrete floating floor on concrete structural floor construction.

Either a concrete or a wood structural floor may have a wood floating floor layer.

- The floating wood floor normally consists of two layers of plywood with staggered joints, glued and nailed to sleepers.

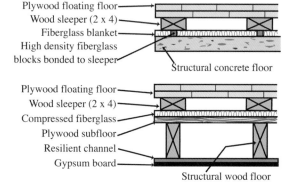

- A wood floating floor provides the following ratings:
    - On concrete floor structure: IIC = 64 and STC = 62
    - On wood floor structure: IIC = 52 and STC = 58

Figure 11.18   Wood floating floor on concrete or wood floor structure.

For example, the concrete screed floor shown in Figure 11.17 is approximately 1½IN thick, poured in situ on a material that must have sufficient strength to remain resilient under the superimposed weight of concrete and normal building live loads. Compressed fiberglass may be used, but should be turned up at the walls to avoid any direct contact between the surface screed and the structural floor or perimeter walls. Alternatively a honeycomb resilient floor board is often used. It consists of a cellulose-like honeycomb core sandwiched between two layers of fiberglass. In this case the separation at the wall boundary is achieved with a perimeter isolation board. Unfortunately, most resilient materials tend to compress after some years of use, and their effectiveness is thus reduced. If the base structure is a concrete slab, then the respective IIC and STC ratings are 74 and 62. However, for a timber-base structure the ratings, particularly the IIC rating, are lower (i.e., 58 and 60, respectively).

Either a concrete or timber structural base may also have a wooden floating floor (Figure 11.18). In either case the flooring boards are nailed to timber sleepers (typically 2IN × 4IN laid on side), which rest directly on the resilient layer such as compressed fiberglass. In the case of a timber structure the gypsum board ceiling may be mounted on the underside of the floor beams, using a resilient channel for additional impact isolation. It should be noted that while the STC ratings are only slightly lower for a timber solution (i.e., about 7 percent), the IIC ratings are significantly lower (i.e., about 23 percent). In other words, the greater mass and stiffness of concrete is useful for impact noise insulation, but only slightly superior to wood construction for airborne noise insulation.

In the case of solid-borne sound produced by vibrating machinery, an attempt should be made to reduce vibration at the source, and if this fails the machine must be isolated from the building structure by means of flexible mountings. It is common practice to place between the source of the vibration and the supporting structure flexible elements, such as springs, rubber pads, or special multiple-layer isolators designed for specific applications. The amplitude of vibration of the source will be proportional to the force causing the vibration, and its own inertia, while the force that is transmitted to the building structure will depend on the dynamic characteristics of the source on its flexible mountings (Bradbury, 1963). It is conceivable that an inappropriate choice of mounting stiffness could lead to an increase rather than a reduction of the transmitted force. As a fundamental rule, it is important that the natural frequency of the source on its flexible mounting should be small compared with the frequency of vibration of the source alone. For simple spring devices the degree of isolation is related to the static deflection of the spring when loaded. As a compromise between cost and vibration isolation, a static deflection given by equation [11.3] is often aimed for:

$$\text{Deflection (d)} = 160 / [f_v^2] \text{ (IN)} \quad [11.3]$$

where f_v cps is the lowest appreciable frequency of vibration.

Care must be taken that the spring has sufficient damping to control the vibration of the machine during starting and stopping. At these times, it is to be expected that the vibration of the source will be momentarily equal to the resonant frequency of the system. A steel spring can be damped by external means such as dash pots.[4] Unfortunately, the behavior of anti-vibration pads (e.g., rubber, cork, or felt laminates) cannot be predicted as simply as in the case of springs, since the static and dynamic stiffnesses differ in most materials. For many of these pads, damping is a function of frequency.

11.5 Noise insulation in practice

Where Transmission Loss (TL) values in excess of 50 dB are called for, such as in recording studios, and less noise-sensitive building occupancies housed in buildings that are required to be located in very noisy environments – such as near airports – the most appropriate acoustical solution may be *discontinuous construction*. This essentially requires the construction of two building shells (i.e., one inside the other). In the case of a timber frame this can be accomplished either with a double wall or the staggering of studs in a wider, single-leaf wall.

Figure 11.19 compares the STC values of a normal single-stud wall (approximately 40) with a staggered-stud wall (approximately 50) and a double wall (approximately 55). As an additional enhancement, sound-absorbing material can be added in the air cavity. The benefit of the absorptive infill is an STC increase of only 3 for the normal single-stud wall, but a much greater increase in the case of the staggered-stud and double-wall construction alternatives (i.e., 9 and 11, respectively).

It is interesting to note that the benefit of adding a second layer of ½ IN thick gypsum board to one side of the wall (i.e., the "1 + 2" columns in Figure 11.19) is more than twice as much for the discontinuous construction alternatives than the normal single-stud wall, while in all three cases the increase in STC value is virtually the same as that provided by the cavity absorption infill. The reason for this is the extra

> The STC rating of a wood stud wall (approx. 40) can be increased by using staggered studs (approx. 50) or double wall construction (approx. 55).

Types of 2" x 4" wood stud wall constructions with one or more layers of 1/2" thick gypsum board.

	Layers of Gypsum Board					
	Without Cavity Absorption			With Cavity Absorption		
	1+1	1+2	2+2	1+1	1+2	2+2
	37	40	43	40	43	46
2 in.	41	48	52	50	54	58
1 in.	46	53	57	57	61	63

Figure 11.19 Alternative stud wall construction methods.

mass provided by the second layer of gypsum board.

In the case of the floor the required constructional discontinuity can be provided by one of the alternative floating-floor constructions described in Section 11.4.2 and depicted in Figures 11.17 and 11.18. However, as noted previously the STC values that can be achieved when the structural floor material is concrete are significantly higher than the corresponding values for a timber structure.

Special care must be taken to avoid air paths in walls that will lead to the direct transmission of noise from one room to another. This is likely to occur whenever electrical outlets for two adjoining rooms are placed opposite each other within the same stud cavity.

As shown in Figure 11.20, the outlet boxes should be sealed with preformed tape around all sides and placed in separate stud cavities. In addition, it is considered good practice to line the stud cavities containing outlet boxes with fiberglass or mineral wool. A similar noise-transmission vulnerability exists for the small

built-in cabinets that are desirable in bathrooms. For this reason, whenever noise insulation is an important design criterion, such cabinets should not be provided in a normal single-stud wall. Cabinets in a staggered-stud or double-stud wall need to be backed with gypsum board on the back and all sides.

A very common noise-transmission problem is encountered in office buildings with suspended ceilings. Even though special care may have been taken, at considerable expense to the building owner, to use prefabricated partition walls with a relatively high STC value (e.g., multi-layered with an interstitial lead sheet), the result can be quite disappointing.

As shown in Figure 11.21, the sound insulation will only be as good as the weakest link in the chain. In this case the effective STC value will be 20 rather than 40, because the noise will travel more readily through the ceiling than through the partition.

Neither of the two remedies suggested in Figure 11.21 is ideal. Extending the partition to the underside of the structural floor above

---

Outlets in the wall of two adjoining rooms should not be placed in the same stud cavity, but should have at least one intervening stud between them.

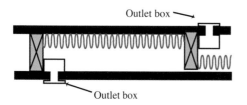

- The back and side surfaces of outlet boxes in sound insulating walls should be sealed (to render them fully air tight) with preformed sealant tape.

- Stud cavities containing outlet boxes should be lined with fiberglass or mineral wool.

Sound insulating construction is highly sensitive to flanking air paths.

Figure 11.20 **Proper sealing of electric power outlet boxes in walls.**

Sound will travel through a false ceiling from one space to another.

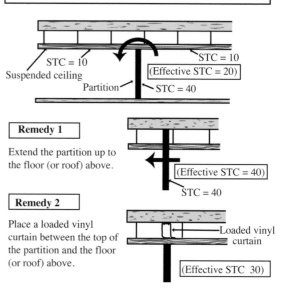

Figure 11.21 **Common sound insulation problem between adjacent office spaces.**

inhibits the flexibility that was intended to be provided through the use of partitions in the first place. The partitions cannot be easily moved to achieve an alternative space layout, because the suspended ceiling is no longer continuous. Adding a loaded vinyl curtain in the space above the partition poses a rather awkward construction challenge and still leaves the ceiling as the weakest link in the chain.

Even more serious is the potential noise-transmission problem that can occur between two adjoining apartments sharing a common attic space.

Here, as shown in Figure 11.22, it is essential that special precautions are taken to fix a solid noise barrier in the attic above the shared wall. Again, it is important that any direct air paths are eliminated by careful attention to the joints where the blocking panel meets the top of the shared wall and the roof above.

Finally, a word of caution about windows in external walls. A typical fixed window with a single ⅛IN glass pane has an STC value of 29. However, if the window is openable, then the

Table 11.2   Reduced increase in STC value of glass of different thicknesses.

Glass thickness	Mass law TL value	Actual STC value
⅛ IN	29 dB	29
¼ IN	35 dB	31
½ IN	41 dB	33

STC value for the window in a closed condition is lowered by 3 to 5 points. Sliding glass doors are particularly prone to air flanking paths. While according to the Mass Law the thicker the glass the higher the TL value, this is not borne out in practice. Unfortunately, for thicker glass the critical frequency of the Coincident Effect is lower and this reduces the STC value disproportionately (Table 11.2). While the Mass Law suggests a TL increase of 6 dB with each doubling of thickness, the STC value increases by only 2 points.

Needless to say, the simplest and most effective means of controlling noise inside buildings is through sound architectural design practices. In particular the following guiding principles are highly recommended:

- Separate noisy rooms from noise-sensitive rooms. For example, in multi-story apartments and condominiums, bedrooms should be separated from community corridors and lobbies.
- Use noisier rooms to buffer noise-sensitive rooms from external noise sources, such as vehicular traffic noise.
- Apply sound absorption to reduce the internally generated noise level in highly reflective (i.e., *live*) rooms. However, be aware of the Law of Diminishing Returns.
- Mitigate very loud internal noise sources through isolation and the treatment of surrounding surfaces with sound-absorbing material.
- Ensure that the transmitted noise level is at least 5 dB below the background noise level of the receiving room, so that the background noise level will not be significantly raised.

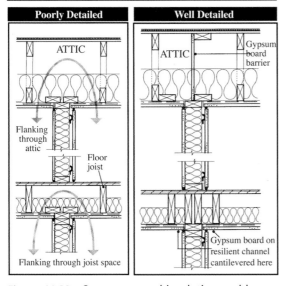

Figure 11.22 Common sound insulation problem between adjacent apartments.

Table 11.3 Recommended STC values for adjoining rooms.

Primary room	Adjoining room	STC value
Classroom	Classroom	45
	Laboratory	50
	Corridor/lobby	50
	Music room	60
Office	Office	50
	General office	45
	Corridor/lobby	50
	Mechanical room	60
Conference room	Conference room	50
	Office	50
	Corridor/lobby	50
	Mechanical room	60
Bedroom	Bedroom	55
	Corridor/lobby	55
	Mechanical room	60

11.6 Common noise sources

It appears that any definite attempt to control noise levels in the community must be accompanied by a determined effort in public education. The reluctance of courts of law and laymen to accept objective measurements as a criterion of annoyance is largely due to uncertainty, since the figures quoted have little relevance to most people. Sound-level meters, like light meters, are relatively costly instruments and are therefore not readily available to members of the community. The situation is perhaps analogous to the hypothetical substitution of wet-bulb temperature as the principal index for weather forecasts. Thermometers are readily available to all persons. Therefore, while dry-bulb temperature is an inadequate measure of thermal comfort (because it neglects air movement and relative humidity), it nevertheless relates to personal experience. Even though wet-bulb temperature is a more precise thermal measure (particularly for hot-humid climates) it has little relevance to the average person, who would be unfamiliar with a sling thermometer. In the 1960s the City of Tokyo in Japan embarked on an interesting public-education initiative. To combat the problem of increasing noise levels, the city authorities set up, for a trial period, sound-level meters in streets and displayed the resultant noise-level readings on large screens attached to adjacent buildings.

Chicago, a pioneer in the control of noise by town-planning legislation, introduced noise-level restrictions in defined areas in the early 1950s. The legislation met with favorable public reaction, no doubt at least partly due to the manner in which it was administered. On the basis of a complaint a city engineer would be sent to investigate the circumstances, without the assistance of a sound-level meter. The engineer would inform the apparent offender that a complaint had been lodged and recommend that the noise level be reduced by taking certain steps. If a second complaint was received, the noise would be analyzed with a sound-level meter to determine whether the noise infringed the current legislation. If so, the offender would be informed of pending legal action unless the noise was reduced within a specified period of time. Finally, if the offender still refused to act, the city would launch a prosecution that had every hope of being upheld in a court of law. Accordingly, the community became increasingly aware that it is possible to be prosecuted for producing excessive noise, with the result that persons tended to refrain from making unnecessary noise. This in itself was a worthy aim, since the community became educated to appreciate the nuisance value of noise.

11.6.1 Ventilation noise

Ventilation and air-conditioning installations are normally responsible for two main noise problems: namely, noise and vibration produced by the fan and motor assembly, and noise transmitted from one area to another by ducts. For convenience, noise sources in ventilation systems may be grouped into three principal categories:

- *Mechanical noise:* Mechanical noise sources such as rotating machinery, bearings, belts, and motors all produce both airborne and solid-borne noise. The solid-borne noise is later radiated into the air of adjoining rooms from the surface of ducts. Although steps might be taken to reduce the noise levels at the source by improvement in balancing or machining, it is often more economical to merely isolate the ducts from the fan and motor assembly, and the latter likewise from the building structure. Flexible couplings are most effective between fans and ducts, although care must be taken to ensure that the coupling is not stretched during fitting, and remains flexible throughout its service life.

- *Vortex noise:* Vortex noise due to air turbulence around fan blades, grilles, and sharp bends forms the major portion of ventilation noise. Accordingly, high-velocity systems (i.e., over 3000 FT/min) produce a considerable amount of vortex noise, especially if outlet grilles are fitted with guide vanes rather than open mesh.
- *Rotational noise:* Rotational noise is generated by the mechanical action of fan blades producing fluctuating pressure changes that are transmitted along the main air stream as a series of pure tones. The principal frequency of rotational noise is related to the number of blades, and the speed of the fan in revolutions per second. Obstructions close to the fan blades tend to aggravate the noise problem. The rotational noise level of both high-speed axial flow and low-speed centrifugal-type fans increases approximately linearly with the power (KW), so that for each doubling of power, the noise level increases by some 3 dB. On the other hand, the frequency spectrum of these two types of fan is fundamentally different, and depends as well on the size of the fan. While the centrifugal fan falls off steadily at about 5 dB per octave band toward higher frequencies, the axial fan rises to a peak in the middle frequency range (i.e., 200 to 1000 cps).

The frequency spectrum of the fan is an important consideration, particularly since nearly all noise-reducing devices are more effective at higher frequencies. It is therefore apparent that from an acoustical point of view alone the centrifugal fan is more amenable to acoustic treatment, despite the fact that it produces potentially more annoying, higher-frequency noise. The simplest method of obtaining an appreciable amount of sound absorption in ventilation systems is to line the duct walls with an absorbent material. Apart from a high absorption coefficient, such linings should have a smooth surface for low air friction and adequate strength to resist disintegration due to the continuous action of the air stream.

Heating, ventilation, and air-conditioning (HVAC) systems commonly used in buildings essentially fall into five categories: namely, window air-conditioning units; fan coil units; rooftop units; packaged air-handling units; and, built-up air-handling units.

Window and fan coil units are commonly found in hotel rooms. Window air conditioners are typically located within a bench-like enclosure immediately below the windowsill. They include a compressor and a fan as an integrated assembly, and require no ductwork. The air is simply drawn into the unit through an air inlet in the external wall and blown directly into the room through fixed angle vanes. While the noise produced by the compressor and the fan cannot be controlled by building design, it may sometimes have the redeeming quality of masking other undesirable noise sources by raising the background sound level in the room. However, window units are often a source of annoyance, particularly if they are not well maintained (i.e., the noise produced by the compressor and fan tends to increase with the age of the unit).

Fan coil units are normally located at ceiling level and incorporate a fan that blows air over coils containing chilled or heated water that comes from a central plant. An alternative to centrally supplied hot water is electric resistance heating that is provided locally within the unit. Although fan coil units are typically located near an external wall with an air inlet, they operate mainly on the basis of recirculated air. The only sources of noise for this type of

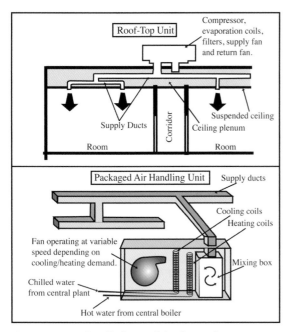

Figure 11.23   Small air-conditioning units.

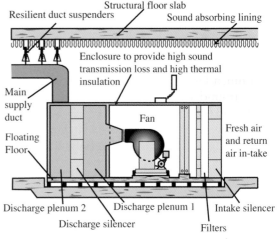

Figure 11.24   Built-up air handling units.

air-conditioning unit are the fan and the possible vibration of the panels that enclose the unit.

As their name implies, rooftop air-conditioning units are usually found on the roof of a building, with the conditioned air delivered to the internal spaces through supply ducts. Return air is drawn into the unit from a ceiling plenum (Figure 11.23, upper diagram). These are self-contained systems complete with compressor, evaporative cooling coils, heat exchanger coils to extract heat from the recirculated air, filters, and ducts (i.e., for both supplying and recirculating air). Fan coil units are commonly used in single-story buildings, where the ratio of the external roof to internal floor area is favorable.

Packaged air-handling units (AHU) are much larger and typically prefabricated as fully assembled units in a factory. They are commonly used in medium-rise buildings to serve one or more floors through ductwork. Chilled water is pumped to the unit from a central plant and heating may be likewise supplied centrally in the form of hot water or steam, or provided locally through electric resistance heating. Fresh air is mixed with return air, filtered, adjusted

for humidity, blown over chilled or heated coils as required, and then transmitted through the connected ductwork to the conditioned spaces (Figure 11.23, lower diagram). Most commonly a packaged AHU incorporates one or more thermostatically controlled mixing boxes that mix cooled air from the AHU with warm return air. The mixing boxes may have their own fans and essentially control the variable fan speed of the AHU through their demand for cool air. To minimize the solid-borne noise that might be produced by the fan-motor assembly it is either mounted directly on vibration isolators, or the entire packaged AHU is mounted on vibration isolation pads.

A built-up AHU is very similar to a packaged AHU, except that it is much larger and therefore assembled on-site. It may include more than one supply fan of the large centrifugal or axial type, and a whole bank of air filters and coils. A complete built-up unit may take up an entire floor of a high-rise building and will require a floating-floor construction (Figure 11.24).

Most of the noise in a HVAC system of the rooftop and AHU type is produced by the fan.

This noise is then potentially transmitted throughout the building by the air stream through the supply ducts and by the vibration of the duct walls. For this reason it is common practice to line portions of the inside surface of a duct with sound-absorption material such as fiberglass (e.g., 1 to 2 IN thick). The resulting reduction in sound (i.e., referred to as *attenuation* or *insertion loss*) is about 4 dB/FT at 1000 cps, but much less at lower and higher frequencies (i.e., around 1 dB/FT at 300 cps and a little less than 2 dB/FT at 4000 cps).

The air stream itself is also a source of noise. Air turbulence due to excessive air speed[5] or poorly designed duct transitions, such as connections and abrupt changes in diameter, will increase the noise generated by air flow. As a general set of guidelines, duct elbows should have rounded corners, right-angle duct branches should be provided with internal guiding vanes, and changes in duct cross-section should be gradual so that the transitional duct wall does not exceed a 15° angle in the direction of the air stream.

The vibration of the duct wall requires further discussion. When the noise generated by the fan is carried by the air stream through the duct-work some of the energy is converted into mechanical vibration of the duct wall. This is referred to as duct *break-out* noise and represents the fan noise that is transmitted by the vibrating walls of a duct and re-radiated into a space as airborne noise. As might be expected, this noise transmission phenomenon is more serious in high-velocity than in low-velocity systems. Duct shape is also a factor. The more compact (i.e., square) or circular the cross-section of the duct, the less break-out noise is generated. Finally, duct stiffness reduces the tendency for the duct walls to vibrate and therefore decreases the break-out noise. To increase its stiffness sections of a duct may be *lagged* with fiberglass wrapping. A typical duct section that combines both the provision for *insertion loss* and break-out noise reduction would include a 1 to 2 IN fiberglass lining inside the sheet metal duct wall and fiberglass sheet wrapping with a loaded vinyl covering around the outside of the duct.

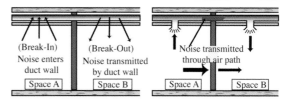

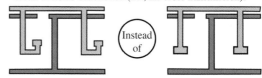

Figure 11.25   Duct break-in and break-out noise.

A duct can also act as a bridge to transmit noise that is generated in one space into an adjoining space. This is referred to as duct *break-in* noise.

As shown in Figure 11.25, this kind of noise transmission can occur either through the walls of a duct or through the direct air path that is provided inside the duct. Since the speed of sound is at least 20 times faster than the flow rate of the conditioned air, the amount of noise transmitted is largely independent of the air-flow direction. External insulation of the duct and duct layouts that increase the noise path will reduce the break-in noise transmitted to some degree. Fortunately, duct break-in noise is normally not a major concern, because the reduction that can be achieved with these two measures is modest.

The ability to reduce or eliminate a sound through interference with another sound that has an identical frequency spectrum, but is 180° out of phase, has been considered conceptually by physicists and acoustic engineers for many years. Although a first patent was awarded in the 1930s, a practical implementation of this concept did not become possible until the 1980s

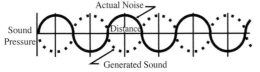

In active noise control noise is canceled out by the production of an identical sound that is exactly 180° out of phase.

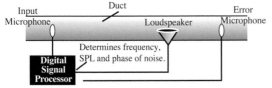

The generated sound must have the same frequency spectrum as the actual noise.

The loudspeaker (i.e., generated sound) must be far enough away from the input microphone to allow adequate time for the signal analysis.

First patent awarded in 1930s but did not become practical until 1980s when computer-based digital signal processors became economical.

Figure 11.26   Active noise control.

when computer-based digital signal processing became economical. While the concept of *active noise control*[6] is quite simple, its practical implementation depends on the ability of computers to analyze noise fast enough so that the interfering noise can be generated in time to cancel the offending noise.

As shown in Figure 11.26, an active noise-control system consists of a microphone located inside the duct, which is connected to a digital signal processor. The latter determines the frequency spectrum and SPL of the noise and generates the required 180° phase shift. The generated sound is then transmitted back into the duct by means of a loudspeaker in time to cancel out the original noise. A second microphone at a small distance behind the first microphone provides feedback to the digital signal processor to increase the efficiency of the noise-canceling operation.

In theory it should be possible to apply active noise control in any sound environment. However, currently its application is limited to the largely low-frequency sound in HVAC ducts and in the sound-cancelling earphones

that are becoming increasingly popular with airline passengers. Unfortunately, further technical advances are necessary before digital signal processing can become a feasible noise-control solution for open sound environments.

The general guidelines for controlling noise sources in ventilation and air-conditioning systems may be summarized as follows:

- Mount fans and other HVAC equipment on anti-vibration pads.
- Use flexible connectors for isolating fans from ducts to reduce duct *break-out* noise.
- Select motors of higher horsepower than is necessary and operate them at less than maximum output.
- Avoid sharp bends and use vanes inside elbows to reduce noise due to air flow in the main supply ducts.
- Line duct sections internally with absorbent material, such as fiberglass.
- Line ducts externally with lagging when they pass through noisy spaces to reduce *break-in* noise.
- Seal around the edges of ducts when they pass through walls, floors, and ceilings.
- Insert bends in secondary ducts to decrease cross-transmission (i.e., duct *break-in* noise) between adjoining spaces.

11.6.2 Industrial process noise

After World War II systematic surveys of industrial noise produced alarming results. In the US, Karplus and Bonvallet (1953) found that in some 40 different (noisy) plants over a wide range of industries, noise levels of between 90 dB and 100 dB were prevalent in about 50 percent of machine-operator positions. Their results indicated that noise generated in mechanical plants is particularly significant in the metal and aircraft industries, where chipping and riveting of large plates and tanks were found to represent the loudest individual noise sources. These findings led to subsequent psycho-acoustic surveys to determine the reaction of individual persons to industrial noise. Davies (1962) distributed questionnaires to more than 500 industrial firms engaged in noisy manufacturing processes. He found that:

- Up to 20 percent of all shop-floor employees in these factories worked in surroundings where normal conversation was not possible.
- In the case of offices, under similar circumstances, less than 3 percent of the workers were affected.
- Methods of noise control were commonly used in the following order of frequency: isolation of machinery mountings (20%); silencers (15%); modifications to machinery (15%); segregation of noise source (5%); and, acoustical treatment and miscellaneous methods (15%).

These and other surveys have shown that industrial machine noise is caused primarily by manufacturing operations that rely on impulsive forces to form metals, abrasive materials to grind surfaces, saws and mills to cut material, and air pressure as a source of power. Forces due to impacts, out-of-balance disturbances, air flow, resonance, and so on, are set up in the machine, and produce airborne sound directly or indirectly due to the vibration of components. Fluctuating gas flows found in combustion engines, compressors, pneumatic hammers, and safety valves are known to produce high-intensity noise levels. Of less significance are noises due to friction and electrical circuits, such as the humming sound produced by transformers.

Systematic analyses of various typical industrial noise sources and their control were published in the 1950s by Aldersey-Williams (1960), Tyzzer (1953), King (1957), and Geiger (1955). Based on these recommendations and other sources (Beranek, 1960; HMSO, 1963; Harris, 1957), steps were taken by governments, employers, and unions to ameliorate adverse noise conditions in industrial environments. Such measures, which soon became commonplace, included noise reduction at the source, substitution of a quiet process for a noisy process, and the mandatory wearing of hearing protectors by workers.

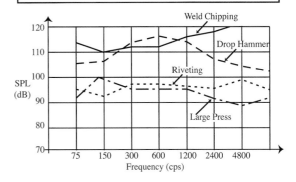

Industrial noise is mostly due to impulsive forces to form metals, abrasive actions to grind surfaces, saws and mills to cut materials, and compressed gasses (e.g., compressors, pneumatic hammers, combustion engines, and safety valves).

Noise reduction at the source is the best strategy (e.g., absorption lined housings, silencers for compressed gas equipment, and substitution of a quiet process for a noisy process).

Figure 11.27 Industrial noise sources.

While at first sight the substitution of a very noisy industrial process with a less noisy process may appear to be more wishful thinking than reality, it was in fact found to be a viable approach.

For example, as shown in Figure 11.27, the use of flame gouging instead of chipping on welded construction, and the substitution of press operations for drop forgings, will be accompanied by considerable reductions in noise level. Moreover, since noise resulting from impact is proportional to the rate of deceleration of the impacting parts (i.e., their mass, size, stiffness, and damping) it was found that resilient buffers could be used to advantage between the impacting surfaces (Aldersey-Williams, 1960). At the same time, isolation of the impacting pieces from the machine frame reduced the risk of resonance. In the case of grinding operations, significant improvements were achieved by damping the component being ground with the aid of clamps or externally applied loads. For cutting tools, the noise level is directly related to the resonant properties of the assembly, while the frequency spectrum is largely determined by the rate at which the teeth of the cutting edge meet the surface being processed. Although it is almost impossible to influence this type of high-frequency noise at the source, some marginal reduction has been achieved by applying large washers to either side of circular saw disks (i.e., thereby damping resonance).

11.6.3 Residential noise

Residential buildings are affected by sources of external and internal noise. Several surveys of residential noise sources were undertaken in the late 1950s and early 1960s. Some of the findings of two of these studies focused on internal noise sources, published by Van den Eijk in the Netherlands (1966) and Lawrence in Australia (1968), are combined in Figure 11.28.

As might be expected, during this post-World War II period radio noise was by far the worst offender. Today, with the prevalent use of earphones, the radio is no longer considered a major source of annoyance. As shown in Figure 11.28, with the notable exception of washing machines, most internal domestic noise sources predominate in the middle and high-frequency sections of the spectrum.

Impact noise in residential buildings is usually the result of footsteps, movement of furniture, and door slamming. Unfortunately, many multiple dwellings (i.e., condominiums and apartment buildings) incorporate foyers and staircases with acoustically hard finishes that will readily transmit and reflect impact noise. Appropriate remedial measures include lining the walls and ceilings of these circulation spaces with sound-absorbing material, and covering floors and staircase treads with carpet. Furthermore, door jambs can be fitted with felt or rubber damping strips to reduce the effect of door slamming.

Referring again to Figure 11.28, a typical push-button water-closet cistern can produce noise levels of 60 dB in the toilet compartment. Although this noise level may be reduced to less than 50 dB in an adjoining room, it can still exceed the ambient background noise level by a sufficiently large margin to produce undesirable interference, particularly at night. The simplest way of dealing with this noise source is to reduce the rate of refilling the cistern, since the velocity of water is directly proportional to the noise level produced. Another source of annoyance in some older dwellings is the shock noises that can be produced by the sudden closing of a faucet. This is commonly referred to as a *water hammer* and is caused by a large volume of water being cut off suddenly. The remedy is to provide an air damper consisting of a length of pipe containing an air cushion at the dead end, mounted on top of a tee-pipe section.

Finally, it is good practice to insulate pipes where they pass through or are fixed inside walls, so that solid-borne sound is less likely to be transferred. Under these conditions noise and heat insulation can often be economically combined.[7]

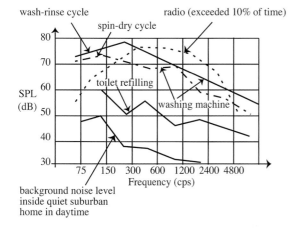

Apart from washing machines most noise sources generated inside buildings are in the mid to high frequency range.

Impact noise is generated inside buildings by footsteps, slamming doors and the movement of chairs.

Figure 11.28   Residential noise sources.

11.6.4   Vehicular traffic noise

Although aircraft can constitute the most severe external noise source in the vicinity of airports

Table 11.4 Vehicular traffic noise (expected 80% of the time).

Type of road and environment	Expected noise levels (80% of the time)	
	Day (8 am – 6 pm)	Night (1 am – 6 am)
Highways and freeways	75–85 dBA	65–70 dBA
Major heavy traffic roads	65–75 dBA	50–60 dBA
Residential roads	55–65 dBA	45–55 dBA
Minor roads	50–60 dBA	45–50 dBA
Residential side streets	50–55 dBA	40–45 dBA

and under direct flight paths, for the majority of city and suburban sites vehicular road traffic will remain the most important and persistent source of external noise. Since road traffic noise is subject to considerable fluctuations due to changes in speed, age, size, and general state of repair of a vehicle, surveys have generally been expressed on a statistical basis. Table 11.4 lists these findings in the form of noise levels recorded for 80 percent of the time. Accordingly, for 10 percent of the time noise levels were found to be higher, and for the remaining 10 percent of the time they were found to be lower than the range shown in the Table. Although mean traffic noise levels are acceptable as a guideline, it is important to also know the maximum levels that will occur whenever a vehicle passes the listener.

It was discussed previously in Chapter 9 (Section 9.3) that a point source of sound in a free field is reduced by some 6 dB for each doubling of the distance between the source and the listener. Unfortunately, traffic noise is more accurately described as originating from a line source, which means that the attenuation with distance is only about 3 dB for each doubling of distance. Further, it should be mentioned that, particularly in city and suburban areas, the noise produced by freely flowing traffic cannot

be rightly considered as an accurate design criterion. In these areas, traffic is subjected to stopping and starting owing to traffic conditions and intersection controls. When accelerating from a stationary position, low gears are used and engine speeds (i.e., revolutions) tend to be high. It must therefore be expected that sound pressure levels are higher under these conditions, accompanied by a slight shift of the frequency spectrum toward higher frequencies.

Basically, the noise produced by vehicular traffic can be reduced in four ways: namely, by reducing the number of vehicles; by eliminating conditions that are conducive to the noisy operation of vehicles; by limiting the noise produced by individual vehicles; and by isolating traffic noise either close to the source or near the listener. Although there appears to be little difference in maximum noise level whether one or more vehicles are passing a given point, the percentage of near-maximum readings is greatly increased for heavy traffic flows.

Present restriction of certain suburban roads to passenger and light commercial traffic, while based on utilitarian premises, could be extended as a means of ameliorating noise conditions. In city and suburban traffic, maximum noise levels occur during acceleration in low gear, whether this is due to a sudden increase in traffic speed or grade. Significant improvements in traffic flow tend to be costly and often difficult to achieve in existing cities, where most land is privately owned. The reduction of noise produced by individual vehicles has long been considered the most fruitful approach. For combustion engines, the noise level is directly related to the engine load and road speed, while in the case of diesel engines there is much less variation (Lawrence, 1968; Priede, 1962). However, there are other sources such as tire noise at high speeds on highways and freeways, horns, and the rattling of bodywork in empty heavy commercial vehicles that need to be considered.

In most cases the reduction of traffic noise is achieved mainly at the listener's end by improving the insulation of the external building walls. Since traffic noise has significant low-frequency components, systems of construction incorporating heavy cavity walls and double-glazed, plate glass windows with substantial cavities (e.g., 8 IN.) are most effective. If a number of closely grouped buildings are involved in the same communal traffic noise problem, consideration might be given to cuttings or a series of free-standing barriers alongside the offending traffic way. Such noise barriers are now quite common in cities to shield residential developments from freeway noise.

As shown in Figures 11.29 and 11.30, the approximate noise reduction that can be achieved by such a free-standing sound barrier can be calculated with the following equation:

noise reduction = 10 log$_{10}$ (20) × (Z / K)   [11.4]

where:

$Z = 2[R((1 + (H^2/R)^{\frac{1}{2}}) - 1)$
$\quad + D((1 + (H^2/D)^{\frac{1}{2}}) - 1)]$
$K = W(1 + (H^2/R))$

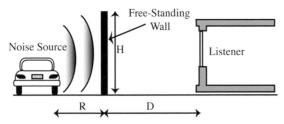

Figure 11.29   Parameters considered in the calculation of the noise reduction provided by external free-standing walls.

Relative Wall Distances (from source and building)	Approximate Reduction at Building		
	Height = 20 FT	Height = 30 FT	Height = 40 FT
100 FT 1000 FT	18 dB	21 dB	23 dB
1000 FT 100 FT	11 dB	14 dB	17 dB

Figure 11.30   Impact on noise reduction of the height and distance from building of an external free-standing wall.

for:

H = height of free-standing noise barrier (FT)
R = distance of barrier from noise source (FT)
D = distance of barrier from listener (FT)
W = wavelength of noise source (FT); – i.e., 1100 (FT) / frequency (cps).

To be effective, free-standing sound barriers need to be at least 20 FT high and are therefore required to withstand considerable horizontal wind forces. For a 20 FT high wall subjected to a wind speed of 50 MPH. the horizontal design load due to wind forces will be approximately 125 LB per vertical lineal FT of wall.[8] The walls are often slightly concave toward the noise source, so as to increase their effectiveness and structural stability. It is also important that the wall is placed as close to the noise source as possible. As shown in Figure 11.30, the difference in effectiveness of a sound barrier that is located 100 FT from the noise source and one that is placed 1000 FT from the noise source is 39 percent for a 20 FT high wall, 33 percent for a 30 FT high wall, and 27 percent for a 40 FT high wall.

11.6.5   Trees and shrubs

Field measurements have verified that trees and shrubs can reduce external noise levels by 5 to 8 dB, which the human ear may perceive as a 50 percent reduction in noise. In particular, carefully planned tree belts in combination with shrubs can provide a moderate buffer for vehicular traffic noise in residential areas. The following guidelines should be followed:

- Tree belts should be 20 to 100 FT wide, depending on the severity of the noise source. Evergreen trees with dense foliage are recommended for year-round noise protection.
- Select taller trees (if permitted), with lower-level shrubs (i.e., 6 to 8 FT high) in front of and between the trees. A soft ground cover such as tall grass is preferable to paving. The trees and shrubs should be planted as close together as the plant species allow.

- The trees and shrubs should be planted as close to the noise source as possible. The same rules as for free-standing sound barrier walls apply in this regard. Ideally, the vegetation belt should be within 20 to 50 FT of the noise source.
- The tree and shrub belt should be at least twice as long as the distance from the area to be protected. In the case of vehicular traffic noise the vegetation belt should extend a significant distance in both directions parallel to the road or highway.

Wind is also a factor that can influence the effectiveness of a tree belt. If the prevailing winds come from the direction of the noise source, then the ability of a vegetation belt to act as a noise barrier will be much reduced.

11.6.6 Aircraft noise

During the 1950s and 1960s, as existing airports were expanded and new airports were built to accommodate an increasing volume of commercial passenger and air-freight transportation, aircraft noise emerged as one of the most severe and politically activated sound-control problems of the late twentieth century. In response, a number of surveys and research studies were undertaken to develop subjective rating scales for aircraft noise (HMSO, 1963; Bishop, 1966; Bowsher et al., 1966). In the US the Composite Noise Rating (CNR) scale was proposed for relating maximum noise levels with the number of occurrences, while in Germany the Q scale was chosen to represent the total weighted noise energy reaching a given point on the ground during any specified period.

It is apparent from these scales that the level of aircraft noise is less important than the number of times the disturbance occurs. Accordingly, in England, on the basis of the Wilson Report (HMSO, 1963), the Noise and Number Index (NNI) was introduced, which for the first time allowed an acceptable aircraft noise rating to be established.

Experiments dealing with the subjective judgment of the noise that occurs during air-

craft fly-overs have resulted in the concept of Perceived Noise (PNdB) level (Kryter and Pearsons, 1963). The perceived noise level is calculated from the spectrum of the noise, so that for aircraft fly-overs the PNdB value would correspond to the maximum sound pressure level. Experimental data have shown that, if *duration* is defined as the time during which the sound pressure level is within 10 dB of its maximum value, a doubling of duration will produce an increase of 3 dB in the PNdB value (Pearsons, 1966). A few years later the perceived noise level was adjusted to allow for the subjective influences of discrete tones as well as the duration of the noise. This became known as the Effective Perceived Noise (EPNdB) level, and has remained to date as the most accurate measure of individual annoyance.

Endnotes

1. Unfortunately, the tensile strength of lead is insufficient to support even its own weight for the ratio of thickness to length required for this application. However, this limitation can be overcome by spraying lead onto a polythene sheet. The resultant laminated lead sheeting can be applied in situations where high transmission loss and flexibility are required.
2. A reverberation chamber is a laboratory with acoustically hard surfaces that facilitate the reflection of sound (i.e., minimize sound absorption). The converse is an anechoic chamber, in which all surfaces (including the floor) are highly absorptive to minimize any sound reflection.
3. The terms solid-borne sound and structure-borne sound are synonymous.
4. A dash pot is a mechanical device that prevents sudden or oscillatory motion of a body by the frictional forces of a fluid (typically a piston moving horizontally or vertically within a cylindrical container that is filled with a liquid of known viscosity).
5. ASHRAE recommends maximum air speeds for rectangular and circular ducts based on the Noise Criteria (NC) rating of the space (ASHRAE, 1989).
6. As opposed to noise insulation, which is referred to as passive noise control.

7. This does not contradict previous statements in this chapter that draw attention to the fallacy of assuming that thermal insulation will also serve well as sound insulation. In this particular case, the sole acoustic purpose of the pipe wrapping is to isolate pipe vibrations from the structural components of the building.

8. The static pressure (P psf) resulting from a wind speed of V mph at 90° to the surface of a wall can be calculated using the equation: $P = 0.00256 (V^2)$, which may be approximated to $P = V^2/400$ (Mehta, 1997). Therefore, for a wind speed of 50 mph the static pressure on the wall is $(50 \times 50)/400$ or 6.25 psf, or 125 LB per vertical lineal foot of wall.

12 Sustainable Architecture Concepts and Principles

The last three decades of the twentieth century have seen the emergence of a relatively new set of building design criteria that are based on ecological concerns. These are driven by a genuine fear that mankind has been recklessly ignoring repeated signs that the delicate balance in nature among plants, animals, and the physical environment is in danger of disruption with serious consequences. Contributing factors that are rapidly gaining widespread recognition include: an increasing world population (approaching seven billion in 2009); a fairly sudden change from inexpensive to much more expensive energy; an increasing realization that environmental pollution and lifestyle will have an impact on health and longevity; the detection of a gradual but steady global warming trend; and the marked transition to an Information Age in which the interests and capabilities of the individual are greatly enabled.

The confluence of these powerful environmental and societal forces is having a profound impact. With the increase in population, agriculture is gradually losing in its competition with residential development. As the cost of land increases, the need for denser habitation also increases the negative human impact on nature. An increasing demand for water, energy, and materials is eroding the availability of natural resources on planet Earth. Moreover, the extraction and processing of the large amounts of raw materials to fulfill these needs not only damages the ecostructure, but also increases the pollution of the atmosphere to a level that has in some localized instances threatened the very existence of animal and human life. In particularly, water has emerged as the most precious resource for habitation, agriculture, and the continuation of life itself.

From a more general point of view the impact of these forces can be recognized as trends to which we adapt in both conscious and subconscious ways. For example, as the economy has shifted from an industrial to a service base, women have entered the workforce in much greater numbers. The smaller two-income family has different household and child-raising needs with direct architectural implications. If we add to this the enablement of the individual through the availability of computers and global connectivity, then it becomes readily apparent that the architectural criteria for the design of buildings and, in particular, homes have already changed and will continue to change as a means of adapting to these trends.

12.1 Human resistance to change

The recognition that we need to consider the impact that our actions have on the natural environment has come only gradually over the past several decades, mostly due to painful experience. Human beings have an aversion to change that is rooted in our biological evolution and deeply embedded in our cognitive facilities. To explore the source of the resistance to change and attendant tensions that inevitably accompany a paradigm shift, it is necessary to understand that we human beings are very much influenced by our surroundings.

As shown in Figure 12.1, we are *situated* in our environment not only in terms of our physical existence, but also in terms of our psychological needs and understanding of ourselves

Building Science: Concepts and Application. Jens Pohl.
© 2011 John Wiley & Sons, Ltd.
Published 2011 by John Wiley & Sons, Ltd.

Figure 12.1   Situated in our environment.

(Brooks, 1990). We depend on our surroundings for both our mental and physical well-being and stability. Consequently, we view with a great deal of anxiety and discomfort anything that threatens to separate us from our environment, or comes between us and our familiar surroundings.

This extreme form of *situatedness* is a direct outcome of the evolutionary core of our existence. The notion of evolution presupposes an incremental development process within an environment that represents both the stimulation for evolution and the context within which that evolution takes place. It follows, first, that the stimulation must always precede the incremental evolution that invariably follows. In this respect we human beings are naturally reactive, rather than proactive. Second, while we voluntarily and involuntarily continuously adapt to our environment, through this evolutionary adaptation process we also influence and therefore change our environment. Third, our evolution is a rather slow process. We would certainly

expect this to be the case in a biological sense. The agents of evolution such as mutation, imitation, exploration, and credit assignment, must work through countless steps of trial and error and depend on a multitude of events to achieve even the smallest biological change (Waldrop, 1992; Kauffman, 1992; Holland, 1995; Pohl, 1999).

In comparison to biological evolution, our brain and cognitive system appears to be capable of adapting to change at a somewhat faster rate. Whereas biological evolution proceeds over time periods measured in millennia, the evolution of our perception and understanding of the environment in which we exist tends to extend over generational time periods. However, while our cognitive evolution is of orders faster than our biological evolution, it is still quite slow in comparison with the actual rate of change that can occur in our environment.

Over the past hundred years there have been many fundamental changes in our human values and the way we perceive our environment (Figure 12.2).

The Industrial Age placed great value on physical products and devised ingenious ways to maximize the manual contributions of the human workforce in a subservient role to a highly automated mass-production process. In the Information Age the focus has moved from the physical capabilities of the human workforce to the intellectual capabilities and potential of its individual members. The attendant symptoms of this profound shift are the replacement of mass production with computer-controlled mass customization, virtual products as opposed to physical products, and the creation and exploitation of knowledge.

In respect to the forces that are driving our increased concern for maintaining a sustainable natural environment, the rate of change has not been constant. For example, while there had been earlier warnings about the need to conserve energy from forward-thinking individuals, it was not until the energy crisis of the 1970s, caused by an Arab–Israeli conflict, that a larger

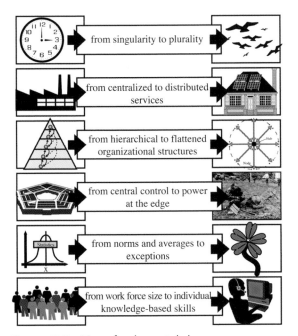

from singularity to plurality

from centralized to distributed services

from hierarchical to flattened organizational structures

from central control to power at the edge

from norms and averages to exceptions

from work force size to individual knowledge-based skills

Figure 12.2 Many fundamental changes .

cross-section of the US population was persuaded to adopt energy conservation measures. Even then it was the pain of increased fuel costs rather than an appreciation of environmental concerns that prompted action. As soon as the fuel prices fell, the consumers again purchased large sports utility vehicles[1] with low fuel-efficiency ratings.

It is therefore very much the foresight and persistence with which the advocates of sustainable development have pursued this important subject that have resulted in public awareness and a general sense of necessary action. However, as discussed at the beginning of this chapter, the availability and cost of energy is only one of the factors that are driving the need to consider sustainability in the design of the built environment. And, even beyond sustainability, there are other equally compelling forces that are changing our lifestyles and thereby the functional requirements of the buildings in which we perform our activities. Foremost among these are the readily affordable information accessibility and exploitation capabilities that advances in computer technology have made available to the individual person, as well as the economic factors that have brought major changes to both the make-up of the workforce and the increasing opportunities for self-employment and entrepreneurship within that workforce. The convergence of these forces produces trends that will continue to dictate the criteria that should be considered in the design of buildings during this century. The most noticeable of these trends and their likely influence on architectural design will be briefly discussed in the next section.

12.2 Discernible trends

The overarching impact of the trends described in this section is that the design of buildings will become an increasingly more complex undertaking. Whereas architects practicing in the twentieth century already had to deal with a host of often conflicting design issues, ranging from space planning and three-dimensional modeling to structural and environmental system selection, twenty-first century architects will have many more considerations added to their plate. For example, they will need to justify the use of every material, not only in respect to cost and serviceability but also based on embodied energy and potential toxicity parameters, as well as the ability to recycle the material. The need to minimize water usage will require the use of graywater with the necessary capture and recycling facilities. Most, if not all, of the energy used in a new residential building will most likely have to be captured on-site. Under these circumstances, the achievement of a building design that would have been acclaimed in the 1990s as an award-winning energy conscious scheme might become a barely baseline solution in the not-too-distant future.

12.2.1 The home as a workplace

One of the most noticeable and exciting aspects of the Information Age is the enablement of the individual. The combination of inexpensive computer hardware, powerful software tools, and freely available global communication via the Internet allows a single person to achieve tasks that required a significant team effort in the not-too-distant past. Of course, to exploit this opportunity the individual person must possess the skills that are necessary to fully utilize the capabilities provided by software tools.

As a result a growing number of young, professionally trained persons are seeking self-employment in preference to employment in a larger commercial or government organization. In addition, an increasing percentage of persons who are employed by commercial companies are able to perform at least some of their work external to the organization's facilities. In either case the home becomes the preferred primary or alternative workplace. The impact of the accompanying lifestyle changes is gradually becoming evident in several ways. First, multiple demands are being made on the functional design of the home. Space planning must take into account the multiple purposes that the home may be required to serve, such as an office where business tasks are performed, a place where children are being educated as an alternative to attendance at a public school, as well as all of the traditional functions of a family home. All of these functional requirements must be served in a manner that allows each function to be performed within its own necessary and desirable environment and yet contribute to the operation of the home as an integrated functional unit.

Second, whereas the land-line telephone previously served as the principal facility for immediate communication over any appreciable distance, most business activities performed in the home require greater communication reach, flexibility, redundancy, and convenience. Not only are these requirements being satisfied by technological advances, but those advances in the form of microcomputers, e-mail, Web services, and cell phones are themselves the main drivers that made the lifestyle changes possible. The home as a workplace is posing new challenges to the building designer in

several ways. How should the need for one or more private workplaces be shielded from other family activities, in terms of space planning and noise control? The parent working in the home requires a productive work environment, but at the same time does not wish to be totally disconnected from the household, particularly if there are children in the family.

Third, building designers need to find effective ways of integrating the new Information Age technology into the building, so that it is readily accessible when needed and yet unobtrusive at other times. This requires not only a deeper understanding of the technology itself, but also a working knowledge of how it could be employed to best advantage by the occupants of the building. For example, this includes the dual local and centralized control of lighting fixtures. The occupants should have the option of automatically switching off all internal lights, radios, and television sets on closing the front door when leaving the house. Relatively inexpensive electronic devices now allow the automated monitoring of almost every activity, the rate of consumption of any resource (e.g., water, electricity, and natural gas), the measurement of most aspects of the physical environment (e.g., temperature, humidity, light levels, noise levels, and pollution), and the ability to alert the occupants to events that might require immediate attention. The question then arises: What should be monitored, how should it be monitored and most importantly, how should these electronic devices be effectively deployed to be readily accessible but not disruptive?

12.2.2 Recycling and waste management

Based on current and historical building construction and occupancy experience it is quite difficult to imagine the design and operation of a building that is not in some measure destructive to the natural environment. Typically: the site is graded to provide convenient vehicular access and suit the layout of the building and its immediate surroundings; the construction materials and components are produced from raw materials that are extracted from nature and consume a great deal of energy during their production; the materials and components are transported to the site consuming more energy in transit; on-site construction generates waste in terms of packaging material and the fabrication of footings, walls, floors, and roof; during the lifespan of the building, energy is continuously consumed to maintain the internal spaces at a comfortable level and power the multiple appliances (e.g., lights, communication and entertainment devices, food preservation and preparation facilities, and security systems); despite some concerted recycling efforts, much of the liquid and solid waste that is produced during the occupancy of the building is normally collected and either treated before discharge into nature or directly buried in landfills; and finally, at the end of the lifespan, when the building is demolished most, if not all, of the construction materials and finishes are again buried in landfill sites.

Let us consider the other extreme, a building that has been designed on ecological principles and is operated as a largely self-sufficient microenvironment. Ecological design has been defined in broad terms as being in symbiotic harmony with nature (Van Der Ryn and Cowan, 1996; Kibert, 2005). This means that the building should integrate with nature in a manner that is compatible with the characteristics of natural ecosystems. In particular, it should be harmless to nature in its construction, utilization, and eventual demolition. The closest we come to being forced to comply with such stringent design and occupancy requirements is in the realm of extraterrestrial habitats, such as an outpost on the Moon or Mars. The constraints imposed by the severe transportation limitations and the hostility of the environment to human, animal, and plant life require careful consideration of even the smallest component or quantity of material, and the most minute energy requirement and need for non-recyclable material. The designers of such extraterrestrial buildings will be faced with design criteria that are only slightly more stringent than those called for by a truly ecological design on Earth. For example:

- In the absence of any excavation equipment the footings of the building will need to adjust to the site topography, rather than the converse. Under these circumstances careful site selection will be a necessary prerequisite to any successful construction project. Also, to accommodate changes in topography that could occur due to environmental influences, the footings will need to be adjustable at least in height. While ecological design on Earth may tolerate a slightly larger building footprint, any significant reshaping of the site topography and certainly larger areas covered by building footings or paving should be avoided.

- The building will need to be designed as a minimum-weight structure, since every pound of material would need to be transported from Earth with an enormous consumption of energy. While the use of on-site materials would circumvent the transportation problem, this alternative is unlikely to be a feasible option, at least during the early stages of extraterrestrial settlement owing to the absence of the necessary extraction and manufacturing facilities. The adoption of minimum-weight structural principles on Earth could also be a desirable ecological design criterion. It would serve to minimize the size of footings, reduce the consumption of energy required for transporting materials and components to the site, and require fewer raw materials to be mined from the Earth's surface.

- The building will need to be largely self-sufficient in terms of the energy required to sustain its occupants. This includes environmental control (i.e., temperature, humidity, air quality, and air composition), food preservation and preparation equipment, water and other waste recycling systems, communication and computer hardware devices, and any other electronic monitoring and control facilities. With the exception of the need to maintain an artificial atmosphere (i.e., air composition) within the building, these requirements are essentially the same as those prescribed by ecological design principles on Earth.

- The occupants of the extraterrestrial building will depend on the treatment and reuse of graywater and the recycling of solid waste to virtually the same extent as a building on Earth that adheres strictly to ecological design principles. In both cases water emerges as one of the most precious and essential resources for the sustainment of human life.
- Apart from the treatment and reuse of graywater, the building will need to incorporate a waste-management system that is capable of sorting dry waste as a precursor to recycling and processing wet waste in an anaerobic or similar treatment facility for composting purposes.
- Regardless of whether or not the building is intended for an extraterrestrial or terrestrial location, it should be designed for a fixed lifespan. The building materials and component products will need to be reusable in some form at the end of that lifespan. To satisfy this ecological design requirement the building must be deconstructable, the materials must be recyclable, the products must be disassemblable, and the materials dissipated from recycling must be harmless (Kibert, 2005, p. 279). The concept of a *closed-loop* building material strategy is central to ecological design and *green building* principles.

A major advantage of a building based on ecological design principles on Earth over an extraterrestrial structure is that the site environment is not hostile and can be used to facilitate the recycling and waste-management processes. For example, the reuse of composted materials in an extraterrestrial building would likely be confined to a small greenhouse facility, while on Earth the opportunities for the effective use of compost extend beyond the confines of a greenhouse structure to the entire site.

12.2.3 Water as a precious commodity

Water is such a precious commodity that even though buildings account for only about 12 percent of the total use of water, there is increasing pressure to reduce this amount through recycling. In fact it is generally suggested that it should be possible to reduce the freshwater draw of buildings by as much as 90 percent in *high-performance* buildings (Kibert 2005, p. 408). There is a need for much education in this area as a precursor to making appreciable progress. Currently, with a few exceptions, neither building designers nor building owners draw a distinction between freshwater and graywater, and simply refer to "water". Increasingly building designers will be required to include water-treatment and recycling facilities in their designs.

However, water conservation in buildings is as much a human behavioral problem as it is a mechanical solution. For example, whether or not the building occupants abide by guidelines that suggest soaping of hands before turning on the water during hand-washing, is a behavioral issue. However, how the waste water from the hand-washing operation is captured, treated, and reused as graywater is a mechanical issue. These issues require different solution approaches.

The solution to the behavioral problem relies mostly on education and motivation. Much can be achieved in this regard by making the building occupants aware of the amount of freshwater that they are using, at the time of usage. The near real-time measurement of the amount of water that has just been used by a building occupant and the concurrent display of this measurement as immediate feedback to the occupant is likely to be more effective in the longer term than automatically stopping the water flow as soon as the recommended freshwater draw has been exceeded. At the same time, communication on a continuous basis of the cumulative water usage to each individual building occupant, in comparison to all other occupants, can motivate occupants to use less water on a competitive basis. Again, inexpensive electronic measurement and alerting devices are already available to meet these objectives.

The capture, treatment, and reuse of graywater are amenable to a range of mechanical solutions that are largely independent of user control. However, all of the solutions that are currently available and even those that may become available in the foreseeable future will result in an increase in capital costs. They all require the addition of plumbing equipment and devices as part of a somewhat more complex water-reticulation system. Nevertheless, within the context of the overall cost of the building, this increase will be a relatively small percentage.[2] On the other hand, faced with dwindling freshwater resources, building codes will increasingly mandate water-conservation measures that will force building designers to give the plumbing design of a building a great deal more attention than has typically been the case to date.

12.2.4   Energy self-sufficiency

Prior to the energy crisis precipitated by an Arab–Israeli conflict in the early 1970s, energy was so inexpensive in the US that its conservation was rarely considered as a design criterion. Buildings were commonly designed with little regard to the climatic determinants of orientation and the performance of the building envelope in respect to heat flow, and daylighting was often at best a secondary consideration. This situation changed drastically in the succeeding 30 years, with the adoption of new building energy codes that mandated building designs based progressively on more and more stringent energy-conservation standards.

During the twenty-first century there will be increasing pressure on architects to devise building designs that aim at energy self-sufficiency. While this goal may not be attainable in less favorable climates, the expectation will be that the requirements for active heating, cooling, and ventilation are minimized. Foremost, this will require a very thorough evaluation of the regional or macro climatic conditions, as well as the micro climatic factors such as the local topography that may apply to a particular site. The specific characteristics of the site's climatic profile will determine the extent to which passive thermal design con-

cepts and principles can be applied in the design solution. The decisions that are made during this detailed climatic analysis will largely determine the overall shape and orientation of the building, the degree to which the building can become energy self-sufficient, and the potential need for additional thermal provisions.

Consideration of passive design approaches and strategies will require not only an in-depth knowledge of the different passive building types and their implementation principles, but also detailed analysis and design tools to simulate different design scenarios for comparative purposes. One focus of this analysis will be to determine how renewable energy sources such as solar radiation and natural air movement can facilitate each alternative passive design solution. The outcome of the simulation results will also determine to what extent the building envelope will need to resist the flow of heat by conduction, convection, and radiation. Most of these determinations will require access to software design tools that not only consider each factor in isolation, but are also capable of considering the impact of each factor on all other factors as an integrated building system. This is a complex undertaking requiring the designer to have both breadth and depth of knowledge, and is unlikely to be achievable without access to subject-matter experts and/or a set of sophisticated design tools.

12.2.5   A healthy building environment

The transition from the Industrial Age to the Information Age is continuing to enable the individual. Increasingly, the assets of an organization are being measured in terms of the ability of the organization to manage the knowledge contributed by its members (Pohl, 2003). Under these circumstances it is not surprising that there should be a parallel concern for health maintenance. Examples include the concerted government campaigns aimed at curtailing and eventually eradicating the smoking and chewing of tobacco, the government-mandated descriptions of the ingredients on the packaging of food products, and the emphasis on diet and exercise by an increasing proportion of the public.

This concern for good health and longevity also extends to the built environment. In a 1983 report the World Health Organization projected that up to 30 percent of buildings worldwide were subject to excessive complaints about indoor air quality (WHO, 1984). A 2002 article by a toxicologist of the US Environmental Protection Agency (USEPA) estimated a productivity loss of over (US) $150 billion per year due to building-related illnesses, taking into account direct and indirect costs (Smuts, 2002). However, it is only in recent years that a spate of lawsuits have brought terms such as Sick Building Syndrome (SBS), Building-Related Illness (BRI), and Multiple Chemical Sensitivity (MCS) into prominence.

There are several potential causes of an unhealthy internal building environment, including: toxic chemical *off-gassing* of materials that might continue for several years after the construction of a building; the growth of allergy-producing molds in moist areas such as those caused by condensation; ductwork that has been contaminated during construction; and glare due to excessive daylight at external windows or inadequately shielded artificial light fixtures. In each case there are readily available remedies that can be applied at the design stage. For example, dehumidification and ultraviolet radiation will reduce the growth of molds and can effectively kill molds and bacteria that have invaded a ventilation system, respectively.

Nevertheless, the selection of construction and finish materials will become a much more demanding and complex design task in future years. Not only synthetic materials may have potentially toxic ingredients, such as volatile organic components. Natural materials may also contain pollutants that are harmful. The selection process for materials is further complicated by the fact that ecological design principles will require the building designer not only to avoid materials that may be toxic in use, but also to consider toxicity during extraction, manufacturing, and deconstruction. This also includes intermediate materials that are used in the production, application, joining, and finishing of other construction materials, such as: paints, solvents, lubricants, adhesives, mastics, detergents, bleaches, and acids.

12.2.6 Quality of life expectations

In addition to the increasing concern for the impact of buildings on the environment, the health of the occupants, the recycling of materials and waste, the minimal use of freshwater, and the avoidance of fossil fuels, the building designer will need to deal with another overarching trend. The enablement of the individual, in a world in which entrepreneurship and self-employment will increasingly replace traditional long-term employment opportunities, is likely to be accompanied by a marked consumer insistence on efficiency and convenience. The quality of life expectations of the individual person are likely to increase as an indirect consequence of the greater value that an Information Age society is placing on the knowledge-based capabilities of each person.

This trend has already started to manifest itself in several ways – for example, the increasing use of the Internet as a convenient shopping mall, with the expectation that the purchased goods will be shipped within 24 hours and packaged in a way that will facilitate their almost immediate use on receipt by the customer. Even relatively major purchases, which in the past would have involved a lengthy period of careful deliberations, are today often concluded in an e-business environment in a matter of hours rather than days. Buildings, particularly the home, will be expected to function with the same level of efficiency, speed, and convenience.

Only electronic devices will be able to deliver the level of monitoring, control, and customization that is required to realize such expectations. This suggests that the building will need to be *electronically enabled* from a functional point of view. Full use of available electronic capabilities will include the monitoring of energy and water consumption, both at the point of utilization and cumulatively over a daily, weekly, monthly, and annual period. In other words, not only will the building occupants wish to know exactly how much water they have just used for washing their hands or for taking a shower, but they will also wish to compare this water usage with their average usage and the usage levels mandated or recommended by the authoritative government agency. It will take some ingenuity by building designers to devise ways for communicating this kind of information to building occupants so that it is readily available when desired and yet unobtrusive at other times.

Similar monitoring and control requirements will apply to environmental systems and devices such as electricity and gas consumption, the movement of blinds and sunshading devices, the dimming of artificial lights, the enabling and disabling of active noise-control systems, and the operation of integrated entertainment suites. In all cases the expectation of the building occupants will be the convenient availability of high-quality monitoring and control facilities for the full range of building services. Particularly the continuous monitoring of energy and water usage will contribute indirectly to the heightened awareness of the ability of each individual person to contribute to the conservation of these resources.

12.3   Fundamental concepts and definition of terms

As discussed previously in this chapter, the *sustainable development* movement is far more encompassing than the design of buildings that are accountable for the natural resources that they consume, the amount of pollution that they produce, and the impact that they have on the health of their occupants. Rather, the increased sensitivity to the natural environment, the concern about global warming trends, and the increasing awareness of the benefits of proactive health maintenance are a direct outgrowth of the enablement of the individual in a knowledge-based Information Age.

It makes a great deal of sense that as the individual members of society gain access to powerful tools and inexpensive global communication facilities, they will also come to value their capabilities and increasingly have higher quality-of-life expectations.

In this section we will define some of the fundamental concepts and new terms that have been coined over the past half-century in the field of sustainable development, as they apply to the built environment.

12.3.1   Sustainability

In the context of the built environment *sustainability* is the overarching concept that acknowledges the need to protect the natural environment for future generations.[3] It proposes that anything that we build today should be sustainable throughout its lifespan. Furthermore, at the end of its lifespan it should be amenable to deconstruction and the reuse of all of its materials in some form. This is indeed a paradigm shift, when we consider that most recycling efforts are still in the earliest and most primitive stages. While the sorting of household, business and public waste into categories such as paper products, bottles and cans, landscaping material, and all other waste, is now reasonably well established in many parts of the world, comparable large-scale recycling programs have yet to be initiated in the construction industry.

Since the 1970s the emphasis has been placed on energy conservation during the lifespan of a structure. Only a very small number of buildings have been certified to date (2010) to comply at least partially with the concept of *sustainability*, and in each case the certification process has been undertaken on a voluntary basis by the building owner. These are very small, first steps in the quest for a sustainable built environment when we consider what needs to be achieved. For a building to meet the full intentions of *sustainability* it would need to:

- be constructed only of materials and products that are reusable in some form or another at the time of deconstruction of the building and, by implication, most of these materials would already contain recycled ingredients;

- be constructed of materials and products that used as little energy (i.e., embodied energy) as possible during their manufacture;
- be constructed of materials that are not subject to toxic off-gassing;
- be as close to energy self-sufficiency as possible, subject to climatic and technology limitations;
- employ water-harvesting, -treatment and -reuse strategies to reduce its freshwater draw to the smallest possible amount (i.e., about 10 percent of existing usage, based on current predictions); and
- incorporate a waste-management system that is capable of recycling most, if not all, of the dry and wet waste produced in the building.

Clearly, it will take some time before the construction industry and its professions will be able to meet these stringent requirements. Supportive industries, such as an economically viable recycling industry, will need to be established. Governments will need to incrementally increase building code requirements, despite industry and potentially even public objections. Owing to the intrinsic human aversion to change it is unlikely that building owners will be willing to voluntarily meet requirements that do not serve their needs during the ownership period of the building. These are just some of the reasons why full acceptance of the concept of *sustainability* will witness a change in lifestyle that will evolve during the twenty-first century. While this change is inevitable, it is difficult to predict how long it will actually take.

12.3.2 Ecological design

Van Der Ryn and Cowan defined *design* as "… the intentional shaping of matter, energy, and process to meet a perceived end or desire", and *ecological design* as "the effective utilization of resources in synchrony with natural processes in the ecosystem" (Van Der Ryn and Cowan, 1996). These two definitions distinguish between

a design process that is intent on meeting the objectives of the designer, regardless of what those might be, and one that demands synergy with the natural environment. Based on this definition, *ecological design* is much more complex than what has been practiced by designers in the past. It adds a whole new dimension to design that on the one hand constitutes a new set of design constraints, and on the other hand requires a deep understanding of the nature of natural systems that does not necessarily exist. According to Kibert (2005, p. 110) the "… key problem facing ecological design is a lack of knowledge, experience, and understanding of how to apply ecology to design".

Adherence to ecological design concepts does not mean that we should attempt to slow down technological progress and downgrade our lifestyle. Instead we should build on natural systems in a complimentary manner. What Kibert and others have pointed out is that this is a difficult undertaking when most of our existing knowledge is based on the machine as the model for design (Kibert, 2005; McHarg, 1999; Odum, 1983; Holling, 1978; Mumford, 1967). Nevertheless, the objectives of ecological design are sufficiently clear for the formulation of at least some broad guidelines.

- The built environment should not unduly disturb the natural environment by disrupting ecosystem processes. Any disruption that cannot be avoided should be temporary and reparable by natural processes.
- Materials that are used for the construction of the built environment should not be toxic to the natural environment (including the human occupants of buildings), and should be to a large degree recyclable at the conclusion of the lifespan of the structure that they were part of.
- Freshwater should be drawn from the natural environment sparingly and recycled as its quality progressively downgrades through multiple uses. Certainly, technology will play a major role in maximizing the reuse of water.

- The selection of energy sources and the efficient use of energy should be a major design criterion. The use of fossil fuels should be minimized and avoided wherever possible, because the processes used to harvest, manufacture, and utilize these fuels are typically disruptive to the natural environment. Again, this is an area where technology will be helpful.

The ecological design objectives related to the efficient use of water and energy will be much easier to achieve than those related to materials of construction and site planning. In the first case, designers will be able to build directly on the existing body of scientific and technical knowledge that was developed during the Industrial Age. For example, the efficient use of natural sources of energy (e.g., sun and wind) and the treatment of water for recycling purposes depend largely on the exploitation of man-made technology. However, in respect to materials, urban planning, and even site planning, the available body of knowledge is much more limited. Little is known about the processes and timescales involved in ecological systems that can be readily applied to the design of the built environment. For example, while we do have some understanding of the relationship between pollution of the atmosphere and global warming, we know very little about the extent to which nature is able to utilize its own processes to counteract atmospheric pollution. Once we have gained an understanding of those natural processes, it will be necessary to translate that knowledge into methodologies and strategies that will allow designers to create the appropriate solutions for the built environment.

12.3.3 Eco-efficiency

The term *eco-efficiency* was coined by the World Business Council on Sustainable Development (WBCSD) in the early 1990s to describe competitive goods and services that reduce ecological impacts throughout their life cycle in accordance with the ability of nature to support these impacts (WBCSD, 1996). More specifically, WBCSD established the following eco-efficiency objectives: reduction of both the material and energy requirements of goods and services; maximization of the recyclability of materials and the sustainability of renewable resources; containment of toxic dispersions from materials and processes; and the achievement of improvements in product durability and service intensity of goods and services.

WBCSD believes that these objectives can be achieved through the judicious application of five strategies:

1 *Improved Processes:* The adoption of well-designed manufacturing processes and service deliveries that avoid the generation of pollution in preference to the employment of end-of-process pollution clean-up procedures.
2 *Product Innovation:* The design of new products and redesign of existing products based on resource-efficiency principles.
3 *Virtual Organizations:* The exploitation of information technology to share resources in a networked environment and thereby increase the effective use of physical facilities.
4 *Business Strategies:* The exploration of alternative marketing models, such as the leasing of products as services rather than goods for sale, thereby refocusing the design emphasis on durability and serviceability.
5 *Waste Recycling:* The utilization of the by-products of one process as the ingredients of another process, with the objective of minimizing resource waste.

It is readily apparent that the concepts and principles of eco-efficiency are well aligned with the objectives of *sustainable development* and *sustainability* discussed earlier in this chapter.

12.3.4 Ecological footprint and rucksack

The concept of *ecological footprint* was proposed by Rees and Wackernagel in 1996 as an appropriate measure of the land area required in support of a particular human activity requiring resources (Wackernagel and Rees, 1996). It represents the area of productive land and shallow sea required to support a single person in terms of food, water, housing, energy, transportation, commerce, and waste disposal. As such, it provides a convenient index for comparing the resource consumptions associated with the different lifestyles of nations. For example, Wilson (2002) has estimated the average ecological footprints for the US and for the world population as a whole to be approximately 24 acres and 5 acres, respectively. If the more than five billion people in developing countries were to achieve even half of the US levels of resource consumption, then based on current technological capabilities we would require at least two Earth planets to support the world population.

The term *ecological rucksack* has been proposed to quantify the mass of material required to be moved to extract a particular resource. It is defined by the European Environmental Agency as the material input required by a product or service minus the weight of the product (EEA, 2009). Material input includes the total quantity of natural material that will be displaced during the entire life cycle of the product from raw-material extraction, through manufacture, recycling, to final disposal. Variations of the ecological rucksack among different materials are quite large. For example, the ecological rucksack for new aluminum (85) is more than 20 times greater than for recycled aluminum (4) and more than four times greater than for new steel (21) (Weiszäcker et al., 1997).

12.3.5   Life-cycle assessment and costing

While *life-cycle assessment (LCA)* methods determine the environmental and resource impacts of a building or one of its components (e.g., material or product), *life-cycle costing (LCC)* determines the financial performance of a building. In each case the analysis is performed over a time period that typically encompasses the entire lifespan of the building or component and is quite complex. The LCA analysis of a product such as a television set must consider all energy and material resources that have been used in the extraction of the raw materials

and manufacture of the product, as well as the energy used during its operation, recycling, and the disposal of those components that cannot be recycled. Finally, the impact of all of those material extraction, manufacturing, recycling, and disposal operations on the natural environment must be measured. This is a complex undertaking that not only requires a great deal of knowledge, reliable data, and access to evaluation tools, but also depends on reasonable assumptions in respect to useful life span and utilization.

The objective of LCC is to determine the economics of a product in present value terms. For example, the financial return of a solar hot-water system requires the amortization of the initial cost of the system and its installation over the probable years of operation, taking into consideration projected energy savings and maintenance costs. An appropriate discount rate is selected and the net benefits for each year are tabulated to determine the payback period of the system. Clearly an LCC evaluation is a much simpler undertaking than an LCA analysis, because there are fewer factors involved and these are considered only from the financial point of view. However, sometimes the LCC evaluation is combined with an LCA analysis to determine the combined environmental and financial impact of a particular material, product, component, or entire building.

12.3.6   Embodied energy

The *embodied energy* of a component or product refers to the entire energy that is expended during the extraction of the raw materials, transportation, and manufacture. About 50 percent of the *embodied energy* of a material is used in the production process, and approximately 40 percent of the energy is used in the extraction of the material. The *embodied energy* of a material is an important consideration in the selection of materials and products in respect to sustainability criteria. For example, the *embodied energy* of an aluminum window frame is seven times greater than for a steel window frame, and the *embodied energy* of poly-

	Cellulose	Fiberglass	Polystyrene
Ratio of *embodied energy* consumption	1	4	35
Ratio of thermal insulation effectiveness	1.00	1.08	1.35

Table 12.1 Comparison of embodied energy and thermal insulation effectiveness.

styrene insulation is almost nine times greater than for fiberglass insulation and about 35 times greater than for cellulose insulation. Yet the thermal insulation performance ratio of these materials is quite similar (Table 12.1). In other words, from an ecological design point of view cellulose thermal insulation in the form of milled paper or wood pulp is a far superior choice to polystyrene.

The values of *embodied energy* for specific materials are likely to vary for different countries and different years (Baird et al., 1984). This is due to variations in production sites, climate, raw material quality, extraction and processing methods, distances between extraction and production sites, and transportation methods. According to Adalberth (1997), the transportation energy component can be as much as 10 percent of the manufacturing energy for a construction material. The difficulties encountered in determining the *embodied energy* value for any particular material are discussed in detail by Heidrich (1999). For example, values for thermal insulation materials may be quoted per volume or weight. Such data are not comparable because they involve assumptions about the density of the material, which varies widely for such materials. Methods for estimating the energy cost of materials are discussed by Chapman (1974).

12.3.7 Factors 4 and 10

The concepts of *Factor 4* and *Factor 10* are similar in principle, although suggested by different persons. They both propose in very general terms a course of action for maintaining a balance between human habitation and the natural environment on planet Earth. *Factor 4*, proposed by Weiszäcker and Lovins, requires resource consumption to be reduced to one-quarter for humanity to reach sustainability based on 1997 conditions (Weiszäcker et al., 1997). Their proposal, published in the form of a book, was in fact a report to the Club of Rome. It was intended as a follow-up to a 1972 report to the Club of Rome, which was published under the well known title *Limits of Growth* (Meadows et al., 1972). The latter projected that as a result of resource consumption and environmental impact, growth on Earth would be halted within a century.

Schmidt-Bleek of the Wuppertal Institute in Germany suggested that long-term sustainability will require humanity to reduce its resource consumption to one-tenth.[4] While the *Factor 4* proponents believed that the technology required for reducing resource consumption to 25 percent of current levels was already available in the 1990s, it is generally agreed that the *Factor 10* goals are much more difficult to achieve. Even though it can be shown that by abandoning the common practice of oversizing mechanical equipment (e.g., chillers, pumps, fans) up to 90 percent reductions in energy consumption are possible, this strategy represents only a relatively small part of the measures necessary for achieving *Factor 10* goals (Kibert, 2005, p. 47).

12.3.8 Green high-performance buildings

The term *green building* has been accepted internationally as describing buildings that are designed and constructed based on the principles of sustainability. It is not possible to define in absolute terms what exactly constitutes a *green building*, because the definition is based on what is acceptable and reasonably achievable at any particular point in time. Arguably, the term *green building* represents a goal based on parameters that are measured by what are considered to be attainable resource and energy conservation levels at any particular time. Both the target areas of the concept of sustainability and the desired level to be aspired to in each target area depend on prevailing societal pressures (i.e., economical and political) and government mandates (i.e., codes and regulations).

Since the 1970s the focus has been on post-construction energy conservation, suggesting that we are still very much in the initial stages of the quest for a sustainable planet. While there is some concern for the conservation of freshwater, marked by the more prevalent appearance of low-flow shower heads and dual-flush toilets, water treatment and recycling systems are still rare in buildings. The selection of construction materials based on recyclability, non-toxicity, and minimum embodied energy criteria remains a distant goal, outside the realm of normal consideration. Nevertheless, the *green building* movement is gaining strength. Significant strides have been made in several parts of the world, including the US, since the 1980s.

In Europe, the Conseil International du Batiment (CIB), a well-established international construction research association located in Rotterdam (the Netherlands), and the International Union for Experts in Construction Materials, Systems, and Structures (RILEM) based in Bagneux (France) advocated the need for building assessment tools and standards. In 1992, CIB formed Task Group 8 for this purpose. This was followed by the formation of CIB Task Group 16 to promote the application of sustainability concepts and principles to construction. Since 1998 the International Institute for a Sustainable Built Environment (iisBE) has held biannual Green Building Challenge and Sustainable Building Conferences at which international green building entries are rated using iisBE's Green Building Tool (GBT) assessment method.[5]

Although the beginnings of the green building movement in the US may be traced back to the 1970s,[6] it was really a succession of events that has focused US attention on the environment in more recent times (BDC, 2003). These included the publication of the Bruntland Report (UN, 1987) in 1987, the formation of the Committee on the Environment (COTE) by the American Institute of Architects in 1989, the United Nations Conference on Environment and Development in Rio de Janeiro (Brazil) in 1992, and the World Congress of Architects sponsored jointly by the International Union of Architects and the American Institute of Architects held in Chicago in 1993. The manifesto issued at the conclusion of the Chicago World Congress of Architects represents perhaps the most important milestone in the evolution of the *green building* movement in the US. Under the title of "Declaration of Interdependence for a Sustainable Future" it boldly pronounced the following five commitments (UIA-AIA 1993).

"We commit ourselves as members of the world's architectural and building-design professionals, individually and through our professional organizations, to:

- place environmental and social sustainability at the core of our practices and professional responsibilities;
- develop and continually improve practices, procedures, products, curricula, services, and standards that will enable the implementation of sustainable design;
- educate our fellow professionals, the building industry, clients, students, and the general public about the critical importance and substantial opportunities of sustainable design;
- establish policies, regulations, and practices in government and business that ensure sustainable design becomes normal practice; and
- bring all the existing and future elements of the built environment – in their design, production, use, and eventual reuse – up to sustainable design standards."

The first prominent US examples of green buildings appeared from the mid-1980s onward, with the design of the New York offices of the Environmental Defense Fund organization in 1985 and the Natural Resources Defense Council in 1989. However, it was the renovation of Audubon House in New York City in 1992 by the Croxton Collaborative firm that drew attention to the necessary involvement of a much broader group of stakeholders in the design of a green building. The process employed by the Croxton Collaborative for the Audubon project was documented and became a template model for achieving the extensive cooperation and collaboration that is required in the design of green buildings (Audubon, 1992).

The US Green Building Council (USGBC) was formed in 1993 and, according to available records, started certifying green buildings in 2000. With its Leadership in Energy and Environmental Design (LEED) certification standard, USGBC has become the preeminent green building organization in the US. The strength of LEED lies in the fact that it is controlled by a non-government organization. It was produced collaboratively by representatives of the USGBC's membership, which presumably includes the principal stakeholders. In this respect the LEED standard is market-driven and is therefore likely to continue to reflect at any particular point in time what building owners would like to achieve and what the design professions and construction industry is able to deliver.

The first LEED v1.0 test version was released in 1998. It led to a pilot evaluation project under the auspices of the Federal Energy Management Program. The purpose of the pilot effort was to test the assumptions and assessment framework employed by LEED on 18 building projects representing over 1 million square feet of floor area. As a result of this evaluation and the support of its increasing membership (i.e., over 300 by 2000), USGBC released a greatly improved LEED v2.0 in 2000. This version provided for a maximum of 69 possible credits and four levels of certification, namely: Platinum, Gold, Silver, and Bronze.

From 2002 onward separate LEED certification standards have been released for different construction types and occupancies, such as new construction (LEED-NC), existing buildings (LEED-EB), commercial interiors (LEED-

CI), homes (LEED-H), and core and shell (LEED-CS). For new construction, only slightly modified LEED-NC v2.1 and LEED-NC v2.2 were released in 2002 and 2005, respectively. The roll-out of a more user-friendly LEED v3.0, with Minimum Program Requirements (MPR) and higher standards, commenced in April 2009 (LEED, 2009).

12.4 Assessment of high-performance buildings

As can be seen from the definition of terms in the previous section, the design of a *green* or *high-performance* building is a much more complex undertaking than the design of a building that does not have to consider sustainability criteria. What makes this undertaking particularly difficult is not just the need to consider more issues – such as the carbon content and embodied energy of the construction materials, the treatment and recycling of water and all forms of waste, and the potential impact of the finishes on the health of the occupants – but the relationships among all of the design issues.

The complexity of a building design problem is seldom due to the difficulties encountered in coming to terms with any one design issue in isolation, such as the avoidance of glare in the maximization of daylight, or the provision of sound insulation when a building is located in a noisy environment. Difficulties arise when these solutions have to be combined into an acceptable holistic design solution. For example, the conflict that arises when the maximization of daylight requires large windows but the existence of an external noise source, such as a major freeway adjacent to the building site, calls for a high degree of noise insulation.

The notion of assessing the design and performance of a building is relatively new to the design and construction professions. Apart from design competitions and post-occupancy performance evaluations, typically contracts provide for a defects liability period during which the contractor is obligated to correct construction faults such as cracks in walls, poorly fitting doors and windows, leaking pipes, and non-operational equipment. Even in the case of design competitions there are no commonly accepted evaluation frameworks and individual review committee members are normally left to their own devices on how they will compare the merits of the submissions. The approach has been more formal in respect to assessing the performance of a building during its occupancy, with the proposal of several methodologies (Daisch, 1985; Pena et al., 1987; Preiser et al., 1988; Preiser, 1989; AIA, 2007).

Therefore, the assessment of buildings prior to occupancy for the purpose of gaining a *green building* certification adds a whole new dimension to the building design process. Currently, such certifications are conducted entirely on a voluntary basis, with the incentive that a building that achieves a high *green building* ranking will have greater economic value. Eventually, however, it is likely that many of the sustainability criteria that have been defined by organizations such as USGBC will find their way into national building codes as mandatory requirements.

12.4.1 Assessment framework concepts and principles

Even though the design of a building – and even more so in the case of a green building – must take into account a host of factors and their interrelationships, it is convenient to be able to express the final result of the assessment as a single score. This is the method adopted by USGBC and the basis of the LEED Certified, Silver, Gold, and Platinum ratings. However, the single score is an amalgamation of a points system that allocates individual scores to different categories and subcategories of desirable higher-performance features.

The disadvantage of such an assessment system is that the manner in which a building achieved its final rating is not represented in the rating. It might therefore seem appropriate to include in the certification documentation a graph that shows how the building scored in each category of the assessment framework.

This would also allow the setting of minimum standards that must be reached in each category for the building to qualify for a particular overall rating. However, there is an opposing argument to this concept that also has merit. It may be a desirable incentive for design innovation if a building is able to obtain a certain ranking by gaining very high scores in some categories and much lower ones in other categories.

In any case, there does not appear to be an alternative to the kind of assessment approach adopted by USGBC to form the basis of the LEED certification process. The different features that must be considered in the design of a *green building* such as site planning, water efficiency, energy, materials, and so on are too diverse in nature to be able to be combined into a single index. Each feature has different units of measurement and applies at a physical scale that is directly tied to its unique context (Kibert, 2005, p. 70). For example, it does not appear to make any sense to attempt to combine the building health aspects of a material with its embodied energy and carbon content characteristics. If this is not possible when dealing with the same type of component (i.e., a particular construction material), then it is even less likely that different types of component will be able to be combined into a single index.

12.4.2 The LEED assessment framework

The LEED v3.0 certification process was launched in April 2009, together with a new *Green Building Design and Construction Reference Guide* (LEED, 2009) that now serves as a single guide for LEED-Schools, LEED-NC (i.e., New Construction), and LEED-CS (i.e., Core & Shell). While the feature categories of LEED v2.2 have remained the same in LEED v3.0, their relative weightings and the total number of points allocated increased from 69 to 110.

The structure of the LEED standard includes a set of minimum requirements that must be met for a particular project to be eligible for LEED certification. These requirements are quite general in nature and appear to be intended to ensure that a submitted project does in fact comply with applicable laws and is definable as a component of the built environment. For example, the project must comply with existing environmental laws, minimum building-to-site-area ratios, minimum floor area and occupancy rates, include at least one building, and provide USGBC access to the water and energy consumption data. All except two of the seven feature categories include one or more prerequisites, followed by a list of desirable attributes with assigned credit points. In the case of LEED-NC v3.0 the seven feature categories cover the principal *sustainable development* considerations discussed in Section 12.3, as follows:

Sustainable Sites [26 possible points]: As a prerequisite to certification some pollution-prevention measures are required to be implemented during construction. Multiple credit points are allocated to: development density and proximity to existing community services (5 points); public transportation access (6 points); fuel-efficient and low-emittance vehicles (3 points); and, parking provisions (2 points). The remaining 10 attributes deal with various aspects of site selection and development and carry one point each.

Water Efficiency [10 possible points]: As a prerequisite to certification a 20 percent reduction in freshwater usage is required. The five desirable features are weighted equally with two points each and are concerned with water usage for landscaping, wastewater treatment, and additional freshwater usage reductions by 30 percent and 40 percent

Energy and Atmosphere [35 possible points]: As a prerequisite to certification the submission must provide evidence that specified requirements will be met during the commissioning process and that certain minimum standards will be adhered to in both energy performance and refrigerant management. Multiple credit points are allocated to the enhancement and optimization of energy performance (up to 19 points) and on-site renewable

energy (3 to 7 points). The measurement and verification of energy performance is allocated three points, and the remaining three desirable features – relating to further enhancements in commissioning, refrigerant management, and the generation of at least 35 percent of the electricity requirement from renewable sources – are allocated 2 points each.

Materials and Resources [14 possible points]: As a prerequisite to certification, provision must be made for the on-site or off-site collection and storage of recyclable materials and products. Two credit points are allocated to the building reuse of 75 percent of existing walls, floors, and roof. The remaining desirable features – ranging from additional reuse of external and internal building materials, the diversion of construction waste from disposal to recycling, and the use of regional materials, to the use of rapidly renewable materials and at least 50 percent of wood-based material and products that are certified by the Forrest Stewardship Council (FSC) – are allocated one point each.

Indoor Environmental Quality [15 possible points]: As a prerequisite to certification, the submission must meet specified indoor air-quality requirements[7] and prevent the building occupants from being exposed to tobacco smoke. The 15 desirable features under this category are all rated equally with one credit point each. They include: monitoring of the inlet air flow rates and carbon dioxide content, with the ability to generate an alarm whenever the conditions vary by 10 percent or more from the set-point; increased ventilation rates; protection of the HVAC system during construction and testing of the air contamination level prior to occupancy; selection of low-emitting (VOC[8]) materials for wall, floor, and ceiling finishes; control of the entry of pollutants from the outside, as well as containment and air exhaust facilities for pollutants originating from sources inside the building (e.g., cleaning substances); a high degree of individual lighting and thermal control; a comfortable thermal environment;[9]

a monitoring system of thermal comfort conditions; and, daylight and external views for 75 percent and 90 percent of the internal spaces, respectively.

Innovation and Design Process [6 possible points]: No prerequisites to certification are stipulated in this category. Up to 5 credit points may be obtained by a submission that substantially exceeds LEED-NC v3.0 requirements in one or more feature categories. An additional point may be earned if a LEED Accredited Professional (AP) is a principal member of the design team.

Regional Bonus Credits [4 possible points]: This category takes into account that ecological conditions and priorities may vary from region to region. The USGBC Website (2009; see: www.usgbc.org) provides six features for each US state (by zip code) that have been determined by the regional authority to be of benefit above the point value set by the LEED Green Building Rating System. Compliance with up to four of the applicable priorities adds one point for each claimed agreement, up to a maximum of four credit points.

The maximum number of points that can be earned in LEED-NC v3.0 is 110. The importance assigned to each category, in terms of the number of points allocated and the selection of the desirable features stipulated, is based on the judgment of the LEED-NC committee members who participated in the preparation of the standard. This is both the weakness and the strength of the LEED rating system. Not all of the stakeholders may be represented on the USGBC working groups. In particular, the views of the Government may not be adequately represented. Furthermore, the deliberations, recommendations, and/or decisions made by any of the working groups may be unduly influenced by special interests.

However, on the other hand, the market-driven non-governmental structure of USGBC is also a significant strength. It will tend to ensure that the direction of the evolving LEED standard over the foreseeable future will remain closely aligned with what the AEC industry and the associated architecture and engineering professions are capable of delivering. Based on market-driven incentives and voluntary participation, USGBC and its LEED standard have made quite remarkable progress over the past decade. However, at some point in the future voluntary compliance with sustainability standards may no longer be acceptable and the Government may have to step in and require mandatory compliance with part or all of the standards. Hopefully, this will be accomplished by the gradual absorption of LEED standards into building codes, without negatively impacting the excellent proactive work being performed by USGBC and similar organizations outside the US.

12.5   Energy design strategies

Reduction of energy consumption is currently, and will remain for the foreseeable future, one of the principal goals of green high-performance buildings. In the US the energy consumed by buildings and transportation is approximately equal and accounts for 80 percent of the total national energy consumption. A typical legacy US commercial building consumes about 100 000 BTU per square foot of building area per year (Kibert, 2005, p. 181). A green building based on LEED standards will reduce this annual energy requirement by at least 50 percent to less than 50 000 BTU per square foot, whereas buildings based on Factor 4 and Factor 10 criteria would reduce this energy requirement to 25 000 and 10 000 BTU per square foot, respectively.

Beyond these current energy-saving goals, some advocates of ecological design principles are suggesting that in the future the majority of buildings should be at least energy-neutral (i.e., they should not consume more energy than they generate), and where feasible they should become net energy producers (i.e., they should generate more energy than they consume). This is indeed a tall order, which will require not just a reduction of energy consumption, but a paradigm shift in how architects will need to approach the design of buildings.

In this section, we will briefly explore energy conservation measures that are either already available today or are being actively pursued for near-term application, in four areas, namely: passive building design strategies; building envelope performance; hot-water systems; and lighting design. It will become quite clear to the reader that in virtually all cases the design strategies that are employed will require a much deeper analysis of the technical issues involved. Designers will not be able to achieve this based on intuition, experience, or manual methods alone. Instead, they will require sophisticated simulation tools that are user-transparent and seamlessly integrated as semi-automated services within the kind of intelligent, computer-aided design environment that has been made possible by a distributed Web-enabled environment based on service-oriented architecture principles (Pohl and Myers, 1994; Pohl et al., 2000; Pohl et al., 2010).

12.5.1 Passive building design strategies

Well-known passive solar building types and design strategies have been discussed previously in Chapter 5 (see Section 5.9). The underlying concept of a passive solar solution is to design the building so that it can function intrinsically as a collector, distributor, and store for solar energy. This requires an intricate balance of design parameters related to the shape of the building and internal layout of spaces, the location and size of windows, sun-path angles and shading devices, and the selection of building materials with the appropriate thermal properties.

For this reason, in current tertiary-level architecture degree programs students are taught to undertake an extensive climate analysis study prior to the commencement of the preliminary design phase. The establishment of the regional (i.e., macro) climate profile and the identification of the local site-specific (i.e., micro) factors that may significantly modify the regional climate profile are considered essential prerequisites for the development of a building design solution. The results of such investigations typically include an assessment of the regional vernacular;[10] a summary narrative description of regional climatic conditions and the incidence of special events such as storms and tornadoes; charts of the principal climatic parameters on a monthly scale (i.e., average minimum and maximum dry-bulb temperatures, relative humidity, heating and cooling degree-days, average wind speeds and directions, solar radiation intensities, cloud cover, precipitation (i.e., rain and snow), and daylight levels); and a topographical analysis of the site.

This climate profile information is then used by the students to categorize the type of climate that they are dealing with and to select, at least in general terms, the appropriate thermal design strategy. Of course in many cases the climatic profile is seasonal, requiring a hybrid solution of the potentially conflicting strategies applicable to different climate types. For example, hot-humid summer conditions might call for natural cooling through cross-ventilation (i.e., a building envelope with large openings), while cold winter conditions could require a sealed envelope with maximum thermal insulation.

To translate this information into accurate passive building design decisions is a very difficult undertaking. Apart from the level of complexity, there are a number of obstacles. First, without simulation tools that are capable of taking into account both thermal parameters such as temperature, humidity, and air movement (i.e., wind), and topographical site conditions such as contours, vegetation, and surrounding structures, only general (i.e., rule-of-thumb) design decisions can be made. Second, tools that are able to perform the required thermal analysis and are capable of producing accurate results will require more detailed data, such as hourly temperature variations. Third, there is currently still insufficient knowledge for the design of simulation tools that are capable of accurately modeling the influence of micro-climatic factors and topographical site features to accurately assess their impact on the projected thermal conditions. Without the ability to accurately model these parameters the most accurate thermal analysis based on hourly temperatures can be quite misleading.

The tools that are available today will allow a designer, with the assistance of an expert consultant, to make sound design decisions in respect to the shape, orientation, space layout, window placement and sizing, massing, and solar control of a building. However, the ability to fine tune these decisions for achieving a *Factor 10* or energy-neutral design solution will in most cases require a much more granular design analysis and access to more sophisticated design and simulation tools than are currently available.

12.5.2 The building envelope

The building envelope serves as the interface between the uncontrollable natural environment and the internal building environment, which is desired to be maintained within quite narrow boundaries. While the external environment can be characterized based on statistical data that have been collected over a considerable number of years, the resulting profile does not tell us much about the local micro climate and the sudden short-term weather changes that can radically deviate from the average regional conditions.

The traditional approach to the design of the building envelope has been to reduce the flow of heat out of the building by embedding thermal insulation in the envelope, and to control the heat flow into the building by means of sunshading devices or by treating the building envelope as a heat sink that will shield the desirable constant comfort conditions of the interior building spaces from the diurnal temperature swings of an external arid climate. In the US, since the oil embargo of the 1970s, government building codes have placed the emphasis on thermal insulation and the prevention of air infiltration and heat leakage through the envelope.

Roof overhangs and other sunshading devices are used to shield the envelope and the building interior from direct solar radiation, or in colder climates to control the amount of solar radiation

that is permitted to penetrate into the building interior as a natural source of heat. While manually movable and automatically controlled sunshading devices have been commercially available for many years, their use in buildings is only gradually becoming prevalent. For various reasons, including cost and maintainability, fixed sunshading devices are still prevalent. Manually openable windows and internal blinds are still by far the most common and preferred form of natural thermal and daylighting control in low- to mid-rise buildings.

Fortunately, this leaves considerable scope for the implementation of the far superior thermal-control strategies that will be required to meet the future objectives of sustainable architecture in terms of energy-neutral and net energy-export buildings. First, thermal insulation will need to be considered as a dynamic rather than a static approach for achieving energy efficiency. It should be possible to automatically generate thermal insulation on a near real-time basis as external climatic conditions change.[11] This will require the development of new *thermal insulation on demand* technologies that are tightly coupled with external electronic monitoring devices. Second, the level of fine tuning required to achieve very high degrees of energy efficiency mandates the continuous monitoring of internal and external environmental conditions. The necessary technology to support the precise monitoring of temperature, humidity, air movement, radiation, precipitation, and air quality has been commercially available at relatively low cost for more than a decade. Third, the same level of monitoring and precision will need to be applied to the control of sunshading devices. Much headway can be made in this area by simply taking advantage of existing electronically controlled devices before considering more elaborate technologies, such as the ability of a building or portion of a building to change its configuration in unison with the movement of the sun. This can be achieved by rotational movement or by components of the building receding or protruding in response to changes in external and internal thermal conditions (Fisher, 2009).

The ability of a building to change its configuration in direct response to environmental changes or occupant desires is a more complex issue than would appear at face value. It is certainly not just dependent on innovation and design ingenuity. What will be required is a paradigm shift in attitude of both the building designer and the building owner or occupant. In addition, the construction industry will be required to respond with new manufacturing methods and processes. As buildings become more dynamically responsive to short-term changes in conditions, they will necessarily also become more dependent on mechanical and electronic capabilities. This will require a shift from on-site construction to factory production of integrated prefabricated modules and entire buildings. The building owner will need to be prepared to accept a building on terms similar to a manufactured car. Such a paradigm shift will occur only if driven by the strongest forces (e.g., potential economic loss or threat to human life) to overcome the natural human aversion to change. Finally, the designer will need to be able to cope with the increasing complexity of the resultant design solution. This is not just a matter of academic preparation and experience, but more importantly the ability of the designer to apply sufficient technical depth and breadth to the development of the design solution. Such ability will increasingly depend on the availability of an arsenal of readily accessible and seamlessly integrated design tools.

12.5.3 Hot-water systems

In building types where bathing and showering, washing clothes, or cooking are principal activities there is a relatively heavy demand for hot water. This includes health-club facilities, drycleaners and laundromats, restaurants, and also residences. The two methods that have become quite prevalent in recent years for providing hot water under energy conservation constraints are solar and tankless hot-water services.

The concept and implementation principles of a *solar hot-water service* are quite straightfor-
ward and have been described in more detail in Chapter 5. The heat collector typically consists of a flat metal plate with a matt black finish that sits on top of a set of closely spaced pipes through which water is circulated. By inclining the flat plate at a fixed slope that is as close as possible to maintaining a 90° angle to the rays of the sun during the major part of the day, the plate transfers much of the collected heat to the water circulating on its underside. Assuming a high degree of thermal insulation applied to the sides and bottom of the collector, the efficiency of such an active solar collector varies from approximately 20 percent to 70 percent, depending on the number of glazings (i.e., none, single, double, and triple) and the temperature differential between the incoming water and the collector plate. The greater the temperature differential, the more efficient is the heat transfer between the plate and the circulating water.

In most cases a solar hot-water service will require a storage facility, and since water has very limited thermal stratification properties the storage facility will often consist of two tanks, a large tank and a small tank. The larger tank will at most times be at a temperature that is not sufficiently high for direct usage, while the smaller tank will be at a higher temperature. This requirement would not exist in the case of a solar collector system in which the heat-transfer medium is air instead of water, because the associated rock storage facility has excellent heat-stratification properties. However, the additional requirement of transferring the heat from the air medium to the water that will be used will normally favor a water-based solar collector solution.

The *tankless hot-water service*, as implied by its name, does not require a heat-storage facility. It is based on the concept that water can be rapidly heated at the time that it is required. The heating facility is activated by the flow of water that occurs as soon as the hot water faucet or valve is opened. If the heating facility has been sized correctly, based on the volume of hot water required at the time that it is activated, then the tankless system will deliver a constant and endless amount of hot water at the desired temperature and flow rate. The two alternative heat sources that are readily available to deliver the fairly intense amount of heat that is required to raise the temperature of the water on such an instantaneous basis are electricity and gas. While gas would appear to be the more energy-conservative heat source, its efficiency is significantly lowered unless the need for a pilot light can be avoided through alternative technology.

Virtually all hot-water services, including solar and tankless services, suffer from a potential heat and water wastage problem. The location of the hot-water tank, or heat source in the case of a tankless facility, is typically at some distance from the point of delivery (e.g., faucet or valve). This means that for the hot water to reach the point of delivery it has to fill the entire length of the pipe from the source to the delivery point. After the faucet or valve has been closed the hot water remains in that section of the pipe and gradually cools down, even though the pipe may be well insulated. Later, after an appreciable time interval, when the faucet or valve is opened again the standing volume of water between the heat source and the delivery point is wasted unless special provisions are made for its collection and recycling. In a tankless system this problem can be avoided only if the heat source is placed in very close proximity of the outlet. This tends to be expensive if there are multiple outlets at some distance from each other, requiring several tankless hot-water installations.

12.5.4 Daylight and artificial lighting

Daylight is an abundantly available resource on most building sites. However, its effective utilization for the lighting of interior spaces is not without challenges. First, the actual amount of daylight available varies from hour to hour during the day as the sun appears to move across the sky from east to west.[12] Second, the variations in daylight can be even more radically and suddenly influenced by cloud conditions. Third, although we consider the sky to be the source of daylight, it is the sun that lights up the sky. Therefore, particularly under clear sky conditions the sun will greatly influence the brightness of the sky in its vicinity. Accordingly, the brightness of the portion of the sky seen through a window could vary greatly with the time of day. Fourth, because the sky is likely to be much brighter than the interior building spaces, side windows acting as an interface between external and internal daylighting conditions can easily become a source of glare. Finally, to optimize energy consumption we need to control the transmission of light and heat separately. Fortunately, in recent years much headway has been made in the manufacture of window glass with low-emissivity (Low-E) coatings.[13] Low-E glass can reduce heat transfer by more than 50 percent, while reducing the visible transmittance by less than 25 percent.

The balancing of these somewhat conflicting considerations can be a complex undertaking. This is particularly true in cases where there is a desire to maximize the amount of daylight in deep rooms with minimum ceiling heights. In such rooms there will be a considerable difference between the light levels at the window and in the rear of the space, giving rise to glare conditions. While light shelves can mitigate this condition by reflecting some of the superfluous light at the window into the rear of the room, they typically provide only a partial solution. An alternative and complementary approach is to utilize artificial lighting to reduce the brightness differences in the room by gradually increasing the artificial light level from a minimum required illumination level in the rear sections to whatever level is required to eliminate glare conditions at the window. This approach, referred to as Permanent Supplementary Artificial Lighting of Interiors (PSALI),[14] provides visual comfort at the expense of increased energy consumption and is particularly wasteful of energy in regions where clear skies predominate.

While every effort would be made by the designer to maximize the availability of daylight in a green high-performance building, some degree of artificial lighting is likely to be necessary even during daylight hours. Therefore, after ensuring that all daylighting opportunities have been fully exploited, any additional efforts to reduce the energy consumed by lighting will rely largely on advances in artificial light source technology. As discussed previously in Chapter 8 (particularly Section 8.2), most existing artificial light sources are quite inefficient. For example, the light-production efficiency of a fluorescent lamp is only about 20 percent. Although this is three times the efficiency of an incandescent lamp, in the context of *sustainability* it must still be considered as being unacceptably low. Considerably more efficient artificial light sources will be required to achieve the order of reduction in building post-occupancy energy consumption that is postulated by *Factor 10*, or even *Factor 4*.

Perhaps the most promising candidate for increasing the efficacy[15] of artificially produced light is the Light-Emitting Diode (LED), which is based on electroluminescence principles. The ability of a semiconductor diode to emit light when it is subjected to an electric current was first observed by the Russian engineer Oleg Losev (1903–1942) in the mid-1920s (Zheludev, 2007). However, it was not until the early 1990s that the Japanese firm Nichia Corporation invented the first high-brightness indium–gallium chip that was able to produce white light through the wave shift provided by a phosphor coating. Although the efficacy of current commercially available LED light sources is only in the 20 to 30 lumen/watt (lm/w) range, which is barely comparable with fluorescent lamps, much higher efficiencies are likely to become available in the near future.[16] In 2006 the US firm Cree Inc. (Durham, North Carolina) demonstrated a white LED with an efficacy of 131 lm/w. At the time of writing of this book (2009) Cree is marketing the XLamp (XR-E R2) white LED with a tested efficacy of 100 lm/w.[17]

While the application of LEDs was initially limited to indicators and signs (e.g., digital equipment displays, traffic lights, signs, and vehicle brake lights) they are now increasingly incorporated in the lighting schemes of build-

ing interiors. Particularly attractive from a sustainability point of view are the 50 000-hour life of LEDs, their relatively high efficacy, their lower carbon dioxide emission,[18] and their non-toxicity. However, LEDs also have some disadvantages. Primary among these are their high initial purchase price, their sensitivity to higher ambient temperatures in the operating environment, and their potential health risks. There is some concern that with increasing efficacy blue and cool-white LEDs will exceed eye safety limits in respect to the blue-light hazard.

12.5.5 Active heating, cooling, and ventilation

After exploiting every opportunity for the application of passive building design principles, the need for active heating, cooling, and ventilation requirements will be at least minimized. However, even in the mildest climatic regions the need for HVAC systems will persist in most commercial buildings and many mid- to high-rise apartment complexes. The question then arises: What strategies can be applied to reduce the energy consumption of HVAC systems?

Electric Motors: The answer begins with consideration of the power unit that normally drives the distribution of air in buildings that utilize either a partial or full HVAC system. The electric motor typically consumes energy each year at a cost that is many times its initial purchase price. For example, an electric motor driving a fan fairly continuously for one year is likely to cost more than eight times its purchase price in the consumption of electricity.

Both improvements in the efficiency of the motor and the equipment that it drives can save energy. For example: large-diameter copper wire in the stator can reduce resistance losses; thinner steel laminations in the rotor will reduce magnetization losses; and, high-quality bearings will reduce friction losses. While the increase in overall efficiency of a high-efficiency electric motor may not exceed a standard model by more than 5 percent, even this apparently small increase in efficiency can lead to an appreciable energy saving over time if the motor is in continuous operation.

It is important to note that electric motors perform most efficiently at or near full load. Therefore, the size of the motor should be determined on the basis of the expected load, without making allowance for possible future increases in load. This is in conflict with noise-control strategies discussed in Chapter 11 (Section 11.6.1) that call for the operation of air distribution fans at less than full capacity. We must expect such conflicts between different design objectives to arise quite frequently over the next several decades as *sustainability* considerations increase in priority. The resolution of these conflicts, apart from further increasing the complexity of the design process, will depend largely on technical innovation and design ingenuity.

Chiller Plants: The chiller component of air-cooling systems is the largest energy user in commercial buildings, accounting for more than 20 percent of the total building energy consumption. The impact of the chiller is exacerbated because its greatest energy consumption normally occurs during the day and therefore coincides with peak electric power demand. In addition, there are two design considerations that work against achieving an energy-efficient chiller-plant solution. First, it is a well-established engineering design practice to oversize cooling systems, for fear that assumed loads may be exceeded during the lifespan of the HVAC installation. Second, while chillers have to be designed for peak loads, they operate most of the time under part-load conditions. To compound matters, just as in the case of electric motors, chillers also operate at their greatest efficiency when they are operating at maximum capacity.

Driven partly by building codes and market forces manufacturers have been addressing the energy efficiency of chillers through the incorporation of new technologies such as direct digital control and variable-frequency drives. However, the selection of the most energy-efficient chiller plant for a given set of building design conditions can be a complicated undertaking requiring a great deal of engineering

expertise. Based on the ratio of cooling power to input power, water-cooled rotary screw or scroll-type chillers are more than twice as efficient as electrically operated air-cooled chillers. However, a water-cooled chiller requires a cooling tower to dissipate the heat absorbed from the building interior. While absorption chillers have a much lower cooling-power-to-input-power ratio, they could utilize the heat recovered from other plant components (e.g., solar energy) to significantly increase their overall energy efficiency.

Air Distribution: The energy efficiency of an air-distribution system depends largely on the ability to deliver no more than the required quantity and quality of air to all parts of the given building domain, under often greatly varying operating conditions. US Government guidelines for federal buildings suggest the following design approach for energy efficient air distribution systems (DoE, 2006):

1 Use variable-air-volume systems in preference to constant-volume systems to deliver the precise volume of air, based on actual loads, to each building space.
2 Use local variable-air-volume diffusers with individual temperature control to allow for temperature variations within multi-room zones.
3 Size fans based on actual loads and use electronic controls to match fan speed and torque with variable load conditions.
4 Use a displacement ventilation system to reduce or eliminate the need for ducting by feeding the conditioned air through a floor plenum and returning the used air through a ceiling plenum.
5 Use low-face-velocity air handlers to take advantage of the ability to reduce the air velocity, due to increased coil size. Since the pressure drop across the coils decreases with the square of the air velocity, smaller fans and variable-frequency drives – as well as slightly higher chilled water temperatures – will be acceptable. The savings in capital costs together with the downsizing of the chilled water plant can be significant.

6 Increase the duct size and avoid sharp turns to reduce duct pressure drop and fan size. Since the pressure drop in ducts is inversely proportional to the fifth power of the duct diameter, the savings in energy that can accrue from relatively small increases in duct size are appreciable.

Energy Recovery: Air-conditioning systems have a mandated requirement for fresh air, which means that as much as 50 percent of the conditioned internal air is replaced by unconditioned external air. This can be a considerable energy cost, particularly in hot or cold climates. For example, on a hot-humid summer day external air may be at a temperature of 90°F with a relative humidity of more than 90 percent. At the same time the conditioned internal air that is being exhausted from a building may be at a temperature of 78°F with a relative humidity of less than 60 percent. Under these conditions the preconditioning of the incoming external air with the outgoing internal air should result in considerable energy savings. The same applies in the case of a cold winter day, where the cold external incoming air can be preheated by the conditioned outgoing air. Also, it should be possible to use external air directly for conditioning the building whenever the external climatic conditions are close to the thermal comfort zone.

Technologies that are available to take advantage of these energy-saving opportunities include economizers and energy-recovery ventilators. Economizers are designed to monitor external conditions and shut down those components of the HVAC plant that are not required to operate at any particular time, and then reactivate these components as external conditions become less favorable. The difficulties encountered with this concept are virtually all related to operational failures that can lead to significant energy wastage. Common failures include corroded dampers that stick in place, failure of temperature sensors, and failure of actuators. Past surveys have indicated that less than 50 percent of economizer-based systems may be operating correctly after several years of use.

Energy-recovery ventilators are essentially heat and humidity exchangers that are placed between the conditioned outgoing air and the unconditioned incoming air. They are usually in the form of a fairly large-diameter rotating wheel made of a thermally highly conductive material, such as metal. The wheel is actually a disk with a desiccant material inside it. The desiccant bed is responsible for drying the air and the metal enclosure is responsible for the heat transfer during the air exchange. The technology is mature and not subject to the kind of operational failures that have plagued economizers.

Radiant Cooling: The concept of cooling a building space with air incorporates some intrinsic inefficiencies. Since air has a very low heat capacity and is highly compressible, relatively large volumes of air are required to cool a space and a considerable amount of energy is required to move the air to the space. Water, on the other hand, has a high heat capacity and is incompressible. It can be moved (i.e., pumped) with the expenditure of relatively little energy. Therefore, radiant cooling systems that circulate water through tubes that are embedded in floor, wall and/or ceiling elements have started to be viewed as a more energy-efficient alternative to forced-air cooling systems.

Ground-Coupling: At even fairly shallow depths, in any but the coldest climates, the temperature of the earth and groundwater below the surface of the building site remains relatively stable. This provides an opportunity for using the ground as a heat sink for cooling and as a heat source for heating a building. Both horizontal and vertical ground-coupling systems are possible. In horizontal implementations pipes are placed in trenches in a single or multiple pipe arrangement. More effective are vertical systems in which pipes are placed in boreholes that reach down to the groundwater table. Alternatively, it is possible to bring external air into a building through relatively large-diameter (3 to 6 feet) underground pipes. In addition, hybrid systems that combine the direct ground-coupling approach with the indirect vertical or horizontal strategy are possible. All of these are variations of the same concept, namely to use the natural thermal inertia of the ground to maintain constant thermal conditions inside a building, with the objective of minimizing the energy required for air conditioning.

12.6 Water conservation strategies

While much of the early interest in *green high-performance* buildings has focused on energy conservation, within the next two decades and perhaps sooner the attention may shift to freshwater as an even more important resource. Water is critical for human survival and although four-fifths of the Earth's surface is covered by water, less than 3 percent of that enormous amount of water is freshwater. Almost 90 percent of freshwater is essentially unavailable in the form of ice and snow, as glaciers. In most parts of the world freshwater is being withdrawn at a much faster rate than it can be replenished. There are many examples of serious freshwater depletion, such as: reduction of the size of the Aral Sea in Russia by 75 percent in the 20-year period between 1960 and 1980, due to the Soviet collective farms program for the production of cotton; the annual withdrawal in some regions of the US (e.g., Arizona) of twice as much water as is being replaced by rainwater; and the severe water shortage being experienced by 90 percent of the population in West Asia. In the US, even though the population is continuing to grow at a steady rate, the water consumption has leveled off since the mid-1980s. However, despite this per-capita reduction there are clear signs that the annual withdrawal of around 400 billion gallons of water is not sustainable.

More than 80 percent of the water consumption is for agricultural purposes. Therefore, the leveling off of the water consumption in the US is more than likely due to slight improvements in irrigation systems. However, it is estimated that more than half of all irrigation water is still wasted by evaporation, leaking canals, and mismanagement.

Water is also a major factor in respect to public health and hygiene. Waterborne diseases such as typhoid, cholera, and dysentery are responsible for the deaths of over 2 million persons each year (Gleick, 2002, Hunter et al., 1997, 2000). A large proportion of those death are due to a lack of water-treatment plants in developing countries. Consequently, raw sewage is dumped into rivers at an alarming rate, For example, 300 000 gallons are dumped into the Ganges River in India every minute (Kibert, 2005, p. 245). It is estimated that only 35 percent of wastewater is treated in Asia and less than 15 percent in Latin America. According to a 2000 survey by the World Health Organization, more than 1.1 billion people around the world lack access to safe freshwater and more than 2.4 billion lack access to satisfactory sanitation (WHO, 2000).

12.6.1 Water-consumption goals

The World Health Organization has defined the daily water requirements for bare survival to be 0.5 to 1 gallon per person for drinking and another 1 gallon per person for food preparation. However, for maintaining a reasonable quality of life the US Agency for International Development (USAID) suggests a much higher requirement of 26.4 gallons per person per day. The current daily consumption of water in the US is estimated to be in the vicinity of 100 gallons per person. If we add the use of water for agricultural and industrial purposes, then that estimate increases the US per capita figure to around 1800 gallons per day.

Buildings account for approximately 12 percent of the total freshwater withdrawal. Although this is a relatively small fraction of water usage when compared with the 80 percent consumed by agriculture, it still represents a meaningful target for water conservation measures. The building hydrologic cycle, which includes the irrigation of landscaping and the management of stormwater, is currently very wasteful. For example, the irrigation of landscaping is typically accomplished with potable water from sprinklers or handheld hoses, toilets are flushed almost exclusively with potable water, and the majority of residential buildings have one or more dripping faucets.

Clearly, the prospects for reducing the use of potable water in buildings and introducing water-treatment facilities are quite favorable. As a starting point this will require architects to become familiar with the differentiation of the common term *water* into its multiple forms within the building hydrology cycle (TGF, 2009).

- *Potable Water:* Water of a quality suitable for drinking. It is either untreated (e.g., from a water well) or has been filtered, tested, and possibly mixed with certain chemicals (e.g., fluoride) prior to release into a municipal water system.
- *Freshwater:* Naturally occurring water that by definition contains less than 500 parts per million of dissolved salt. While freshwater is found in naturally occurring lakes, rivers, and underground aquifers, the source of almost all freshwater is precipitation from the atmosphere in the form of mist, rain, and snow.
- *Rainwater:* Water that is collected during rainfall. Rainwater is typically collected on the roof and used directly for landscape irrigation or subjected to purification treatment prior to use as potable water.
- *Groundwater:* Water found below the surface of the ground in aquifers, underground rivers, and between soil particles.
- *Graywater:* Water from showers, bathtubs, kitchen and bathroom sinks, hot tub and drinking fountain drains, and washing machines.
- *Blackwater:* Water containing human excreta, such as wastewater from toilets.

In the US the Energy Policy Act of 1992 (EPAct) requires all plumbing fixtures to meet specific water-consumption standards, as follows:

While these standards (Table 12.2) constitute a welcome increase in code requirements, *green high-performance buildings* will generally improve on them by employing strategies such as specifying ultra-low-flow fixtures and drought-tolerant landscaping plants that require minimal or no water.[19] The cost benefits of these strategies can be determined on the basis of a fairly

Table 12.2   EPAct water usage standards for plumbing fixtures.

Plumbing fixture	Maximum flush and flow requirements
Water closets (toilets)	1.60 gallons per flush
Urinals	1.00 gallon per flush
Showerheads	2.50 gallons per minute at 80 psi water pressure
	2.20 gallons per minute at 60 psi water pressure
Faucets	2.50 gallons per minute at 80 psi water pressure
	2.00 gallons per minute at 60 psi water pressure
Replacement aerators	2.50 gallons per minute
Metering faucets	0.25 gallons per cycle

simple life-cycle cost (LCC) analysis that may consider only the cost of potable water. A more detailed and complex LCC would also take into account reductions in the energy required to move and treat both wastewater and potable water.

Based on Kibert (2005, pp. 250–1), the following additional steps for developing a building hydrologic design strategy are suggested:

- Step 1: Selection of the appropriate water source (i.e., type) for each purpose. Potable water should be used only for human consumption such as drinking, cooking, washing, and cleaning.
- Step 2: For each water usage the technology that ensures minimum water consumption should be employed. For example, the specification of low-flow and no-flow fixtures, as well as sensors for control purposes.
- Step 3: Consideration of the implementation of a dual wastewater system that will automatically separate graywater from blackwater as a prerequisite for water treatment and recycling.
- Step 4: Consideration of the implementation of a wastewater treatment facility. For example, at the very least consideration should be given to the provision of a constructed wetland[20] to process effluent.

The primary objective of the hydrologic design strategy is to minimize the consumption of potable water by reducing the flow rate of plumbing fixtures and finding ways of recycling wastewater for all uses that do not require potable water.

12.6.2 Lower-flow-rate fixtures

If we consider plumbing fixtures that comply with the EPAct of 1992 to be low-flow fixtures, then plumbing fixtures that exceed these standards can be referred to as ultra-low-flow fixtures. The kinds of plumbing fixture that are becoming increasingly available as commercial products in the ultra-low-flow category are dual-flush toilets and electromechanical flush toilets. The dual-flush concept is based on the recognition that the most frequent use of toilets is for urinating, which requires a much smaller volume of water for flushing. Electromechanical flushing systems incorporate electrically powered pumps and compressors that require less than 1 gallon of water to remove blackwater under increased pressure.

Relatively new technologies, such as chemical toilets that use no water at all, and composting toilets, are still relatively rare and generally not yet considered suitable for normal building application. However, the technology for waterless urinals has matured to the point where office, school, and recreational facility applications are not only feasible but economically attractive. A waterless urinal utilizes an odor trap with a biodegradable oil that allows urine to pass through, but prevents odors from escaping into the restroom.

Showerheads that reduce the flow rate to between 1.0 and 2.5 gallons per minute and provide adjustable spray patterns have been commercially available for some time. What is required in addition are technologies that will eliminate the wastage of water that occurs during soaping and while waiting for hot water to reach the showerhead or faucet from the hot-water source. Manual and electronic controls could eventually solve part of this problem, but are unlikely to overcome the hot-water delay issue. It appears that the latter will require a different solution approach.

12.6.3 Graywater systems

The key requirement for graywater management is the separation of graywater from blackwater at the origin, before the two are mixed. This requires a dual waste-pipe system that collects the graywater and carries it to a holding tank in a central location. Once that first step has been taken, several additional second-step options are available. The graywater can be pumped directly to an irrigation system for landscape maintenance purposes, or it can be treated and then recycled within the building.

Some municipalities already provide reclaimed water to buildings. In these cases, consideration should be given to the converse possibility of sending all or a portion of the graywater produced in the building to the municipal wastewater treatment plant. If piping already exists for the delivery of reclaimed water from the municipal plant to the building, then the provision of piping for the transmission of graywater from the building to the plant is worthy of consideration. Certainly in the future such two-way piping connections, at least between larger buildings and municipal wastewater treatment plants, are likely to become available. To achieve *Factor 10* water- and energy-conservation goals, the greater efficiency that should be able to be realized in larger-scale water-treatment plants is likely to be necessary.

12.6.4 Rainwater capture

Rainwater harvesting systems have been used in rural communities when a municipal water system is not available and well water is fragile or scarce. Such systems have been used extensively in Australia for many years and in the more arid states of the US, such as Texas, but are mostly confined to single-story buildings (Texas-WDB, 1999). The principal components of a rainwater harvesting system include:

- A large *catchment area*, such as the roof of a building. Since the roof area has to be quite large, rainwater systems are typically limited to low-rise buildings. Metal roof surfaces are most suitable, because they are smooth and provide less opportunity for the growth of algae, mold, and moss.

- A *roof-wash system* that prevents the initial run-off during rain from being collected. In other words, the initial run-off is sacrificed for purposes of cleaning the surface of the roof.
- Protection of open inlets with *pre-storage filtration devices* such as stainless steel screens, to prevent leaves and other debris from entering the storage tank. Depending on site conditions, leaf guards over gutters may need to be included.
- A *storage tank* that is large enough to supply sufficient water in between rainfalls. The tank may be located inside the building or external to the building, and normally constitutes the most expensive component of the system.
- A *booster pump* to deliver the water under pressure (ideally at least 60 psi) from the tank to the point of use. Seldom is a gravity-feed arrangement possible, because the tank would need to be at least 60 feet above the point of use.[21]
- A *water-treatment facility* to protect plumbing and irrigation lines. Such a facility typically consists of a filtration unit to remove particulates in the case of graywater uses, and a considerably more sophisticated treatment unit in the case of potable water uses (e.g., microfiltration, reverse osmosis, ozonation, ultraviolet sterilization, chemical treatment, or any combination of these).

Since rainwater, like solar energy, is readily available in virtually all regions it presents an opportunity for taking advantage of a natural source of water. Therefore, it is likely that green high-performance buildings will in coming years increasingly incorporate rainwater harvesting systems.

12.7 Closed-loop building materials

While the concept of closed-loop building materials is sound and highly laudable, a compre-

hensive implementation of this concept based on the current body of knowledge does not appear to be feasible. As mentioned previously in Section 12.3.6, the definition of embodied energy is very broad and includes not only the energy consumed during the extraction of the raw materials. It also includes the energy used during the transportation and initial processing of the raw material, the preparation of the final construction material or product, the marketing and distribution of the material or product, and the transportation to the building site. The current barriers are numerous.

General Variations: The embodied energy of a material or product varies from country to country and with time. Factors that influence this variation include the quality of the raw material, the climate, processing methods, age and type of plant, distances between extraction, production and construction sites, and transportation modes.

Transportation Modes: The proportion of energy consumed by transportation depends not only on the transportation mode, but also on the weight (i.e., density) of the raw material. For example, according to Adalberth (1997), the transportation component of embodied energy accounts for from 5 to 10 percent of the manufacturing energy. To arrive at this estimate he assumed 2.7 MJ/km[22] for distances less than 50 km, 1.0 MJ/km for distances greater than 50 km, 0.5 MJ/km for coastal vessels, and 0.2 MJ/km for ocean-going vessels.

Units of Measurement: The units of measurement for embodied energy have not been internationally standardized to date (2009). Some sources provide their data per material volume (MJ/m^3) and others per material mass (MJ/kg). For example, the embodied energy for bricks is given in volumetric terms (MJ/m^3) in Australia and in weight terms (MJ/kg) in Germany, while the US first published brick data per volume in 1967 and then changed to per mass in 1996. Although the US has not generally changed to the metric system of units, it has adopted metric units for embodied energy values.[23] A comparison

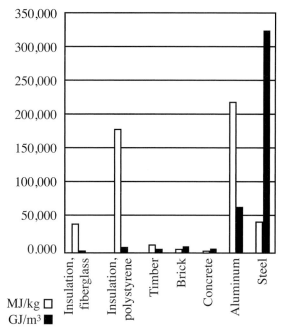

MJ/kg □
GJ/m³ ■

Figure 12.3   Volume versus mass.

Table 12.3   Embodied energy in volume and mass.

Material	MJ/kg	GJ/m³
Insulation, fiberglass	35.360	0.460
Insulation, polystyrene	177.240	4.254
Timber	6.230	3.425
Brick	3.480	5.918
Concrete	1.020	2.346
Aluminum	214.270	58.067
Steel	39.040	305.800

of embodied energy by volume and mass is shown in Figure 12.3 and Table 12.3 (Heidrich, 1999).

The data based on volume provide a clearer impression of the amount of energy that would be embodied in a building constructed of these materials.

Continuous Change: Industry is continuously striving for greater energy efficiency and has achieved significant reductions over the past several decades. In 1993 Cole reported the following substantial improvements: chemical industry (40%); iron and steel (8%); cement (27%); glass (33%); petrochemicals (39%); textiles (26%); and, wood products (39%). Therefore, to maintain at least a reasonable level of accuracy, embodied energy values for materials and products need to be updated on a regular basis.

Assessment Complexity: Virtually all of the individual components that make up the total embodied energy of a material or product, from extraction through production to on-site delivery, are difficult to assess because of the number of variables involved and the indefinite nature of most of those variables. For example, the methods used in the growth, extraction, and preparation of structural timber can vary widely not just from country to country, but even within the same country. If the source of the timber is a plantation forest, then large quantities of fertilizers, herbicides, and water may have been used to accelerate the growth cycle. The accessibility of the timber source will be a major factor in determining the type of equipment used and the energy cost incurred in hauling the rough timber logs to the sawmill for initial preparation.

The first step in determining the embodied energy of a material or product is to establish the boundaries for each component stage in the path from extraction to delivery to the construction site, including the boundaries of the overall end-to-end process. The wider the overall boundaries are drawn, the more complex is the process and the less definite the outcome.

12.7.1   Methods for determining embodied energy

Several methods have been used to determine the embodied energy of materials and products. Owing to the factors discussed in the previous section, the results obtained by the application of two or more different assessment methods to the same material can vary widely (Chapman, 1974). If the energy measurements are in terms of primary sources such as coal or crude oil, then the loss of energy during conversion to electricity should be considered. Therefore, in countries using mostly hydroelectric power the embodied energy will be lower than in countries that depend mostly on fossil fuel as the primary source of energy. In the case of nuclear power, the boundaries drawn for assessment in respect to the period of maintenance of the power plant and the management of the nuclear waste material can have an appreciable impact on the end result. The following four assessment approaches are described in the literature.

Process Analysis: This approach considers both direct and indirect energy consumptions. Direct energy refers to the energy that is directly related to a particular process. For example, the energy used in a smelter during the manufacture of steel is considered to be direct energy. The direct energy component can normally be determined with a fairly high degree of accuracy. However, the indirect energy consumed during the extraction of the iron ore, transportation, and the manufacture of the equipment and facilities used during the production of steel requires many assumptions to be made. As a very general rule of thumb, Baird et al. (1984) have suggested that approximately 40 percent of the embodied energy is consumed during extraction, 50 percent during manufacture, and 10 percent for the equipment employed. This method is time-consuming, because of the level of detail required for a complete analysis. It can be argued that the effort involved is not justifiable owing to the potential vagueness of the assumptions that have to be made in the analysis of the indirect energy component.

Input–Output Analysis: This method is based on examination of national financial data that track the flow of money in and out of the energy-consuming and energy-producing sectors. In this way the monetary output value of each sector can be equated with the energy consumed by that sector. The results tend to be superficial, because they are based on industry groups rather than individual material types or products.

Hybrid Analysis: This method attempts to combine the process analysis method with the input–output method. Starting with the data that are readily available, such as the information relating to material preparation or product manufacturing processes, the method proceeds with process analysis. When the readily available data have been exhausted the hybrid approach switches over to the input–output method. The quality of the results depends on how much of the less granular input–output data had to be used.

Statistical Analysis: This approach relies on published statistical data relating to the energy profile of a particular industry (i.e., energy consumption and industrial output). Similarly to the input–output method, the analysis is based on industry groups rather than on a particular material or product. It therefore lacks detail. However, order-of-magnitude estimates can be rapidly generated.

Clearly, these methods are only approximate. While the process analysis method has the potential of providing fairly accurate results for the direct energy component, it suffers from the same problem as the other three methods in respect to the indirect energy component. From that point of view, all four of the methods are useful for indicating trends and identifying materials that should be avoided because of their relatively high embodied energy, rather than determining precise embodied energy values.

12.7.2 Deconstruction and disassembly

The need to consider the recycling of all of the materials that have been used in the construction of a building at the end of the lifespan of that building is an onerous requirement. Historically, building components such as the structural frame, external and internal walls, floors, and ceilings have not been designed for disassembly. Buildings are typically custom-designed and the manufacturing industry has found ways to adapt to an increased desire for customization without any appreciable cost increase. This has been made possible by computer-controlled manufacturing that allows for customization during a mass-production process. While this serves the interests of the customer, it complicates the reuse of building components. For example, the customization of window sizes makes it very difficult to recycle complete window units. The availability of the required number of reusable window units would need to be known at the design stage of a new building. With the very large variation in window sizes and configurations, such a dependency between new construction and the deconstruction of existing buildings is not commercially viable.

The lifespan of a building is normally not predictable and can often exceed 50 years. In fact, one of the criteria of the *green* building movement is to consider the renovation or remodeling of an existing building in preference to the construction of a completely new one. For example, LEED New Construction 2009 allocates 4 points to building reuse under the Materials & Resources category (LEED, 2009). Over such a relatively long life-span, deconstruction and recycling assumptions that were made at the design stage may no longer be applicable at the final deconstruction stage. Few would argue with the notion that profound technological, economic, and societal changes are occurring at an increasing rate.

Given the indefinite nature of some of the issues involved, the concept of deconstruction and disassembly requires careful consideration at the building design stage. In his doctoral thesis Crowther (2002) suggests a framework of 27 principles for considering deconstruction at the building design stage. The proposed framework can be divided into several categories of consideration:

- *Overall Design:* Adopt a modular design approach that includes prefabricated sub-assemblies within a clearly defined grid layout. The design emphasis should be on an open building system that provides flexibility through interchangeable components.
- *Material Selection:* Reduce the number of different types of material and place the emphasis on existing materials that have been recycled and can be again reused after deconstruction. In addition, criteria for material selection should include the avoidance of toxic and hazardous materials, as well as composite materials that cannot be easily separated into their component parts after deconstruction. This includes avoidance of secondary material finishes.
- *Structural Layout:* Use a standard structural grid and separate the structure from the building envelope.
- *Structural Frame:* Use mechanical (e.g., bolted, nailed, screwed) in preference to chemical (e.g., welded, glued) connections. Design components to facilitate assembly and disassembly, with particular regard to component size (for ease of handling), number of connectors and types (limit the number of different connector types), and joint tolerances.
- *Deconstruction Provisions:* Design joints and connectors to facilitate disassembly and allow for parallel deconstruction sequences. Use assembly technologies that are compatible with standard building practices and capabilities (by default this will equally apply to deconstruction).
- *Documentation:* Provide standard and permanent identification of each material type and each component. Record and retain comprehensive descriptions of the building and its components, the assembly and disassembly sequences, and component handling procedures.
- *Maintenance:* Apart from drawings and descriptions of the principal building components, allocate storage space for maintaining at least a minimum inventory of critical spare parts.

Crowther's framework treats a building as a set of components that can be as easily disassembled as they can be assembled during the initial construction of the building. In the past such design criteria have been applied by architects only in very special cases, such as temporary and mobile structures. Typically, still today by far the majority of buildings are designed and constructed with little thought (if any) to how they might be deconstructed, let alone how their materials and principal components such as the structural frame and envelope might be salvaged for recycling.

12.7.3 Selecting green building materials

Conceptually a *closed-loop* building material or product should consist of materials that are non-persistent, non-toxic, and originate from reused, recycled, renewable, or abundantly available sources (ORTNS, 2004; Kibert, 2005, pp. 277–8). The material or product should not be new, but a remanufactured or refurbished version of a previous use. The emphasis is on recycling, not only in terms of past use but also in respect to future use. In other words, the material should also be able to be recycled at the end of the lifespan of the building. The notion of "renewable" requires the material to come from a source that will be regenerated in nature at a rate that is greater than or at least equal to the rate of consumption. Finally, the material should be abundantly available in nature so that the human use of the material is small in comparison with its availability.

How will the architect be able to consider all of these additional construction material selection criteria that are a prerequisite for meeting sustainability objectives? Certainly the architect will have neither the time nor expertise to calculate embodied energy values for materials and products from first principles. Instead, the building designer will have to rely on material vendors and product manufacturers to take responsibility for researching and certifying their offerings. It could be quite misleading for the building designer to assume this responsibility. For example, when conducting a comparative analysis of the embodied energy of different materials it would appear that there

are specific materials that should be avoided. Regardless of the variations among different data sources (see the discussion at the beginning of Section 12.7.1) certain materials such as aluminum, polystyrene and fiberglass insulation, paper, and steel almost always appear among the top 10 most energy-intensive materials. However, this does not mean that these materials should be necessarily avoided in new building construction. There are several other factors that could reverse such an a priori decision. First, the energy intensive material may be the best choice for the function to be performed, and the amount of the material required to perform this function may be relatively small. Second, the material may lend itself to recycling and may in its present form already be a product of recycling. If it is already a product of recycling, then its embodied energy is likely to be much reduced. For example, the embodied energy of recycled aluminum is only 5 percent of the energy consumed when aluminum is produced from bauxite ore. Third, there may be additional factors such as maintenance, commercial availability, cost, and energy savings related to other components that are indirectly influenced by the selection of the energy-intensive material, which should be considered in the final design decision.

Endnotes

1. A sports utility vehicle (SUV) is an automobile, similar to a station wagon, mostly equipped with four-wheel drive for occasional off-road driving. SUVs are considered light trucks and have in the past been regulated less stringently than passenger cars under the US Energy Policy and Conservation Act for fuel economy standards, and the US Clean Air Act for emissions standards.
2. If the plumbing costs (including fixtures) of a typical home are currently about 5 percent of the total cost of the building, then even a 40 percent increase in plumbing costs is only a 2 percent increase in the capital cost of the building.
3. The Bruntland Report (1987) defined *sustainable development* as "… meeting the needs of the present without compromising the ability of

future generations to meet their needs" (UN, 1987: "Our Common Future". United Nations, World Commission on Environment and Development, A/42/427 Supplement 25, 4 August, New York, NY).

4. The *Factor 10* concept continues to be promoted by the Factor 10 Club and the Factor 10 Institute, whose publications are available at: www.factor10-institute.org.

5. The iisBE Web site address is: www.iisbe.org. The next Green Building Challenge Conference is scheduled for London, UK in 2011.

6. In 1970 Earth Day was founded in the US by Senator Gaylord Nelson (D-Wisconsin) as an environmental teach-in. Since then Earth Day has been celebrated in the US on April 22 each year. In other countries Earth Day is celebrated in spring in the northern hemisphere and in autumn in the southern hemisphere.

7. For LEED-NC v3.0 the minimum requirement for mechanically ventilated buildings is ASHRAE Sections 4–7 (62.1-2007) and ASHRAE Section 5 Paragraph 5.1 (62.1-2007) for naturally ventilated buildings.

8. Volatile Organic Compounds (VOC) are gases or vapors emitted by various solids or liquids, which may have a deleterious health impact. Typical building materials that emit VOC include paint, paint strippers, glues and adhesives, floor coverings, building materials, and furnishings.

9. To obtain the allocated single credit point the HVAC system must be designed to meet the requirements of ASHRAE Standard 55-2004.

10. The regional vernacular "built environment" is often an indicator of indigenous architectural prototypes that reflect historical solutions to ambient climatic conditions, such as adobe construction in desert regions (see Chapter 3, Section 3.2 and Chapter 4, Section 4.9).

11. In 1967 Laing proposed an approach for generating *thermal insulation on demand* through multi-layered membranes in which the width of interstitial air cavities is controlled by either electrostatic or pneumatic forces (Feder D. (ed.), 1967, Proceedings of the 1st International Colloquium on Pneumatic Structures, IASS, University of Stuttgart, Stuttgart, Germany, (pp. 163–79)).

12. This is of course an illusion. The sun appears to move across the sky when viewed from Earth. In fact, planet Earth rotates around the sun.

13. See Chapter 3, Section 3.3, for a more detailed explanation of Low-E glass.

14. See Chapter 8, Section 8.7, for a more detailed explanation of the PSALI concept.

15. Efficacy defines energy efficiency in terms of the light flux (lumen) produced per electric power (watt) consumed (i.e., lumen/watt).

16. However, there are some technical barriers that have to be overcome before the full potential of LED lighting can be realized. For almost a decade researchers have been trying to understand why the efficiency of bluelight-emitting diodes drops off sharply with increasing current (Stevenson, 2009). This phenomenon, referred to as *droop*, currently defies explanation, with several competing theories under discussion. It is one reason why LED technology has been used most effectively in low-power applications such as the backlit screens of mobile telephones and indicator panels.

17. Based on 20 000 hours of continuous testing, Cree Inc. estimates that the brightness deterioration of the XR-E series of LED lamps is about 30 percent over a life span of 50 000 hours.

18. While a 40-watt incandescent lamp will generate about 196 pounds of carbon dioxide per year, a 13-watt LED with comparable light output will produce only about 63 pounds of carbon dioxide per year.

19. Also referred to as *xeriscaping* or *xerogardening*, which is an environmentally friendly form of landscaping that relies on the use of indigenous and drought-tolerant plants, shrubs, and ground cover.

20. An artificially constructed wetland is a landscaping area that is saturated by wastewater and takes advantage of natural processes involving soil development and plant growth.

21. A 60-feet height difference would result in a water-head, owing to gravity of a little under 30 psi.

22. Megajoules per kilometer (MJ/km). For conversion to American units of measurement 1 MJ/km is approximately equivalent to 592.4 BTU/mile or 0.174 kWH/mile, or 149.3 Cal/mile.

23. The prevalent units of measurement for energy in the American system are British Thermal Unit (BTU), Kilowatt Hour (kWh), and Calorie (Cal). In respect to embodied energy the conversion factors from metric to American units are as follows: $1 MJ/m^3 = 26.84 BTU/FT^3 = 0.0079 kWh/FT^3 = 6.762 Cal/FT^3$; and $1 MJ/kg = 429.9 BTU/LB = 0.126 kWh/LB = 108.5 Cal/LB$.

References and Further Reading

Adalberth K. (1997) "Energy Use During the Life-Cycle of Buildings: A Method", *Building and Environment*, **32**(4), 317–20.

AIA (2007) *Design for Aging Post-Occupancy Evaluation*. American Institute of Architects, Wiley Series in Healthcare and Senior Living Design: Wiley, Hoboken, NJ.

Aldersey-Williams, A. (1960) *Noise in Factories*. Factory Building Studies No. 6. Building Research Station, HMSO, London, UK.

ANSI (1969) *Methods for the Calculation of the Articulation Index*. American National Standards Institute, ANSI S3.5.

ANSI (1989) *Methods for Measuring the Intelligibility of Speech over Communication Systems*. American National Standards Institute, ANSI S3.2.

ASHRAE (1978) *Procedure for Determining Heating and Cooling Loads for Computerizing Energy Calculations*. American Society of Heating, Refrigerating, and Air-Conditioning Engineers, Atlanta, GA.

ASHRAE (1989) *Handbook of Fundamentals*. American Society of Heating, Refrigerating, and Air-Conditioning Engineers, Atlanta, GA.

ASI (2007) *Mass Loaded Vinyl*. Acoustical Surfaces Inc., 123 Columbia Court North (Suite 201), Chaska, MN 55318.

ASTM (1990) *Standard Test Method for Measurement of Airborne Sound Insulation in Buildings*. American Society for Testing and Materials, ASTM Standard E 336-90.

Audubon (1992) *Audubon House: Building the Environmentally Responsible, Energy-Efficient Office*. Croxton Collaborative and National Audubon Society, Wiley, New York, NY.

Baird G., M. Donn, F. Pool, W. Brander, and C. Aun (1984) *Energy Performance of Buildings*. Center for Resource Solutions, CRS Press, San Francisco, CA.

Baume, M. (1967) *The Sydney Opera House Affair*. Nelson, Melbourne, Australia.

BDC (2003) "White Paper on Sustainability: A Report on the Green Building Movement", *Building Design and Construction*, May (www.bdcmag.com/).

Bedford, T. (1936) *The Warmth Factor in Comfort at Work*. Industry Health Research Board, Report 76.

Bedford, T. (1951) "Equivalent Temperature"; *Heating, Piping and Air Conditioning*, **95**(23).

Beranek, L. (1960) *Noise Reduction*. McGraw-Hill, New York, NY.

Beranek, L. (1966) *Concert and Opera Halls: How They Sound*. The Acoustical Society of America, Woodbury, NY.

Beranek, L. (2004) *Music, Acoustics and Architecture*, 2nd edn, Springer-Verlag, New York, NY.

Bishop, D. (1957); "Use of Partial Enclosures to. Reduce Noise in Factories", *Noise Control*, **3**(2), March, 65–9.

Bishop, D. (1966) "Judgments of the Relative and Absolute Acceptability of Aircraft Noise", *Journal of the Acoustical Society of America*, **40**, 108–22.

Bowsher J., D. Johnson, and D. Robinson (1966) "A Further Experiment on Judging the Noisiness of Aircraft in Flight", *Acustica*, **17**, 245.

Bradbury, C. (1963) *Engine Noise: Analysis and Control*. Temple Press, London, UK, pp. 50–66.

Brooks, R. (1990) "Elephants Don't Play Chess", in Maes, P. (ed.) *Designing Autonomous Agents*. MIT/Elsevier, Cambridge, MA, pp. 3–7.

Bryan, M. and R. Parbrook (1959); "The Masking of One Tone by Another", in Cremer, L. (ed.), *Proceedings of the 3rd International Congress on Acoustics*, 1, Elsevier, London, UK, pp. 103–5.

Bryan, M. and R. Parbrook (1960) *Acustica*, **10**, 87.

Cardarelli, F. (1997) *Scientific Unit Conversion*. Springer-Verlag, London, UK.

Carr R. (1967); "Acoustical Conditioning", *Proceedings of the 3rd Australian Building Research Congress*, Melbourne, Australia, August, pp. 249 –52.

Caudill, W. and R. Reed (1952) *Geometry of Classrooms as Related to Natural Lighting and Natural Ventilation*. Texas Engineering Experiment Station, Report 36.

Chapman, P. (1974) "Energy Cost: A Review of Methods", *Energy Policy*, June, 91–103.

Connor, R. (1987) *The Weights and Measures of England*. HMSO, London, UK.

Crowther, P. (2002); "Design for Disassembly: An Architectural Strategy for Sustainability", Ph.D. thesis, School of Design and Built Environment, Queensland University of Technology, Brisbane, Australia.

Building Science: Concepts and Application. Jens Pohl.
© 2011 John Wiley & Sons, Ltd.
Published 2011 by John Wiley & Sons, Ltd.

Cushman, W. and D. Rosenberg (1991) *Human Factors in Product Design*. Elsevier, Amsterdam, The Netherlands.

Daisch, J. (1985) *Bibliography on Post-Occupancy Evaluation of Buildings*, 2nd edn. School of Architecture, Victoria University of Wellington, Wellington, New Zealand.

Datta and Chaudri (1964) *Sun Control and Shading Devices*. Architectural Science Review, Department of Architectural Science, University of Sydney, Australia, September.

Davies, D. (1962) *Noise Problems: Industry's Attitude*. National Physical Laboratory Symposium No. 12: "The Control of Noise", Paper E 5; HMSO, London, UK, pp. 311–23.

Day, B., R. Ford, and P. Lord (1969) *Building Acoustics*. Elsevier, London, UK.

Doelle, L. (1965) *Acoustics in Architectural Design*. National Research Council of Canada, Division of Building Research, Canada.

Drew, P. (2000) *Jorn Utzon and the Sydney Opera House: As It Happened, 1918–2000*. Inspire Press, Sydney, Australia.

Drysdale, J. (1967) "Progress and Noise: Some Building Problems", 3rd Australian Building Research Congress. Melbourne, August.

Duek-Cohen, E. (1967) "Utzon and the Sydney Opera House: A Statement in the Public Interest", University of New South Wales, Sydney, Australia.

Duffie, J. and W. Beckman (1974) *Solar Energy Thermal Processes*. Wiley-Interscience, New York, NY.

EEA (2009) European Environmental Agency: http://glossary.eea.eu.int/EEAGlossary/.

Egan, J. and R. Hake (1950) *Journal of the Acoustical Society of America*, **22**, 622.

Flyvbjerg, B. (2005) "Design by Deception: The Politics of Megaproject Approval", *Harvard Design Magazine*, Spring/Summer, pp. 50–9.

Furrer, W. (1964) *Room and Building Acoustics and Noise Abatement*. Butterworth, London, UK.

Geiger, P. (1955) "Noise Reduction Manual", Monograph, Engineering Research Institute, University of Michigan, Ann Arbor, MI.

Gleick, P. (2002) "Dirty Water: Estimated Deaths from Water-Related Diseases 2000–2020", Research Report, Pacific Institute for Studies in Development, Environment, and Security, 15 August (www.pacinst.org).

Hall, P. (1973) "The Design of the Concert Hall of the Sydney Opera House", *Journal and Proceedings, Royal Society of New South Wales*, **106**, 54–69.

Hand, I. (1948) "Charts to Obtain Solar Altitudes and Azimuths", *Heating and Ventilating*, **86**(45), October.

Harris, C. (1957) *Handbook of Noise Control*. McGraw-Hill, New York, NY.

Hay, H. (1973) "Energy technology and Solararchitecture", *Mechanical Engineering*, **94**, 18.

Hay, H. and J. Yellott (1970) "A Naturally Air Conditioned Building", *Mechanical Engineering*, **92**, 19.

Heidrich, A. (1999) "Embodied Energy and Operational Energy in Low-Rise Residential Buildings in California", Master of Science in Architecture Thesis, Architecture Department, California Polytechnic State University, San Luis Obispo, CA, December.

HMSO (1963) "Noise: Final Report", Committee on the Problem of Noise, HMSO, London, England.

Holland, J.H. (1995) *Hidden Order: How Adaptation Builds Complexity*. Addison-Wesley, Reading, MA.

Holling, C. (1978) *Adaptive Environmental Assessment and Management*. Wiley, London, UK.

Hopkinson, R.G., P. Petherbridge, and J. Longmore (1966) *Daylighting*. Heinemann, Oxford, UK.

Horvath, A. (1986) *Conversion Tables of Units for Science and Engineering*. Macmillan Reference Books, Macmillan, London, UK.

Houghton, F. and C. Yaglou (1923) "Determination of the Comfort Zone", ASHVE Report 673, ASHVE Transactions, (29)361.

Houtgast, T. and H. Steeneken (1984) "A Multi-Language Evaluation of the RASTI Method for Estimating Speech Intelligibility in Auditoria", *Acustica*, **4**.

Hunter, P., B. Robey, and U. Upadhyay (1997) "Solutions for a Water-Short World", Population Reports, Series M, No. 14, John Hopkins School of Public Health, Population Information Program, Baltimore, MD, December.

Hunter, P., J. Colford, M. LeChevallier, S. Binder, and P. Berger (2000); "Panel on Waterborne Diseases: Panel Summary from the 2000 Emerging Infectious Diseases Conference in Atlanta, Georgia", *Emerging Infectious Diseases Journal*, **7**(3) Supplement, 544–5.

IEC (1961) "Recommendations for Sound-Level Meters", International Electrotechnical Commission, Publications 123, POB 131, CH-1211, Geneva 20, Switzerland.

Ingerslev (1952) *Acoustics in Modern Building Practice*. The Architect Press, London, UK.

Jones, G., T. Hempstock, K. Mulholland, and M. Stott (1967) *Acoustics*. English Universities Press, London, UK.

Jordan, V. (1973) "Acoustical Design Considerations of the Sydney Opera House", *Journal and Proceedings, Royal Society of New South Wales*, **106**, 33–53.

Karplus, H. and G. Bonvallet (1953) "A Noise Survey of Manufacturing Industries", *American Industrial Hygiene Association Quarterly*, **14**(4), US 1953, 235–63.

Kauffman, S.A. (1992) *Origins of Order: Self-Organization and Selection in Evolution.* Oxford University Press, Oxford, UK.

Kibert, C. (2005) *Sustainable Construction: Green Building Design and Delivery.* Wiley, Hoboken, NJ.

King, A. (1957) "Reduction of Noise and Vibration in Engineering", Metropolitan Vickers Electrical Company Ltd, Research Series No. 43, Manchester, UK, pp. 1–17.

Klein, H. (1975) *The World of Measurements.* Allen and Unwin, London, UK.

Knudsen, V. (1955) "Noise, the Bane of Hearing", *Noise Control*, **1**(3).

Knudsen, V. and C. Harris (1962) *Acoustical Designing in Architecture.* Wiley, New York, NY.

Knuttruff, H. (1979) *Room Acoustics.* Applied Science Publishers, London, UK.

Koch, W. (1950) "Binaural Localization And Masking", *Journal of the Acoustical Society of America*, **22**, 801.

Kreider, J. and F. Kreith (1975) *Solar Heating and Cooling: Engineering, Practical Design, and Economics.* McGraw-Hill, New York, NY.

Krochmann, J. (1963) "Über die Horizontalbeleuchtungsstärke der Tagesbeleuchtung", *Lichttechnik*, **15**, 559–62.

Kryter, K. and K. Persons (1963) "Some Effects of Spectral Content and Duration on Perceived Noise Level", *Journal of the Acoustical Society of America*, **35**, 886.

Kuhl, W. and U. Kath (1963) "The Acoustical Requirements of a Concert Hall and their Realization in the N.D.H.'s Large Studio in Hannover", (translation), Institute for Broadcasting – Techniques, Special Report DK 534.861:534.84:72, Vol. 5, Hamburg, Germany.

Lawrence, A. (1968) "Regulating for Noise Control", 3rd Australian Building Research Congress, Melbourne, Australia, pp. 259–62.

LEED (2009) *LEED for New Construction 2009.* US Green Building Council, Washington, DC, April.

Libby-Owens-Ford (1951) *Sun Angle Calculator.* Libby-Owens-Ford Glass Company.

Louden, M. (1971) "Dimensional Ratios of Rectangular Rooms with Good Distribution of Eigentones", *Acustica*, **24**, 101–4.

Lynes, J.A. (1968) *Principles of Natural Lighting.* Elsevier, Architectural Science Series; London, UK.

MacPherson, R. (1962) "The Assessment of the Thermal Environment", *British Journal of Industrial Medicine*, 151–64.

Mariner, T. and A. Park (1956) "Sound-Absorbing Screens in a Marginal Industrial Noise Problem", *Noise Control*, **2**(5), September, 22–7.

Mason, C. and L. Moir (1941); "Acoustics of Cinema Auditoria", *Journal of the Institute of Electrical Engineers*, **H8**, 175.

McHarg, I. (1999) *Design with Nature.* Natural History Press, Garden City, NY.

Meadows D. H., D. L. Meadows, J. Randers, and W. Behrens (1972) *The Limits of Growth.* Universe Books, New York, NY.

Mehta, M., J. Johnson, and J. Rocafort (1999) *Architectural Acoustics: Principles and Design.* Prentice Hall, Upper Saddle River, NJ.

Mehta, M. (1997) *The Principles of Building Construction.* Prentice Hall, Upper Saddle River, NJ, p. 46.

Meyer, E. (1954); "Definition and Diffusion in Rooms"; *Journal of the Acoustical Society of America*, **26** (pp. 630).

Mumford, L. (1967) *The Myth of the Machine.* Harcourt, New York, NY.

Nickson A. (1966) "Noise and the Community", *Australian Building Science and Technology*, **6**(4), April, 19–26.

Nickson, A. and R. Muncey (1964) "Criteria for Room Acoustics", *Journal of Sound and Vibration*, **1**(3), 292–7.

Odum, H. (1983) *Systems Ecology.* Wiley, New York, NY.

Olgyay, A. (1952) "Housing and Building in Hot-Humid and Hot-Dry Climates", *BRAB Conference Report 5*, November.

ORTNS (2004) *Using the Natural Step as a Framework Toward the Construction and Operation of Fully Sustainable Buildings.* Oregon Natural Step Construction Industry Group, Oregon (www.ortns.org).

Parkin, P. and H. Humphreys (1958) *Acoustics, Noise and Buildings.* Faber and Faber, London, UK.

Parkin, P. and K. Morgan (1965) "Assisted Resonance in the Royal Festival Hall, London", *Sound and Vibration*, **2**(1), 74–85.

Parkin, P., W. Scholes, and A. Derbyshire (1952) "The Reverberation Times of Ten British Concert Halls", *Acustica*, **2**, 97.

Pearsons, K. (1966) "The Effects of Duration and Background Noise Level on Perceived Noisiness", Technical Report, FAA-ADS-78.

Pena W., S. Parshall, and K. Kelly (1987) *Problem Seeking: An Architectural Programming Primer.* AIA Press, Washington, DC.

Pickwell, D. (1970) "Landscaping and Sound Conditioning Offices", *Building Materials and Equipment (Australia)*, April, 39–43.

Piess, R., J. Rose, and N. Murray (1962) "Hearing Conservation in Noise", Report C.A.L., No. 19, Commonwealth Acoustics Laboratories Australia, Melbourne, Australia.

Pleijel, G. (1954) "The Computation of Natural Radiation in Architecture and Town Planning", Meddelande 25, Statens Nämnd för byggnadsforskning, Stockholm, Sweden.

Pohl, J. (1999) "Some Notions of Complex Adaptive Systems and Their Relationship to Our World", in J. Pohl and T. Fowler (eds.) *Advances in Computer-Based and Web-Based Collaborative Systems*. Focus Symposium: International Conference on Systems Research, Informatics and Cybernetics (InterSymp-99), Baden-Baden, Germany, August 2–6, pp. 9–24.

Pohl, J. (2003) "The Emerging Knowledge Management Paradigm: Some Organizational and Technical Issues", InterSymp-2003, Pre-Conference Proceedings, Focus Symposium on Collaborative Decision-Support Systems, Baden-Baden, Germany, July 28–August 1.

Pohl, J. (2008) "Cognitive Elements of Human Decision-Making", in L. Jain and G. Wren (eds.) *Intelligent Decision Making: An AI-Based Approach*. Springer Verlag, New York, NY.

Pohl, J. and L. Myers (1994) "A Distributed Cooperative Model for Architectural Design", in G. Carrara and Y. Kalay (eds.) *Knowledge-Based Computer-Aided Architectural Design*. Elsevier, Amsterdam, pp.205–42.

Pohl, J., H. Assal, and K. Pohl (2010) "Intelligent Software for Ecological Building Design", 2nd KES International Symposium, Inner Harbor, Baltimore, MD, 28–30 July.

Pohl, J., A. Chapman, and K. Pohl (2000) "Computer-Aided Design Systems for the 21st Century: Some Design Guidelines", 5th *International Conference on Design and Decision-Support Systems for Architecture and Urban Planning*, Nijkerk, The Netherlands, August 22–25.

Preiser, W. (1989) *Building Evaluation*. Plenum, New York, NY.

Preiser, W., H. Rabinowitz, and E. White (1988) *Post-Occupancy Evaluation*. Nostrand Reinhold, New York, NY.

Priede, T. (1962) "Noise of Internal Combustion Engines", in *The Control of Noise*, N.P.L. Symposium No. 12, HMSO, London, UK.

Richards, S. (1957) "Minimum Ceiling Heights in South Africa", National Building Research Institute, Bulletin 15, South Africa, January.

Roux, A., J. Visser, and P. Minnaar (1951) "Periodic Heat Flow Through Building Components", National Building Research Institute, Report DR-9, South Africa.

Schön, D. (1983) *The Reflective Practitioner: How Professionals Think in Action*. Basic Books, New York, NY.

Smuts, M. (2002) "Sick-Building Syndrome Gains a Growing Level of National Awareness", *Boston Business Journal*, August (www.bizjournals.com/boston/stories/2002/08/19/focus9.html).

Somerville, T. (1951) "Acoustics in Broadcasting", Building Research Congress, Division 3 (Part 1), p. 53.

Somerville, T. and J. Head (1957) "Empirical Acoustic Criterion (2nd paper)", *Acustica*, 7(195), 96.

Steeneken, H. and T. Houtgast (1985) "RASTI: A Tool for Evaluating Auditoria", Technical Review, No. 3, Bruel and Kjaer Instruments, Inc., Marlborough, MA.

Stevens, S. (ed.) (1951) *Handbook of Experimental Psychology*. Wiley, New York, NY.

Stevenson, R. (2009) "The LED's Dark Secret", *IEEE Spectrum*, 46(8), 26–31, August.

Texas-WDB (1999) *Texas Guide to Rainwater Harvesting*, 2nd edn. Texas Water Development Board, Austin, TX (www.twdb.state.tx.us/publications/reports/RainHarv.pdf).

TGF (2009) *Groundwater Glossary*. The Groundwater Foundation, Lincoln, NE (www.roundwater.org/gi/gwglossary.html).

Tyzzer, F. (1953) "Reducing Industrial Noise: General Principles", *American Industrial Hygiene Association Quarterly*, 14(4), 264–85.

UN (1955) *World Weights and Measures*. Statistical Office, United Nations, New York, NY.

UN (1987) "Our Common Future", United Nations, World Commission on Environment and Development, A/42/427 Supplement 25, 4 August, New York, NY.

Van den Eijk (1966) "The New Dutch Code on Noise Control and Sound Insulation in Dwellings and Its Background", *Journal of Sound and Vibration*, 3(7).

Van Der Ryn, S. and S. Cowan (1996) *Ecological Design*. Island Press, Washington, DC.

Wackernagel, M. and W. Rees (1996) *Our Ecological Footprint*. New Society Publishers, Gabriola Island, BC, Canada.

Waldrop, M. (1992) *Complexity: The Emerging Science at the Edge of Order and Chaos*. Simon and Schuster, New York. NY.

WBCSD (1996) "Eco-Efficient Leadership for Improved Economic and Environmental Performance", World Business Council for Sustainable Development (www.wbcsd.org).

Wegel, R. and C. Lane (1924) *Physics Review*, **23**, 266.

Weiszäcker, E. von, A. Lovins, and L. Lovins (1997) *Factor 4: Doubling Wealth, Halving Resources Use.* Earthscan Publications, London, UK.

Wente, E. (1935) "The Characteristics of Sound Transmission in Rooms", *Journal of the Acoustical Society of America*, **7**, 123.

WHO (1984) "Indoor Air Pollutants: Exposure and Health Effect". World Health Organization, EURO Reports and Studies 78, WHO Regional Office for Europe, Geneva, Switzerland, January.

WHO (2000) "Global Water Supply and Sanitation Assessment 2000 Report", World Health Organization (www.who.int/water_sanitation_health/ Globassessment/GlobalTOC.htm).

Wilson, E. (2002) "The Bottleneck", *Scientific American*, February, 82–91.

Zheludev, N. (2007) "The Life and Times of the LED: A 100-Year History", *Nature Photonics*, **1**(4), 189–92. (see: www.nanophotonics.org.uk/niz/publications/zheludev-2007-ltl.pdf.)

Zwicker, E. (1961) "Subdivision of the Audible Frequency Range into Critical Bands", *Journal of the Acoustical Society of America*, **33**.

Further Reading

Adkins, P. (1963) "Transformer Noise Reduction with a Close-Fitting Mass-Law Enclosure", *IEEE Transactions*, Paper 63-200, February.

Arnold, F. (1980) "Dehumidification in Passively Cooled Buildings", in *Passive Cooling Handbook*, US Department of Energy Publication #375.

ASHRAE (1995) *Heating, Ventilating, and Air-Conditioning Applications.* American Society of Heating, Refrigerating, and Air-Conditioning Engineers, Atlanta, GA.

ASTM (1990) *Standard Test Method for Laboratory Measurement of Airborne Sound Transmission Loss of Building Partitions.* American Society for Testing and Materials, ASTM Standard E 90-90.

ASTM (1991) *Standard Practice for Determining the Acoustical Performance of Exterior Windows and Doors.* American Society for Testing and Materials, ASTM Standard E 1425-91.

ASTM (1992) *Standard Practice for Use of Sealants in Acoustical Applications.* American Society for Testing and Materials, ASTM Standard E 919-84(92).

ASTM (1993) *Standard Practices for Mounting Test Specimens During Sound Absorption Tests.* American Society for Testing and Materials, ASTM Standard E 795-93.

ASTM (1994) *Classification for Rating Sound Insulation.* American Society for Testing and Materials, ASTM Standard E 413-87(94).

ASTM (1994) *Standard Classification for Determination of Impact Isolation Class (IIC).* American Society for Testing and Materials, ASTM Standard E 989-89(94).

Ausubel, J. and H. Sladovich (eds.) (1989) *Technology and the Environment.* National Academic Press, Washington, DC.

Beranek, L. (1962) *Music, Acoustics and Architecture.* Wiley, New York, NY.

Beranek, L. (1988) *Noise and Vibration Control.* Institute of Noise Control Engineering, Washington, DC.

Bruckmayer F. (1963) "Estimation of Noise Annoyances by Reference to the Background Noise Level", *Österreichische Ingenieur Zeitschrift*, 315–21.

Caudill, W. (1954); *Toward Better School Design.* Architectural Record Book: Dodge, New York, NY.

Chalkley, J. and H. Cater (1968) *Thermal Environment for the Student of Architecture.* Architectural Press, London, UK.

Cotton, H. (1960) *Principles of Illumination.* Chapman and Hall, London, UK.

Cowan, J. (1994) *Handbook of Environmental Acoustics.* Van Nostrand Reinhold, New York, NY.

Cremer, L. and H. Müller (1978) *Principles and Applications of Room Acoustics*, Vol. 1. Applied Science Publishers, Barking, UK.

Crocker, M. and A. Price (1975) *Noise and Noise Control*, Vol. 1. CRC Press, Cleveland, OH.

Croome, D. (1977) *Buildings and People.* Pergamon Press, Oxford, UK.

Davis, A. and I. Schubert (1974) *Alternate Natural Energy Sources in Building Design.* Van Nostrand Reinhold, New York, NY.

Davis, R. and S. Silverman (1947) *Hearing and Deafness.* Holt Rinehart, New York, NY.

De Boer E. (1959) "Measurement of the Critical Band Width in Cases of Perception Deafness", in Cremer, L. (ed.), *Proceedings of the 3rd International Congress on Acoustics, 1*, Elsevier, London, UK, pp. 100–2.

DIN (1966) "Precision Sound Level Meter", German Standard DIN 45633, DK 793:681.88, November.

DoE (2006) *Greening Federal Facilities*, 2nd edn. Federal Energy Management Program, US Department of Energy (www.eere.energy.gov/femp/technologies/sustainable_greening.html).

Doelle, L. (1972) *Environmental Acoustics.* McGraw Hill, New York, NY.

Edwards, B. (ed.) (2001) *Green Architecture: An International Comparison.* Wiley, Hoboken, NJ.

Egan J. (1975) *Concepts in Thermal Comfort.* Prentice Hall, Englewood Cliffs, NJ.

Egan, M. (1988) *Architectural Acoustics*. McGraw Hill, New York, NY.

Faulkner, L. (1976) *Handbook of Industrial Noise Control*. Industrial Press, New York, NY.

Fisher, D. (2009) "Dynamic Architecture" www. dynamicarchitecture.net/home.html.(Also:Chicago Tribune, 16 July, 2009 (www.chicagotribune.com); and archimagazine, 11 April 2007 (www. archimagazine.com/arotating.htm).

Fletcher, H. (1953) *Speech and Hearing in Communication*. Van Nostrand, New York, NY.

Gelin, L. (1997) "Active Noise Control: A Tutorial for HVAC Designers", *ASHRAE Journal*, August, p. 44.

Gissen, D. (2002) *Big and Green: Toward Sustainable Architecture in the 21st Century*. Princeton Architectural Press, New York, NY.

Harris, C. (1994) *Noise Control in Buildings*. McGraw Hill, New York, NY.

Harris, D. (1991) *Noise Control Manual*. Van Nostrand Reinhold, New York, NY.

Haselbach, L. (2008) *The Engineering Guide to LEED-New Construction: Sustainable Construction*. McGraw-Hill, Columbus, OH.

Hemond, C. (1983) *Engineering Acoustics and Noise Control*, Prentice Hall, Englewood Cliffs, NJ.

Hopkinson, R.G. and J.D. Kay (1969) *The Lighting of Buildings*. Praeger, London, UK.

IEA (2000) *Daylight in Buildings: A Source Book on Daylighting Systems and Components*. International Energy Agency (IEA), Energy Conservation in Buildings and Community Systems Program, IEA SHC Task 21 / ECBCS Annex, Morse Associates Inc., 1808 Corcoran Street (NW), Washington, DC 2009, 29 July.

Jones, R. (1984) *Noise and Vibration Control in Buildings*. McGraw Hill, New York, NY.

Jordan, V. (1980) *Acoustical Design of Concert Halls and Theatres*. Applied Science Publishers, London, UK.

Keighley, E. (1966) "The Determination of Acceptable Criteria for Office Noise", *Journal of Sound and Vibration*, 4(1), July, 73–87.

Kellog-Smith, F. and F. Bertolone (1986) *Bringing Interiors to Light: The Principles and Practices of Lighting Design*. Whitney Library of Design, Watson-Guptill, New York, NY.

Kinsler, L. and A. Frey (1962) *Fundamentals of Acoustics*. Wiley, New York, NY.

Kryter, K. (1959) "Scaling Human Reactions to the Sound from Aircraft", *Journal of the Acoustical Society of America*, **31**, 1415.

Kryter, K. (1966) "Psychological Reactions to Aircraft Noise", *Ekistics*, November, 345–57.

Kuttruff, H. (1979) "Room Acoustics"; Applied Science Publisher, Barking, UK.

Laing, N. (1967) "The Use of Solar and Sky Radiation for Air Conditioning of Pneumatic Structures", IASS, *Proceedings of the 1st International Colloquium on Pneumatic Structures*, University of Stuttgart, Stuttgart, Germany, 11–12 May, pp. 163–79.

Langdon, F. (1965) "A Study of Annoyance Caused by Noise in Automatic Data Processing Offices", *Building Science*, **1**, January, 69–78.

Lawrence, A. (1970) *Architectural Acoustics*. Elsevier, Barking, UK.

Lawrence, A., L. Hegvold, and R. Green (1968) "Prediction of Traffic Noise Spectrum Levels for Use in Building Design", 6th I.C.A., F-23.

Leckie, J., G. Masters, H. Whitehouse, and L. Young (1975) *Other Homes and Garbage*. Sierra Club Books, San Francisco, CA.

Lee, J. (1974) "Information Theory: Wavefront Reconstruction and the Concert Hall Problem", *Acustica*, **30**(4), 196–200.

LEED (2003) *Green Building Rating System 2.1*. US Green Building Council, Washington, DC, January.

Lyle, J. (1994) *Regenerative Design for Sustainable Development*. Wiley, New York, NY.

MacPherson, R. (1965) "Physiological Aspects of Thermal Comfort", Third Conference of the Australian and New Zealand Architectural Science Association on Climate Comfort and Environment, Architectural Science Review, Department of Architectural Science, University of Sydney, Australia, December.

Mather, C. (1968) "The Acoustical Environment of Four Modern City Office Buildings", *Architectural Science Review*, June. p. 42.

Mendler, S. and M. Lazarus (2005) *The HOK Guidebook to Sustainable Design*, 2nd edn. Wiley, New York, NY.

Moore, J. (1978) *Design for Good Acoustics and Noise Control*. Macmillan, London, UK.

Moore, J. (1961) *Design for Good Acoustics*. Architectural Press, London, UK.

Moreland, J. and R. Musa (1972) "The Performance of Acoustic Barriers", *Proceedings, International Conference on Noise Control Engineering*, Washington, DC, pp. 95–104.

Muncey, R. and A. Nickson (1964) "The Listener and Room Acoustics", *Journal of Sound Vibration*, **1**(2), 141–7.

Northwood, T. (ed.) (1977) *Architectural Acoustics*. Hutchinson, and Ross, Stroudsburg, PA.

Nuckolls, J. (1983) *Interior Lighting for Environmental Designers*, 2nd edn. Wiley, New York, NY.

Orr, D. (2002) *The Nature of Design: Ecology, Culture, and Human Intention.* Oxford University Press, New York, NY.

Page, J. (1963) "Human Thermal Comfort", *Architect's Journal*, June, p. 1301.

Parkin, P., W. Allen, H. Purkis, and W. Scholes (1953) "The Acoustics of the Royal Festival Hall, London", *Acustica*, **3**(1).

Phillips, D (1964) *Lighting in Architectural Design.* McGraw-Hill, New York, NY.

Pritchard, M. (1969) *Lighting.* Environmental Physics Series, Longmans, Green and Co., London, UK.

Reynolds, D. (1981) *Engineering Principles of Acoustics.* Allyn and Bacon, Boston, MA.

Sabine, W. (1964) *Collected Papers on Acoustics.* Dover, New York, NY.

Sassi, P. (2006) *Strategies for Sustainable Architecture.* Taylor and Francis, London, UK.

Spiegel, R. and D. Meadows (1999) *Green Building Materials: A Guide to Product Selection and Specification.* Wiley, New York, NY.

Stein, B. and J. Reynolds (2000) *Mechanical and Electrical Equipment for Buildings.* Wiley, New York, NY.

Straten, J. van (1967) *Thermal Performance of Buildings.* Elsevier, London, UK.

The Energy Resources Conservation Development Commission of California (2005) Title 24 – *Building Energy Efficiency Standards.* Sacramento, CA.

UIA-AIA (1993) "Declaration of Interdependence for a Sustainable Future", see www.uia-architectes.org/).

Vallero, D. and C. Brasier (2008) *Sustainable Design: The Science of Sustainability and Green Engineering.* Wiley, New York, NY.

Van Der Ryn, S. and P. Calthorp (1986) *Sustainable Communities: A New Design Synthesis for Cities, Suburbs and Towns.* Sierra Club Books, San Francisco, CA.

Vickers, A. (2001) *Handbook of Water Use and Conservation.* WaterPlow Press, Amherst, MA.

Walsh, J.W.T. (1961) *The Science of Daylight.* MacDonald Publishing, London, UK.

Warren, J. (1983) *Lighting: Basic Concepts.* Department of Architectural Science, University of Sydney, Sydney, Australia.

White, H. and D. White (1980) *Physics and Music.* Holt Rinehart and Winston, New York, NY.

Williamson, T., A. Radford, and H. Bennetts (2003) *Understanding Sustainable Architecture.* Spon Press, London, UK.

Wilson, C. (1989) *Noise Control: Measurement, Analysis, and Control of Sound and Vibration.* Harper and Row, New York, NY.

Yerges, L. (1978) *Sound, Noise, and Vibration Control.* Van Nostrand Reinhold, New York, NY.

Zwicker, E., G. Flottorp, and S. Stevens (1957) "Critical Band Width in Loudness Summation", *Journal of the Acoustical Society of America*, **29**.

Keyword Index

"n" after a page number indicates notes

Building Science: Concepts and Application. Jens Pohl.
© 2011 John Wiley & Sons, Ltd.
Published 2011 by John Wiley & Sons, Ltd.